D1474012

SCHOOLING IN SOCIAL CONTEXT:

Qualitative Studies

edited by

George W. Noblit
University of North Carolina at Chapel Hill

William T. Pink
National College of Education

ABLEX PUBLISHING CORPORATION
NORWOOD, NEW JERSEY 07648

Library of Congress Cataloging-in-Publication Data

Schooling in social context.

   Bibliography: p.
   Includes index.
   1. Education—United States—Aims and objectives.
2. School management and organization—United States.
3. Education and state—United States. 4. Education—
Social aspects—United States. 5. Industry and
education—United States. I. Noblit, George W. II. Pink,
William T.
LA217.S293   1986   370.19'0973   86-10890
ISBN 0-89391-326-X

Ablex Publishing Corporation
355 Chestnut Street
Norwood, New Jersey 07648

Contents

Chapter 12   Fitting into a Job: Learning the Pace of Work   265
              Kathryn M. Borman

Chapter 13   Authority Relations in Adolescent Workplaces   284
              Jane Reisman

Chapter 14   Life's Not Working: Cultural Alternatives to Career
              Alternatives   303
              Harry F. Wolcott

              Author Index   325

              Subject Index   330

Foreword

There are those rare, almost illusive, moments in the development of a line of research or the formation of a new way of understanding when one senses that a threshold has been crossed, a new perspective has taken hold. Such is my reaction to the materials included in the present volume. As I read and study the chapters brought together here by the editors, George Noblit and William Pink, I am persuaded that qualitative research in education has achieved that "critical mass" so necessary for the further expansion of its influence. A substantial intellectual contribution is made in these chapters. It is evident in the breadth of topics covered, in the manner in which qualitative data inform the development of theoretical insights, and in the clearly drawn linkage between field research and policy implications.

The editors are correct to argue that educational research, especially as it is predominantly conducted in the United States, has found itself recently in something of an intellectual cul-de-sac. As research efforts turn more and more in circles staging fierce symbolic battles over the nuances of various aspects of quantitative research, the force is spent. Sterility, irrelevance, and obscurity are words not too strong to characterize much of what is self-appointed as educational research. The result is that the end products of educational research are generally not read by policymakers, believed by practitioners, or used by other researchers.

Interestingly, the response (by others than those who remain convinced that the intellectual vitality of quantitative research is not spent) has been roughly of two types. On the one hand are those who see a need for a broad theoretical framework that establishes the boundaries and parameters for research, and in so doing, escapes the shallow empiricism rampant in much present work. Central among the proponents of this approach are those who argue for theories that focus on the role of education in reproducing the social class structure of the society. The intellectual foundation of this work is largely derived from Marx. Alternatively, other educational researchers believe that a movement toward an orientation grounded in qualitative research can overcome the futility of the rush to empiricism. Here the focus is not on abstract measures of outcomes but on the careful study of the processes and content of the educational experience. The intellectual strength of this tradition is drawn from Weber, Simmel, and Mead.

I see this present volume as an exemplary indication of the coming of age of this second response to the crisis of positivism.

Of special importance in this regard is that the authors have not traded one set of shackles for another. Whereas they clearly fault quantitative research for its lack of attention to the social and cultural context in which individual behavior occurs, i.e., the various meanings that individuals bring to their own experience, they do not overcompensate by presenting so much of the context that one loses sight of the individuals in a cloud of environmental description. There is a middle ground in these studies. Context is provided, but so also is the description of the ways in which individuals create their own meaning, frame their own constructions of reality, and sometimes respond in unpredictable ways. The authors have rejected psychological reductionism as well as sociological superstructures.

Perhaps the single most ambitious aspect of this volume (and thus its most contentious statement) is offered by the editors in their Introduction where they state their intent to "reframe the policy debate of the 1980s." While this could be dismissed as the wishful thinking of some academics who are necessarily removed from the policy arena (and who are already a half a decade late), it would be premature to do so. And while no one volume of research is likely in and of itself to reshape a policy dialogue, what is presented here does have critical implications for the discussion on governmental involvement in education. What the material presented here forces to the front of our attention is that the traditional perspectives on the methods and assumptions of educational policy making seem singularly ill-equipped to explain and respond to current conditions in American education.

Rather than yet another effort at "top-down," hyper-rational, organizational engineering of education that posits how schools ought to be organized to function and what kinds of graduates to produce, the present work begins with the conviction that policy can only grow from first understanding the day-to-day realities of education as they actually exist. Stated differently, there is a need to reorient ourselves to an inductive approach to policy formulation, constantly recognizing the interplay between broad societal objectives and the way in which the organization is actually functioning. A book such as this helps us understand schooling and education as it is. That is something of a provocative statement, given the extent to which our discussion of education is based solely on what we think is going on.

The approach offered here is one of developing policy based on a continuing set of reality checks grounded in day-to-day events, particularly at the local level— the level the authors see as critical to any successful policy implementation, the level where there are actually teachers, kids, buildings, school books, and parents.

The volume moves in the opposite direction from conventional thinking on educational policy making. It seeks a direct linkage between theory and practice, and this is my reason for seeing it as such an important contribution to educational research. It is counterintuitive time and again. But maybe that is so only because we have held for so long to an outmoded perspective on the contribution educational research can make to the policy dialogue. The present work, then, gives reason for optimism.

Ray C. Rist
Washington, DC
February, 1985

An Introduction

GEORGE W. NOBLIT
WILLIAM T. PINK

INTRODUCTION

Education has recently become the object of considerable national scrutiny. The various national commissions and foundation reports on the current status of schooling have all had suggestions for reforming schools (e.g., Boyer, 1983; National Commission on Excellence in Education, 1983). Educational policy at the state and district levels is currently being altered to correspond with several of the proposed reforms (e.g., strengthening graduation requirements and lengthening the school day and year). Yet Jonathan Sher (1983) reminds us to never mistake policy for genuine action. Certainly it is true that policy is symbolic and may serve as a guiding device for action, but it is also true that the action most relevant to students and educators is the social organization of their school experience. Those who wish to improve the quality of schooling, i.e., student test scores, must do more than increase standards. They must detail ways to alter key processes in occupational socialization, and school and district organization. They must give "standards" an operationalized meaning. They must detail ways to prepare students more appropriately for life after schooling. This volume is designed to promote an understanding of each of these issues.

The perspective of this volume is rather unique. As qualitative researchers, each author in this volume has studied schooling and its outcomes directly—trying to describe and understand the dynamics of schooling as it is played out in the everyday life of schools. The result is a series of studies, portraits if you will, of schooling. The intent of this volume is to reframe the policy debate of the 1980s by examining schooling in its social context. Much educational research, however, ignores context and how it shapes the behavior of students, teachers, administrators, and parents. In fact, much positivistic research is "context stripping" (Mishler, 1967, p. 1) and thus gives the false impression that context is but a confounding factor. Yet ethnographers and other qualitative researchers have repeatedly revealed that context is the source of both social meaning and the basis of behavioral decisions as well as the limits which shape the outcomes of behavior. Moreover, it is the social context which guides us to be concerned about some problems and not others. The options we perceive for resolving problems, for example, or our weighing of the options and choosing one—as well as the effects of implementing that option—are all similarly affected by social context. One need only examine the recent national commissions and foundation reports to see that the educational problems of the 1980s are not those of the 1960s. In short, the context has changed.

Social context can be conceived broadly or narrowly. The broad context, of course, gives us perspective on national and state policy. Yet schooling in the United States is largely a function of local policy. Within state guidelines, local districts enact policy, and local schools are responsible for implementing that policy. Yet, as we will discuss later, schooling is "loosely coupled" (Weick, 1976). That is, what happens at a higher level in an organization does not necessarily directly affect what happens at a lower level. Policy and practice are often rather different and often for very good reasons. Our approach in this volume has been to start at the level of teachers, classrooms, and schools and to ask in what ways contexts affect their operations. Thus, we can be sure that the social contexts we uncover are relevant to schooling even though practice is loosely coupled from policy.

Focusing on studies grounded in schooling practice is not the usual way to study educational policy. Traditionally, researchers start with policy considerations and then examine practice to see if practice corresponds to policy. We would argue that this approach has been discredited by recent developments in educational research. We suggest that the approach presented in this volume is a more productive strategy for understanding schooling and therefore for generating policy. Moreover, we suggest that the studies in this volume represent new developments in (a) the study of educational organizations; (b) the study of educational policy; and (c) the methodology for studying both policy and social organization.

THE "NEW" ORGANIZATIONAL THEORY

It is apparent that organizational theory is currently undergoing a reformation. Perrow (1982) argued that we have been deluded by theory into the conception that organizations are rational. Much recent research has supported his position (cf. Meyer, Freeman, Hannan, Meyer, Ouchi, Pfeffer & Scott, 1978). The role of educational organizations in this controversy is not incidental. As Metz (1984) pointed out, educational organizations have always challenged the prevailing rational paradigm by being "loosely coupled" (Weick, 1976). Yet, recently, theorists have been less likely to treat schools as an anomaly and more likely to see them as the basis of the critique of rational and neorational theories.

It is apparent that education was first seen by organizational analysts as a convenient venue for conducting research. Schools are found in abundance in all communities, and researchers, if they could negotiate access, could test their organizational theories on schools. They treated schools as simply one case to illustrate or test a more general theoretical issue. This view changed, however, when it became apparent that schools were special cases that did not seem to adhere to the rational principles of organizational theory. What started out as a convenient place for testing theory emerged as a critical incident in the repudiation of the assumed universality of organizational theory (cf. Perrow, 1982).

Such a realization, of course, was not self-evident. It required some champions to promote and shape such an interpretation. In this case, the champions were

Karl Weick and James March. Both shared the conviction that organizations were more involved than rational organization theory admitted, but each developed his ideas somewhat differently. March had already developed his "garbage can" model prior to turning his attention to educational organizations (Cohen & March, 1974; Cohen, March, & Olsen, 1972). By contrast, Weick had been exploring "organizing" as an alternative way of understanding organizations as "loosely coupled systems" (Weick, 1969, 1976). Yet both found that through studying educational organizations, a new organizational theory could be elicited. In short, through exploring schools they developed new theory to be applied to the study of all organizations.

Other organizational theorists, of course, were aware of problems with organizational theory and were actively seeking alternatives. In 1978, Scott declared that a new theoretical model was emerging that was concerned with "the explanation of *formal* structures" (p. 26, emphasis in the original). This new model attempted to explain how organizations came to be both rationalized and formalized. Yet the research Scott heralded was not ethnographic. Meyer et al. (1978) argued that this research was characterized by:

> the definition of organizations, as opposed to individual people, as the unit of analysis; the study of many organizations using quantitative approaches as opposed to qualitative case studies; the application of multivariate statistical techniques to organizational data; and the use of panel studies and time series to trace changes in organizations over lengthy intervals. (p. 3)

These analysts were also aware that their approach was at variance with Weick and March. As Scott (1978) footnoted: "However, some analysts, such as Weick (1976) and March and Olsen (1976) are calling anew for more in-depth case studies of actual decision making and behavior and more 'deep descriptions' of the context and meaning of organizational activities" (p. 26). Further, Scott (1978) concluded that even the quantitative research on schools that some researchers included as part of their approach challenged the ideas they were promoting:

> Also, in common with March and Olsen (1976) and Weick (1976), Meyer and Rowan raise the question as to just how tightly connected the various structural units and levels of organization are. Many contemporary organizations appear to consist of quite loosely coupled segments—so much so that March and his colleagues refer to them as "organized anarchies"—capable of relatively independent actions and subject to varying environmental contraints. This conception not only challenges the rational system conception of structure but also raises the issue as to how meaningful the organization is as a unit of analysis. . . . (p. 23)

Meyer and Rowan (1978) argued that in schools and school systems the formal structure is primarily for legitimation of the schools' activities and controls only "ritual classifications" (p. 78). Given the disagreement over appropriate instructional methods, schools protect themselves from the environment by "decoupling" and using a "logic of confidence" (Meyer & Rowan, 1978, p. 98). That is, the social context of schools is seen as sufficiently turbulent as to interfere with instruction. To prevent this, administrators control the organization so that certified teachers teach specified types of students, and in so doing, administrators act as if these controls were adequate to control instruction. They also attempt to manage the "interference" of factors outside of the school.

For us, the important point is that educational organizations have required a new organizational theory, regardless of the preconceptions that analysts themselves brought to the study of schools. Further, if we are to understand schools as organizations, we must conduct in-depth, qualitative studies on what actually occurs.

In many ways, the new organizational theory requires that we study *social* organization—the structure of social relationships and social beliefs in schools—and then consider how formal organization affects and is affected by the social relationships and beliefs. Further, it requires that we differentiate between the boundaries that schools draw around themselves and the actual boundaries at which context factors influencing the daily life of schools end. That is, we must recognize that the social context and environment are implicated in the actions of educators inside the walls of school buildings rather than buffered out by organizational boundaries.

The studies in this volume reveal, for example, that the dynamics of interaction frequently create social structures that may contrast with the structures that administrators desire. They also illustrate that this interaction is frequently the basis for the development of alternative formal structures. The chapters by LeCompte and Ginsberg, Kyle, Green, Harker, and Golden, and Van Galen all reveal patterns of emerging social organization that are the basis of teaching. The chapters by Whitford, Brieschke, Dwyer, Smith, Prunty, and Kleine expand on our organizational emphasis by revealing how organizational identity, innovation, and environments have their own processes of social organization that limit what is possible even while creating opportunities for new possibilities. The chapter by Sizemore is a particularly adept introduction to the organizational concept of school effectiveness. While demonstrating that organizations often assumed to be ineffective need not be so, she details the organizational dynamics which create an effective school. The three other studies of effective schools by Noblit, Pink, and Garibaldi illustrate in different ways the point made by Sizemore that a tight control on beliefs about what is possible, together with a building wide focus on making that occur, is more important to effectiveness than any specific curriculum or instructional innovation. Finally, the chapters by Borman, Reisman, and Wolcott complete the challenge to the rational model. Rather than narrowly assuming that achievement test scores measure the quality of schooling, they document in various settings that schools as organizations might only be as effective as their ability to help students in the transition to their life after school. In developing this position, the authors explore the learning dynamics that function as young workers enter jobs. Further, Wolcott empathetically reminds us that the working world is not always hospitable to the young worker.

These studies are an important part of the "new" organizational theory that seeks to understand and explain how *formal* structures are created and modified and how they in turn interact with *informal* structures. These studies also remind us that order is evident even in the absence of rational structures, a point both educators and organizational theorists need to consider more carefully.

GROUNDED EDUCATIONAL POLICY

In every epoch schools are buffeted by the larger shifts in society and politics (James & Tyack, 1983). Recently, both the legislated and proposed education policy reflect a rather conservative and elitist agenda (Edson, 1983). The National Commission on Excellence (1983) report, *A Nation at Risk*, for example, casts the problems of schooling in terms of insufficient standardization: Raising standards, a return to the supposed rigors of yesteryear, is seen as the means to reverse declining student test scores and regain America's intellectual supremacy in the economic marketplace. To achieve this goal the Commission recommends two related educational reforms: raising graduation standards and extending the school day and year. Such recommendations assume that (a) higher exit standards and (b) more required courses in the basics are necessary to improve student achievement. While this reform strategy has some intuitive appeal, we should not overlook the fact that many schools are presently highly effective in the absence of these proposed reforms. Moreover, such a policy recommendation is based neither on research evidence nor on a conceptualization of what constitutes good teaching. Notwithstanding the interest shown by state legislators in this recommendation, the chapters by Sizemore, Noblit, Pink, and Garibaldi all indicate that educational excellence is primarily the product of effort at the local school site and not the result of state or district policy mandates regarding school improvement.

A second recommendation of the Commission is for states to adopt uniform exit requirements. The notion here is that 4 years of English, for example, is in some way better than 3 years of English, and that requiring 4 years will result in higher test scores. Such a recommendation ignores, however, both the issue of *what* is taught in classrooms, i.e., content of the curriculum as well as *how* it is taught, i.e., the instructional formats employed by teachers. Moreover, the Commission also ignores the problems of implementing a uniform policy without regard to the contextual factors operating within each district and at each school site.

The important issue here is the kind of data available to guide policy for reforming schools. We suggest that much of the available educational data cannot inform such policy. The result, as we see in these national reports, is simple answers to complex problems about improving schools. Simply stated, our position is that data cannot adequately inform policy, if the data are not grounded in the social context of schools. More specifically, research which ignores the school as an organization and is insensitive, for example, to questions about what is taught in the classroom and how decisions are made about what to teach students grouped according to assumptions about differential educability has limited utility to inform policy. Rather, we argue, research which focuses on the school and classrooms as the units for investigation and uses observational or ethnographic methods to detail the daily life of schools is perhaps best suited to understand schools and thereby inform policy. This book presents such an examination of schools: The research reported here attempts to explain how different aspects of schooling actually function (e.g., teacher socialization, the implementation and effects of innovation, school effectiveness, and the transition to the world of work). The result is a challenge to the prevailing knowledge base about schools.

We must acknowledge that educational research has matured rather rapidly in the last 30 years: Beginning in the early fifties, it was the discipline of sociology which showed the most interest in education. While straining to gain respectability at that time, researchers interested in understanding schooling borrowed heavily from the philosophy and methods which generated the "scientific model" used in the physical sciences. Grounded in this empiricism and the structural functionalism as elaborated by Talcott Parsons, the early concerns about schooling focused on issues of social integration into the normative structure and the development of consensus about shared values. As might be expected, however, the questions about schooling changed over time. Concerns in the sixties for equal access to educational opportunity, for example, brought with it alternative paradigms and methodologies. Functionalism sank into disrepute, and the scientific model was challenged by case study and ethnographic data-gathering methods. In more recent years, questions have surfaced about the relationship of both the organizational form and curriculum content of schools to the reproduction of the social class structure and the maintenance of a capitalistic economy. Different paradigms (e.g., Marxist or neo-Marxist conflict and correspondence paradigms as well as sociology of knowledge paradigms) and different field-based research methods, borrowed most heavily from anthropology (e.g., participant observation, ethnography) have developed to address these new questions about both the process and outcome of schooling. A brief examination of this evolutionary process will illustrate how important grounded data are to policy development.

The work of Blau and Duncan (1967), Coleman, Campbell, Hobson, McPartland, Mood, Weinfeld & York, (1966) and Jencks, Smith, Ackland, Bane, Cohen, Gintis, Heyns, & Michelson, (1972) are examples of the functionalist view of schooling. Blau and Duncan (1967) developed the use of path analysis to assess the movement of different generational waves of males from status origins to status destination. They found schooling to be relatively unimportant independent of social origins to occupational status. Only statistics regarding the years of completed schooling contributed much to explaining occupational status: Only time spent in school was measured, however, not what students did or learned when they were in school. Blau and Duncan included in their analysis no measure of the *quality* of schooling. In fact, their only measure of life in school, replete with all the built-in biases of track location and differential expectations, is earned grade point average (gpa). The use of these data to educational policy, we suggest, is extremely limited. At best, these data suggest that the quality of the schooling experience is unimportant to subsequent occupational success: The implication for improving schools is nonexistent.

Coleman et al. (1966) were charged by Congress to fill the gap in our knowledge about the impact of the quality of schooling on student achievement. The central charge was to assess the impact of schooling on the difference in achievement between students attending predominantly black schools and students attending predominantly white schools. Using traditional survey techniques to gather data from a representative national sample, together with sophisticated statistical procedures, Coleman et al. concluded that a range of indicators of schooling quality (e.g., years of teacher training and service, expenditures per pupil, availability of libraries and science laboratories) were unrelated to student achievement. Missing from this analysis, however, were key data about family and schooling experiences. Thus the data are unable to answer questions about the contribution of family or schools to achievement beyond the limited range of self-report measures surveyed. They are unable to directly inform policy on school reform, because they offer no insight into the organization, content, and context of classrooms and schools.

In a similar vein, Jencks et al. (1972) submitted several previously collected data sets to new and sophisticated statistical analysis. As others had before them, Jencks et al. concluded that schooling played a relatively unimportant role in determining occupational status. While viewing schools as "marginal institutions" for creating a more egalitarian society (e.g., they reasoned that improving the quality of schools would not significantly affect the achievement of students currently performing poorly), they acknowledged that they "ignored not only attitudes and values, but the internal life of schools" (Jencks et al., 1972, p. 13). As a consequence of these omissions, these data are also unable to inform policy to reform schools. Again, lacking details of life in classrooms and schools, these data tell us nothing about what might be changed or how it might be changed to make schools more effective.

Perhaps the most significant shift in the policy relevance of educational research occurred when questions raised by researchers working out of new paradigms (e.g., a class reproduction, or sociology of knowledge paradigm), generated a disenchantment with traditional quantitative research methods. In seeking out new ways to capture events in naturally occurring settings, educational researchers turned to what until then had been methods used by anthropologists. More specifically, as questions were asked about (a) *how* classroom teachers treated students from varied social class and racial background, and (b) *how* decisions were made about placing students into academic versus commercial tracks, researchers began to use methods that involved long-term and detailed observations of the major actors and key interactions in schools. Simply stated, questions about the process and content of schooling demanded different and more specific information than could be generated by using standard survey techniques and standardized instruments.

Field studies, or qualitative studies, have gained in popularity over the last several years with researchers, practitioners, and policymakers. This popularity is grounded as much in the power of the method to provide data to answer critical questions about life in schools as in the ability of the data to inform policy for school improvement. Two different strands can be identified in this movement. One strand is the emergence of a group of sociologists who have used qualitative methods to detail both the internal workings of schools as well as the meaning structures used by actors in schools. The work of Bossert, Dwyer, Rowan & Lee, (1982), Herriott and Gross (1979), Metz (1978), Noblit and Johnston (1982), and Rist (1970, 1978) illustrates this tradition. A second strand is the emergence of educational anthropology. Here, anthropologists have turned from studying foreign cultures and have brought both their traditional concerns with culture and the ethnographic method to investigating schools. The result has been studies of schooling in social context which attempt to translate knowledge about schools into action. The work of Erickson (1982), Gearing and Epstein (1982), Peshkin (1978, 1983), Spindler (1974, 1982), Wilcox (1982), and Wolcott (1973, 1977) illustrates this strand.

These two developments have led to the growth of studies we might label educational ethnography: They also bring together scholars from differing disciplines who are beginning to work collaboratively. The importance of this work is that it provides (a) a view of schools firmly grounded within the social context in which they function, and (b) specific information about the dynamics of schooling that can inform policy about school reform. The chapters in this book extend this work.

THE QUALITATIVE APPROACH

In some ways, this recent shift to well-grounded, interpretive methodologies pioneered by both sociologists and anthropologists is the natural result of the success of positivism. Positivism was a great enabler for social scientists, because it elaborated its philosophy of science, methodology, and technique. But the return to qualitative research highlights that such success also reveals the limits of positivism. Positivism appropriately serves theory through its hypothesis-testing logic. Yet positivism relies on the gradual accumulation of knowledge to generate theory. Unfortunately, as Kuhn (1962) long ago revealed, the paradigms from which theory emanates are not simple summations of studies. The paradigms are based in world hypothesis and domain assumptions (Gouldner, 1970) as well as in research-generated knowledge. Social context affects knowledge in the same way it affects schooling. Positivism reached its limits because it cannot generate the new paradigms: It can only elaborate an existing one. The new theories that are being generated are based in empirical studies of *what is* and in critical analyses of who benefits from this state of affairs. Qualitative research, we suggest, is best able to accomplish these analyses and has become the primary methodology of both interpretive and critical research (Bredo & Feinberg, 1982; MacNeil, 1984).

As Rist warns us, however, the use of ethnography in education has become something of a social movement. It is this very popularity however, which threatens to trivialize the approach. Researchers rush to join the band wagon of ethnography without conceptualizing a sound research design, or the appropriate use of data-gathering methods. A qualitative approach does have criteria. Spicer (1976), for example, suggests that:

In the study there should be the use of the emic approach, that is, the gathering of data on attitudes and value orientations and social relations directly from the people engaged in the making of a given policy and those on whom the policy impinges. It should be holistic, that is, include placement of the policy decision in the context of the competing or cooperating interests, with their value orientations, out of which the policy formation emerged. This requires relating to the economic, political, and other contexts identifiable as relevant in the sociocultural system. It should include historical study, that is, some diachronic acquaintance with the policy and policies giving rise to it. Finally, it should include consideration of conceivable alternatives and how other varieties of this class of policy have been applied with what results, in short, comparative understanding (p. 341).

Harry Wolcott (1976) has approached the issue of what is an ethnography in a different way. He describes four criteria that are essential to an ethnographic approach. First is the appropriateness of the problem to the researcher. He argues that an ethnographer must be free to "discover what the problem is" in the course of the fieldwork (Wolcott, 1976, p. 25). Second is the appropriateness of the ethnographer. Since in ethnography the observer is the primary instrument of data collection, Wolcott argues it is essential that the researcher be thoroughly grounded in the ethnographic literature in anthropology (and sociology) as well as experienced in professional ethnography and the preparation of ethnographic accounts. Third is the appropriateness of the research climate. The climate, Wolcott argues, should (a) personally involve the ethnographer in the setting, data collection, and analysis; (b) allow for extensive time in the field as well as an equal amount of time for analysis of the data; and (c) permit professional autonomy. Fourth is the appropriateness of expectations for the completed study. Wolcott argues that the completed study should (a) involve a range of data collection techniques, primarily observation and interviewing; (b) seek to study a range of topics encompassing social organization and belief systems in an effort to be holistic; (c) be objective but not necessarily neutral; (d) analyze contrasts and/or paradoxes surfacing in the data, and finally (e) employ a "wealth of primary data" (Wolcott, 1976, p. 40).

These criteria are stringent. But Wolcott cautions that we must not equate a qualitative study with an ethnography. Many studies are "toward" an ethnography rather than full ethnographies in themselves. We must acknowledge that frequently studies using qualitative methods such as observation and interviewing may be so restricted in both the scope of the study and time at the school that they cannot support the depth of analysis suggested by Spicer or Wolcott. This distinction is important in interpreting the work that we have called educational ethnography. Where proponents identify themselves alternatively as educationalists, anthropologists, and sociologists, investigators rely as much on using qualitative data to construct case studies as on full ethnographies. As the chapters in this volume attest, both kinds of studies are part of the tradition of educational ethnography.

Qualitative research is often equated with relativism and critiqued on that count. The studies in this volume reveal that this is a vacuous critique. Qualitative research does not demonstrate that "anything goes," as critics often intimate (Willower, 1981). It is certainly true that in most collective settings there is more than one perspective. However, the fact that there is a multiperspectival reality does not mean that anything goes. The complexity revealed by qualitative research indicates that simple truths are not self-evident, regardless of what positivists and rationalists wish to be the case. The chapters in this volume reveal that if qualitative research is to be equated with relativism, then it is a limited relativism, limited by the contending forces in the setting.

The research in this volume is quite varied. The chapters by Garibaldi, Noblit, and Pink are all essentially comparative case studies. With case studies the purpose is not only to capture the integrity of each case, but also to compare cases with one another. Usually, therefore, the depth of each case is sacrificed in favor of presenting multiple cases. However, case studies can also be part of a more intense ethnographic study, and this applies to the chapters by Borman, Sizemore, and Whitford. In these studies, the cases are used to reveal the lessons of the ethnography. In various ways, the cases are the vehicles for the analysis rather than that to be analyzed, as with the Garibaldi, Noblit, and Pink chapters.

Intensive studies of a single case are more traditionally seen as ethnographies. The chapters by Brieschke, Dwyer, Smith, Prunty, and Kleine, Kyle, LeCompte and Ginsberg, Reisman, Van Galen, and Wolcott are all within this modality, but vary in degree. With more intensive studies the analysis usually takes the form of a within-case comparison. Different groups and/or experiences are compared to reveal the dynamics of the case and the lessons we should learn.

Most importantly, however, each study in this volume reveals that qualitative researchers are both theorists and methodologists. The theory is both grounded as well as metaphoric, while the methodology is adapted to the issues studied. In this way qualitative research, like all research, justifies its method based on what seems to be the case under study. Unlike positivistic research, however, qualitative researchers base both theory and method in empirical studies of what is going on.

ABOUT THIS VOLUME

This volume is organized into four sections. The first section, The Occupation of Teaching, focuses on becoming and being a teacher. The second section, The Organization of Schooling, focuses on the school and the district and the implementation of change. The third section, Focusing on Effective Schools, attempts to establish how effectiveness is defined and operationalized in practice. The fourth section, Moving from School to Work, concerns the transition to adulthood and explores the ways young workers learn on the job. Certainly this volume does not cover everything that should be included; space precludes it. Nevertheless, each chapter is a carefully crafted "portrait" of schooling selected to contribute to an understanding of schooling in its social context and thus policy to reform schools.

REFERENCES

Blau, P., & Duncan O.D. (1967). *The American occupational structure.* New York: Wiley.

Bossert, S.T., Dwyer, D., Rowan, B., & Lee, G. (1982). The instructional management role of the principal. *Education Administration Quarterly, 19,* 34–64.

Boyer, E. (1983). *High school: A report on secondary education in America.* Princeton, N.J.: Carnegie Foundation for Advancement of Teaching.

Bredo, E., & Feinberg, W. (Eds.) (1982). *Knowledge and values in social and educational research.* Philadelphia: Temple University Press.

Cohen, M.D., & March, J.G. (1974). *Leadership and ambiguity.* Berkeley, CA: Carnegie Commission on Higher Education.

Cohen, M.D., March, J.G., & Olsen, J.P. (1972). Garbage can model of organizational choice. *Administrative Science Quarterly, 17,* 1–25.

Coleman, J.S., Campbell, E., Hobson, C., McPartland, J., Mood, A., Weinfeld, F., & York, R. (1966). *Equality of educational opportunity.* Washington, DC: U.S. Government Printing Office.

Edson, C.H. (1983). Risking the nation. *Issues in Education, 1, 2, & 3,* 171–184.

Erickson, F. (1982). Classroom discourse as improvisation: Relationships between academic task structure and social participation structure in lessons. In L.C. Wilkinson (Ed.), *Communicating in the classroom.* New York: Academic Press.

Gearing, F., & Epstein, P. (1982). Learning to wait: An ethnographic probe into the operations of an item of hidden curriculum. In G. Spindler (Ed.), *Doing the ethnography of schooling.* New York: Holt, Rinehart, & Winston.

Gouldner, A.W. (1970). *The coming crisis of western sociology.* New York: Basic Books.

Herriott, R., & Gross, N. (Eds.) (1979). *The dynamics of planned educational change.* Boston: Apt Associates.

James, T., & Tyack, D. (1983). Learning from past efforts to reform the high school. *Phi Delta Kappan, 64,* 400–406.

Jencks, C., Smith, M., Ackland, H., Bane, M., Cohen, D., Gintis, H., Heyns, B., & Michelson, S. (1972). *Inequality: A reassessment of the effects of family and schooling in America.* New York: Basic Books.

Kuhn, T.S. (1962). *The structure of scientific revolutions.* Chicago: University of Chicago Press.

March, O.G., & Olsen, J.P., (1976). *Ambiguity and choice in organizations.* Bergen, Norway: Universitets Forlaget.

MacNeil, L. (1984). *Critical theory and ethnography in the classroom.* Paper presented at the meeting of the American Educational Research Association, New Orleans, LA.

Metz, M. (1978). *Classrooms and corridors.* Berkeley, CA: University of California Press.

Metz, M. (1984). *Ethnography, organizational theory, and educational innovation.* Paper presented at the meeting of the American Educational Research Association, New Orleans, LA.

Meyer, M., Freeman, J., Hannan, M., Meyer, J., Ouchi, W., Pfeffer, J., & Scott, W. (Eds.) (1978). *Environments and organizations.* San Francisco, CA: Jossey Bass.

Meyer J., & Rowan B. (1978). *The structure of educational organizations.* In M. Meyer, Freeman, J., Hannan, M., Meyer. J., Ouchi, W., Pfeffer, J., & Scott, W. (Eds.), *Environment and organizations.* San Francisco, CA: Jossey-Bass.

Mishler, E. (1979). Meaning in context. *Harvard Educational Review, 49.* 1–19.

National Commission on Excellence in Education, (1983). *A nation at risk: The imperative for educational reform.* Washington, DC: Department of Education.

Noblit, G., & Johnston, B. (Eds.) (1982). *The school principal and school desegregation.* Springfield, IL: Charles Thomas.

Perrow, C. (1982). Disintegrating social sciences. *Phi Delta Kappan, 64,* 684–688.

Peshkin, A. (1978). *Growing up American: Schooling and the survival of community.* Chicago: University of Chicago Press.

Peshkin, A. (1983). *Fundamentalist Christian schooling: Truth and consequences.* Paper presented at the meeting of the American Educational Research Association, Montreal, Canada.

Rist, R. (1970). Social class and teacher expectation. *Harvard Educational Review, 49,* 411–451.

Rist, R. (1978). *The invisible children: Social integration in American society.* Cambridge, MA: Harvard University Press.

Rist, R. (1980). Blitzkreig ethnography: on the transformation of a method into a movement. *Educational Researchers, 9(2),* 8–10.

Scott, W.R. (1978). Theoretical perspectives. In M. Meyer, Freeman, J., Hannan, M., Meyer, J., Ouchi, W., Pfeffer, J., & Scott, W. (Eds.), *Environment and organizations.* San Francisco, CA: Jossey-Bass.

Sher, J. (1983). On the danger of thinking policy is reality. *Rural America, 8,* 10.

Spicer, E. (1976). Beyond the analysis and explanation. *Human Organization, 835(4),* 335–343.

Spindler, G. (Ed.) (1974). *Education and cultural process.* New York: Holt, Rinehart, & Winston.

Spindler, G. (Ed.) (1982). *Doing the ethnography of schooling.* New York: Holt, Rinehart & Winston.

Weick, K. (1969). *The social psychology of organizing.* Reading, MA: Addison-Wesley.

Weick, K. (1976). Educational organizations are loosely coupled systems. *Administrative Science Quarterly, 21,* 1-19.

Wilcox, K. (1982). Differential socialization in the classroom: Implications for equal opportunity. In G. Spindler (Ed.), *Doing the ethnography of schooling.* New York: Holt, Rinehart, & Winston.

Willower, D.J. (1981). Educational administration: Some philosophical and other considerations. *Journal of Educational Administration, 19,* 115-139.

Wolcott, H. (1973). *The man in the principal's office: An ethnography.* New York: Holt, Rinehart, & Winston.

Wolcott, H. (1976). Criteria for an ethnographic approach to research in schools. In J.I. Roberts & S.K. Akinsanya (Eds.), *Schooling in the cultural context.* New York: McKay.

Wolcott, H. (1977). *Teachers versus technocrats: An educational innovation in anthropological perspective.* Eugene, OR: University of Oregon.

PART I
THE OCCUPATION OF TEACHING

The occupation of teaching has long been portrayed as embattled. In large part this is because schools in general and teachers in particular are subject to conflicting expectations. Lipsky (1980) reminds us that this conflict, together with other conditions found in schools, is such that teachers develop routines to simplify their work. Curriculum, instructional methods, and volunteer programs are examples of the formal routines that are generally seen as necessary. Teaching occurs, however, in a dynamic social context that requires teachers to develop routines and understandings that are not as formal as curriculum, methods, and programs. In fact, teachers select their own model for how they ought to behave. They also learn the pace of the job even as they try to buffer the environmental constraints on their classroom activities. These elements of the craft of teaching are rarely revealed in positivistic educational research. Recent evidence from naturalistic studies of schooling has suggested, by contrast, that it is such factors which play a major role in shaping (a) *how* teachers teach, and (b) how they make decisions about *what* to teach. Thus, by defining teaching as a context, improvement efforts might focus profitably on shaping the context and teaching practices to maximize the learning of students. The four chapters in this section address these critical issues.

LeCompte and Ginsburg carefully examine college students in a teacher education program. Their interest centers on the degree to which teachers in training become involved in using their own experience to define the role of teacher. They contrast symbolic interactionism and functionalist theories and find some support for symbolic interactionism's emphasis on active and creative processes. However, they find that student teachers selectively construct the idealized model used as the basis for personal standards. This suggests that socialization to the role of teacher is a dynamic process involving both passive reception and active social construction. LeCompte and Ginsburg conclude that for teacher preparation programs to have a dramatic impact on the quality of teaching, they must be conceived as teacher socialization rather than teacher education.

Kyle uses a standard anthropological analysis, i.e., "a day in the life," to reveal the complexity of teaching. She illustrates with vivid description that teaching is more than instruction. Teaching includes clerical tasks, schoolwide duties and responsibilities, management tasks, and a complex pattern of events we call instruction. Further, much of teaching involves unexpected events, interruptions, and unclear and conflicting expectations, all of which must be accommodated by the teacher in the isolation of her classroom. Kyle details how Ms. Carr uses routines to manage all this, and as a result, seems to mismanage important dimensions of instruction.

Green, Harker, and Golden take us deep into "micro" ethnography and enable us to see how sociolinguistic, semantic propositional, and literary-text analysis complement and supplement each other in revealing how the construction of a lesson affects student learning. This chapter reveals that the recent emphasis on using time on task to improve student learning may be misguided. They argue that the content of the lesson is as important as the time available. Green, Harker, and Golden demonstrate that a specified instructional system does not guarantee uniform achievement, because teachers must infuse the system with a social definition of the lesson. When a teacher emphasizes a clear definition of task and organizes the lesson around that definition, higher achievement seems likely.

Finally, Van Galen demonstrates how teachers actively manage their environments. She suggests that regardless of the rhetoric about community and parent involvement, teachers structure the nature of parent involvement so that it legitimates the teacher's role rather than generating input to alter teacher decision-making. Van Galen uses a case study of a single school to explore how teacher and administrator perceptions of the ability of parents shape the options extended to parents to participate in schooling. She reminds us that the environment may be managed, but at some cost in terms of responsive schooling.

These chapters provide detailed portraits of teaching. They suggest very strongly that efforts to improve schools must focus on teaching as a context rather than a set of behaviors. In short, they argue that teaching is too complex to reduce to a mechanistic view of the occupation.

REFERENCES

Lipsky, M. (1980). *Street-level bureaucracy.* New York: Russell Sage Foundation.

1

How Students Learn to Become Teachers: An Exploration of Alternative Responses to a Teacher Training Program*

MARGARET D. LeCOMPTE
University of Cincinnati
MARK B. GINSBURG
University of Houston—University Park

INTRODUCTION

Does teacher training really make a difference in the quality of teachers? Many practicing teachers say that it does not and describe their teacher preparation and methods courses as an intellectual wasteland, a necessary, if boring obstacle course between the first two years of college and their careers. In fact, the content of teacher training programs may be a major deterrent to becoming a teacher in the first place; able students who might become teachers use the poor reputation of education courses as an excuse to choose other fields. Once in the college of education, they often find the experience distasteful enough to go elsewhere.

There is some evidence that ordinary people right off the street can teach as well or better than people who have had specialized training (Popham, 1971). In addition, most people can remember especially fine teachers who were influential by the very force of their pedagogy and personality; these individuals serve as models for aspiring teachers who end up teaching as they were taught. In some cases, good teachers teach as they were *not* taught; they will go to great lengths to avoid inflicting upon children the unpleasant school experiences they had themselves. Regardless of how they learned how to teach, most teachers minimize the impact of teacher training on their present behavior, attributing their good—or bad—teaching to everything—except what happened in college.

Despite these conventional beliefs, we think that some models for teaching, both positive and negative, come from the positive and negative experiences which pro-

*A revised version of paper was presented at the Southwestern Sociological Association, Houston, April 2-5, 1979. Gratitude is expressed to Pham Thi-Hue, Carol O'Connor, and Peggy Bradfield for their help in data collection. Comments by Edie Archer, Katherine K. Newman, and Paul F. Secord also helped improve this paper. We would also like to express our appreciation to the University of Houston Limited Grants-in-Aid Program and the College of Education for providing funds to support the research.

spective teachers have had in teachers' colleges. This is a study of 53 graduates from a college of education and how their courses and professors as well as their student teaching assignments influenced how they planned to teach the following fall.

These former students were chosen for the study, because they were among the first graduate of a program which was specifically designed as a model for the teaching styles of its graduates. The unofficial motto of the college was "exemplify what you explicate," which, simply put means that the program was established to provide instruction and educational experiences to prospective teachers in the very same way they would be expected to teach. We were interested in the program, because it was not intended to operate on the assumption that simply *telling* people how to teach was sufficient; instead, students were to be immersed in the "how-to's"—to have ample opportunity to observe and practice and to have practiced upon them what they were to be doing on the job.

The college of education which we studied was part of a large state university located in a fast-growing city in the southwestern United States. It was located in the inner city, though most of its students were commuters from the suburbs.

The program was housed in a new, open-concept building; its architecture was designed to provide an appropriate backdrop for what was planned as competency-based and individualized instruction. The dean of the college of education had helped to plan the building.

Several hallmarks of the program included an initial period of observation in the classroom, intended to help students decide whether teaching really was the right career choice for them; organization of students into teams with a faculty team leader and instructors who were to follow them through their training; and modularized instruction, focused around specific program-wide instructional objectives. A particularly important course was devoted to generic teaching skills, which were said to be distilled from all good teaching and required for any teacher regardless of subject matter or level taught. Several aspects of competency-based education as it usually is envisioned could not be implemented. One was continuous progress, because students were given grades at the end of each semester and could not remain in courses as long as they failed to master the content. The other was complete individualization of instruction. A strong attempt had been made, however, to provide "alternative delivery systems" for instruction, so that if a student had difficulty learning material in one way, other methods usually were available, as were opportunities for remediation. All of these were intended to prepare students for team teaching in open-concept schools and to enable them to tailor instruction to the needs of individual students.

One issue which emerged in the course of this study was the fact that not all the student teaching assignments received by the students were congruent with the open-concept model. Because of this mismatch, some students felt as though they had been trained for teaching situations which did not exist. Others, who had disliked the college of education model throughout their training, abandoned it altogether upon graduation. Theirs was the relief which derives from having had one's personal convictions about an issue finally affirmed; they had not been able to use in student teaching what they had learned in teacher training and felt their college training to be irrelevant.

POPULATION AND DATA COLLECTION PROCEDURES

At the time these data were collected, the college of education was being converted to a competency-based undergraduate teacher preparation program. Two groups of students from the teacher preparation program constituted the population for this study. They were chosen because the curriculum for these groups was viewed by the program designers as the most coherent and well-organized in the college and therefore was felt to be the most likely to have an impact upon students. Each student group also had the same team leader for the entire two years of teacher education.

The two faculty members who served as team leaders were among the architects of the more general competency-based teacher education (CBTE) program. They were interviewed first to determine program structure and content as well as the general philosophy which informed the program. Both team leaders strongly stressed that the entire program was to serve as a model for prospective teachers. They were to be taught in a manner which they, in turn, were expected to model in their student teaching and later careers. Moreover, students were not to model any specific teacher or group of teachers; they were to model their teaching after the program as a whole.

In May, 1975, just prior to the normal graduation time for this cohort, interviews were conducted with 53 of the 60 students who could be contacted; 14 of the 74 students who still were involved with the two teams could not be reached using the addresses and telephone numbers available from the university. The population consisted of 48 females and 5 males. While most were in their twenties, there were a few women in their forties. Almost all subjects lived in the metropolitan area and had chosen to attend this university because it was relatively near where they lived.

Interviews were conducted by three graduate students who had been trained in techniques of unstructured interviewing. They were to record as nearly as possible the *verbatim* responses of the subjects. Respondents were contacted at their homes, and, for the most part, interviews were set up at the university. A few were interviewed by telephone, and one who had already moved from the area responded by mail.

The interview schedule, which was developed by one of the authors after interviewing the two team leaders, was designed to elicit in an open-ended fashion the following information: (a) students' motivation for entering the teacher preparation program and the university; and (b) students' descriptions and evaluations of their experiences during different phases of their program.[1]

---

[1] It must be mentioned that the finding that a dearth of students seem to adopt others' standards for evaluation may stem from our efforts to tap into this dimension by the use of

THEORETICAL ISSUES AND RELATED RESEARCH

Our primary interest in this study was whether or not individuals involved in occupational training programs were active or passive participants in their indoctrination. This question is related to a longstanding debate in the philosophy of social science and is implicit in debates between scholars from two major schools of thought in sociology; structural functionalism and symbolic interaction. In the pages which follow, we outline what these schools of thought are and describe how the debate over agentry structured this particular research project. In this study, the term *agentry* refers to the extent to which individuals are actively or passively involved in directing the course of their lives and careers.

In recent years, perspectives used in the field of occupational socialization have been shifting. Traditionally, studies of occupational socialization have been based, however implicitly, on a model which assumed that training programs (and other less formal occupational socialization experiences) were the most important factors in molding and shaping the ideas and behavior of prospective members of an occupation. This traditional, or functionalist, model[2] of socialization is perhaps best illustrated by Brim and Wheeler's (1966) statement about socialization after childhood: "The function of socialization is to transform the human raw material of society into good working members" (p. 5). Taken to an extreme, it assumes that participants in a training program more or less blindly incorporate into their behavior everything the program tells them about their chosen field. As Merton, Reader, and Kendall note, socialization is the process through which individuals are inducted into their culture. It involves the acquisition of attitudes and values, of skills and behavior patterns making up social roles established in the social structure (pp. 40–41). (See also Eddy, 1969, p. vi.)

While the functionalist view of occupational socialization seems to have remained influential, especially among those responsible for developing and coordinating training programs, an alternative model with roots in symbolic interaction has begun to evolve. Adherents to this model of occupational socialization suggest that even though trainees may be shaped and molded by the program, they also are:

> Working at constructing their own identities. While aware of constraints and problems with their situation, the basic subjective experience of trainees is that they are actively managing their work and controlling their situation with a growing sense of mastery. (Bucher & Stelling, 1977, p. 270)

---

post hoc interviews. It may be that, even if trainees have adopted others' standards for evaluation, they would be unlikely to indicate this explicitly during an interview. Thus, an expression such as: "I like this," while different from the expression: "I learned from him to like this," may be indicative of the same processes occurring.

[2]Oleson and Whittaker (1970) observe that "sociologists concerned with professional socialization [often use] concepts suffused with implicit [deterministic] models from childhood socialization" (p. 189). This has occurred despite the fact that some studies of childhood socialization have raised questions about the validity of the images of the child as an empty vessel, a passive agent and of the process as a one-way, parent-to-child form of influence (see Lewis & Rosenbaum, 1974).

[According to this model,] socialization is not merely the transfer from one group to another in a static social structure, but the active creation of a new identity through a personal definition of the situation: (Reinharz, 1979, p. 34)

Thus trainees are not blind followers or unthinking recipients of information.

It is important to note that although the alternative model posits an active, creative actor who is undergoing socialization experiences, it does not discard completely what Bucher & Stelling (1977) call a "programming effect," or the notion that participants accommodate to the demands of a program for a greater or lesser period of time.

The symbolic interactionist and the functionalist models of occupational socialization can be placed toward opposite ends of three dimensions. These dimensions are:

active———passive
creative———conformist
manipulative———accommodating

Taken together, they help explain the way trainees begin to think about and act in their jobs. Specifically, they delineate the following:

1. The extent to which trainees establish their own personal standards for their own or others' performance rather than accepting the standards of others, including their trainers.
2. The extent to which trainees (a) selectively and partially model the behaviors of their trainers; (b) globally and fully model the behavior of a particular trainer; or (c) model the image provided by the entire training program.
3. The extent to which students solve problems encountered in their training program publicly—whether individually or collectively—rather than seeking solutions privately, especially by individual strategies of internalized adjustment.

As we discuss each of these dimensions, we will give attention to whether all individuals can be conceived of as operating near one end of each continuum at all times or whether people might be seen to vary either among themselves, over time, and/or across circumstances. We believe that the degree to which individuals are active or passive may depend upon the type of program, the way it is implemented, and the motivations individuals have for participation in it. For example, teacher trainees may be more willing to accommodate rather passively to a program with which they are unhappy, if their goal for being in it is very important. Being a teacher—and consequently having to endure teacher education courses—may be more important than short-term goals of fighting policies within the college of education. Similarly, people may relate differently to consciously chosen training programs than to ones about which they feel they had little choice.

Indeed, the controversy between contrasting perspectives may be unimportant, since knowledge of both may be necessary in order to understand how people really behave. A training program may reproduce in people a certain similarity in behavior as they may be transformed themselves by the actions of the same individuals. Such a view of human action as transformative as well as reproductive (see Bhaskar, 1979; Giddens, 1979) seems potentially more valid than one which adheres rigidly to either end of the continuum. In this research, we attempt to test the validity of both views.

Developing One's Own Personal Standards
Versus Accepting the Standards of Others

A central aspect of the functionalist model is the "assumption that the individual seeks social approval and that persons move in the direction of resolving the demands upon them by conformity to the greatest pressure" (Brim & Wheeler, 1966, p. 16). Implicit in this assumption is the idea that individuals accept others' standards for performance in a relatively passive manner.

By contrast, the symbolic interactionist model asserts that trainees are far more active during their preparation program. For example, in their study of graduate students in psychiatry, biochemistry, and internal medicine training programs, Bucher & Stelling (1977) conclude that trainees "were not passive recipients of messages from the accorded agents of socialization . . . These young professionals were constantly making judgments" about the teachers who were trying to socialize them (p. 134). Moreover, Bucher & Stelling note that trainees soon became the ultimate judges of their own competence and effectiveness. Such a practice is congruent with the on-the-job experience of teachers. Lortie (1975) has remarked upon the tendency for teachers to act as the ultimate judges of their own performance. He attributed this in part to the isolation teachers experience in their work settings. Evaluation, if it takes place at all, is in the form of ritualized assessment procedures rather than ongoing constructive feedback. Criteria for evaluating the effectiveness of teaching also have been poorly defined, either by professional educators or researchers, making it more likely that teachers develop their own personal standards to fill the vacuum.

There are variations in the self-evaluation dimension. Bucher & Stelling conclude that self-evaluation increases as students become more deeply involved in the program. However, other researchers suggest that some trainees actively discount the evaluation of others, while other trainees internalize the assessments made of their competence and performance by other people. For example, Loevinger (1976) posited that people who are at the "conscientious" level of ego development tend to have "self-evaluated" standards, while people at the "conformist" level of ego development tend to act in a manner exhibiting conformity to external rules defined and prescriped by others. A third alternative might be one in which trainees accept evaluations of others in certain areas of practice, while in other areas they set their own standards for behavior and performance.

Selective Versus Global Modeling or Influence

This dimension involves the extent to which trainees wholeheartedly adopt the model for behavior which their training program presents. In the case of this study, the poles of the dimension would be represented by two groups of students, one which fully embraced the notion of open-concept, competency-based education and another which picked and chose specific aspects of the program to copy. We have termed the former case *global modeling* or influence; and the second we call *selective modeling*. Here, the analogy of trainees as supermarket shoppers may be helpful. Let us assume that the trainees (shoppers) have been listening to a great deal of advertisement from a particular supermarket. From the functionalist perspective, the shoppers (or trainees) will believe everything they hear; form an identification with the market or its manager (who reads the advertisements over the radio); and put into their baskets everything the store has to sell. However, from the symbolic interactionist perspective, the shoppers or trainees are "persons engaged in conscious choice making" (Oleson & Whittaker, 1970, p. 208). Far from believing everything they are told and buying everything offered, the shoppers or trainees select those items which they view as better and/or more suited to their tastes and styles. One way a trainee can be selective is to identify one instructor in the program and model everything that that single individual displays. Another form, probably more commonly used, involves modeling only certain behaviors displayed by some of the instructors.

Selectivity may even involve deciding that what is displayed is something that one would never want to model (see Bucher & Stelling, 1977, p. 272, for their discussion about "negative models"). A great deal of information training can take place by means of such negative modeling, even though trainees may not be aware that they are learning by identifying with role models. In the case of the teacher training program, role models included the team leader, professors, supervisors, and the teachers with whom the student teachers taught.

Since the range of items available in any given store (or program) may be limited, the shoppers or trainees may decide to look for needed or desired items at other markets or from more informal sources, just as their initial choice may have been guided by what was available or what friends and associates told them. By choosing to enter some establishments and not others, the shoppers or trainees control to some extent the kind of items they may see displayed and from which they may select (Bucher & Stelling, 1977, p. 256; Lacey, 1977, pp. 104–106). Students usually can pick and choose professors and courses; however, they do not have much opportunity to change "stores," unless they choose to go to another university or college, one which may not be so convenient or desirable.

A note of caution must be sounded at this point. When the research primarily involves interviews with trainees, as is the case with our study, it may be that the limited amount of modeling or instructor influence reported by the students is a consequence of efforts by trainees to manage a favorable presentation to interviewers as well as to other students, faculty, and the community (see Thielens, 1977, pp. 167–172). It may also be that the students were too close to their own experiences to see clearly which individuals had influenced them most.

Given this note of caution, it is even more important to look for variations among individuals in the extent to which trainees reported modeling or being influenced by instructors over time and across task and content areas. (See Spatig, Ginsburg, & Liberman, 1982, for research indicating that teachaers-in-training at different levels of ego development vary in the extent to which they are influenced by instructors.) It may be that such variations indicate actual differences in modeling and influence or merely that some trainees subscribe more strongly to a time-honored norm of independence in the culture of the United States, which holds that for an adult "to reach a decision properly . . . inward deliberation should be the key, and outward influence should be avoided" (Thielens, 1977, p. 172). The existence of this norm does not mean that students are immune to the influence of instructors, but that they may discount such influence when interviewed.

Approaches to Problem Solving:
Manipulation Versus Accommodation
A third dimension which distinguishes the two models of occupational socialization pertains to the method of solving problems encountered by trainees in the program. On one side of the continuum, trainees may be viewed as adjusting privately, or accommodating, to the demands of the situation. This is called *situational adjustment,* and in certain senses it conforms to the functionalist approach. It is important to note, as Lacey (1977, p. 72) does, that there are two different forms of situational adjustment. One form is termed "internalized adjustment," in which the individual complies with situational or institutional constraints and believes that they are for the best. This is probably the closest position to that of the traditional structural functionalist. The second form is labeled "strategic compliance," in which the individual complies with the dictates of authority figures and situational constraints *but* retains private reservations about them. This second form, of course, has quite different implications for social change, since when and if the situation or authority figure changes, there is likely to be an "underground" group of strategic compliers ready to support proposed changes.

Bucher & Stelling (1977) discussed how, when the source of the trainees' problem was a supervisor, they often would act first in ways to maximize what could be learned from that person, in spite of any difficulties they were having with their work. They might ask the instructor for help, or they might try to listen selectively, attending to aspects of instruction they thought useful and paying less attention to information which they felt was not.

> But when these strategies for maximizing learning failed, trainees fell back on strategies for minimizing trouble, or, in the language of the respondents, they 'manipulated' supervisors . . . The most common tactic was that the trainees psyched out what the supervisor wanted to hear, and presented their material accordingly. (Bucher & Stelling, 1977, pp. 107–109)

In contrast to the accommodative approach to problem solving just described is the symbolic interactionist view that trainees openly and publicly resist adjusting to difficult situations. They not only resist adjusting, but seek to change whatever seems to be causing the problem. Lacey (1977) refers to this social strategy as "strategic redefinition," which "implies that change is brought about by individuals who do not possess the formal power to do so. They achieve change by causing or enabling those with formal power to change their interpretation of what is or should be happening in the situation" (p. 73). This would occur, for example, if trainees convinced their professors to eliminate a particular course or practice which the trainees found objectionable (see Becker, Geer, Hughes, & Strauss, 1961).

Somewhere in the middle of this dimension is a view wherein trainees publicize their problems but not to those who hold the power to resolve them. For example, some students teachers complained about their assignments to each other, their boyfriends, but not to their supervisors, team leaders, or to their cooperating teachers out in the schools.

We should note that these different points along the problem-solving dimension may represent the actions or strategies of different types of people, of the same person at different points in time, and/or the same person facing problems in different aspects of their training experience. Lacey (1977) explains that among his sample of teacher trainees in England, "some . . . remain true to one or the other of these basic strategies throughout the program, though many shift from one to another position, depending upon the situational constraints" (p. 86).

DATA ANALYSIS APPROACH

Data were analyzed using a content-analytic approach. After reviewing the literature and reaching consensus on the theoretical issues, the authors read the interview protocols in detail. Working independently, each author took one of the two groups of student interviews and recorded all statements which were relevant to one or more of the three dimensions outlined earlier: active or passive agentry, creative or conforming agentry, and manipulative or accomodating agentry.

After individually reviewing each others' work, the two authors cross-checked the recording for consistency between themselves and with the theoretical issues described earlier. Then a typology of responses made by the trainees to their training program was developed. These were arrayed along the active–passive dimension. As Figure 1 indicates, we defined as passive agents those students who adopted the standards of others rather than maintaining their own; who unquestioningly internalized the message and model presented by the training program in the college; who dealt with problems and conflicts simply by accepting for the moment what the college said to do; or who reorganized their behavior and belief to be congruent with college demands, so the problems did not exist any more for them. Students who picked and chose among models, developed their own standards of evaluation, and tried to change situations which created conflict for them were defined as active agents.

	Type of Agentry		
Source of Standards	Self	Self and others	Others
Type of Modeling	Selective of persons	Global of persons	Global of program and persons
Method of Problem Solving	Strategic redefinition	Strategic compliance	Internalized adjustment

Figure 1. Typology of Trainee Responses to Program

While these were not the only possible ways the student teachers could have acted, these distinctions were initially helpful in categorizing the subjects of our study. Each author placed each respondent at some position on each of the three dimensions. While respondents often could be classified according to the typology, some respondents were placed in a "mixed" position, indicating, for example, that a respondent's statements made reference to (a) the use of both strategic compliance and strategic redefinition as means of problem solving, or (b) both the adoption of others' standards and the assertion of one's own standards in making evaluative judgments. After all the student teachers had been classified by both authors, the instances of disagreement over classification of a respondent were discussed and reconciled.

FINDINGS

In presenting the findings, we have provided illustrations of the various positions on each of the three dimensions. Our emphasis has been on illustrating the range of positions, not upon categorizing every statement made by every respondent or presenting every statement which represented a given position. We have used the data to clarify the criteria we used to classify respondents, but we also wanted to provide a sense of the way these student teachers felt about their experiences. In the conclusion, we have displayed the frequency of respondents classified in each position and indicated how a respondents' position on one dimension may be related to their position on each of the other two dimensions.

Source of Standards
The first dimension deals with the extent to which trainees establish their own personal standards rather than accepting the standards of others, particularly their trainers. As was noted earlier, the strict functionalist position with regard to socialization implies a one-way process in which the trainee passively internalizes the evaluative criteria employed by trainers. However, we did not find that our data conformed well to such an "oversocialized" model (Wrong, 1961). Our data indicated that teachers, often described in research literature as highly conforming and said to undergo a "crippling form of professional socialization" (Zeigler & Peak, 1970), tended not to reject the standards with which they had entered the program. Thus, the functionalist model seems to understate the degree of the

autonomy exhibited by teacher trainees with respect to the referents they choose for evaluation.

We found that most trainees fell into two categories: a group which always seemed to evaluate their experiences (e.g., the nature of the program and its instructors as well as their own academic and teaching performance) in accordance with their own personal criteria, and a second group which seemed to accept or internalize certain criteria imposed upon them by their trainers, but which also used their own criteria for evaluating other facets of their experience.

The self-evaluators were the students who seemed, on the basis of statements made during the interview, to have some notion of their own standards or bases for comparison and who used these exclusively to make judgmental statements about the program or their own behavior. For example, one student commented about the program: "There were lots of promises made regarding CBTE that didn't pan out." Another claimed: "The whole program was a joke. . . . The courses were just too easy."

These statements reflect generally negative feelings about the program, which most of the students seemed to share. We were not able to determine how much of this negativism students brought with them upon entry to the program and how much of it developed as they progressed through their studies. For example, as the trainees had more opportunity to discuss the program together and complain about it, they may have begun to generate norms which precluded saying anything favorable about their experiences. Some negativism simply could have been a reflection of an anti-institutional, antischool bias common among students in the late 1960s and early 1970s. By contrast, a more positive response which still indicated the use of personal standards came from a student who referred to a particular course as a "really good course." Another described a methods teacher as "the best . . . she was so well organized."

Like Bucher & Stelling's (1977) findings among students in internal medicine, biochemistry, and psychiatry programs, our interviews with teacher education students revealed a tendency, which increased over time, for trainees to adopt their own standards to evaluate their performance. One self-evaluator explained: "I felt inferior a lot, because of all I had to do; I felt maybe I wasn't in the right field sometimes," but added that:

> In observation and interacting with kids, from that point on I felt good. Now I feel that I have control over any classroom. I have lots of confidence in myself; this developed over the year.

For some teacher trainees this increasing sense of self-determined confidence led them to seek an early completion to their student teaching experience. In discussing her beliefs, one student said that since the program was "competency-based," a student should "be dismissed when you felt competent and your supervisor agreed." For some trainees, being their own primary evaluator meant that they would discount or ignore others' criticisms. One trainee, after describing how her cooperating teacher's instructional style was teacher-centered rather than learner-centered, stated: "I felt guilty when I was part of it [the classroom]. I was criticized for lack of classroom control, . . . but the atmosphere created by the cooperating teacher wasn't conducive to learning."

Although the tendency toward self-evaluation seemed to increase over time, there are indications that even in the early phases of the program some trainees were asserting their own criteria for assessing personal performance. One trainee described her experience in one course in a manner indicating that she valued her work more highly in comparison with her peers than her instructor did. She criticized: "I would work very hard, and someone else would not work as hard but would get the same grade." Importantly, trainees were also critical when their self-evaluations were lower than instructors' formal evaluations. In commenting on the early videotaped simulation lesson assignments, a trainee explains: "We hadn't had methods yet. I got overprepared. I got started and realized I didn't know what I was doing. I felt like a complete flop. I made A's but got nothing out of it."

However, at another point in the interview, the trainee just quoted indicated that she did not rely solely on her own standards to assess her performance in all situations. Despite viewing student teaching as a "farce" and describing her supervisor as a "stumbling block," she expressed a desire for more "immediate feedback" and stated: "I wanted to know what I was doing wrong." This trainee thus exemplified a mixture of both passive and active images. At some times she asserted her own standards for evaluation, while at others she adopted, or at least sought out, the assessment of others in her performance. We do not know, however, whether she would have agreed with or accepted her supervisor's assessment.

By looking at these comments, we obtained a clearer picture of how the standards of others played a role in trainees' evaluative comments. The most frequent mixture of responses among our sample involved employing one's own standards to evaluate the program, while accepting (or seeking out) others' standards to use in assessment of one's own competence.

Expressions indicating that trainees accepted or sought out the standards of others for their own performance were most frequent when they spoke about their cooperating teachers. Some statements were positive:

My cooperating teacher was most helpful in giving me honest feedback about good and bad points.

My cooperating teacher was most helpful in giving me constructive criticisms of my lessons.

Other statements were negative or critical:

The most difficult aspect of student teaching was the fact that I was never really sure what I needed to improve, since no one ever gave me negative criticism.

I wanted more feedback on degree of teaching quality. . . . She didn't critique me enough as either good or bad.

Nevertheless, both types of statement point to an acceptance of, or at least a concern with, standards which the cooperating teacher had for teaching performance.

It might be suggested that when the cooperating teacher provided a formal assessment of the student teacher's instructional competence and thus exercised considerable power over the student's academic fate, it was natural for student teachers to be concerned with their cooperating teachers' evaluation of classroom activities. Another reason why students may have been more receptive to the assessment of cooperating teachers was that these teachers were felt to be on the firing line, closer to the real experience of teaching children than their professors were, and hence were more credible in their judgments than university-based personnel.

It is worth repeating, however, that some of our respondents never indicated such a concern for their cooperating teachers' standards. As indicated earlier and as Bucher & Stelling's (1977) research also suggested, trainees in professional school programs often actively discount others' evaluations of their competence.

Modeling/Influence Processes

A second dimension concerned the way in which trainees dealt with the examples of behavior and ideas they encountered. At the passive end of the continuum, we hypothesized that trainees would model and be influenced by all aspects of the program, taking in everything they saw and heard and incorporating it into their practice as teachers. As already mentioned, this was the image of trainees seemingly held by the organizers of the program; they felt that if they presented specific material in certain ways, trainees would wholeheartedly embrace it. The data revealed, however, that only one of our respondents fit this image, at least as described in the interviews. At one point in the interview this respondent seemed to indicate that she had globally modeled the entire program: "I really was introduced to a whole new facet. I had no idea about the makings of education. I incorporated a system within myself for preparing for teaching." However, this response seemed to be an exception. In following sections, we describe alternative ways in which students felt they were influenced by role models.

Global Modeling of Individuals. A few of the trainees in the teacher preparation program found one person who served as the major model for behavior or ideas for their approach to teaching. Sometimes this modeled or influential person was the instructor of one of the trainees' courses. One respondent made reference to a social studies methods instructor: "really super . . . taught us like we would teach kids. I used it in the schools." Other times the global modeling/influence was linked to the trainees' cooperating teacher. One respondent suggested that she "grew professionally" most during the program when "I was watching my (cooperating) teacher. She was really a good model." Teachers encountered by trainees during the student teaching experience also served as negative global models. "In the school where I taught," one respondent reports, "there are really some terrible teachers out there, and there are a lot of good ones. The terrible ones did everything I would not."

Selective Modeling of Individuals. Notwithstanding the potentially profound influence of global models which were either positive or negative, most of our respondents were more selective than those just described in copying behaviors or ideas to which they were exposed. Just like the shopper in our supermarket analogy, many trainees picked and chose behaviors and ideas from a variety of people with whom they came in contact. Some ideas and behaviors were purposely discarded; others were selected and put into practice because of their quality or value as perceived by the trainee; and still others were selected, but only on a trial basis (see also Lortie, 1975). For example, one trainee seemed initially to describe global modeling/influence: "I was not very close to anyone in the program, except my cooperating teacher, who influenced me a lot." However, this trainee explained later in the interview that it was important "to work with (any idea) so you can see if you like it or not."

Generally, trainees referred to incidents of what we call selective modeling and influence in terms of a cooperating teacher or university professor who provided "a lot of good ideas," "New ideas," or "materials, good ideas."

It is apparent that for some trainees the modeling/influence processes were not only selective but bidirectional. For example, one trainee commented that "I shared my ideas with my cooperating teacher and vice versa." Another trainee related that her cooperating teacher "kepy many of my programs to use them for next year."

Selective modelers showed no signs that they incorporated the ideas and examples of any single person. One respondent remarked that her cooperating teacher was most helpful in terms of "discipline and bulletin boards; offering helpful opinions to me *to take or leave as I saw fit.*" She also talked about problems she experienced in class discipline during her student teaching:

> I brought it up with my student teacher supervisor and [cooperating] teacher. We talked about the situation. After discussing discipline as a topic I felt much better to handle the problem as *I saw* fit. I tried various methods that I felt would work, until finally I found the technique best suited for handling my discipline problem.

Another trainee explained that if the approach "doesn't work when I use it with children, . . . I throw it out and learn something else. I created my own method." This comment provides an important contrast with the statements made by other trainees, who seemed to model globally the entire program or one of the people encountered during their experience in it.

Approaches to Problem Solving

Responses on this dimension resembled those on the other dimensions in that respondents did not generally adopt what we have called the passive approach, i.e., internalized adjustment. In fact, none of our respondents were so classified; respondents either tried strategic redefinition, strategic compliance, or a combination of the two.

Strategic Redefinition. Data collected at the end of a program are unlikely to pinpoint anyone who was totally disaffected with, or involved in strenuous efforts to change, the program. If unable to make any fundamental changes in the program, disaffected students would have either voluntarily or involuntarily left the program much earlier. Thus our data may not reflect the level of discontent or the amount of strategic redefinition attempted.

Only one rather dramatic collective effort to change things was mentioned by the respondents in the study. A group of students developed a petition in response to the unhappiness with the mathematics methods course and delivered it to one of the team leaders. Very few of the respondents in this study actually signed the petition; most did not even mention it during their interview. More generally, confrontation, or active attempts to redefine the situation, were limited to attempts by individual students to solve their own personal problems. To this end, the preferred method was to talk to the team leader, the instructor, or cooperating teacher involved. Sometimes the solution involved a grade change; other solutions involved transfer to another school for student teaching, an extension in course assignment deadlines, or permission to complete student teaching early. Active efforts appeared to be effective in resolving minor individual matters; they were almost totally ineffective, however, in producing major changes in program structure, content, mode of instruction, or personnel during students' sojourn in the program. As one student said: "I signed a petition, went to talk with [the team leader], but nothing helped." The fact that relatively few efforts toward strategic redefinition were attempted and fewer were successful may indicate that even though there was considerable discontent among students, they simply chose not to mobilize their resources sufficiently to bring about a change.

Strategic Compliance. Individuals exemplifying this strategy exclusively or in part constituted the majority of the respondents. While they may have griped occasionally to instructors and on a daily basis with student peers and while many sought solace in the support of friends, husbands, or boyfriends (see also Oleson & Whittaker, 1968), in general they "resolved things the best way I could," "tried to live through it," "worked as hard as I could," and "had to flow with the tide or sink." Their displeasure with the program was publicized in a sense, but only to student peers or outsiders and not to those in positions of authority. Some individuals engaged in temporary subterfuge to disguise their unwillingness to go along with the program: "I would teach the way they wanted me to when they observed me." Others ignored things they did not like or withdrew when the pressure was too much to bear.

There was no course in which I really felt gypped. (The course wasn't required) and I dropped it.

I should have gone in to talk with the principal (about his concern over lack of discipline in her class), but I never did. I just withdrew from student teaching.

SUMMARY AND CONCLUSIONS

We have tried to assess whether the dominant student response to socialization practices in this teacher training program was passive or active. If it were primarily passive, we could have substantiated, for this population, the functionalist belief that content and delivery of training are the primary factors in shaping new occupants of a career, and we could have made the architects of the open-concept, competency-based approach to training quite secure in the belief that their message had been received. If it were primarily active, however, supporting a more symbolic interactionist position, the direct and predictable impact of teacher training would be less clear. Table 1 shows how we categorized the 53 teacher education students on each of the three dimensions. It demonstrates that with regard to the evaluation, or source of standards dimension, no respondents engaged in wholesale adoption of the standards of other people. It should be remembered, however, that these data may represent how the students wanted to present themselves to interviewers rather than a depiction of their true experience. The interview protocols do nevertheless provide a strong indication that many ($n = 31$) respondents felt they assessed their own standards in an active manner when evaluating the program, the activity of other people, and their own performance. Twenty-two respondents exemplified the use of both their own and the standards of others in making assessments of performance.

One of the objectives of university training is to impart knowledge and skills and to provide evaluation to students on the degree to which these knowledge and skills have been acquired. However, if students discount both the value of what their professors want them to learn and the college's assessment of their own achievement, it may be difficult to predict the degree to which a training program really influences their future behaviors as professions. On one hand, students simply may not be conscious of the degree to which they actually have been shaped by their

Table 1. Frequency of Cases Classified Along Each Passive–Active Dimension

Dimension	Active ─────────────────────────────────────── Passive			
Source of standards	Self (31)	Mixed (22)		Others (0)
Type of modeling[a]	Selection of persons (37)	Global of person (4)		Global of program (1)
Response to problem[b]	Strategic redefinition (11)	Mixed (18)	Strategic compliance (23)	Internalized adjustment (0)

[a] Eleven cases could not be classified on this dimension on the basis of comments they made during interview.
[b] One case could not be classified on this dimension on the basis of comments they made during interview.

training and by the evaluations they received in it. Disclaimers such as those we heard, made before they had any extensive work experience as teachers, may not be congruent with behavior they exhibited later on. We were not able to observe any behavior changes made by individual students as a consequence of teacher feedback during their course work, nor were we able to follow them into the classroom to see what they did the following year.

On the other hand, the degree to which a training program turns out successful teachers may be purely accidental, or a function of the initial quality of recruits, rather than of the direct socialization impact of the program. Short of having to maintain the minimum grade point average—at this time, a "C"—to stay in school, students could safely ignore what their professors told them.

On the second dimension, only one respondent was classified at the extreme passive end or appeared to model or to be influenced by the program as a whole, even though this had been one of the primary goals of the program. The interview data also provided only four examples of trainees who globally modeled individual college of education or public school faculty. In most cases that could be classified ($n = 37$), trainees were located at the active end of this continuum; they seemed to model selectively or be influenced by several individuals. In a sense, respondents indicated that they selectively "purchased" a few behaviors and ideas from a wide range of the people to which they were exposed.

One possibility involved negative modeling, as mentioned earlier. While the college purported to have an open-concept approach with competency-based education, ample feedback, and alternative forms of instruction, there was considerable evidence that it was not as well-developed or integrated an example of that type of educational experience as it was portrayed to be. By selectively ignoring aspects of the program which did not match with their initial expectations or with which they did not agree, students may have learned to teach in ways more congruent with what the college really wanted than the negative comments we collected would indicate. In a way, some students modeled the ideal, rather than the actual, aspects of their education experience.

With respect to the third dimension, none of the trainees presented an extremely passive image of continuous internal adjustment to program authorities' demands in the face of problems or conflict experienced. Eleven respondents were classified at the extreme active end of the continuum as engaging solely in efforts toward strategic redefinition. Most trainees engaged in strategic compliance either all the time ($n = 23$) or part of the time, in combination with efforts toward strategic redefinition ($n = 18$).

Overall, the results lend little credence to the extremely passive view of trainees which is associated with the functionalist perspective approach. The extreme active view associated with symbolic interactionalist/phenomenological perspectives approach receives more support, but the descriptions many respondents gave of their experiences were not completely congruent with an active type of agentry. In particular, the number of trainees classified in the "mixed" category on the "source of standards" and "response to problems" dimensions illustrates the need to draw on both perspectives when seeking to understand the socialization process. This point is reinforced further by the fact that the trainees' classifications on one passive–active dimension are not related significantly (chi-square probability for cross-classifications are .40, .95, and .97) to their classification on any other dimensions. Thus while a few respondents exemplified very active types of agentry on a particular dimension, most trainees exhibited some combination of activeness and passiveness on all three dimensions.

Although the self-descriptions of trainees in the program cannot be characterized as extremely passive, there still may be what we have earlier described as a programming effect (Bucher & Stelling, 1977), or an accommodation by students to demands of their training. That is, the trainees were selecting ideas and behavior from a limited range of models. This effect may be enacted consciously or unconsciously. For example, even when selectively modeling, or using their own screening devices to choose from among behaviors exhibited by instructors in the program, the trainees were selecting primarily those ideas and behavior provided by the program. This may be particularly important in terms of the way trainees come to view teaching and schooling in the context of contemporary society; they come to see their chosen field and its place in society in ways similar to those views held by their faculty and supervisors.

One of our respondents commented: "It seemed that the program tried to reinforce the idea that we are professionals. This hit one more than anything else." Being a professional teacher, however, means more than simply possessing the requisite bachelor's degree in education. It implies a way of thinking, acting, and even dressing which the outside world and especially other teachers view as appropriate for a member of the profession. According to Popkewitz, Tabachnick & Zeichner, 1979), "Teacher education articulates not only 'skill' competence, but communicates ways of reasoning about teaching that contain principles of authority, legitimacy and control" (p. 58). These constitute a prevailing orthodoxy. What this means is that education may be an essentially conservative enterprise in that its role, at least in the public schools, has been to transmit to new generations those values and basic cognitive skills deemed legitimate and necessary by dominant groups in society. Colleges, as trainers of teachers, and teachers, as participants in this enterprise, reinforce existing authority structures, patterns of control, and ways of thinking (Ginsburg & Newman, 1985). Even in the most innovative of school settings, teachers can rarely teach values or skills which outrage certain segments of the community, nor can they easily arrange their instruction in ways which violate schoolwide norms of order, timeliness, task orientation, and control (LeCompte, 1978) without jeopardizing their jobs.

Colleges of education are under similar constraints. While professors and deans might subscribe to and write about radical conceptualization of the teaching/ learning process, they must still prepare their students for actual teaching situations. Further, most education professors and administrators have undergone the same socialization as they are providing for their students, albeit some years earlier.

Thus it is unlikely that any teacher training program will, in its basic structure, be a dramatic or revolutionary departure from conventional practice (see Bartholomew, 1976).

The perspective on teacher training already outlined has rather profound implications for the direction of the teaching profession. To develop into a substantially different type of teacher, aspirants to the profession may have to transcend their early training; to develop a substantially different structure for the profession, its relationship to the established order may have to change.

A number of our respondents seemed to feel that they were thinking through the process of their training and establishing their own unique view of teaching. However, colleges and universities may not really present a valid training ground for alternatives to prevailing orthodoxies. It is more likely that teacher trainees tended to subscribe to a rather conservative ideology, even while actively asserting their autonomy in selecting behaviors and ideas to model. This is because the models to which they were exposed in the program, while heterogeneous, did not represent the whole range of ideologies available. "Deschooling," for example, or the idea that gifted individuals might not need certification to teach, were not options. Even though the college in this study executed its ideas about teaching in a somewhat novel fashion, they were arrayed in a fairly traditional framework. The focal points of authority and control had not changed; students still had to do what teachers said and accept their evaluations. Students also had little, if any, voice in the content or direction of training. Their experience was, in our opinion, good preparation for the authority structure and constraints of a real-life teaching career.

Further, if teachers still are, as they once were, servants of the community, their aspirations for increased status, professional autonomy, and control over the standards to which they are held accountable may be difficult to realize (Ginsburg, Meyenn & Miller, 1979). This is especially true insofar as professional teacher education continues to deemphasize, as even the innovative college we studied did, systematic, collective, and expressive modes of problem solving, and to expect students to participate in their training in what we have called a traditional structural functional, or rather passive, manner.

The free spirits leave early or never enter; the disaffected live with their discontent. Long experience with such accommodation may lead educational systems to reproduce themselves.

REFERENCES

Bartholomew, J. (1976). Schooling teachers: The myth of the liberal college. In G. Whitty & M. Young (eds.) *Explorations in the Politics of School Knowledge*. Nafferton, Driffield. England: Nafferton.

Becker, H., Geer, B., Hughes, E., & Strauss, A. (1961). *Boys in white: Student culture in medical school*. Chicago: University of Chicago Press.

Bhaskar, R. (1978). On the possibility of social scientific knowledge and the limits of naturalism. *Journal for the Theory of Social Behavior, 8*(2) 1-28.

Brim, O., & Wheeler, S. (1966). *Socialization after childhood*. New York: Wiley.

Bucher, R., & Stelling, J. (1977). *Becoming a professional.* London: Sage.

Eddy, E. (1969). *Becoming a teacher: The passage to professional status.* New York: Teachers College Press.

Giddens, A. (1979). *Central problems in social theory.* Berkeley: University of California Press.

Ginsburg, M., Meyenn, R., & Miller, H. (1980). Teachers conceptions of professionalism and trades unionism: An ideological strategy. In *Explorations in the sociology of the school.* London: Croom Helm.

Ginsburg, M., & Newman, K. (1985). Social inequalities, schooling and teacher education. *Journal of Teacher Education, 36* (2), 49-54.

Lacey, C. (1977). *The socialization of teachers.* London: Methuen.

LeCompte, M.D. (1978). Learning to work. *Anthropology and Educational Quarterly, 9,* 22-37.

Lewis, J., & Rosenblum, L. (Eds.). (1974). *The effect of the infant on its care-giver.* New York: Wiley.

Loevinger, J. (1976). *Ego development.* San Francisco, CA: Jossey-Bass.

Lortie, D. (1975). *School teacher: A sociological analysis.* Chicago: University of Chicago Press.

Merton, R., Reader, G., & Kendall, P. (1975). *The student physician: Introductory studies in the sociology of medical education.* Cambridge, MA: Harvard University Press.

Oleson, V., & Whittaker, E. (1968). *The silent dialogue: A study in the social dialogue of professional education.* San Francisco, CA: Jossey-Bass.

Oleson, V., & Whittaker, C. (1970). Critical notes on sociological studies of professional socialization. In J. Jackson (Ed.), *Professions and professionalization.* London: Cambridge University Press.

Popham, W.J. (1971). Teaching skills under scrutiny. *Phi Delta Kappa, 52,* 599-602.

Popkewitz, T., Tabachnick, B.R., & Zeichner, K. (1979). Dulling the senses: Research in teacher education. *Journal of Teacher Education, 30,* 5, 52-60.

Reinharz, S. (1979). *On becoming a social scientist.* San Francisco, CA: Jossey-Bass.

Spatig, L., Ginsburg, M., & Liberman, D. (1982). Ego development as an explanation of passive and active models of teacher socialization. *College Student Journal, 16* (4), 316-325.

Thielens, W. (1977). Undergraduate definitions of learning from teachers. *Sociology of Education, 50,* 159-181.

Wrong, D. (1961). The over-socialized conception of man in modern sociology. *American Sociological Review, 26* (2), 183-193.

Zeigler, H., & Peak, W. (1970). The political functions of the educational system. *Sociology of Education, 43,* 129-142.

2
Life as Teacher: Ms. Carr's Second Grade

DIANE W. KYLE
University of Louisville

INTRODUCTION

"Busy" and "unpredictable" are terms commonly used for characterizing teachers' daily lives. A teacher's world often includes ringing bells, frequent announcements, numerous reports and forms, lunch and bus duty, parent conferences, faculty meetings, spur-of-the-moment schedule changes, and, of course, instructional demands. And these illustrate only general events; many others emerge each day within each teacher's unique classroom setting.

The study reported here took place during the 1978-1979 school year in a rural southern school. The setting was initially studied to determine class-size effects on instruction (see Cahen, Filby, McCutcheon, & Kyle, 1983). Concurrently, additional data was collected in order to focus on understanding and describing a second-grade teacher's activities and subsequent emergent problems (Kyle, 1979). The specific questions providing the framework for the research included:

1. What does a teacher *do*; that is, what is the nature of the activities a teacher engages in at school? In studying these activities, what patterns emerge? What influences external and internal to the classroom seem to affect a teacher's activities?
2. As a teacher engages in various teaching activities, what problems develop, from both the observer's and the teacher's view? How does a teacher resolve these problems? What alternatives does a teacher consider?
3. What effects on the curriculum occur as a result of a teacher's activities and emergent problems?

Why study teachers' activities? What insights might one develop from such inquiry? Given the complexity of teaching tasks, it seems logical to assume that teachers often confront problems, some even requiring almost immediate solutions. Certainly a variety of influences affects what teachers do—administrative demands, promotion policies, interruptions. A clearer portrayal of teachers' activities and influences on those activities may facilitate an understanding of how teachers' problems emerge, how teachers tend to resolve those problems, and what appear to be the implications of these choices.

Previous researchers using questionnaires, surveys, and time-sampling techniques have contributed needed insights about the range and types of teachers' activities, the diversity of teachers' responsibilities, and the demands on teachers' time (Daniel, 1958; Etten, 1958; Hawkins, 1975; Sheldon, 1969, 1970). Other researchers, interested in how the classroom context affects teachers, have shown the ways in which environmental demands such as time constraints, instructional tasks, and student behavior influence what a teacher does (Adams & Biddle, 1970; Bossert, 1977; Doyle, 1977; Jackson, 1968; Kounin, 1970; Ross, 1978).

Research on teachers' problems is more limited (Biddle, 1970; Coates & Thoresen, 1976; Lee, 1974, 1975). Through questionnaires and interviews, teachers have identified some sources of job-related anxiety and role conflicts, but these methods have been insufficient for rendering the combination of situations which may contribute to or result in a problem.

The purpose of this study, then, was to spend an extensive amount of time observing the naturally occurring events of a classroom in order to understand more fully the relationships among the teacher's activities, the effects of influences on those activities, and the types, sources, and results of any problems the teacher confronted. Qualitative research methods provided a way of disclosing these aspects of the classroom and are described more fully in the following section.

Research Methods

Educational criticism (Eisner, 1977, 1979; McCutcheon, 1976, 1979a; Ross, 1984) was the research methodology used to conduct the study. This approach is a multidisciplinary one, combining and adapting methods from anthropology and aesthetic criticism and applying them to the study of educational settings and materials. As Ross (1984) notes, the function of the educational critic is "to describe the essential qualities of the phenomenon studied, to interpret the meanings of and relationships among those qualities, and to provide reasoned judgments about the significance and value of the phenomenon" (p. 47).

Data collection techniques include those typically associated with qualitative field research such as extensive observations, interviews, and the examination of educational artifacts. In this study, for example, observations were recorded in field notes over a 5-month period. During the first 2 months, the classroom was observed twice each week. The next 3 months included day-long observations each day for 3 consecutive weeks followed by less frequent visits to gather additional supporting evidence.

Additionally, scheduled and structured interviews with the teacher took place once weekly with other unscheduled discussions taking place when possible throughout the school day. Informal interviews took place with children, the teacher's aides, and the principal. All interviews were recorded in field notes.

In order to gather further data about the teacher's activities and influences on those activities, a variety of documents was collected and examined. These included instructional materials, the teacher's lesson plans, student work, and administrative memos.

The field notes were initially organized according to observation and interview data. However, as patterns emerged, the field notes were organized by category such as types of activities, influences on activities, and teacher's problems. Subcategories followed as they became apparent and as supporting evidence occurred. The categories used were based both on those cited in the literature such as Edgerton's (1977) identification of role conflict as a source of teacher anxiety and on those which emerged due to their significance in this particular setting such as the sources of classroom interruptions.

The written account of an educational criticism includes three interrelated processes. Through detailed and vivid description, the critic recreates the experience and qualities of the educational setting, attempting to describe events so evocatively that the reader can almost see and hear what the critic has encountered. This description also serves as a basis for the other two processes, interpretation and appraisal.

Based on the data described, the critic offers interpretations of the patterns of events, the meaning of behavior, and the relationship between events within the setting and external considerations. Furthermore, the critic appraises the classroom, offering a reasoned judgment of the effects and significance of what has transpired. The following educational criticism, therefore, provides a description, interpretation, and appraisal of the activities and problems encountered by a second-grade teacher.

LIFE AS TEACHER:
MS. CARR'S SECOND-GRADE SETTING

A rural elementary school, built in 1941, provides the setting for Ms. Carr's second year of teaching. Although the high ceilings give a sense of spaciousness, the building is actually quite small; one hall connects all classrooms except for one room downstairs designated for the learning disabilities teacher. The school houses grades K-4, approximately 180 children, 10 classroom teachers, 1 reading teacher, 1 learning disabilities teacher, and 2 parent aides.

Although the stands of pine trees and spacious fields offer an attractive visual background for the school, other aspects of life in this rural location are less desirable. Few employment opportunities exist due to a decline in agriculture and logging and the absence of industry, except for two small textile factories. The area also lacks recreation facilities and public transportation.

The school's student population is 65% black and 35% white, and in the 1978-1979 school year, 93 of 176 children received free lunch. One half of the children live with both parents; one fourth live in an extended family situation, and one fourth live in a single-parent household. Ninety-five percent ride the bus to school.

Ms. Carr also taught second grade at the school the year prior to this study. During the 1978-1979 school year, she agreed to participate in a study of class-size effects on instruction. At the beginning of the year she had 20 students on her roll; in January a new second grade was formed, and Mr. Carr's class was reduced to 13. Although these class sizes are significantly less than what many second-grade teachers face, several of the students had academic and behavioral problems and demanded a great deal of attention. In this context, the study was conducted of the activities and problems Ms. Carr encountered.

STARTING THE DAY

Ms. Carr's morning routines give us a glimpse of the range, types, and interplay of activities making up her life as a second-grade teacher. Let's look in as a typical day begins.

At 8:10 a.m., another school day starts as Ms. Carr rushes into the classroom and, in one almost continuous movement, reaches out to flip on the overhead light, shrugs off and hangs up her coat, and finds a place to set down an armload of graded papers. During the next hour, she seems to be occupied constantly .vith morning preparations of putting up board work, making hurried trips throughout the school to the office and supply areas, and readying the room for the day's activities. By 8:20, early-arriving students begin to enter, usually asking for a moment of Ms. Carr's attention.

Tony: Look at my finger, Ms. Carr. It got smashed in the car door.
Ms. Carr: That really looks sore. Have you done anything for it?
Tony: No, but I might have to go to the doctor.

Students continue to straggle in until all are present by 8:40 a.m. Myriad sounds pervade the room. The constant squeak-bang, squeak-bang of the coat closet door opening and closing as children store their belongings for the day and the grinding of each handle turn of the pencil sharpener underscore childish giggles, chatter, and jostling until everyone settles down for board work.

Jennifer hands Ms. Carr a note from home; Andrew needs to borrow a pencil, and Ms. Traylor comes in from next door with a question about filling out monthly registers. These events occur while Ms. Carr takes roll, collects money for pencils and erasers, cuts out red construction-paper hearts for the classroom calendar, glances over the day's lesson plans, sends four students to the special reading teacher, and answers student questions about the board work. And, then, the first-grade teacher enters: "May I make an announcement? Some people have lost library books; maybe you can help find them. One is *Charlie Brown's All-Stars.* Thank you." A few minutes later, the school secretary knocks softly on the door and comes in to announce, "Mr. Patten (a parent aide) won't be here today." Ms. Carr sighs, frowns slightly, and responds, "He usually reads with one group while I work with another. Guess I'll have to find something else for them to do." But reading class is more than an hour away; now it's time to start the day officially. Turning to the class, Ms. Carr asks, "Are you ready to stand for the pledge?"

This scene of one day's beginning reflects several of the activities and problems characterizing this teacher's life at school. How have these activities evolved? What problems emerge from them? How does Ms. Carr view these activities and problems? Does she, in any way, contribute to the problems she confronts as a teacher? These questions guide our study.

CLERICAL, SCHOOL-WIDE, AND MANAGEMENT ACTIVITIES: TYPES, SOURCES, AND EMERGENT PROBLEMS

Clerical Tasks

Clerical tasks are the teacher's record-keeping jobs. These tasks, ranging from time-consuming activities such as completing report cards and compiling a substitute teacher folder to briefer demands such as placing film orders and updating students' immunization records, occupy much of Ms. Carr's time and attention.

Some of the numerous tasks requiring her daily attention include checking the roll, collecting absence and tardy slips, and recording the information in the register. In discussing this responsibility, Ms. Carr reports:

> We have to keep a roll book. Also, we keep the excuses for absences and tardies and turn them in at the end of the month with our register. However, we don't know if we'll have to do all the numerical calculations in the register until right before they're due—like maybe the day before. Sometimes the aide does them.

The importance of maintaining these records accurately has been emphasized in a faculty memo from the principal:

> *Registers:* Attention has been called on updating and inking registers after each report. There are some still incomplete on data concerning pupils. Please see that this is done. Caution please: Numeral formation needs to be small, uniform, and kept in proper columns.

In addition to checking roll each morning, Ms. Carr spends several minutes collecting money from her students, asking, "Does anyone want to buy a pencil or eraser today?" On Fridays, this activity takes even longer—Fridays are ice cream days and, for 15 cents, a child can look forward to a frozen popsicle afternoon treat. When students pay for workbooks or other instructional materials, Ms. Carr records the purchase in an account book, following administrative instructions. And, as the following memo indicates, correct bookkeeping is important:

> *Account Books.* Each teacher make an appointment with (the teacher aide) and update today.

Other clerical tasks, although not a part of the daily routine, occupy a great deal of preparation time. Report cards, perhaps, are the best example. Every nine weeks, Ms. Carr fills in checklists and writes comments about each child's attendance, academic achievement, and social habits. However, as the following memo for one reporting period indicates, sending home a report card often involves more than evaluating student progress.

> In the Report Card Pak, please send:
> 1. A parent/teacher conference form.
> 2. Bills for any books or supply fees.
> 3. Absence records warning (10 days +).

4. Workbooks with parent evaluation form clamped to the last page worked.
5. Sample worksheets showing parents how to help at home.

A similar set of forms and notes to parents goes home halfway through each grading period, when teachers complete progress reports—instead of report cards—for each child. Although several weeks separate reporting periods, preparing the supplementary materials occupies a great deal of Ms. Carr's time.

Other clerical tasks occur infrequently, sometimes in response to school or system-wide events. These, too, require that Ms. Carr find a place for them in an already busy schedule. The following examples, taken from faculty memos, exemplify the varied nature of these tasks:

1. Parent–Teacher Conferences—Continue to send these requests. Complete your resumes, and give the secretary these records along with a master list of parents seen.
2. Requested task—Please give principal a complete resume of your formal instruction.
3. Referrals must be written. Always use Basic Form with whatever else your specific request may be.
4. Review revised report cards carefully. Write your comments in your notebook before writing them on these reports for review.
5. A.E.W. Observance—November 12–18—Open House Parent/Teacher Conference—Thursday, November 16.
6. Send P/T Conference notices again to parents who have not responded. In *red pencil* write the word *PLEASE!* Explain importance to child.

Ms. Carr's activities, then, include many, varied clerical tasks, some completed daily, some required only once or twice a year, and some scheduled at regular intervals throughout the school year. The time necessary to complete these tasks can range from a few minutes to several hours of concentrated attention. In order to find this time, Ms. Carr often utilizes the first half-hour of the day, assigning board-work activities for her students. According to Ms. Carr, "I have so much to do in the morning, I need something quiet for them to work on."

Clerical tasks, however, represent only one aspect of this teacher's activities. Next, we examine her school-wide duties and responsibilities.

School-Wide Duties and Responsibilities
Ms. Carr teaches in a small elementary school with only 11 faculty members. The teachers often rotate school-wide duties, and teacher aides are available to share some of these responsibilities; nevertheless, each week's schedule contains blocks of time when Ms. Carr monitors bus and lunch duty and engages in a variety of other activities characterizing a part of her role as a teacher.

On Thursdays, for example, Ms. Carr arrives at school earlier than usual for bus duty beginning at 7:50 a.m. During the next 40 minutes, she might show a movie or read a story aloud to the 40 kindergarten, first, and second-grade children who wait in her room until dismissed to their own classrooms. In any case, she cannot follow her usual morning routines of getting ready for the day. Bus duty also interferes with her afternoon routines of grading papers, checking over plans, and straightening the room, since these 40 children return from 3:00 until 3:40 p.m.

Certain duties seem to be part of a day's typical scenario—monitoring students' bathroom breaks, for example. Other responsibilities occur less often than daily or weekly; nevertheless, they exemplify further the range and types of a teacher's activities. Faculty meetings, for instance, usually take place every other week, sometimes lasting for an hour and a half or more. These sessions typically involve announcements of forthcoming events, reports from in-school committees and from representatives to system-wide committees and organizations and discussions of various administrative issues affecting the operation of the school.

Attending faculty meeting illustrates only one aspect of school-wide responsibilities related to being a faculty member; others include both serving on committees and responding to requests from other committees. The following faculty memo entries represent only a few of the committees teachers might join:

> *Testbook Adoptions:* Need chairman for each subject: English [and] Social Studies. These chairmen will also serve on county committees.
>
> *SOQ Committee* for planning in-service for teachers. Need representative in addition to principal.
>
> *Houghton-Mifflin County Committee:* Need representation to this county committee immediately.
>
> *In-Service Survey Follow Through:* Our school needs a teacher representative on this committee.

In addition to faculty meetings, Ms. Carr attends system-wide, grade-level meetings three times during the year. These take place after school. And, seven times during the year, teachers are expected to be present for evening meetings of the Parent Teacher Organization (PTO). The following memo illustrates what this activity sometimes involves:

> PTO—Thursday—7:30 p.m.—Please observe and carry out your responsibilities. If you are Hostess, then you will need to be at the school by 7 p.m. and meet the patrons in attendance as you would welcome them into your home.

Duties and school-wide responsibilities, therefore, require both in-school and out-of-school time. Next, we begin to examine the activities more closely associated with Ms. Carr's involvement with students.

Management Tasks

Management tasks constitute the supervisory, administrative jobs in a teacher's life. According to Jackson (1968) such tasks form a large category of teachers' activities. The findings of this study support Jackson's view. What types of management activities exist in Ms. Carr's teaching day?

First, Ms. Carr watches her wristwatch, keeping track of when it is time for changing classes, lunch, bathroom breaks, switching from discussion to seatwork, and all the other events of the day. Establishing a daily routine appears, for this teacher, to provide a way of dealing with the demands of managing time. For example, the morning bathroom break always occurs between 9:00 and 9:02 a.m., and hearing, "It's time to stand for the pledge" tells us, with a remarkable degree of accuracy, that it is 9:15 a.m.

Many activities throughout the day, then, occur on a strictly scheduled basis, necessitating Ms. Carr's continuous awareness of time. Furthermore, deviating from the schedule could affect other teachers who operate within the bounds of the school-wide schedule. Recognizing this possibility provides an additional incentive for being an efficient timekeeper.

In addition to managing the daily routines, Ms. Carr must remember any special features of the schedule. For instance, Sarah and Frank attend a gifted program on Mondays and need some individual attention on Tuesdays to "catch up;" Tammy has an appointment with the speech therapist at 10:35 a.m. on Thursdays, and four students leave at 8:45 a.m. each morning to work with the special reading teacher—except on Fridays. Ms. Carr juggles these and other special occurrences such as when the music teacher visits or when the students are scheduled to practice for the Christmas or May Day programs.

Management tasks involve more than managing time; Ms. Carr also keeps track of supplies and organizes the "housekeeping" chores of the classroom. Second-grade classrooms are busy settings, containing a variety of materials and supplies necessary for conducting the day's activities. Ms. Carr makes certain, for example, that an adequate supply of green, lined, writing paper remains available throughout the day for children's use. She also checks the availability and condition of the extra pencils, dittos, games, puzzles, art supplies, workbooks, and texts scattered and stored around the room. Although her students help with keeping the classroom supplies in order, Ms. Carr allocates and monitors this and other housekeeping chores—washing the blackboard, cleaning erasers, straightening desks, and generally tidying up at the end of the day.

A variety of activities seems apparent in Ms. Carr's classroom, even in just the first hour of the school day. Not only does she complete a number of clerical tasks, distribute materials, and generally set the day in motion, she also interacts with colleagues, mentally processes the day's subject matter information, and responds to students' personal needs. According to Ms. Carr, she views this variety as a problem, even after almost three years' experience: "Sometimes I feel I have so *much* to do, I don't get *anything* done—or done well."

This perception has been echoed by two of Ms. Carr's colleagues during lunchtime discussion of why teachers joke about—and often act on—the need for "mental health" days. In their view,

The pressure just builds up. There are so many demands—every day!

You have all the paperwork and jobs to do, but then you also have all these individual little personalities to deal with—and some of them are *really* amazing! I think the pressures in teaching are *every bit* as great as for surgeons or lawyers.

How does Ms. Carr cope with the problem of varied activities vying for her attention? The most apparent strategy seems to be the attempt to establish routines (although, of course, *other* contextual factors often interfere with putting them into practice).

Certain periods of the day, for instance, are devoted to particular groups of activities—mornings for preparing materials and checking over lesson plans, afternoons for grading papers, revising or making lesson plans, and attending meetings. And, during certain other times, Ms. Carr seems more accessible to her students for personal encounters—for example, when the children arrive and leave and while everyone gets ready for lunch. Doyle (1977a, 1977b) uses the term "chunking" to describe this practice of grouping discrete events into larger units in order to manage their variability.

Another way Ms. Carr deals with the responsibilities she faces is to take much of "school" home with her. However, Ms. Carr might be able to deal with this problem within her own classroom by considering other ways of accomplishing some tasks. For instance, many children could assume responsibility for collecting money for supplies and ice cream, taking the roll, checking the condition and availability of materials, and many of the classroom's housekeeping chores. Although it may take more time initially to teach children these tasks and to establish a sense of responsibility for them, the long-term effect may be to provide Ms. Carr with a greater amount of time for more student-oriented activities.

Moreover, Ms. Carr may be contributing to this problem of so much to do. For instance, the board-work activities she assigns add to the number of papers she must grade, as do the dittos she uses to supplement her math program. Also, other teachers, perhaps through more efficient use of available time or perhaps because of different priorities, allocate their activities in order to enrich their curriculum, continually trying out new ideas or approaches. Certainly the demands of many activities can create anxiety for a teacher; nevertheless, we must recognize that they can also become an excuse for devoting less time to developing and maintaining a stimulating environment for learning.

Changes in administrative policies, too, might offer possible solutions. For example, perhaps some of the bookkeeping and clerical work now occupying so much of Ms. Carr's time could be reduced by having an aide assume these tasks. And, maybe a bulletin board or memo could be used for announcements rather than scheduling a faculty meeting, further reducing the demands placed on teachers' time.

Many other tasks in Ms. Carr's day relate specifically to instructional matters. We consider these features next.

INSTRUCTIONAL ACTIVITIES

Preparing for Instruction

According to the findings reported in McCutcheon's (1979b) study of teacher planning, teachers spend an extensive amount of time preparing for instruction. Apparently, they consider a number of factors in deciding what and how to teach;

they think about the characteristics of their students, about available materials, time limits, textbook content, testing programs, the season of the year, and administrators' requirements. Ms. Carr reports taking similar factors into account when she plans:

> Some things I'm able to plan for a week at a time—like spelling—but for reading and math I really plan day by day. Either we don't get to everything because something interrupts or I have to check how far we got in a skill or in a story. And if the kids have trouble with something, I have to find other materials—dittos, or games, or flash cards—for more practice.

Ms. Carr plans for a variety of subjects, deciding on activities and finding the materials necessary for implementing her plans. What does this involve? For reading, math, spelling, and language arts, Ms. Carr relies on the adopted textbook series or program, utilizing available supplementary workbooks, dittos, and assessment tests. For morning board work, she uses spelling words from the text but makes up her own sentences for practice exercises. Only occasionally does she introduce new materials into the curriculum. According to Ms. Carr, she often does not know what materials are available in the school:

> Last year the LD and reading resource teachers made a list of all the materials they had, but we haven't gotten any list like that this year. And then new materials come in I don't know about.

Ms. Carr feels particularly limited in ideas for art lessons: "Sometimes it's really hard to think of anything. A lot of the ideas I use come from a resource like the *Instructor.*"

And, of course, planning for instruction involves more than making decisions about page numbers, activities, or instructional strategies. Preparing the materials adds further to this dimension of Ms. Carr's activities as she runs stencils, makes a Valentine pattern for Firday's art lesson, and finds a new set of books and read-along cassettes for the listening station.

We might also consider the activities not apparent in this phase of Ms. Carr's teaching. We don't observe, for example, much variety in her preparations; textbooks, dittos, and written assignments predominate. We see no evidence of ongoing classroom projects or the setting up of special interest areas.

What reasons might account for what we *do not* see in Ms. Carr's planning? She may lack certain knowledge and skills needed to do these things. Furthermore, she believes she is required to follow the adopted textbook series for reading and math. When asked about choices for students who may need an instructional style different from these series, she responds, "I could only use something else in addition to the series, not instead of." Moreover, she believes that the principal wants teachers to follow closely the instructional format of the series with the accompanying dittos and assessment forms.

However, Ms. Carr acknowledges little administrative control over the remaining aspects of her curriculum. Perhaps, then, her limited choices stem from few creative ideas of her own and little awareness of resources she might use for new ideas.

Instructing

When we think of teachers' activities, perhaps our first image is of teachers and students interacting during a lesson. As the following scenes illustrate, periods of instruction involve much more than merely "covering" the content. First, the teacher has to organize the students and materials.

Organizing for instruction

Ms. Carr gets one reading group started at the listening station, adjusting headphones and volume controls ("Ms. Carr, that's too *loud*!"), and checking on the whereabouts of Nick.

Five children in the other reading group gather around the front table, hopping from place to place in musical-chairs fashion until Ms. Carr notices, "OK, you all up there get settled. Nat, is that your seat? Then get in the right place." Soon taking her own place at the end of the table, Ms. Carr distributes the stack of workbooks and phonics dittos in front of her.

Once organized, the lessons can proceed, but managing the situation is a continuous process.

Managing groups and behavior

One reading group works on phonics dittos and board work while Ms. Carr and the other group read, "My Dog is a Plumber," a poem about aspiring to be what you want to be. Ms. Carr asks, "What could you be when you grow up?" But before Claire can answer, Ms. Carr notices three students wandering around the room. "All right, I don't want to see all these people up. Some are trying to see the board." The children take turns reading the poem, but soon five in the other group finish their work and whisper softly to one another or get up to explore. Again, Ms. Carr notices, "If you have finished, find something, but *do not* get up every five seconds." With hardly a pause, she turns back to ask, "What does the dog do that makes you think he's a boy?"

In the midst of organizing and managing the instructional scene, however, the teacher focuses on subject matter, as this math lesson shows.

Introducing new skills

Ms. Carr passes out dittos and says: "We're going to go over the first page together. This is something a little different. David, read this. The rest of you listen."

David reads the word problem.

Ms. Carr: "How do we find the answer to the problem David read? Barry?"

Barry: "Put down 335 and 338 and add them."

Ms. Carr: "Yes, let's solve it."

After going over two more problems together, Ms. Carr hands out a ditto and begins moving around the room, answering questions and offering help when needed.

Evaluating Student Progress

In several ways, system-wide policies affect Ms. Carr's activities in evaluating student progress. As mentioned previously, every four to five weeks Ms. Carr is required to provide checklist information and narrative comments regarding each student's work. Additionally, she administers and scores system and state-wide tests of academic achievement. And, the adopted textbook series for reading includes an extensive set of assessment tests. All of these tasks supplement the more routine evaluations Ms. Carr makes as she talks with students, checks workbook pages, and looks through the always-high stack of student papers calling for her attention at the end of the day.

Instruction-Related Problems

In the descriptions of instruction in Ms. Carr's classroom, certain patterns of problems that occur seem related to simultaneous events and in-class interruptions.

Simultaneity. The following example illustrates the everything-happening-at-once feature of Ms. Carr's classroom:

Ms. Carr readies the room for reading, stacking workbooks and dittos on the front table, where five children wait restlessly, and setting up the listening station in the back. Seven boys rush through the door, laughing and shoving as they enter.

Ms. Carr: "OK, you all sit up here in the desks, and you three go on over to the listening station." She hands a ditto to the ones doing seatwork.

Ms. Carr sits down at the front table. Just as she begins, "Today we want to review these two sounds," Kevin, obviously confused, shouts from the listening station, "Ms. Carr, they went on the number two."

Nathaniel, too, calls out: "It's too loud, Ms. Carr."

Ms. Carr gets up, goes to the back of the room, checks the volume setting on the tape-recorder, makes sure everyone's on the right page, and returns to her reading group.

Again she starts, but a soft knock on the door draws her attention and, also, she notices Sharon leaving her desk to wander the room. On her way to see who is at the door, Ms. Carr reminds Sharon, "There's too much going on for you to be up walking around." During the next minute, Ms. Carr reads and responds to a memo and once more returns to the by-now-noisy reading group, this time with a command, "All right. I'm not going to have so much noise in here. Tommy, turn back around."

The group at the listening station finishes, and an insistent Malcolm yells, "Teacher, we're at the end of the tape."

Ms. Carr, with an audible sigh, leaves the group at the front to go turn over the tape. Glancing over her shoulder, she watches three boys talking instead of working, and says: "Andrew, Steven, and Carl, no one can work here while you're talking."

Back with her reading group, Ms. Carr continues once again, "Let's go over these *fr* words."

According to Doyle's (1977a, 1977b) findings, successful student teachers adapt to simultaneity with "distractible" behavior, meaning they often do not appear to be attending solely to one activity but instead scan the room frequently during small-group instruction, spotting potential problems before they occur. Kounin (1970) uses the terms "withitness" to describe teachers' ability to convey to students their awareness of what is taking place in the classroom and "overlap" to describe the way teachers cope with simultaneous events.

Ms. Carr exhibits some of these traits; even while attending to one discussion, she glances around the room, monitoring where students are and what they are doing. At times, Ms. Carr deals with one event and ignores the other; for example, she might continue listening to John read and not respond to Jerome's raised hand. On other occasions, she tries to do two things (or maybe more) at once—such as writing the afternoon's spelling assignment on the board while making certain everyone takes turns washing their hands for lunch. She does acknowledge, however, that "One of the *biggest* problems for me is having to deal with so much that's happening at the same time."

Finding successful adaptive strategies in response to this problem represents one option available to a teacher, certainly a necessary and beneficial one since, no matter what changes can be incorporated, simultaneous events are not likely to disappear from the classroom scene. For instance, intrusions from outside the classroom, from the larger school context, often contribute to this problem but are not within Ms. Carr's power to control. In other instances, however, Ms. Carr's management techniques appear to cause several events happening at once. In other words, in addition to adapting, the possibility also exists of finding ways to limit the degree of simultaneity, perhaps through alternative classroom routines and management techniques—teaching children how to turn over a cassette tape, for example.

Instead of establishing procedures to enable children to handle supplies and equipment or to make their own decisions about when to sharpen a pencil, go to the restroom, or get a drink of water, Ms. Carr retains authority over these incidents. This need for control produces more demands on Ms. Carr's attention and reduces the time she can devote to any one. Furthermore, such classroom management may limit the opportunities available for children to develop a sense of responsibility and to practice effective decision-making skills. Perhaps Ms. Carr does not know how to make such changes or, perhaps, she does not believe changes are necessary or even appropriate.

Contending with many activities occurring at once often means the teacher interrupts one child to deal with the problems of another or races back and forth between two small groups. In any case, this problem often results in breaking the continuity of a lesson and, perhaps, limits the extent of what children can learn from the experience. Furthermore, Ms. Carr's practice of dividing her attention among many simultaneous events means she has less time to focus her attention on the children's need for adequate time and opportunities to express themselves fully and to ask questions.

In-Class Interruptions. Reinforcing the simultaneous events are the interruptions occurring within the classroom. Usually these take place when Ms. Carr organizes the class for small-group instruction:

> Ms. Carr (to one reading group): "OK, today we want to talk about words with these sounds *ad* and *dr*. Who can tell us an *ad* word?"

> Paul (in another group doing board work) walks up to Ms. Carr: "Ms. Carr, what's that third word?"

> Ms. Carr turns around, glances at the board, reads the word, and turns back to the group.

> Sandy moves up to the reading group next, asking, "Ms. Carr, can I sharpen my pencil?"

> Ms. Carr stops, checks the pencil point, and responds: "You have other pencils there; use one of them."

> Paul returns, needing help with another word; soon he is joined by two classmates who also need help, and by Chad who wants permission to leave for the restroom.

> Ms. Carr tries to ignore them: "Shh, I want to hear Donna read this sentence."

As this example illustrates, classroom management also relates to the existence of in-class interruptions. These occur most often when one group finishes an assignment before Ms. Carr finishes working with another group. With few options within their control and with few supplementary activities available in the room, many of the students interrupt with questions. If these children had interesting supplementary activities to turn to when finished with an assignment and better understood their responsibilities, fewer interruptions may take place.

Ms. Carr views as problems the many, often simultaneous tasks occupying so much of the school day. Furthermore, the frequency of interruptions concerns her. While she may be able to reflect about these problems and to develop some alternative strategies for dealing with them, she also may benefit from suggestions from other sources, especially other teachers who have found effective solutions.

EMERGENT PROBLEMS

Unpredictability

Much of what occurs in the course of Ms. Carr's day at school involves unexpected events originating from a variety of sources. Certainly, some of these are unavoidable; this feature of the school setting simply reflects a characteristic of life in general, the inability to control or foresee all possibilities.

So when Randy leans out of his desk and gets quite sick during a language arts lesson, Ms. Carr, although unprepared, responds almost instinctively. Picking Randy up and rushing him from the room, she sends Cynthia for the custodian and directs the rest of the class, "You all stay quiet now." And, when a sudden snowfall causes early school dismissal, Ms. Carr stops the lesson, allowing the children to watch out the window, "oohing" and "aahing" as the snow gets deeper.

In other instances, however, Ms. Carr believes administrative policies create some of the unforeseen problems she contends with. Consider the following early morning battle with the duplicating machine:

> Ms. Carr, in the midst of getting the materials ready for the day, hurries to the office to run off six stencils. The machine, however, doesn't cooperate; it wrinkles the paper and leaks fluid.
>
> Ms. Rogers (a fourth-grade teacher): "Guess the paper supply is running low."
>
> Ms. Carr: "What about all these boxes under the table?"
>
> Ms. Rogers: "That's next year's supply."
>
> Ms. Carr: "Well, they better put it away 'cause I just might use it. This machine just doesn't work unless you've got a big stack of paper."
>
> After spending 25 minutes to run off six stencils, Ms. Carr shares, "I am *thoroughly* frustrated. I guess Ms. Sullivan (the principal) gets flak from the central office about supplies and tells the aides to tell us we're out of everything. We know it's here, though. That machine won't work unless there's a big stack of paper, but I couldn't get any to run off these six stencils. And look at the time I spent when I needed to be doing other things."

In Ms. Carr's view, therefore, certain administrative policies can influence the feature of unpredictability; for example, being able to depend on a workable duplicating machine requires the provision of adequate supplies. An additional example of administrative influence involves decisions regarding report cards.

As mentioned previously, every four to five weeks, some type of report goes home, either a progress report or the official report card, accompanied by various other forms, workbooks, and requests. The principal, however, does not announce the exact date for sending everything home until the day arrives. Ms. Carr discusses the problems this creates for her:

> I just can't figure out why she keeps it such a secret. I really thought report cards would go home last Thursday. Instead, they went home Monday. I had already stapled the pink slip in the math workbooks for the parents to check that they'd looked over the work. When I went on and used the workbooks Friday, the kids got all confused.

Recently, Ms. Carr faced unpredictability in a different sense—with the addition of a subject to the curriculum. During an afternoon language arts lesson, Ms. Carr received a memo from the principal, asking her to write a description of how she teaches handwriting and then to meet with her after school. In the conference, Ms. Carr learned she was expected to teach formal handwriting lessons. Later, she expressed her feelings about this:

> This thing about handwriting really gets me. I asked for books and never got them, so I've checked their writing in other lessons. I just never knew I was

supposed to have formal lessons, and now I have to find time *somehow* to teach this.

As we can see from the examples, unpredictability is, at times, an unavoidable problem for a teacher; little can be done to alter certain influences affecting the flow of classroom events. In other cases, however, intervention may be possible. Administrators, for example, may be able to modify some of their decisions, if they are provided with evidence of problems such decisions seem to create for the teacher.

External Interruptions and Disruptions

Interruptions occurring throughout Ms. Carr's school day seem to come from several sources external to the classroom setting. For example, other adults in the school comprise one major source, because they enter the classroom on a variety of errands. The following three examples represent only a fraction of the number actually occurring during several weeks of observation.

1. The fourth-grade teacher comes in to ask Ms. Carr to switch lunch periods with her today. Ms. Carr agrees. Seven minutes later, the other second-grade teacher enters, concerned about how the switch affects the afternoon schedule.

2. The Title I aide stops by to include reading reports with students' report cards. Although Ms. Carr is in the midst of helping her students with their math assignment, the aide announces, "These are the only ones in alphabetical order. Thank goodness."

3. The first-grade teacher comes in to ask if any of the children have seen a purse one of her children has lost.

On other occasions, teachers send their students to ask a question or to return or borrow materials. Each time an interruption occurs, Ms. Carr must shift the focus of her attention. In the following scene, we can see how such intrusions affect instruction:

Ms. Carr sits with her reading group at the front table. The school secretary enters to ask a question. During the two minute conversation, Franklin and Steven start giggling and pushing their books across the table; Paul tips his chair far back against the blackboard.

Turning back to the group, Ms. Carr says sternly: "OK, you all settle down. Paul, one day you'll move back like that and fall and hit your head."

Eight minutes later a parent comes to the door, then walks away. The secretary re-enters. Ms. Carr responds then turns back to the group, "Everyone should be following along."

Two minutes later the visitor returns and again walks away. Soon the principal steps through the doorway, glances around and leaves. Ms. Carr hasn't seen her, but Cliff has: "Hey, Ms. Carr, Ms. Sullivan just came in."

Ms. Carr: "I wish you all would be quiet and pay attention."

Ten minutes later the parent returns, expecting a conference. Ms. Carr leaves; the class gets noisier until an aide walks in to watch them.

What are the possible reasons for so many interruptions from colleagues? First, few scheduled opportunities exist during the school day for contact with other adults; teachers, for the most part, remain isolated in their classrooms. Perhaps stopping by to ask a question or to borrow a book is a way to seek out needed adult companionship. Also, some teachers may not view interruptions in their own classrooms as a problem and, therefore, do not perceive the problem they may be causing for a colleague.

A second reason such interruptions occur may stem from administrative policies. The principal's concern for contact between school and students' homes, for instance, permitted an unscheduled parent-teacher conference during class time. This visit resulted in the secretary, the principal, and the parent entering the classroom and distracting children's attention from their work. The principal can create other interruptions, too. For example, she might enter the classroom with a question or for a brief conference. And her special interests such as having an elaborate May Day program can result in interruptions of the regular schedule to provide rehearsal time for the students.

In addition to interruptions from colleagues and other adults, faculty memos and bulletins constitute another major source of external interruptions. Since this school does not have an intercom for general announcements, many times the teacher must read a memo immediately, initial it, and send it on. The following is a typical example:

For Your Attention:

At any time when it is necessary for you to answer the telephone, please write the message on the pink form (sample attached) which you will find on the secretary's desk.

Sign and send on right away.

Ms. Carr views interruptions as a key problem in her life as a teacher.

All the memos really get to be a problem. Some days there are so many, and they always seem to come at the busiest time—then you have to take your attention away from the group.

I'm so aware of the many interruptions. They take so much time, and then I have to get the kids interested again. It's really the kids who suffer, too. It takes *their* time.

Interruptions, then, appear to result from varied sources, influencing the continuity of life in this classroom and resulting in feelings of frustration and annoyance for Ms. Carr. Not only does she believe students lose valuable instructional time, she also must cope with students' misbehavior and inattention after an interruption of a lesson. And, interruptions affect Ms. Carr's planning; she reports, "They *often* cause me to carry over activities from one day to the next."

Another problem Ms. Carr faces involves the *scheduled* disruptions of the daily routine, necessitating a range of adjustments. These disruptions are varied in nature and impact. For instance, preparing for the Christmas program affects the daily schedule for over a week, but the SCA brownie sale takes only 10 minutes of a spelling lesson.

The next problem focuses on a more subtle, less easily discernible conflict for a teacher—role conflicts. Ms. Carr shares her view of this problem in the following section.

Role Conflict

Edgerton (1977) perceives role conflict as a major source of teacher anxiety. In her view, teachers must often assume mutually exclusive roles—as executives, representing the organization, enforcing rules, and evaluating student progress and as counselors, focusing more on student needs and interests. Evidence from the classroom, supported by Ms. Carr's comments, indicates this is indeed a problem for this teacher. As Ms. Carr explains: "It's hard sometimes when you want to let them talk when they seem to want to—like in reading—but you also have to get on with the lesson." The press of time and demands, it seems, contributes to conflicts as Ms. Carr tries to listen to the children and also tries to maintain the flow of a lesson or the day's events. So David's story about a favorite pet is interrupted in reading class by directions for the phonics ditto, and Jennifer's concern about her sore arm occupies only a moment of Ms. Carr's attention before she turns to direct the other homeroom students, "OK, let's settle down and get to work now."

The conflict between the executive and counselor roles continues throughout the school day as Ms. Carr maintains authority ("I want the noise in here to stop"), attempts to stimulate interest ("Who has an interesting library book they'd like to share?"), evaluates academic and social development ("Marc, do you and Chad want to work together for a while?"), and cares about her students' lives ("Steven, did you have fun on your family's trip?").

According to Ms. Carr, the system-wide promotion and grading policies add to conflicts in her roles as a teacher.

> We're told in education courses to help children feel good about themselves, not to make them feel like failures. Then we have to use a grading system where we have to mark "Needs Improvement," if the child isn't on grade-level in reading and math. So, no matter how hard a child has worked, no matter how many "Smiley" faces he or she gets on papers, the report card says it's not quite good enough. You know that must make a child feel bad."

As Edgerton has explained, a variety of roles will continue to define the life of a teacher; however, helping pre-service teachers recognize and understand this phenomenon may facilitate their ability to deal with it. Furthermore, such understanding may help teachers

> be less traumatized by the "unknown" forces they confront during their first teaching experience. As they remain in the classroom, an understanding of

role conflict will enable them to be aware that the debilitating problems and tensions they experience are not due solely to their own personal weakness or inadequacies. (Edgerton, 1977, p. 122)

Teachers' skills in adjusting to a variety of roles may mean they convey fewer conflicting messages to their students. As a result, students may feel more comfortable and secure in the classroom environment.

SUMMARY AND IMPLICATIONS

The three key questions guiding this study provide a useful organization for summarizing the findings.

What Do Teachers Do?

Ms. Carr's life as teacher includes many events and requires wearing a number of different "hats." As we have seen, the role encompasses far more than instructional responsibilities such as planning, finding appropriate materials, explaining and discussing lessons, managing groups, monitoring student behavior, and evaluating student progress. In addition, Ms. Carr collects money, fills out reports, runs off stencils, keeps the classroom supplied with materials, watches the clock, and, occasionally, plays hostess to visitors. And, Ms. Carr attends to some of the more personal needs of her students—getting zippers unstuck, tying shoelaces, and listening to the special stories children tell, sharing the excitement and disappointments of their lives. Combine all of these activities with the time taken up by lunch duty, bus duty, textbook evaluations, county meetings, and parent conferences, and we have an illustration of the busyness teachers often allude to when discussing the nature of their professional lives. For Ms. Carr, to be a teacher also means to be a secretary, a bookkeeper, a custodian, a nurse, a guard, a counselor, a diplomat, a facilitator, a comedian, and, at times, a mind reader. As she explains,

> When I went out to do student teaching, I just didn't know what to expect, did you? I mean, it would be so great if you could know all you have to do as a teacher, so you wouldn't be so surprised by it all.

We read with surprise and amusement (as well as gratitude for progress) reports of the duties expected of teachers during the 1800s—stoking the fire, toting in drinking water, scrubbing the floors. Ms. Carr can be thankful for societal changes. Nevertheless, her experiences reveal that much is expected of today's teachers. Cuban (1971) believes that the nature of some demands on teachers conveys a negative message about teachers' roles as professionals. Reading faculty memos reminding teachers not to make absence marks "too tall" in registers, to write invitations to parents with a red-pencil *PLEASE*, and to be conscientious in playing hostess may cause some to concur with Cuban.

What teachers do seems to be influenced, in part, by administrative policies and decisions. Faculty memos and meetings provide evidence of an emphasis in this setting on accurate record keeping, maintaining contact with students' homes, and assuming responsibility for related professional duties such as serving on committees, and each task further extends the realm of teachers' activities.

Additional evidence, however, indicates the influence of teachers themselves. Ms. Carr, for instance, has chosen to do many of the tasks she could delegate to her students and, as a result, has increased her own workload. Furthermore, not all teaching activities are externally imposed; teachers can still make many choices regarding instructional strategies or management routines. Consequently, a teacher's own decisions can affect the activities encompassing his or her professional life.

What Problems Do Teachers Face?

Evidence from this classroom indicates various sources of problems—from the number of diverse activities the teacher has responsibility for, from simultaneous, often unpredictable events, from interruptions and disruptions of the routine, from role conflicts, and from lack of preparation or ingenuity to deal with it all.

While many of her concerns about the multitude of teaching activities may be valid, evidence in this setting indicates Ms. Carr may contribute to the problem of "so much to do." For example, board-work assignments predominate and increase the teacher's paperwork. Furthermore, Ms. Carr does not appear to explore ways in which the children or the aide could handle many tasks for which she retains responsibility. The possibility exists that she permits her tasks to be more difficult than they inherently are, and, as a result, devotes less time and effort to the more intellectually rigorous activities necessary to enrich her curriculum.

Ms. Carr seems particularly concerned about dealing with the many simultaneous events in her situation, particularly during reading instruction when students work in small groups. In discussing this problem, she attributes its occurrence mainly to her students' immaturity and lack of self-discipline. She has not suggested, in these conversations, alternatives she might try to implement to resolve the problem such as providing opportunities for students to develop the self-discipline that she perceives they lack.

Certainly not all problems originate with the individual teacher's limitations; other sources of problems exist and influence teachers' lives. In this setting, we can see the effect of certain administrative policies. For example, the principal's decision not to reveal in advance the date for sending home report cards creates uncertainty for Ms. Carr who must also contend with repeatedly hearing, "Is *today* report card day?" from her impatient second graders. And, the principal could choose to have fewer faculty meetings, thus demanding less time of the teachers, and could delegate many of the teachers' clerical tasks to the paraprofessionals working in the school.

Additionally, Ms. Carr identifies interruptions as a major irritant in her life and as a source of classroom problems; in her view, the continuity of lessons is broken, and behavioral problems occur as students' attention is diverted. Interruptions appear to come from several sources. Other adults in the school enter and leave on a variety of errands to ask questions, to borrow or return materials, or just to chat. Adults from outside the school, perhaps unaware of their effect, also interrupt;

parents stop by for an unexpected conference, or resource personnel arrive late for a scheduled appointment. And, interruptions occur as the extensive number of faculty memos circulate the school, requiring immediate attention from the teacher.

Some of the problems evident in this classroom may be due, in part, to limited opportunities in the teacher's pre-service education for understanding roles teachers assume other than the instructional role, for developing skills in reflective thinking and problem solving, and for exploring alternatives for instructional practices. The evidence indicates that the problems emerging from a teacher's activities originate in external influences affecting the teaching context and in the individual teacher's skill in meeting those demands. The ability to reflect about perceived problems, to consider possible contributing factors (including personal limitations), and to search for alternative solutions appear to be significant attributes in a teacher's life.

How Do Teachers' Activities and Problems Affect the Curriculum?

A teacher's response to the activities of teaching affects, in part, what the children in the classroom have an opportunity to learn. For example, Ms. Carr tends to respond by focusing on routine tasks and, in order to find time for her own work, assigns "busywork" for the children. Such responses limit curriculum possibilities. Teachers who view themselves as too busy and hassled may assume that developing new approaches or a variety of activities for the students would create more work for themselves. However, the evidence in this classroom fails to support such an assumption and suggests, instead, that greater variety in the curriculum might alleviate some of the behavioral and management problems Ms. Carr confronts.

Teachers' role conflicts can also affect the curriculum. If a teacher exhibits extreme vacillation between counseling and controlling roles, some children attempting to adjust to and understand the discrepant, double messages may be hesitant about interacting or participating as fully as possible.

Furthermore, effects on the curriculum may stem from external influences which create problems for the teacher, typified in this study by the number and nature of interruptions occurring throughout Ms. Carr's school day. Evidence suggests these interruptions break the continuity of a lesson and affect children's attention, thus, perhaps, limiting their possible degree of learning.

Implications

For Intervention. The findings of this study indicate a number of possible points of intervention for lessening the problems teachers confront. Teacher education is one area. As mentioned previously, Ms. Carr has revealed a lack of awareness, prior to teaching, of what the role of teacher actually encompasses. The lack of variety in her curriculum, her apparent need for control, and her limited exploration of alternatives may not indicate complacency or unwillingness to attempt new ideas, but, instead, may be evidence of weaknesses in her preparation for teaching.

What does this suggest for teacher educators? In the best of all worlds, we might hope those educating future teachers would maintain contact with classrooms and with the concerns of in-service teachers and would share such experiences with their students. In this way, pre-service teachers would have access to the reality of problems existing in teachers' lives. An alternative or addition would be for teacher educators to use the growing number of descriptive studies of classrooms as discussion starters, allowing students to analyze and discuss the various educational issues revealed. For example, students could focus on the origin of teachers' problems, could speculate about the possible options the teacher might employ, and could consider the likely resulting effects on the curriculum. Such activities could be combined with students visiting classrooms, conferring with teachers, and reflecting and talking about what they've seen and heard.

Administrators might also provide some intervention. The findings indicate, for instance, the way administrative decisions (about reading programs, parent conferences, faculty memos, etc.) can contribute to problems in teachers' lives. Provided evidence of such effects, administrators might be able to speculate about other possible policies or procedures. Furthermore, administrators could be instrumental in providing opportunities for teachers to identify, discuss, and attempt to resolve some of the problems concerning them most. For example, Ms. Carr might benefit greatly from discussions with colleagues about classroom management strategies. And, the entire faculty could undertake a study of the sources of interruptions and possible ways of reducing them.

Teachers, too, could intervene to resolve some of their concerns. Instead of waiting for administrators to convene meetings or to provide the impetus for problem solving, teachers, if motivated and if willing to invest the necessary time and energy, could organize their own problem-solving groups. However, this implies the teachers would perceive such an activity as an appropriate aspect of their roles as teachers. Perhaps teachers' hesitancy in initiating problem-solving endeavors stems, not from lack of willingness or interest, but from views about role definition.

REFERENCES

Adams, R.S., & Biddle, B.J. (1970). *Realities of teaching: Explorations with video tape.* New York: Holt, Rinehart, & Winston.

Biddle, B.J. (1970). Role conflicts perceived by teachers in four English-speaking countries. *Comparative Educational Review, 14,* 30–44.

Bossert, S.T. (1977). Tasks, group management, and teacher control behavior: A study of classroom organization and teacher style. *School Review, 85,* 552–565.

Cahen, L.S., Filby, N., McCutcheon, G., & Kyle, D.W. (1983). *Class size and instruction.* New York: Longman.

Coates, T.J., & Thoresen, C.E. (1976). Teacher anxiety: A review with recommendations. *Review of Educational Research, 46,* 159–184.

Cuban, L. (1971). Teaching the children: Does the system help or hinder? In V.F. Haubrich (Ed.), *Freedom, bureaucracy, and schooling.* ASCD 1971 Yearbook. Washington, DC: Association for Supervision and Curriculum Development.

Daniel, C.I., Jr. (1958). An analysis of nonteaching duties of elementary school teachers in the first-class districts of the state of Washington (Doctoral dissertation, University of Washington, 1958). *Dissertation Abstracts International, 19,* 76.

Doyle, W. (1977). Learning the classroom environment: An ecological analysis. *Journal of Teacher Education, 28,* 51-55.

Edgerton, S.K. (1977). Teachers in role conflict: The hidden dilemma. *Phi Delta Kappan, 59,* 120-122.

Eisner, E.W. (1977). On the uses of educational connoisseurship and criticism for evaluating classroom life. *Teachers College Record, 78,* 345-358.

Eisner, E.W. (1979). *The educational imagination.* New York: Macmillan.

Etten, J.F. (1958). *A time study and job analysis of teachers' activities in a selected elementary school.* Unpublished doctoral dissertation, Loyola University, Chicago, Illinois.

Hawkins, W. (1975). Research on the determinants of classroom processes. *Classroom Interaction Newsletter, 11,* 15-17.

Jackson, P.W. (1968). *Life in classrooms.* New York: Holt, Rinehart, & Winston.

Kounin, J.S. (1970). *Discipline and group management in classrooms.* New York: Holt, Rinehart, & Winston.

Kyle, D. (1979). *Life-as-teacher: The disclosure of teachers' activities and emergent problems.* Unpublished doctoral dissertation, University of Virginia, Charlottesville.

Lee, C.S. (1975). An investigation of the frequency, bothersomeness, and seriousness of classroom problems as perceived by first and fifth year secondary teachers (Doctoral dissertation, University of South Carolina, 1974). *Dissertation Abstracts International, 35,* 6576A.

McCutcheon, G. (1979a). Educational criticism: Methods and application. *Journal of Curriculum Theorizing, 1,* 5-25.

McCutcheon, G. (1979b). How do elementary teachers plan? The nature of planning and influences on it. *The Elementary School Journal, 81(1),* 4-23.

Ross, D.D. (1978). *Teaching beliefs and practices in three kindergartens.* Unpublished doctoral dissertation, University of Virginia, Charlottesville.

Ross, D.D. (1984). An introduction to curriculum criticism. *Journal of Thought, 19*(2), 47-60.

Sheldon, D.M.H. (1970). A study to identify activities performed in the elementary school as teaching or as non-teaching activities (Doctoral dissertation, University of Utah, 1969). *Dissertation Abstracts International, 30,* 3842A-3843A.

3
Lesson Construction: Differing Views

JUDITH L. GREEN
The Ohio State University
JUDITH O. HARKER
VA Medical Center Sepulveda
JOANNE M. GOLDEN
University of Delaware

In the last decade, a variety of new approaches have emerged that extend our ability to examine how individual teachers and their students work together to carry out everyday activities that make up life in classrooms. These approaches, grounded in disciplines such as anthropology, linguistics, literary analysis, psychology, and sociology, have been adapted to meet the demands of research on everyday educational settings. The value of these approaches is that they extend our ability to explore the regularities, details, and variations of classroom life; the nature of the demands for appropriate participation in instructional activities; and social and academic outcomes and consequences of such participation.

In this chapter, three of the recent approaches were used to explore the nature of one instructional event: a sociolinguistic, a semantic propositional, and a literary text analysis approach. The goal of this multiple perspective approach to the analysis of instruction was twofold: (a) to compare and contrast the lessons of two teachers who taught the same story to a group of students from their respective classes and whose students differed in their story-retelling performance; and (b) to explore the nature of the descriptions obtained when complementary systems of analysis were used to explore different aspects of the same instructional activity.

The chapter is the culmination of a series of individual and collaborative efforts in which the nature of teaching–learning processes as explored from a variety of theoretical perspectives: Green from sociolinguistics and discourse analysis, Harker from semantic analysis and comprehension of text, and Golden from text analysis and reader response theory (Golden, in press a; Golden & Green, 1983; Green, Weade, & Graham, in press; Green & Harker, 1982; Harker, in press; Harker & Green, 1985). These efforts led to an awareness of a common thread that ran through each of our fields of interest—the concern for how meanings are constructed. This awareness led to the conclusion that our combined theoretical and methodological approaches provide a much richer description and understanding of the complexities and consequences of instructional process than our separate efforts could provide.

The discussion of the multiple perspective analysis is presented in three sections. In the first section a brief discussion of the common perspective on meaning construction that underlies the separate analyses is presented. In the second section a brief description of each approach and representative findings from each study are provided. As demonstrated in this section, the findings in each of these separate analysis are often overlapping and convergent as well as unique. In the third section the contributions of the different systems to the comparison of the two lessons will be discussed as will implications of a multiple perspective analysis for observing teaching.

THE COMMON THREAD: THE CONSTRUCTION OF MEANING

Central to the three studies brought together in this chapter is the view that meaning is constructed by teacher and students as they interact with one another and with objects during instructional events (e.g., books, pictures, written materials). In the two story-reading–discussion lessons explored in this chapter, the instructional event involved a teacher, a group of 6 students from the teacher's classroom, and a text (*The Way the Tiger Walked,* Chacones, 1970). In these lessons, the meaning construction process was the result of interactions among different combinations of contributors as the lesson evolved over time (e.g., teacher and student; teacher and group; teacher, student, and text; teacher, group, and text). The section that follows provides a brief discussion of the nature of meaning construction and factors involved in this process that are common to the three separate analysis approaches and theoretical perspectives discussed in this chapter.

Lessons as Constructed Events

In instructional events, the construction of meaning refers to both academic and social aspects of lessons. That is, as teachers and students interact with each other and with instructional materials, meanings are being constructed and interpreted on a variety of levels simultaneously (e.g., Bloome & Theodorou, in press; Erickson, 1982; Green & Harker, 1982; Wallat & Green, 1982). On the social level, the teacher and students are constructing the activity (cf. Erickson & Shultz, 1981; Florio & Shultz, 1979; McDermott, 1976) and defining expectations and norms for participation (cf. Green & Wallat, 1981b; Wallat & Green, 1982). On the academic level, the teacher and students interact with each other and with instructional materials to meet the academic goals of the curriculum. In other words, as teachers deliver the academic content, they also signal who can talk, when, where, about what, in what ways, with whom, for what purpose. Conversely, as students contribute to the evolving flow of the lesson, they also signal their understanding of content (academic level) and appropriate participation (social level). In this way, academic and social aspects of lessons are interwoven, and instruction is viewed as a process of meaning construction.

Lessons, from this perspective, are not unitary activities; rather, they evolve over time and have differentiated parts with varying demands for participation and content (e.g., Bales & Strodtbeck, 1967; Erickson, 1982; Florio & Shultz, 1979; Green, 1977; Green & Harker, 1982; Green & Wallat, 1981a; Mehan, 1979; Wallat & Green, 1982). For example, the two lessons explored in this paper had different organizational or participation structures (cf. Erickson & Shultz, 1981; Philips, 1972 and 1982). Teacher G had a two-part lesson structure (an introductory phase and a story-reading–discussion phase), and Teacher S had a four-part structure (an introductory phase, a transition phase, a story-reading–discussion phase, and a post-story-reading–discussion phase). Each phase had different content demands and different expectations for participation.

Students' Tasks

The task for students in the lesson construction process is multifaceted. Students must extract from the ongoing stream of activity the nature of the activity being constructed at any given point in the lesson (e.g., we are engaged in a story-related discussion about the animals and not in discussion about animals in the zoo) and the expectations for participation within the activity (e.g., respond to teacher questions versus initiate topics for discussion). They must also process and interpret accurately the information being presented (e.g., verbal and nonverbal, social and academic, oral and written). Once the students interpret the academic and social information that has been presented, their task is still not complete. The construction of meaning and interpretation of information is continuous. In addition, students must use information from their repertoire of strategies to select appropriate ways of participating (cf. Gumperz, 1982; Hymes, 1974). They must then use this information to present academic content in an appropriate form (e.g., raise hand vs. call out information; give answer in a complete sentence vs. respond with a single-word answer). In other words, students are involved with the process of meaning construction on both an intrapersonal and interpersonal basis (e.g., Bloome & Green, 1984; Cazden, 1981).

Teachers' Tasks

The teachers' task is also multifaceted. It is both similar to the task for students and different. The difference comes from the difference in roles required of students and teachers. In addition to being an active participant, the teacher is curriculum developer, instructional planner, instructional leader, and coordinator of instructional events. Within a lesson, the teacher presents information, orchestrates participation, assesses student performance, modifies the lesson based on perceived student needs, and maintains the direction of the evolving lesson. These demands co-occur and require continuous decision-making and information processing across a variety of co-occurring channels of communication (e.g., verbal and nonverbal; social and academic; oral and written). Therefore, within lessons, teachers are constructing their own meanings about lesson content, lesson direction, and individual student performance while simultaneously helping students to construct meanings, interpret information, and participate in lessons. For teachers as for students, the meaning construction process is intrapersonal and interpersonal, as well as ongoing and dynamic.

Frames of Reference

Another way to think about what is involved in the meaning construction process is from the perspective of the frames of reference used by participants in lessons to help them "read" the academic and social content and requirements of the lesson (eg., Frcdcriksen, 1981; Green, 1983; Green & Harker, 1982; Green & Wallat, 1981b; Heap, 1980; Tannen, 1979). The first frames of reference are brought to the task by participants. One type of frame of reference used by participants in lessons is the personal frame. A *personal frame* can be thought of as the set of expectations for interacting and learning derived from past experiences, knowledge, perceptions, emotions, values, abilities (e.g., cognitive, linguistic, social, physical), and so forth that participants bring to the instructional situation. A second type of frame involves materials used in the lesson. *Material frames* are constructed by the person who designed and/or wrote the materials. Materials have form and content that are presented in deliberate ways. Materials, therefore, bring a frame that contributes to the construction of meaning within lessons.

Additional frames are generated by participants as they interact with each other and with materials to reach the instructional goals of the lesson. The frames that follow were adapted from an earlier collaborative effort (Golden & Green, 1983). The first of the lesson-generated frames is the *local frame,* which is derived from the messages and actions immediately surrounding the message/action under construction. This frame is related to the topic/theme under construction (e.g., we are discussing how the elephant walked as opposed to how the tiger looked). The second type of lesson-generated frame, the *academic frame* of the lesson, includes academic content constructed from the beginning of the lesson to the specific point under construction. The third type of lesson-generated frame parallels the academic frame—the *instructional frame.* This frame focuses on instructional strategies and demands that have been developed in the lesson (e.g., in the introductory segment of the lesson, students are expected to "focus" on the book, "observe" the way titles are written, "discuss" prior knowledge of books). The fourth type of lesson-generated frame is the *social frame.* This frame is related to interpersonal aspects of lessons and parallels the historical and instructional frames. This frame establishes the norms for participation (e.g., who gets to talk, when, where, with whom, in what ways) that develop within and across the different parts of the lesson. The last lesson-generated frame is one that is extracted from participation in and across lessons. This frame, *frame from previous lessons,* can be social, instructional, and/or academic. It provides a set of expectations for what to do and how to do it in subsequent lessons that appear similar in content and/or form.

From this perspective, frames of reference constructed during lessons are part of the information acquired in lessons. This information becomes part of the individual's personal frame. The interaction between personal frames and lesson-generated frames can lead to the modification, change, suspension, or replacement of an individual's personal frame within a lesson or at specific points in a lesson or can lead to modification of the lesson itself. Interactions among frames can also lead to frame clashes and to misunderstandings and miscommunication (e.g., Cook-Gumperz, Gumperz, & Simons, 1981; Collins, 1983, Green & Wallat, 1981b; Hymes, 1981; Mehan, 1979; Scollon & Scollon, 1984). Each of these possibilities can influence what is learned, how students participate, actions teachers take, evaluations teachers make about students, and the nature of the interactions among lesson participants (teacher, students, materials).

These issues and constructs lay the foundation for the three analyses that follow, as well as point to the need for in-depth exploration of teaching–learning processes as they evolve throughout a lesson.

LESSON CONSTRUCTION: THREE VIEWS

In this section, two teachers' lessons are analysed using three different approaches: (a) a sociolinguistic approach was used to explore social-instructional aspects of lesson structure and lesson delivery (Green); (b) a semantic propositional approach was used to explore thematic and instructional aspects of lesson introduction and story beginning (Harker); and (c) an episodic text analysis approach was used to explore text structure, text construction, and reconstruction aspects of the story-reading–discussion segments of the lesson (Golden). Each analysis produced both unique information and information that overlapped and/or confirmed the findings from one of the other analyses. Therefore, in the discussion that follows, there is a degree of redundancy of information about certain aspects of the lessons. However, in most instances of overlap (redundancy), the findings from one analysis provided clarification or greater specificity for the other.

A Description of the Data

The raw data were videotapes obtained from a study in which 11 teachers taught the same lesson (a story-reading–discussion lesson) to students from their classrooms (Green, 1977). This study can be thought of as a natural experiment; that is, while the story-reading-discussion lesson is a naturally occurring classroom event, this specific lesson was undertaken for research purposes and is an experimental occurrence of an everyday event.

The present study involves an in-depth, secondary analyses of two teachers who formed a planned contrast. Both were participants in an 18-month, in-service training project that was field-based in their school (Ruddell & Williams, 1971). During this training project, the two teachers received training in the area of comprehension and questioning. The lesson selected for secondary analysis was the third lesson of this type that was videotaped and was made at the end of the training period. The lesson was taped in a room near the teachers' classrooms. The groups were constructed to reflect the ethnic population of the school, were balanced in terms of males and females, and were multigrade (Teacher G had 2 first-grade and 4 second-grade students; Teacher S had 2 first-grade, 3 second-grade, and 1 third-grade student).

The teachers were selected for inclusion in the present study on the following basis: (a) they were considered effective teachers by the director of the in-service project; (b) they differed in terms of student performance on a retelling task (Teacher G was the top-ranked teacher and Teacher S was ranked eighth in the sample of 11 teachers when student performance on a story-retelling task was considered) (Green, 1977); (c) the two groups of students could be defined as equivalent in that no difference was found between the groups in terms of ethnic group membership, student ability levels (as measured by performance on standardized tests), and age (Green, 1977; Schmidt, 1972).

Each researcher was provided with a transcript and copy of the videotape and a copy of the story text. Transcripts of student retellings were also made available. The raw data were then subjected to in-depth analysis from the three separate analytic perspectives.

LESSON CONSTRUCTION 1: A SOCIOLINGUISTIC PERSPECTIVE

The perspective on lesson construction in this section is grounded in sociolinguistics, ethnography of communication, and discourse analysis and research on the study of teaching. It is part of a growing body of work that seeks to understand the nature of teaching-learning processes from a communicative perspective (e.g. Barnes & Todd, 1977; Bloome, 1986; Cazden, 1986; Cazden, John, & Hymes, 1972; Cochran-Smith, 1984; Collins, 1983; Cook-Gumperz, 1986; Gilmore & Glatthorn, 1982; Green, 1983; Green & Wallat, 1981b; Heap, 1983; Hymes, 1981; Mehan, 1979; Morine-Dershimer, 1985; Philips, 1982; Stubbs, 1983; Wilkinson, 1982). From this perspective, the classroom is viewed as a social system in which instruction and learning are products of interactions among participants (students, teachers, materials). This research seeks to identify and understand processes and events that make up everyday life in classrooms from the perspective of the participants and to explore factors that constrain and support participation and learning.

The goal of this section is to compare the two lessons in terms of patterns of instruction and demands for participation in order to understand factors that contributed to the differences in student outcomes obtained in the original study (Green, 1977). In this section, findings from the sociolinguistic microanalysis of communication during the two lessons will be highlighted along with the procedures for analysis of the lesson.

Procedures

Analysis of instruction from a sociolinguistic perspective is a multifaceted process. The analytic process involves a variety of tasks: (a) "freezing" the evolving lesson through development of a transcript that includes all conversation and relevant nonverbal behaviors; (b) segmenting the ongoing stream of conversation and action into units of varying types; (c) developing systematic maps (concrete representations) of the evolving lesson based on sociolinguistic constructs and consideration of interrelationship of various types of units obtained in Task B; (d) extracting patterns of communication between students and teacher; (e) constructing variables grounded in the observed patterns in the data; and (f) developing a descriptive model that can be examined across other instances of similar events (e.g., Erickson & Shultz, 1981; Florio & Shultz, 1979; Green & Harker, 1982). Units were identified by a team of researchers. All disagreements were resolved.

Figure 1 provides a sample of the transcription, segmentation, and representation process. The basic unit is the *message unit* (001; 002; 003; ... 012), which is the minimal unit of meaning. This unit is identified by considering contextualization cues—e.g., pitch, stress, intonation, pause, nonverbal gestures and actions, proxemics, verbal content (cf. Corsaro, 1981 1985; Gumperz, 1982; Gumperz & Herasimchuk, 1973). Once the individual message units have been identified and

Transcript Line	Text	Potentially Divergent Messages	Thematically Tied Messages
001	ALL RIGHT BOYS AND GIRLS (places book under chair)		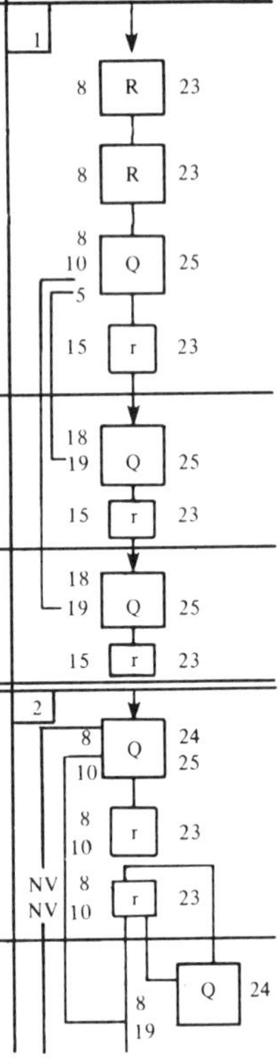 1 → 8 [R] 23
002	THIS MORNING I'VE BROUGHT SOME THINGS WITH ME (sets out cutout animals)		8 [R] 23
003	CAN ANYONE TELL ME WHAT THIS IS? (shows cutout animals in turn)		8 10 [Q] 25 / 5 / 15 [r] 23
004	All: A giraffe		
005	AND THIS ONE?		18 19 [Q] 25
006	All: An elephant		15 [r] 23
007	AND THIS ONE?		18 19 [Q] 25
008	All: A tiger		15 [r] 23
009	WOULD YOU LIKE TO TELL ME ALL YOU CAN ABOUT THESE ANIMALS?		2 / 8 [Q] 24 / 10 25
010	All: (raise hands)		8 10 [r] 23
011	J: Unhh (said as he raises his hand)		NV 8 NV 10 [r] 23
012	JOHN?		8 [Q] 24 / 19

Figure 1. Map segment teachers.

transcripts constructed, the transcript and videotape are used to identify additional units of varying type and length within the unfolding stream of conversation and action. (See Cochran-Smith, 1984 and Ochs, 1979 for a discussion of transcript construction issues.) These units include: (a) *interaction units* (sequences of conversationally tied message units: 001–004; 005–006; 007–008; 009–011); (b) *instructional sequence units* (sequences of thematically tied interaction units: 001–008— identify and name the animals); (c) *phase units* (sequences of pedagogically tied instructional sequence units—e.g., introductory phase, storyreading-discussion phase); and (d) *lesson units* (sequences of instructionally tied phase units). Simultaneously, the instructional content of messages can be identified—e.g., 8R (frame), 8R (focus), 8Q (request-focus), 10Q (request-confirmation). Once the units are identified, they are placed on the transcript either in a column that reflects goal-directed messages (*thematically tied messages*) or in one that reflects potentially off-task messages (*potentially divergent messages*). Thus, transcription, segmentation, and mapping are heuristic tools that provide a means of graphically representing the unfolding instructional conversation. (For a complete discussion of analysis procedures see Green, 1977 and Green and Wallat, 1981.)

Microanalysis of the relationship between and among units provides the means of systematic exploration of how the social, instructional, and academic aspects of lessons are woven together and the influence of these processes on participation and learning. Microanalysis also provides the basis for hypothesis generating and testing within the lesson (e.g., identification of a pattern and exploration of pattern recurrence across phases of lesson).

Representative Findings

Findings presented in this section are illustrative. They are presented as a series of contrasts that focus on differences in (a) lesson structure and (b) social and instructional demands within the lesson as reflected in questioning patterns. These contrast points were extracted from the summary of representative variables identified during microanalysis and were used to identify places in which the descriptive data (the transcripts and videotapes) could be re-entered for further systematic, in-depth exploration of what contributed to the differences in student performance identified in the original study (Green, 1977).

Contrast 1: Lesson Structure. Contrast 1 focuses on the general structure of the lessons and the distribution of talk within and across the phases of the lessons. As illustrated in Table 1, the two teachers had contrasting lesson organizations. Teacher G had a two-part structure, an introduction and a story-reading-discussion phase, and Teacher S had a four-part structure, an introduction, a transition to story reading, a story-reading–discussion phase, and a discussion phase following the story. Exploration of Table 1 shows that differences also existed in the types of units constructed and their distribution within and across all phases of the lesson. For example, while Teacher S had a larger proportion of overall talk in terms of message units (17% vs. 12%) and interaction units (18% vs. 15%) in Phase

Table 1. Units and Questioning Patterns

	Units			Question Direction			Question Type					
	Message	Interaction	Instruc. Sequence	To Any Student	To Specific Students	Student Initiation	New	Rephrased	Same	Variation	Clarifying	Totals
Introduction												
Teacher G	70 (12%)	22 (15%)	5 (13%)	13 (17%)	3 (10%)	0	7 (14%)	4 (17%)	0	0	2 (01%)	13 (13%)
Teacher S	112 (17%)	30 (18%)	3 (11%)	10 (32%)	16 (19%)	0	4 (19%)	0	12 (39%)	3 (50%)	6 (16%)	25 (25%)
Transition												
Teacher G	0	0	0	0	0	0	0	0	0	0	0	0
Teacher S	26 (04%)	7 (04%)	1 (03%)	2 (07%)	3 (04%)	3 (09%)	1 (05%)	0	0	0	1 (03%)	2 (02%)
Storyreading Discussion												
Teacher G	495 (87%)	124 (83%)	33 (85%)	62 (83%)	27 (90%)	6 (86%)	43 (84%)	19 (83%)	5 (100%)	4 (100%)	18 (90%)	89 (86%)
Teacher S	397 (61%)	98 (57%)	19 (68%)	15 (48%)	36 (43%)	26 (81%)	12 (58%)	3 (75%)	10 (32%)	3 (50%)	18 (48%)	46 (46%)
Poststory Discussion												
Teacher G	1 (00%)	1 (01%)	1 (025%)	1 (01%)	0	1 (14%)	1 (03%)	0	0	0	0	1 (01%)
Teacher S	113 (17%)	36 (21%)	5 (18%)	4 (14%)	28 (34%)	3 (09%)	5 (23%)	1 (25%)	9 (29%)	0	12 (32%)	27 (27%)
Total												
Teacher G	566	147	39	76	30	7	51	23	5	4	20	103
Teacher S	648	171	28	31	83	32	22	4	31	6	37	100

I (Introduction), Teacher G had more instructional sequence units (13% vs. 10%). That is, Teacher S had more talk but covered less content (two less topics). The difference in content coverage becomes more pronounced in the subsequent phases of the lesson (Teacher S had 28 instructional sequence units vs. 39 for Teacher G). The effect of this and other differences to be discussed later is cumulative and is related to student performance within the lesson and on the retelling task used to measure outcome (Golden, in press a; Green, 1977; Green, Weade & Graham, in press; Harker, in press). Comparison of the amount and distribution of units in the remaining phases of each lesson confirms the fact that while the groups were equivalent, the story the same, the teachers similar in training, and directions for the lesson the same, the two lessons were not the same lesson.

The difference in the number of phases in the two lessons suggested a contrast point for further exploration. To explore the meaning of this difference, the nature of activity and the content of the talk were considered for each phase of the lesson as was the relationship of activity and talk between phases. By considering what happened in the introduction and story-reading-discussion phases in Teacher S's lesson, the need for the transition phase to the story-reading-discussion phase became evident. Teacher S began the lesson by placing the book under her chair, placing three cardboard animals before the students, and asking, "Would you like to tell me all you can about these animals?" (see Figure 1). The introduction proceeded until all students had a turn to tell something about the animals. The focus of this phase, then, was not on story but on relating personal knowledge about the animals represented by the cutouts.

In the transition phase, the teacher took the book from under her chair where she had placed it at the beginning of the introduction and attempted to begin story: "All right. This morning, boys and girls, we have a story for you. Has anyone ever read this story?" These actions were similar to those at the beginning of the introduction (see Figure 1, lines 001-003) and thus appear to signal the start of a new activity. However, no overt bridge was made between the animals in the introduction and those in the story, and no change of activity occurred. In fact, students began to offer spontaneous comments about the animals rather than focus on the book being introduced. The student behaviors suggest that the students continued to use an *instructional frame* from the introduction: "Tell about the animals." This frame "clashed" with the teacher's expectations, thus producing the transition phase. One source of verification of the *frame clash* was found in the teacher's comments at the end of the transition phase, "And let's think, listen to the story, and then we'll come back and talk about it a little bit more. Okay?" While the teacher's comments focused students on the story, they also left open the possibility of using earlier frames in other parts of the lesson ("We'll come back and talk about it a little bit more.").

Exploration of student performance within and across subsequent phases of the lesson confirmed the use of the frame by students: Tell all you know about the animals. The use of inappropriate frames at particular points in the lesson indicates that at times some students did not share a common definition of task with the teacher. This lack of shared expectations led to instances of inappropriate participation and to periodic interruptions in the goal directed flow of the lesson. (For further discussion of this issue see Green, Weade, & Graham in press, and Green and Weade, 1985.)

In contrast, Teacher G moved smoothly from the introduction to the story-reading–discussion phase. She used the book as the focus of the introduction and discussed the cover picture, title, title page, illustrator, and dedication with the students. That is, she moved systematically through the parts of a book, focusing students on content and providing them with the opportunity to practice discussing book content. The story-reading–discussion segment was simply the next step in a sequence of steps. For Teacher G, the story began as she turned a page in the book. The task for students was similar in the two parts of the lesson—observe and discuss the content of the book. The majority of talk and topics occurred in the story-reading-discussion phase in which the text was available to students for reference (85% instructional sequence units vs. 68% for Teacher S). Teacher G's lesson did not contain instances of behavior that led to similar frame clashes; rather, the behaviors of teacher and students appeared to reflect a shared understanding of the lesson goal throughout the lesson.

The contrast point suggested by the quantitative differences in lesson structure when combined with a qualitative analysis of content and activity showed a difference in control and intent of lesson phase, content coverage, and instructional structure. These differences influenced lesson fluidity and the demands on students academically and socially. In other words, Teacher G's lesson phases supported one another and were logically related; activity in phase 1 set the frame for activity in phase 2. Teacher S's lesson phases were more disjunctive. Students had to shift the nature of activity from one part of the lesson to the next—from discussing animal cutouts to listening to and discussing story with no overt bridge provided to help students make the transition to story.

Contrast 2: Social and Instructional Patterns. Contrast 1 led to the conclusion that the two lessons were not the same lesson. In contrast 2, this finding will be considered further. In contrast 2, the social and instructional demands for participation identified in an analysis of questioning patterns are presented.

Table 1 provides a summary of information about questions. The variables in Table 1 were constructed from patterns of language use related to questioning within instructional sequence units. The types of questions were identified by comparing and contrasting questions across interaction units. From this analysis five types of questions were identified: new questions, rephrased questions, same questions, variation questions, and clarifying cycle questions. *New questions* opened a new topic. In *rephrased questions* the content and intent of a previous question were paraphrased. *Same question* involved a literal restatement of an earlier question. *Variation questions* were questions that had the same form but changed object of focus (e.g., in Figure 1, animal names for cutouts). *Clarifying cycle questions* required students to clarify information presented. In addition to question type, the person(s) to whom the question was directed was considered: question to specific students, questions to any student, student initiation. As indicated in Table 2, these ways of viewing questions further helped to differentiate the two teachers and the two lessons. To make the differences clearer, the number of questions for each category for Teacher S were subtracted from those for Teacher G. The difference scores are presented in Table 2.

As indicated in Table 1, the total number of questions identified across the categories was similar for the two teachers (103 for Teacher G and 100 for Teacher S). However, when the distribution of questions across phases of the lesson was considered, differences were identified that reinforce the conclusion that the instructional events were not the same lesson. If questions are seen as indications of what is important to know or focus on (e.g., Morine-Dershimer & Tenenberg, 1981), then the students in the two lessons were not exposed to the same content or were exposed to content in different ways. The difference in content is reflected in the difference in distribution of questions by phase. Teacher S asked 25% of all questions in an introduction that focused on animal cutouts (one of which was not in the story) and asked students to relate personal knowledge about the animals. As shown previously, no direct connection was made between the introduction and the story; therefore, the density of questions in this area contributes little to the comprehension of story. She also asked 46% of all questions in the story-reading–discussion phase and 27% in the poststory discussion phase. In contrast Teacher G asked 13% of the questions in the introduction and 86% in the story-reading–discussion phase; in this way, the teacher focused primarily on the content of the story. In addition, the types of questions used within and across phases differed (see Table 1).

When the types of questions used and the ways in which questions functioned to

Table 2. Comparison of Teachers G and S:
Variables Related to Involvement of Students

Variable	Teacher G	Teacher S
Questions to any student	+45	–
Questions to specific students	–	–53
Student initiation	–	–25
New questions	+29	–
Rephrase questions	+19	–
Clarifying cycles	–	–17
Same questions	–	–26
Variation questions	–	–2

Note: Teacher G (+) and Teacher S (–): Direction of difference.

distribute turns at talk were considered, differences in instructional and social patterns related to academic content were identified. As indicated in Table 2, Teacher G exceeded Teacher S in the number of new questions (+29) and rephrased questions (+19). She used more questions directed to the total group (+53 questions to any student). In contrast, Teacher S designated responders more frequently (−60), permitted students to spontaneously initiate more turns at talk (−25), used more variation questions (−2) and clarifying cycles (−17), and repeated the same question frequently (−26). Analysis of question content and function and questioning patterns indicates that questions in Teacher G's lesson were generally open to any student, were used to support student attempts to respond to teacher questions (as indicated by the number of rephrased questions), and were exposed to more content (as indicated in the number of new questions asked). In contrast, questions in Teacher S's lesson were used to control who responded (as indicated by the number of questions to specific students), required students to clarify the information, and frequently provided each student with a chance to give an opinion or answer to the question asked (as indicated by the number of instances of the same question being asked). In addition, students were permitted to spontaneously initiate information.

The numeric difference indicated another contrast point for qualitative analysis. When the conversational content was considered, the difference in overall patterns suggested that students in Teacher G's lesson were being asked to focus on various aspects of the story content (e.g., on the author's words, on predicting outcomes), were asked to do this as a group, and were asked to attend to the responses of other students. In contrast, Teacher S's students were expected to contribute information primarily about the content of pictures and definition of terms. Students were also permitted to initiate talk more often than in Teacher G's lesson. However, these initiations often involved asking a question about the picture—"Is that a porcupine? It looks like a fox upside down." The clarifying cycles were often related to these initiations; that is, the teacher had to ask students to explain what they meant. In the two lessons, therefore, the teacher strategies differed, the way in which the talk functioned to signal content differed, and the rights and expectations for student participation differed. One way to think about the difference is that Teacher G helped students focus on the story and prepare for exploring the story, while Teacher S used the book to stimulate discussion. The difference in outcome discussed previously indicates these differences in instructional and social demands influenced what was retold about the story. Further discussion of the relationship of teacher strategies and student performance is presented in the sections on semantic analysis (Harker) and text analysis (Golden) that follow.

This brief analysis presents a sample of the kinds of analyses which are possible using a sociolinguistic ethnographic system. The findings presented for the other systems of analysis both extend the information about the similarities and differences between the two lessons and provide convergent validation for the information presented in this section.

LESSON CONSTRUCTION 2:
SEMANTIC PROPOSITIONAL ANALYSIS

The perspective presented in this section is grounded in discourse analysis at the microlevel. At this level a number of systems have been designed to *represent the meanings conveyed in discourse* (e.g., Frederiksen, 1975; Harker, Hartley, & Walsh, 1982; Kintsch, 1984; Kintsch & Van Dijk, 1978). The purpose of such representation systems is to go beyond the surface level of the language in which a message is stated and to provide a well-defined representation of the meaning which underlies the message. One advantage of a system of discourse analysis, such as the system of propositional analysis (cf. Frederiksen, 1975) used in this study, is the ability to examine the complexity of language in terms of the meaning load it carries—for example, the number of embedded propositions and the logical nature of the relationship contained within and across propositions. For example, research on propositional structure has shown that even a set of apparently simple messages can be quite complex, especially when they contain rhetorical devices such as ellipsis, anaphora, and pronominal reference. Analysis of the underlying propositional structure of messages, therefore, provides one way of identifying and clarifying the magnitude of the cognitive task set for readers and listeners in lessons such as the story-reading–discussion lesson discussed in this chapter.

The purpose of this section is to examine the informational content of the lesson events in terms of the type of information presented and its distribution across parts of the lesson. The goal is to contrast the content of the two teachers' presentation of information in the introduction and beginning episode of the story, to highlight similarities and differences in lesson construction, and to identify factors between the two groups on the story retelling task.

Microanalysis of Discourse Structure. The propositional representation system employed in this study is an heuristic tool for representing the meaning of discourse in the instructional event under consideration—the introduction and beginning episode of the story-reading–discussion event. This system provides one way of freezing the flow of conversation and of exploring meanings contained in the messages exchanged by teachers and students. The value of this system lies in its ability to provide a systematic, reliable representation of meanings of interest.

The starting point for this analysis was the transcript of the videotaped lesson and the videotapes. As discussed in the previous section on sociolinguistic analysis, transcripts were segmented into message units based on contextualization cues (cf. Corsaro, 1981; Green, 1977; Green & Wallat, 1981; Gumperz, 1982; Gumperz & Herasimchuk, 1973; Gumperz & Tannen, 1979). These message units served as the beginning point for the present propositional analysis of the verbal and nonverbal messages that made up the lesson content (cf. Green & Harker, 1982).

Data analysis began with segmentation of the lesson information contained in the message units into microlevel units called propositions, according to an adaptation of Frederiksen's (1975) system. (A more expanded discussion is presented in

Green and Harker, 1982, and in Harker, in press.) Propositions are composed of a finite set of relations which operate on and connect an unlimited set of possible concepts and have a general form of *concept*-RELATION-*concept* (see Table 3 for examples). The concepts comprise what is being talked about; the relations describe how the concepts are connected. Relations can include: (a) *case relations* (agent, patient, object, instrument, dative); (b) *relations which describe events or states* (result, goal, theme, location, manner); (c) *relations describing objects* (category, attribute, number, extent, degree); and (d) *logical relations* (conjunction, disjunction, identity, equivalence, ordinal, causal, conditional). The proposition can be thought of as an event or state or the logical relations between events or states. Complex propositions may have event, state, or logical propositions embedded within them. The first six propositions in Table 3 show three such pairs of complex propositions.

Classification of Propositions. The second level of data analysis explored how propositional units were distributed across the categories of topics which made up the lesson. The first major topic category extracted from the evolving lesson involved the propositional context of the *story text* itself as woven into the fabric of the story-reading-discussion phase of the lesson. Three types of story content were identified and examined: actions, descriptions, and thoughts. The second major category extracted from the story-reading-discussion phase(s) was *story-related* discussion and questions. The content of this category was also divided into actions, descriptions, and thoughts. These categories were common to both lessons.

However, while the two lessons were similar in the use of these topics, they also contained markedly different topics. Analysis of the information in the introduction showed that the two teachers placed the story within very different thematic contexts; therefore, two categories had to be generated to account for these differences. Teacher G used the book itself as introduction and discussed the parts of the book (e.g., title page, dedication, author). *Theme-Book*, then, was a third

Table 3. Sample Transcript and Its Propositional Structure

Transcript Line		Proposition No. and Structure	
113	The porcupine	154	porcupine PAT watch OBJ 155
114	watched the tiger walk.	155	tiger PAT walk
115	He saw the tiger's golden coat velvety thick and soft.	156	porcupine PAT see OBJ 157
		157	tiger HASP coat CAT golden, CAT velvety EXT thick, EXT soft
116	"How beautifully the tiger walks," the porcupine thought.	158	porcupine PAT thought THEME 159
		159	tiger PAT walks MAN beautifully
117	DO YOU THINK HE THINKS HE WALKS PRETTIER HE DOES?	160	Q: you (class) PAT think THEME 161
		161	porcupine PAT thinks THEME 164
		162	tiger PAT walks EXT pretty
		163	porcupine PAT walks EXT pretty
		164	162 ORD 163
118	Students: Uh-hum	165	R: yes, 160-164, confirm.

major category of proposition. Teacher S began her lesson by showing and discussing cutouts of animals; therefore, the category *Theme-Animals* was constructed (category 4). The two final categories were constructed to permit classification of propositional units not accounted for in the above categories. Category 5 included *control* statements which refocused or directed student behavior; and category 6, *other,* included statements which allocated turns, confirmed responses, or were other comments about lesson procedures.

Representative Findings

The findings presented here were obtained from an analysis of a segment of the two lessons. The segment of the lessons chosen for semantic propositional analysis begins with the introductory phase of the lesson and continues through the discussion of the first episode of the story. (See Harker, in press, for a more complete analysis of this lesson.) One way to think about this segment is that it introduces the task(s) involved in the lesson to the students. The data are rich and provide the base from which many questions can be addressed and hypotheses generated about content demands of lessons. In the discussion that follows, two questions will be considered. The first question provides a global view of the two lesson segments: How are these two teachers' lessons different in terms of the amounts and kinds of information presented? The second question provides a detailed look at one specific aspect of instruction: How are these teachers similar or different in their questioning styles and strategies?

Global View of Lesson Content. On the surface, there are several similarities between the lessons. The segments were equivalent in length (271 and 281 propositions for Teacher G and S respectively). The teachers asked an equivalent number of questions (41 and 46), and received an equivalent number of responses to questions (21% vs. 24% of total propositions). However, when the source of propositions was considered, differences began to emerge. In Teacher G's lesson, 55% of the propositions were stated by the teacher, whereas 25% were stated by the student, a better than 2:1 ratio of teacher to student talk. In contrast, Teacher S stated 43%, while her students contributed 36% of the total propositions. (For both teachers, the remaining propositions were contributed by the story.) These patterns reflect a difference in lesson organization and demand. Teacher G's lesson was teacher directed, while Teacher S's had a more equal distribution of teacher-to-student talk.

When the relationship of the discussion to the content of the story was considered, differences were also found that provide further information about the patterns already described. Sixty-two percent of Teacher G's question propositions are related to the story, in contrast to only 32% of Teacher S's. Teacher G's students produced more than twice the amount of story-related responses (53%) than did Teacher S's (23%). Although Teacher S's students were participating at a high rate, neither her questions, nor their responses were closely focused on the story content. In other words, while Teacher S had more student talk, less of this talk was related to the story than for Teacher G's students. This difference, then, indicates a difference in focus or lesson emphasis in terms of content.

Table 4. Distribution of Propositions Across Topics: Introduction and Episode I

	Story-Related		Theme					
	Action	Description	Thought	Book	Animal	Other	Control	Totals
Story text propositions								
Teacher G	30	17	9					56 (20.7)
Teacher S	32	19	9					60 (21.3)
Teacher G propositions								
Questions	20	13	15	23	1	5	0	77
Responses	20	10	5	23	7	1	0	66
Other	6	1	0	45	5	15	0	72
Total	46	24	20	91	13	21	0	215
% of Total	17.0	8.8	7.4	33.6	4.8	7.7	0.0[a]	79.3[a]
Teacher S propositions								
Questions	7	12	4	1	36	11	2	73
Responses	10	2	2	2	36	8	0	60
Other	0	15	2	8	20	35	8	88
Total	17	29	8	11	92	54	10	221
% of Total	6.0	10.3	2.1	3.9	32.7	19.8	3.6	78.7[a]

[a]Percent of propositions in teacher talk and propositions in text equals 100%.

The full distribution of propositions across topics is presented in Table 4. When all story-related propositions were examined in relation to the total set of propositions, 32% of Teacher G's lesson was story-related, in contrast to 19% for Teacher S. When talk is combined with propositions in story text presented by the teacher, 54% of Teacher G's lessons were story-related as opposed to 41% for Teacher S's lesson. Again, this suggests that Teacher G's lesson was more closely tied to the story content. When the propositions in the story text were broken down according to action, description, or thought, the majority of *story text* propositions were given to action (54% of the text propositions in this segment), followed by description (30%) and thoughts (16%). In her story-related discussion, Teacher G followed this order with 51% of her text-related propositions devoted to action-related propositions, 27% description-related, and 22% thought-related. In contrast, Teacher S emphasized description-related propositions (54%), followed by action-related (32%) and thought-related (19%) propositions of all text-related propositions. In other words, the teachers emphasized different aspects of the story.

The differences in story-related propositions in the beginning episode provide only part of the picture of differences. When the introductory phase was considered, additional differences in content were found. The introductory contexts developed by each teacher is clearly revealed in the columns labeled "Theme-Book" and "Theme–Animal." The largest number of propositions for both teachers in this part of the lesson as devoted to their chosen theme: *book* for Teacher G and *animal* for Teacher S. These themes established different foci for the two lessons and therefore placed the remaining parts of the two lessons in different contexts.

Noticeable differences between the teachers were also found in the number of "Other" and "Control" propositions. "Other" statements mainly functioned to reinforce participation and allocate turns. Teacher S, who tended to direct questions to one student at a time, had a rate nearly three times the number of control themes than that of Teacher G. Teacher G's technique of directing questions to the group at large and allowing simultaneous responses eliminated much of the need for allocating turns, and her students were not required to frequently raise their hands and bid for a turn to speak. Thus the difference in strategies for turn allocation contributed to the differences in the two lessons. The Control statements also provide an understanding of the differences in the two lessons. Control statements were used to refocus students on the task at hand when the discussion ranged off the topic and when students misbehaved. The 10 Control statements by Teacher S (vs. none for Teacher G) revealed another way in which the two lessons differed.

The differences in lesson focus (topics) and the amount of control and other statements reflect a difference in lessons that appears to be one of the contributing factors to the difference in student retell performance. One way to characterize the two lessons is in terms of fluidity and focus. Teacher G's lesson appears more fluid in that it is more story centered and contains fewer procedural propositions than Teacher S's lesson. This difference suggests that the thread of the story might be more difficult for Teacher S's students to discern. This observation can become a hypotheses which can be tested as the lesson continues to unfold. Analysis of propositions in the first episode of the story and the introduction, therefore, can lead to the identification of patterns, questions, and hypotheses that can be explored in later phases of the lesson as well as in other lessons (see Harker, in press). These patterns can also be related to student performance both within lessons and on outcome measures.

Question Complexity.   This discussion highlights global-level similarities and differences between the two lessons in terms of general categories of propositions (topics). In this section, a closer look at one factor that differentiates teacher style and also provides a means of exploring lesson complexity (questioning patterns) will be considered. The overall number of questions (including tag questions) and the number of propositions contained in the questions were examined for each teacher. A summary of this information is presented in Table 5. Question complexity was defined in terms of the number of propositions contained in a question. A simple question contained one or two propositions (e.g., "What did he do?" "What do you think he did?"). Complex questions contained three or more propositions (e.g., "What do you suppose he wanted to do?" How would doing that help him to walk like the tiger?").

Although the teachers have an equivalent number of questions, there is a fairly large difference between them when the number of propositions embedded in questions was considered, that is, how structurally and conceptually complex

Table 5. Similarities and Differences in Question Complexity
(Introduction and Episode 1)

Question Complexity	Teacher G	Teacher S
Total *N* questions	41	44
Total *N* questions propositions	80	65
Simple Questions		
N of questions	31	40
N of propositions	41	51
% of total questions propositions	51.25	78.46
Complex Questions		
N of questions	10	4
N of propositions	39	14
% of total questions propositions	48.75	21.54

they are. Of Teacher G's 77 propositions, 54% were in simple questions, and 45% were in complex questions—a fairly even split. Teacher S had fewer total propositions (73) of which 68% were in simple questions and 31% were complex. Overall, Teacher G had 31 simple and 10 complex questions (3.5:1 difference), whereas Teacher S had 40 simple and 4 complex (5.5:1 difference). Structurally, then, Teacher S's questions were simpler than those of Teacher G and addressed different information. Many of Teacher S's questions emphasized vocabulary and looking at the illustrations ("What is a——?" Can you see the ——?"). The level of her lesson was simpler and appeared to be aimed at the youngest children in her group. In contrast, Teacher G can be described as teaching "up" to the older students (second graders) in the group by using a more complex questioning style and by more closely addressing the actions of the story text. These observations suggest an hypotheses for further study both within this lesson and in other similar lessons. (See Harker, in press, for a more extensive discussion of this finding across the remainder of the lesson.)

This brief analysis presents a sample of the kinds of analyses which are possible using a propositional system. The findings relating to control and turn-allocation statements reinforce the sociolinguistic analysis presented in the previous section. The questioning analysis presented here also extends the information about lesson structure and content described in the sociolinguistic analysis section. These analyses reinforce the conclusion that the two lessons were not the same lesson either socially or academically. In the section that follows, these findings and those of the sociolinguistic analysis will be complemented by the episodic analysis of the literary text, lesson text, and the student recall protocols.

LESSON CONSTRUCTION 3:
CONSTRUCTION AND RECALL OF THE LITERARY TEXT

In this section, the structure of the literary text, the presentation of the text by the teacher (reader) and the retelling of the text by the student (listener) are examined. The theoretical frame for this work comes from reader-response theory, which provides insights into how readers read and interpret literature. From this perspective the reader is viewed as actively constructing the meaning of a literary text guided by text cues and by prior knowledge (e.g., Golden, 1983; in press-a, in press-b; Iser, 1978). Information about characters or plot, for example, is integrated as the text develops. The reader makes inferences and predictions while "reading between the lines."

In a story-reading lesson this process is mediated since students do not interact directly with the text. In such a lesson, the teacher (reader) interprets the text through the oral reading performance. If the teacher has additional goals for the lesson (vocabulary development, group discussion skills), these goals may also influence the story presentation. The student (listener) is thus presented with an experience in which three texts are intertwined: the author's original text, the teacher's (reader's) oral interpretation of that text, and the instructional text. The student's task is complex—to construct the meaning of the literary text from the instructional experience, and then to restructure the text by orally retelling the story.

Procedure

The analysis of the different texts focused on the story-reading and story-discussion segment of the lesson. This analysis, therefore, explored the part of the lesson directly related to story presentation and discussion; the introductory phase (and other phases for teachers) was not included in the analysis of the construction and reconstruction of text. The episode was selected as a unit of analysis, because it provided a workable, clear means for uncovering the structure of the original literary text, the teacher's instructional text, and the students' reconstructions of the text (see Golden, in press, for a complete discussion).

The analysis process involved a series of steps: (a) episodic analysis of the literary text; (b) analysis of instructional units of the teacher-presented text; and (c) episodic analysis of student recalls. Central to each step was the exploration of episodic structure. This common element in the analysis permitted the comparison of texts and the exploration of the relationship among the elements of the text. This approach extends episodic analysis from a static view of text meaning and structure to a dynamic view of meaning as it occurs in the evolving lesson.

Episodic Analysis. A story generally consists of a sequence of episodes which combine to form the major story components: beginning (setting and frame), middle (complication and development), and ending (resolution). The episode, a story within a story, also has a structure and boundaries which are marked in specific ways. One way to analyze episodic structure is from a story grammar frame. From this perspective, episodes are goal-oriented (Mandler & Johnson, 1977; Rumelhart, 1975; Stein & Glenn, 1979; Thorndyke, 1977) and are comprised of a set of structural elements. Elements that are central in an episode's structure are a *goal* (stated or implied), an *attempt* to achieve that goal, and an *outcome* of the goal attempt. Other elements may also be included in episodes—beginnings, reactions, and endings. Episode boundaries are marked by a variety of cues, including changes in cast, events, location, and time (Kintsch, 1977; Van Dijk, 1982).

In the study that follows, the original literary text and the students' story retelling protocols were segmented into episodes according to markers for episodes, and episodic elements (beginnings, goals, attempts, reactions, outcomes, endings) were then identified. Since the students recalled less than the whole story, a criterion was needed to guide the analysis of episodes. The criterion for episode in student recalls was the presence of a goal attempt and an outcome given the goal-based orientation of an episode. A total of 14 episodes containing 55 episodic elements were possible for recall. The analysis of the episodic structure of the literary text was also used as the basis for the segmentation and analysis of the teacher's instructional text.

The Story-Reading Event: Instructional Units. In the section on sociolinguistic analysis, the lesson was segmented into instructional sequence units based on contextual, pedagogical, and thematic cues. In this analysis, teacher talk in the story-reading segment of the lesson was also divided into instructional units. Instructional units were identified by considering the topics of the talk that occurred during story presentation. Within each instructional unit, the themes of these units were identified (more than one theme per unit was possible). Of interest here was (a) whether the teacher's instructional units coincided with the episodic boundaries of the literary text; that is, whether the teacher's presentation matched or clashed with the text structure; and (b) whether the themes of the instructional units were episodic-based, text-related, or extratextual; that is, how closely the themes followed the content of the story.

Representative Findings

The similarities and differences between the two teachers' presentations of the literary text were examined in terms of the match between instructional units and episodes and the relation of the themes of the instructional units to those of the story. The student recalls were then analyzed in terms of the number of episodes and the elements they contained. The goal was to explore the interrelationship among the author's text, the teacher's instructional text, and the students' reconstructed text.

Structure of the Literary Text. The literary text is comprised of 14 episodes and 55 episodic elements within those episodes. Three episodes (1, 4, and 7) met the criteria for well-formed episodes with a beginning, reaction, goal, attempt, outcome, and ending. Ten episodes consisted of either 3 or 4 elements. One episode (6) contained 2 elements. The distribution of the elements in the episodes is presented in Table 6. The first 10 episodes of the story (part 1) focused on the three characters' imitation of the tiger's walk. The remaining four episodes (part 2) concerned the tiger's imitation of the other characters' walks; these characters, in turn, imitated the "tiger's" walk.

Match Between Instructional Units and Episodes. Both teachers were sensitive to the episodic structure of the stories. This sensitivity is reflected in the fact that

Table 6. Comparison of Text Structure, Lesson Structure, and Student Recall Across Episodes

	E1	E2	E3	E4	E5	E6	E7	E8	E9	E10	E11	E12	E13	E14	Totals
Structure of the story text: Episodic elements per episode															
N of Elements[b]	6	4	4	6	3	2	6	3	3	3	4	4	4	3	55
Structure of the lesson: Instructional themes per episode															
Teacher G	9	0	3	3	0	3	2	2	0	0	4	2	2	2	32
Teacher S	5	1	1	3	0	3	1	1	0	1	2	0	0	1	19
Total	14	1	4	6	0	6	3	3	0	1	6	2	2	3	51
Structure of recall protocol: Episodic elements summed over 6 students															
Teacher G	14	0	4	14	6	4	10	0	0	2	7	9	8	7	85
Teacher S	14	0	0	13	2	1	13	4	3	1	4	3	4	0	62
Total elements possible[c]	36	24	24	36	18	12	36	18	18	18	24	24	24	18	330

Episode Number[a]

[a] Episodes 1–10 are in part 1; episodes 11–14 are in part 2 of the story.
[b] Episodes 1, 4, 7 are well-formed episodes which had a beginning, reaction, goal, attempt, outcome, and ending. Other episodes were less well formed.
[c] Total equals n of elements times n of students in each group ($n=6$).

in the majority of instances, the teachers broke into the story text either at boundaries of episodes (33% and 44%, respectively, for Teacher G and Teacher S) or at
boundaries between elements of episodes (30% and 44% respectively, of Teacher
G's and Teacher S's instructional units). In relatively few cases did either teacher
break into the middle of an episodic element (11% and 12%). One major difference
between the teachers is Teacher G's reference to information in prior episodes. In
22% of her instructional units, Teacher G made cross-episode relational ties, whereas Teacher S made none. In other words, Teacher G made links between episodes
for students, whereas Teacher S tended to treat each episode and related instructional units as separate entities.

Distribution and Content of Instructional Themes. The distribution of instructional themes across episodes is presented in Table 6. This table reflects the
teachers' choices as to which parts of the story text to elaborate and discuss.
Teacher G had an average of 2.3 themes per epsiode. Her discussion of story included 22 themes in the first half of the story (69%) and 10 in the second half
(31%). In contrast, Teacher S had 1.4 themes per episode and spent more time discussing the first half of the story (16 themes or 84%) than the second half (3
themes or 16%). As noted previously, the emphasis on the first part of the story is
partially related to the way in which the text is structured. Part 1 contains episodes
(1–10) that introduce the characters (tiger, porcupine, elephant, zebra) and their
goals (imitating the tiger's walk). Part 2 contains episodes (11–14) in which the
tiger imitates the animals. Seventy-one percent of all episodes (10) 73% of all
episodic elements (40) occur in the first part of the story; 27% of the episodes
(4) and 15 episodic elements occur in the second part of the story.

When the distribution of themes is compared by episode, a second pattern of
influence on lesson organization was identified. Both teachers had the greatest
number of instructional themes in episode 1 (9 for Teacher G and 5 for Teacher
S). There were no instructional themes for either teacher in episodes 5 and 9. In
episodes 1, 11, and 12, Teacher G had twice as many themes as Teacher S and, as
indicated previously, Teacher G emphasized the second part of the story more
than Teacher S. In other words, lesson organization was influenced by both the
text structure and teachers' choices as to which part of the story to emphasize.

Several additional contrasts were identified related to information presented in
instructional units for the two lessons. One such contrast is presented to provide
further information about similarities and differences between the two lessons. This
contrast involves the types of themes considered. Teacher G had 32 themes: 18
themes (56%) referred directly to episodic information in the story; 13 themes
(41%) were text-related (relevant to the story but not referring to information in
an episode); and only 1 theme was "other," since it referred to lesson procedures.
Within these themes, she focused on episodic information and directed children
toward information in the story text. In the text-related themes, she required
students to discuss vocabulary, speculate about characters' reactions, and project
personal views into the story (e.g., "What would you do?"). She also invited dif-

ferent kinds of thinking about the information in the text and encouraged children's interaction with the story on a number of levels.

Teacher S, in contrast, had 19 themes: 6 (32%) were episodic-based, 12 (63%) were text-related, and the remaining 1 was extratextual ("Have you ever seen a porcupine?"). Her text-related themes were both similar to and different from those of Teacher G. Like Teacher G, she discussed vocabulary. However, the two teachers differed in that Teacher S used a strategy that directed students to look at the animals in the illustrations (e.g., "See the tiger . . . "), whereas Teacher G used a strategy that focused students on the story itself. The differences in strategies reflect a difference in content emphasis and support the conclusion that the two lessons were not the same lesson. The effect of such differences become clearer when the structure of student recalls is considered.

Structure of Student Recalls. Before discussing the student recall performance, this work needs to be placed in an historical context. Past work on recall indicates that primary-grade students tend to recall only a small portion of the episodes or episodic elements in a given story (e.g., Mandler & Johnson, 1977; Stein & Glenn, 1979). These findings have been obtained from tasks in which the text was relatively brief (e.g., stories of less than 150 words) and contained a single protagonist. In the study being discussed, the literary text was both long and complex. That is, the text contained 1,041 words and had 14 episodes with multiple protagonists.

There were differences between the two groups of students in terms of the total number of episodes and episodic elements recalled. Recall data is also presented in Table 6. Teacher G's group recalled 14 (17%) episodes, and Teacher S's group recalled 7 (8%) episodes. Eighty-five (26%) elements were recalled by Teacher G's group, whereas 62 (19%) elements were recalled by Teacher S's group. Teacher G's group generally recalled more than Teacher S's group as measured in the mean number of episodes (2.3 vs. 1.2) and in the mean number of elements (14.2 vs. 10.3). Data should be interpreted in light of the wide range of performance in both groups (e.g., 3 to 26 elements in Teacher G's group and 4 to 21 in Teacher S's group), as would be expected with multiage groups and an open-ended recall task.

When the number of episodic elements recalled in the two parts of the story was considered, both similarities and differences were identified. The number of elements recalled in part 1 was similar for both groups (23% for teacher G's group and 21% for Teacher S's group). However, when the number of elements recalled in the second part of the story was considered, a different pattern was identified. Teacher G's students recalled 34% of the elements, whereas Teacher S's students recalled 12%. This pattern parallels the pattern of emphasis previously described.

Other patterns of episodic recall were common to both groups. First, well-formed story episodes (numbers 1, 4, 7) which had a beginning, reaction, goal, attempt, outcome, and ending were recalled best by both groups of students. These three episodes were the most elaborated in the story text. The 6 students in Teacher G's group recalled a total of 14, 14, and 10 elements in these three episodes, respectively; the 6 students in Teacher S's group recalled 14, 13, and 13 elements in these episodes. This finding is consistent with that of Black and Bower (1979), who found that episodes which were more elaborate were recalled better than those with less subordinate detail.

These data suggest that both the teacher and the text influenced what occurred. If the teacher had been the sole source of influence then there would have been a perfect match between episodes in which the text was discussed or text-related talk occurred and those recalled by students. Conversely, if the text had been the sole source of influence on recall, students would be expected to recall all elements in each episode. Exploration of the match between discussion/talk and recall, and conversely, lack of talk related to story, revealed a difference between the two teachers. Teacher G's students recalled elements in 9 of the 10 episodes in which the teacher discussed text. They also recalled elements in 1 episode in which no talk about the text occurred. In contrast, Teacher S's students recalled elements in 7 of the 10 episodes in which the teacher engaged in talk. They also recalled elements in 4 of the episodes in which no instructional themes occurred. The fact that students in both groups recalled elements in a majority of the episodes in which no elaboration occurred suggests an influence of both teacher and text. (See Golden, 1986, for a more complete discussion of this pattern.)

Recall of Element Type. Consideration of the proportion of element types also produced a pattern of similarities and differences between the two groups. The proportion of elements recalled by both groups is presented in Figure 2. Outcomes had the second highest proportion recalled by both groups (Teacher G's group had 32% and Teacher S's group had 23%). Reactions were among the elements least well recalled by both groups (19% for Teacher G's group and 14% for Teacher S's group). Endings were equally well recalled by both groups (21%). Attempts were less well recalled than outcomes by both groups (23% for Teacher G's group and 14% for Teacher S's group). These findings are similar to those described in Mandler and Johnson (1977), who found outcomes were better recalled than reactions and endings. They also found that attempts were less well recalled than outcomes by first graders, although this difference was not as apparent by fourth grade.

Differences between the two groups in the recall of types of elements were also evident. Teacher G's group recalled over twice as many beginnings as Teacher S's group (33% vs. 15%). Teacher G's group also recalled more attempts (23%) and outcomes (32%) than Teacher S's group (14% attempts and 23% outcomes). Beginnings for Teacher G's group were the best recalled element and for Teacher S's students, beginnings were among the least well recalled elements. Attempts were the third best recalled element for Teacher G's group and the least well recalled (along with reactions) for Teacher S's. A reverse pattern is evident when goals are examined; Teacher G's group recalled no goals and Teacher S's group recalled 25% goals.

When teachers' instructional units are analyzed, some of these differences might be explained. Teacher G emphasized beginnings and attempts more than the other

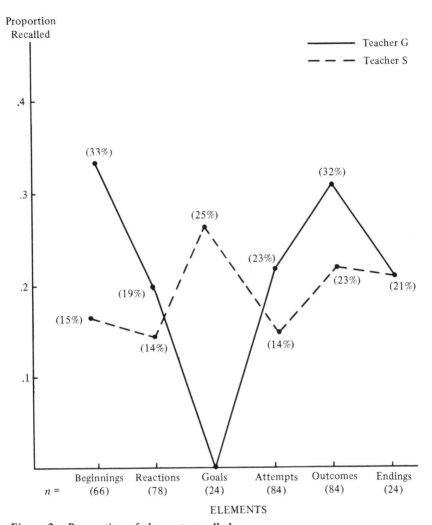

Figure 2. Proportion of elements recalled.

elements. Goals, reactions, outcomes, and endings received almost half the attention than beginnings and attempts. The high recall of outcomes despite the
teacher's lack of emphasis may be related to the salience of outcomes in children's
story recall without a teacher's mediating influence. The reason for the higher
recall of goals for Teacher S's group is less clear since this teacher had no instructional units which focused on goals. Moreover, studies of children's story recall
indicate that goals are among the least well recalled elements. Two students in
Teacher S's group recalled three goals each, therefore, individual differences rather
than a group pattern are evident. These similarities and differences in the recall of
element types highlight ways in which the teachers and the text structure influence
what was recalled.

Influences on Recall. This analysis shows that story recalls are affected by many factors which have their sources in characteristics of the students, the story text, and the teacher's instructional text. Given the same text and similar students, differences in recall outcomes between those groups was traced to differences in the lessons presented by the teachers. In this planned contrast of two teachers, Teacher G's emphasis on episodic information such as beginnings and attempts was reflected in her students' overall recall rate and higher recall of beginnings and attempts. This finding suggests a need for further study of the effect of teacher style on recall, of the context in which stories (and other lesson content) is presented, and of the meanings that are actively constructed.

MULTIPLE PERSPECTIVE ANALYSIS: ISSUES FOR RESEARCH

The three analyses presented in the previous sections provide an in-depth analysis of two instances of what appeared on the surface to be the same instructional activity, a story-reading–discussion lesson of *The Way the Tiger Walked* (Chacones, 1970). Each analysis produced a detailed description of specific aspects of the work required of teachers and students as they interacted to construct the various parts of the lesson. Taken together, the multiple analyses of these two events showed that the two events, while equivalent in group composition, teacher background, material used, and length of lesson (time on task), were not the same lesson. The analyses provided descriptions that showed the ways in which the teachers and students interacted with each other and with materials (e.g., the book, props) to construct the evolving lesson produced different lessons and that these differences in lesson delivery and meaning construction produced different outcomes for the two groups of students.

Space does not permit discussion of all aspects informed by multiple perspective analysis, therefore one area has been selected to highlight the value of this approach. One area of difference between the two lessons focuses on the difference in organizational structure. The three analyses provided information about the social and academic structure of the two lessons. Sociolinguistic analysis showed that the lessons were differentiated events. Lessons were shown to have phases, and phases were shown to have specific content and demands for participation. Lesson phases in the lesson of the top-ranked teacher supported one another; activity and expectations established in phase 1 set the frame for what was expected in phase 2. In contrast, the lesson phases in the teacher of lower rank were only loosely related. That is, the first part of the lesson established a pattern of interaction that was specific to that phase only; the expectations in the second phase differed, but the teacher did not signal overtly the difference of shift to the students. As a result of this set of actions, the teacher was forced to create a formal transition between the two phases. Organizational differences were also found when questioning patterns were explored. Teacher G used questioning patterns that permitted students to participate spontaneously throughout the lesson in response to questions. In contrast, Teacher S used questioning patterns that required students to "bid" for turns to answer.

Propositional analysis of the introduction and the beginning of phase 2 contributed further information about the two lessons. This analysis showed that the content demands of the two phases differed. The two teachers introduced different themes. The top-ranked teacher focused on the theme of the book, while the second teacher focused on a set of animal cutouts. Students in this lesson were expected to contribute personal knowledge about the animals. In other words, the two teachers placed the content of the story within different historical contexts. Organizational differences, therefore, were identified in terms of distribution of theme. Propositional analysis of questions also showed an organizational difference. Teacher G tended to use more complex questions than simple questions, thus placing greater cognitive demands on students. Teacher S, in contrast, tended to ask simpler questions. Propositional analysis, therefore, provided information about organizational structure and complexity of the lesson.

When combined, these analyses show that the two teachers established different historical (content) frames for the two lessons and different instructional and social frames. To be students in each of these lessons meant that they had to attend different types of information and had to respond in specific ways.

When the episodic analysis of the original text, the teacher-presented text, and student-reconstructed text are added to the sociolinguistic and propositional analyses, additional organizational aspects of lessons become clear. This analysis showed that teachers presented different stories. The two teachers broke the original text in different places during presentation and discussed different aspects of the story. The difference in presented themes and in episodic elements (e.g., beginnings, goals, outcomes, reactions, attempts, and endings) showed that while the same story text served as the basis of the lesson, the story that the two groups heard was not the same. Analysis of the story retellings showed that student reconstruction of the story reflected elements stressed. Exploration of the structure and organization of the original text also identified factors reflected in the retellings. Certain episodes in the story, episodes that were well formed in terms of elements (e.g., they had a beginning, a goal, an attempt, and an outcome) were recalled better than less well formed episodes. In other words, the structure and organization of the materials in this lesson influenced what students recalled about the story.

The three analyses, when taken together, demonstrate that differences in the way two teachers structured lessons, distributed content, and established expectations for participation influenced what was learned. However, the teacher and students were not the sole source of influence. The text used in the lesson was also shown to be a contributor to lesson development and meaning construction. The three analyses provided both unique information about lessons and convergent information. In instances in which findings converged, findings from one analysis extended, confirmed, and/or provided greater specificity to the findings from one of the other analyses. When the analytic systems are complementary, that is, they have a common theoretical base, it is possible to move back and forth across analyses to explore the relationships of various units to the whole. Another way to think about a multiple perspective analysis approach is that each analysis provides the researcher with the ability to "peel back" a different layer or aspect of the event under observation.

REFERENCES

Bales, R., & Strodtbeck, R. (1967). Phases in group problem-solving. In E.J. Amidon & John Hough (Eds.) *Interaction analysis: Theory, research and application.* Reading, MA: Addison-Wesley.

Barnes, D., & Todd, F. (1977). *Communication and learning in small groups.* London: Routledge & Kegan Paul.

Black, J.B., & Bower, G.H. (1979). Episodes as chunks in narrative memory. *Journal of Verbal · Learning and Verbal Behavior, 18,* 309–318.

Bloome, D. (1986). *Literacy, language and schooling.* Norwood, NJ: Ablex.

Bloome, D., & Green, J.L. (1984). Directions in the sociolinguistic study of reading. In P.D. Pearson, R. Barr, M.L. Kamil, & P. Mosenthal (Eds.), *Handbook of reading research.* New York: Longman.

Bloome, D., & Theodorou, E. (in press). Multiple layers of classroom discourse: Where teachers and students stand. In J.L. Green, & J.O. Harker (Eds.), *Multiple perspective analysis of classroom discourse.* Norwood, NJ: Ablex.

Cazden, C. (1981). Social context of learning to read. In J. Guthrie (Ed.), *Comprehension and teaching: Research reviews.* Newark, DE: International Reading Association.

Cazden, C. (1986). Classroom discourse. In M. Wittrock (Ed.), *Handbook for research on teaching.* Englewood Cliffs, NJ: Macmillan.

Cazden, C., John, V., & Hymes, D. (1972). *Functions of language in the classroom.* New York: Teachers College Press.

Chacones, D. (1970). *The way the tiger walked.* New York: Simon & Schuster.

Cochran-Smith, M. (1984). *The making of a reader.* Norwood, NJ: Ablex.

Collins, J. (1983). *A linguistic perspective on minority education: Discourse analysis and early literacy.* Unpublished doctoral dissertation. University of California, Berkeley.

Cook-Gumperz, J. (1986). *Social construction of literacy.* New York: Cambridge University Press.

Cook-Gumperz, J., Gumperz, J., & Simons, H. (1981). *School/home ethnography project.* Final Report to the National Institute of Education (NIE G-78-0082). Washington, DC: National Institute of Education.

Corsaro, W. (1981). Entering the child's world: Research strategies for field entry and data collection. In J.L. Green & C. Wallat (Eds.), *Ethnography and language in educational settings.* Norwood, NJ: Ablex.

Corsaro, W. (1985). *Friendship and peer culture in the early years.* Norwood, NJ: Ablex.

Erickson, F. (1982). Classroom discourse as improvisation: Relationships between academic task structure and social participation structure in lessons. In L.C. Wilkinson (Ed.), *Communicating in the classroom.* New York: Academic Press.

Erickson, F., & Shultz, J. (1981). When is a context? Some issues and methods in the analysis of social competence. In J.L. Green & C. Wallat (Eds.), *Ethnography and language in educating settings.* Norwood, NJ: Ablex.

Florio, S., & Shultz, J. (1979). Social competence at home and at school. *Theory Into Practice, 18* (4), 234–243.

Frederiksen, C. (1981). Inference in preschool children's conversations—a cognitive perspective. In J.L. Green & C. Wallat (Eds.), *Ethnography and language in educational settings.* Norwood, N.J.: Ablex.

Frederiksen, C.H. (1975). Representing logical and semantic structure of knowledge acquired from discourse. *Cognitive Psychology, 7,* 371–485.

Frederiksen, C.H. (1977). Semantic processing units in understanding text. In R.O. Freedle (Ed.). *Discourse production and comprehension* (Vol. 1). Norwood, NJ: Ablex.

Gilmore, P., & Glatthorn, A. (1982). *Children in and out of school.* Washington, DC: Center for Applied Linguistics.

Golden, J.M. (1983). If a text exists without a reader, is there any meaning? In B.A. Hutson (Ed.), *Advances in reading/language research.* Greenwich, CT: J.A.I.

Golden, J.M. (in press). The construction of a literacy text in a storyreading lesson. In J.L. Green, J.O. Harker, & C. Wallat (Eds.), *Multiple perspective analysis of classroom discourse.* Norwood, NJ: Ablex.

Golden, J.M. (1986). An exploration of reader-text interaction in a small group discussion. In D. Bloome (Ed.), *Literacy, and schooling.* Norwood, NJ: Ablex.

Golden, J.M., & Green, J.L. (1983). *Factual questions in context.* Paper presented at the American Educational Research Association Meeting, Montreal, Canada.

Green, J.L. (1977). *Pedagogical style differences as related to comprehension performance: Grades one through three.* Unpublished doctoral dissertation, University of California, Berkeley.

Green, J.L. (1983). Research on teaching as a linguistic process: A state of the art. In E. Gordon (Ed.), *Review of research in education.* Washington, DC: American Educational Research Association.

Green, J.L., & Harker, J.O. (1982). Gaining access to learning: Conversation, social, and cognitive demands of group participation. In L.C. Wilkinson (Eds.), *Communicating in the classroom.* New York: Academic Press.

Green, J.L., & Wallat, C. (1981a). *Ethnography and language in educational settings.* Norwood, NJ: Ablex.

Green, J.L., & Wallat, C. (1981b). Mapping instructional conversations. In J.L. Green & C. Wallat (Eds.) *Ethnography and language in educational settings.* Norwood, NJ: Ablex.

Green, J.L., & Weade, R. (1986). In search of meaning: The sociolinguistic perspective on lesson construction & reading. In D. Bloome (Ed.), *Literacy and schooling.* Norwood, NJ: Ablex.

Green, J.L., Weade, R., & Graham, C. (in press). Lesson construction and student participation. In J.L. Green, J.O. Harker, & C. Wallat (Eds.), *Multiple perspective analysis of classroom discourse.* Norwood, NJ: Ablex.

Gumperz, J.J. (1982). *Discourse strategies.* London: Cambridge University Press.

Gumperz, J.J., & Herasimchuk, E. (1973). The conversational analysis of social meaning: A study of classroom interaction. In R. Shuy (Ed.), *Sociolinguistics: Current Trends and prospects. Georgetown University Monographs in Language and Linguistics.* Georgetown, VA: Georgetown University Press.

Gumperz, J.J., & Tannen, D. (1979). Individual and social differences in language use. In C.F. Fillmore, D. Kempler, & W.S.-Y. Wang (Eds.), *Individual differences in language ability and language behavior.* New York: Academic.

Harker, J.O. (in press). In J.L. Green, & J.O. Harker (Eds.), *Multiple perspective analysis of classroom instruction.* Norwood, NJ: Ablex.

Harker, J.O. & Green, J.L. (1985). When you get the right answer to the wrong question: Observing and understanding communication in the classroom. In A. Jaggar & M.T. Smith-Burke (Eds.), *Observing the language learner.* Newark, DE: International Reading Association; Urbana, IL.

Harker, J.O., Hartley, J.T., & Walsh, D.A. (1982). Understanding discourse: A life-span approach. In B. Hutson (Ed.), *Advances in reading/language research* (Vol. 1). Greenwich, CT: JAI Press.

Heap, J. (1980). What counts as reading? Limits to certainty in assessment. *Curriculum Inquiry 10,* 265–292.

Heap, J. (1983). On task in discourse: Getting the right pronunciation. Paper presented at the annual meeting of the American Educational Research Association. Montreal, Canada, March 1983.

Hymes, D. (1974). *Directions in sociolinguistics: An ethnographic approach.* Philadelphia: University of Pennsylvania Press.

Hymes, D. (1981). *Ethnographic monitoring project.* Final Report to the National Institute of Education. (NIE F-78-0038). Washington, DC: National Institute of Education.

Iser, W. (1978). *The act of reading: A theory of aesthetic response.* Baltimore, MD: Johns Hopkins University Press.

Kintsch, W. (1977). On comprehending stories. In M.A. Just & P.A. Carpenter (Eds.), *Cognitive processes in comprehension.* Hillsdale, NJ: Erlbaum.

Kintsch, W. (1984). *The representation of meaning in memory.* Hillsdale, NJ: Erlbaum.

Kintsch, W., & Van Dijk, T.A. (1978). Toward a model of text comprehension and production. *Psychological Review, 85,* 363–394.

Mandler, J., & Johnson, N. (1977). Remembrance of things parsed: Story structure and recall. *Cognitive Psychology, 9,* 111–151.

McDermott, R.P. (1976). *Kids make sense: An ethnographic account of interactional management of success and failure in one first grade classroom.* Unpublished doctoral dissertation, Stanford University, CA.

Mehan, H. (1979). *Learning lessons.* Cambridge, MA: Harvard University Press.

Morine-Dershimer, G. (1985). *Talking, listening, and learning in the elementary classroom.* New York: Longman.

Morine-Dershimer, G., & Tenenberg, M. (1981). Participant perspectives of classroom discourse (Final Report, Executive Summary, NIE G-78-0161). Washington, DC: National Institute of Education.

Ochs, E. (1979). Transcription as theory. In E. Ochs & B. Schleffelin (Eds.), *Developmental pragmatics.* New York: Academic Press.

Philips, S.U. (1972). Participant structures and communicative competence: Warm Springs children in community and classroom. In C. Cazden, V. John, & D. Hymes (Eds.), *Functions of language in the classroom.* New York: Teachers College Press.

Philips, S.U. (1982). *The invisible culture: Communication in classroom and community on the Warm Springs Indian reservations.* New York: Longman.

Ruddell, R., & Williams, A. (1971). *A research investigation of a literacy teaching model, Project DELTA, Developing Excellence in Literacy Teaching Abilities, kindergarten through grade three.* (EPDA Project No. 005262) Washington, DC: U.S. Department of Health, Education and Welfare, Office of Education.

Rumelhart, D.E. (1975). Notes on a schema for stories. In D.G. Brown & A. Collins (Eds.), *Representation and understanding: Studies in cognitive science.* New York: Academic Press.

Schmidt, B. (1972). *The relationship between questioning levels and listening comprehension in K-3 children.* Unpublished doctoral dissertation, University of California, Berkeley.

Scollon, R., & Scollon, S. (1984). Cooking it up and boiling it down: Abstracts of Athabaskan children's story retellings. In D. Tannen (Ed.), *Coherence in spoken and written discourse.* Norwood, NJ: Ablex.

Stein, N., & Glenn, C. (1979). An analysis of story comprehension in elementary school. In R. Freedle (Ed.), *New directions in discourse processes.* Norwood, NJ: Ablex.

Stubbs, M. (1983). *Discourse analysis: The sociolinguistic analysis of natural language.* Chicago, IL: University of Chicago Press.

Tannen, D. (1979). What's in a frame? Surface evidence for underlying expectations. In R. Freedle (Ed.), *Advances in discourse processing* (Vol. 2). Norwood, NJ: Ablex.

Thorndyke, P. (1977). Cognitive structures in comprehension and memory of narrative discourse. *Cognitive Psychology, 9,* 77–110.

Van Dijk, T.A. (1982). Episodes as units of discourse analysis. In D. Tannen (Ed.), *Analyzing discourse: Text and talk, Georgetown University Roundtable on Languages and Linguistics.* Georgetown, VA: Georgetown University Press.

Wallat, C., & Green, J.L. (1982). Construction of social norms. In K. Borman (Ed.), *Social life of children in a changing society.* Hillsdale, NJ: Erlbaum.

Wilkinson, L.C. (1982). *Communicating in the classroom.* New York: Academic Press.

4
Maintaining Control:
The Structuring of Parent Involvement

JANE VAN GALEN
University of North Carolina at Chapel Hill

In spite of the almost total disregard for the relationships between the home and the school in the recent wave of reform proposals (Adler, 1982; Goodlad, 1984; National Commission on Excellence in Education, 1983; Task Force on Education for Economic Growth, 1983; Twentieth Century Fund Task Force, 1983), elementary teachers believe that parents can either support or undermine the work of the school (Lightfoot, 1978, pp. 30-34; Lortie, 1975, p. 181). To strengthen parental support, schools often encourage parents to take part in their children's education through such activities as school volunteer programs, advisory councils, parent-teacher organizations, parent-teacher conferences, and structured home-school communications.

Discussions in the literature of these structured opportunities for parent participation generally focus on educators' perceptions of the relative effectiveness of one of these mechanisms over another or on innovations in the basic format of one of the channels of parent participation (see, e.g., Becker & Epstein, 1982; Epstein, 1984; Gray, 1984; Moles, 1982). What this literature does not consider is the competing interest of teachers in maintaining control and authority over the domain of their classrooms (Licata, 1982; Lightfoot, 1978, pp. 25-30; Lortie, 1975, p. 191). Programs which draw parents into this domain also threaten to infringe upon teachers' sense of prestige and legitimacy as professional education "experts." With these conflicting interests rarely articulated in the traditional parent involvement literature, few researchers have looked beyond the formal goals of parent involvement programs to examine the actual interaction of parents and teachers in schools. Yet, given the explicit goal of increasing parents' opportunity for involvement in the school and the more implicit goal of protecting teacher autonomy, it is likely that explanations for why a program does or does not "work" will be found not in the formal structures of the programs but rather in the informal, unwritten rules that the teachers employ for managing the dichotomy between independence from, and dependence upon, the parents of children in their classrooms. These informal rules and their importance in the structuring of the parent involvement programs of one elementary school will be described in this chapter.

METHODS

During the spring of 1984, I observed the teaching and administrative staff of an elementary school. In these observations, I was primarily interested in the staff's perceptions of their students' parents and whether these perceptions help to shape the formal and informal rules around which their parent involvement programs are organized. I visited the school at least once, and often twice, a week from January through April, usually spending several hours at the school on each visit. I attended a parent-volunteer recruiting meeting and observed the administration's presentation of school programs to visitors from a neighboring school system. I observed parents coming and going from the school's office, talking informally with teachers, and working as volunteers. I also examined the school's newsletters and form letters that are sent to parents regularly. I also noted slogans and other messages intended for parents on the school's bulletin boards and other display areas. I requested but was not given access to parent-teacher conferences. Finally, I conducted in-depth, unstructured interviews with the president of the Parent Teacher Organization (PTO), the principal, the assistant principal, and at least one teacher from each grade level. My role during the study was that of a graduate student interested in parent involvement programs.

MESNER SCHOOL

Mesner School is located in Duplin County, a rural county in a southeastern state. It is the only elementary school in the county school system that is outside the corporate limits of the county seat 10 miles away. The school is located 25 miles from a major state university and 15 miles from a large private university. The building includes an older wing and a new wing that was completed seveal years ago. The building is bright and cheery, and visitors often comment on its warmth and attractiveness.

I had met several of the administrators and teachers from the school when they were enrolled in the same graduate courses as I. I had also supervised undergraduate students doing observations at the school. Through these contacts, it became apparent that the school not only welcomed, but even encouraged visitors from the university. Students who had visited the school had noted that the staff strongly emphasized its positive relationship with the community to visitors, and university faculty recommended Mesner as a place where "things are happening" between the school and community. The school's openness to visitors, my acquaintance with members of the staff, and my interest in an area that was also of interest to the staff contributed to my unchallenged and uneventful entry into Mesner.

Three hundred children in grades kindergarten through five attend the school. The school district maintained a racial balance in its schools that reflected the racial balance of the county: Approximately 60% of the students are black; the remaining 40% are white. White students are bused to the school from an area on the far side of the county to achieve this racial balance. The community from which the children come is generally poor, with small middle- and upper-middle-class groups. Many parents work in nearby textile mills.

The teachers at the school were generally young, and many were hired when the current principal came to the new school shortly after the new wing was completed. Only one of the teachers I interviewed had grown up in Duplin County. Those who had come from elsewhere generally considered it to their advantage in dealing with parents that they were "outsiders" to the community. One of the teachers I spoke with was black; the rest were white. All of the teachers at Mesner were female.

Academic achievement test scores for Mesner students were lower than those of the other schools in the county—a comparison spoken of defensively by the school staff. While showing me a compilation of the county's test scores for the previous year, the assistant principal, Mr. Berry, explained that the other schools had higher scores because they had students from families associated with the nearby universities. The PTO president was also defensive about these scores. She lamented that "everybody thinks of us as a poor cousin, because we're stuck way out here." She went on to claim that the school's test scores were better than those of the rest of the county because they showed more growth. The principal later made this same point.

The school had fewer parents actively involved in school activities than did other schools in the district. The PTO president offered the following explanation for this difference:

> It's just the difference in the community. It's not that we're doing anything wrong, it's just that we have different people to draw from. It's just a shame, but that's the way it is.

The staff's account of the children's lower-than-average achievement and the socioeconomic background of the parents provided the context within which the parents and the staff of the school interacted. The school offered the parents the opportunity to participate in the school through the PTO, a parent volunteer program, and parent-teacher conferences held twice yearly. However, the teachers rarely mentioned the PTO during interviews. They focused instead on the volunteer program and the conferences with which they were more directly involved.

VOLUNTEERS

The parent role most often mentioned by the school staff was that of the parent volunteer in service to the school. The primacy of the staff's definition of parents as volunteers was illustrated by the teachers' and administrators' perceptions of my interest in the study of the school. Although I was careful to describe my project as dealing with parent *involvement,* staff members often introduced me to their colleagues as someone looking at the parent volunteer program. During several interviews, broad questions about parents were interpreted and answered with reference to volunteers. For example, in response to the question, "What did you learn through academia about what to expect when working with parents?" a teacher said:

> I think through academia, very little. In fact the more I think about it, the less I think it really trained me to work with volunteers, be they just volunteers or parent volunteers.

The number of volunteers fluctuated during the year. The staff estimated that there were 30 volunteers early in the year, but fewer than 20 were still active. Both Mr. Berry and the principal, Mr. Johnson, claimed that the school had employed as many as 60 volunteers a few years earlier. Most of the parents who volunteered were recruited directly by a classroom teacher. A PTO parent volunteer committee recruited others for special events for teachers without homerooms.

The tasks of the volunteers were consistently defined by the school's staff. Sherry, the teacher coordinator of the PTO volunteer committee, described the suggestions given to the staff when they were surveyed to determine their need for volunteers:

> Do you want someone for clerical work, or for reading with the children, or cutting out letters for bulletin boards, or putting up bulletin boards?

Other teachers described similar activities performed by volunteers in their classrooms:

> They help with parties. If they can't come and help to supervise, they'll send things.

> We had one at the beginning of the year volunteer to build a bookcase. That was really helpful.

When asked how their classrooms would be different if more parents were involved, teachers envisioned more of the same type of volunteer help.

> I would use them mainly for relieving paperwork, monitoring behavior, making games, doing what I never get around to doing.

In only a few instances did teachers describe volunteers working directly with children on instruction. One mother (who formerly worked at the school as a counselor) occasionally drilled a small group of children on material taught by the teacher. Elsewhere, the mother of a kindergarten student helped her child's class to plant seeds. These two instances were exceptions to the rule, however, for in all other descriptions of the volunteers efforts, the work of the parents was distinctly different from the work of the teacher. Limited to clerical and decorating jobs that were only incidental to the children's learning, the parents' responsibilities were subordinate to the work of the professionals.

Sherry explained her views on the logic of assigning these tasks to volunteers:

> We have to, for lack of a better word, maintain a degree of control, because we are professionals, and at the same time we want to pull in all our re-

sources. We want to make sure not everyone feels, "well I could do that," because they haven't been through the schooling, or the training, or whatever.

Volunteers were expected to commit themselves to consistent schedules and to regular availability. Parents serving on the volunteer committee noted that parents who could come to the school only occasionally or who could volunteer for only limited time periods would not be recognized in the end-of-the-year recognition awards. While the staff expressed a desire for more parents to volunteer, these scheduling requirements limited the parents who could volunteer at the school to those who had few other responsibilities or demands on their time. As one teacher explained:

> A lot of the parents we see involved here, the mothers don't work. That's who we see here as our volunteers.

Thus, the structure of the program systematically excluded those parents the teachers described as being in the majority—those who worked, those who were poor, and those with young children to care for.

In summary, distinctions between the professional educators and the parents were maintained through the volunteer program, not on the basis of demonstrated differences in the skills of teaching children, but in preventing parents from performing work that involved these skills at all. By invoking time restrictions and a narrow definition of appropriate tasks for volunteers, the staff was able to control the parents who might otherwise intrude into the professional's domain.

PARENT-TEACHER CONFERENCES

The distance between teachers and parents was reinforced in the parent-teacher conferences held every spring and fall. The 15-minute conferences were the one formal mechanism through which parents and teachers met to consider the work of the child. Turnout rates varied, however, from teacher to teacher. Mr. Berry estimated a 40-50% turnout for the school (which he considered good). One teacher boasted a 90% turnout, while others estimated that 40-60% of the parents come to at least one of the conferences.

There was a notable consistency in the descriptions teachers gave of their conferences. In every case, much of the time was taken by the teacher's description of the child's work to the parent. Four teacher responses to the question, "What do you talk about during your conference?" illustrate this point:

> I try to think of the things that (the children) are doing well. Positive things. I give them ideas of how they can improve their weaknesses.

> We try to point out—to keep things not altogether negative . . . we try to point out positive things. And weaknesses and ways of improving.

> If they have no concerns, and we try to answer their questions first, we usually begin with their academics, their strengths and weaknesses, and then give them some guidance.

We usually try to come up with strengths and weaknesses for each child. And we give recommendations for what the child has.

When asked to describe bad conferences, the teachers told of experiences in which a parent disagreed with the teacher's definition of the child's performance. These dissenting parents annoyed and frustrated the staff:

I've had one parent, she just did not listen. She had it in her head . . . what she was, she was angry, and she never got over it the whole conference.

Interviewer: So what did you say to her?

You just kind of sit there and listen. You keep repeating what the problem is . . . the only thing to tell them is the facts when you have a conference like that.

Mr. Berry described a similar conference that he had fielded for a teacher:

The teacher had been quite honest about just what the child was doing, and the parents, they just didn't want to accept that.

In every account of conflict between parents and teachers, the staff maintained that their position was "fact" while insisting that parents were too subjective.

The credibility of parents was not questioned, however, when parents offered approval and support during the conference. The teachers agreed that being complimented by a parent was a key ingredient of a "good" conference:

Several parents mentioned that their kids really enjoyed our class and that made us feel like we'd really been doing a good job, and they showed sincere appreciation.

When they say their child is happy and they say their child enjoys my classroom, and is doing good this year, or really improved from last year . . . or if a parent sees a notable change, and knows the child is happy, then that makes a good conference.

No instances were mentioned of parents changing the minds of teachers, but in no case was the objectivity of parents questioned when the parents were pleased with the school's work with their child. This conditional acceptance of the parents' judgment, the domination of the teacher during the conference, and the short time allotted for conferences (one teacher even suggested that cutting the time in half— to 7½ minutes—would be adequate) challenged the assumption that the primary purpose of the conference was to draw parents into meaningful participation in the child's academic program. The more symbolic function of bringing the parents to the school in a gesture of support and deference to the teacher was suggested by several teachers. They noted that they particularly appreciated parents coming in even when their child was doing well and there was little to talk about. The PTO president, who spent an entire day every week volunteering in her child's classroom, was one of these parents:

I'm here all the time, and I wouldn't miss a conference. They don't even think they have to schedule me, because I'm here all the time.

For this parent, conferences had little to do with discussing her child's progress, but much more to do with showing her concern and support for the teacher. Thus, "involvement" of parents in this situation was their gesture of giving approval to the teacher for making decisions.

The staff was critical of parents who did not come on conference days and therefore did not offer this deference to the teacher. This was seen as particularly problematic if they were parents of children having trouble in school:

> The parents we'd like to see at conference time are the ones who don't come in.
>
> Usually the ones who we need to see don't usually come to these things.
>
> It's not the ones you'd want to come, or the ones you *need* to see.
>
> We see a lot of parents that we would not quite call to see. The children that are having problems, it's real hard to get those parents in.
>
> The ones you *need* to see are the ones that don't come in.

These comments, all unsolicited, came early in our discussions about conferences, usually immediately after the teachers told me how many parents came to the conferences. In making these claims, the staff was suggesting that children were doing poorly in school because their parents had not sought the advice traditionally dispensed by teachers. Yet this concern for these "needy" parents was not matched by effort to get the noninvolved to attend conferences. When asked how they had tried to work with these parents, the teachers answered that they did not know how to get through to them, or they described using some form of coercion, such as threatening to fail the child.

As with the volunteer program, parent-teacher conferences were not designed to facilitate contact with the parents of children who were having the most difficulty in school. The conferences served instead to strengthen the teachers' authority over the "good" children whose parents readily came to the school on the teachers' terms. At the same time, uncooperative parents could be blamed for the failure of less successful students. When little concerted effort was made to work with these uninvolved parents, teachers reduced the threat of potentially negative encounters with the parents of the children least adequately served by the school.

ACCOUNTING FOR NONINVOLVEMENT

Whether they were discussing parents who did not come to conferences, who did not volunteer, or who did not appear to be encouraging the child's efforts, the staff attributed noninvolvement to personal characteristics of the parents. The parent's job, socioeconomic status, educational background, and "attitudes" were all given as explanations for why some parents failed to take advantage of the opportunities for participation offered by the school. In addition, the staff had different expectations for the children's fathers than their mothers. These factors can each be considered in greater detail.

Gender

The staff of the school used the terms *parent* and *mother* almost interchangeably. Consequently, when the teachers singled out one of the parents, it was nearly always the mother who was held accountable for the child's behavior or for cooperating as the staff expected:

> What he was supposed to be doing, he wasn't, and mom and dad weren't too concerned that we were expecting a certain level out of him. And I really don't know when the mother expected the child to get it.

> Now if something happens over and over, and I'm not getting anywhere with (the student), then I'll write a note home and see if the mother can talk to them about it.

While acknowledging that it was necessary for many mothers to work, the teachers' expectations were still rooted in traditional conceptualizations of full-time motherhood. Accordingly, when mothers went to work, communications channels between the school and home broke down:

> A lot of our parents are working parents, both parents are working. They work shifts. It's very difficult. When we call, we cannot even get them to the telephone where they work.

Adherence to such practices as only meeting at school, during the day, and relying solely on phone and written communication (which the teachers admit is ineffective) made participation difficult for working parents. But it was not the practices of the school that were questioned; rather, working parents themselves were blamed for not being more actively involved.

The staff made some concessions to the working parent such as holding conferences in both the afternoon and the evening. Such concessions, however, did not represent any real effort to formulate new solutions to meet the needs of the growing numbers of working mothers. One teacher mentioned an idea discussed by some teachers to approach the area textile mills about allowing parents to spend their lunch hour or other release time at the school. The idea was not pursued, because the staff felt that it was more important at the time to concentrate their efforts on the available volunteers who were not working. The teacher went on to explain that she still thought the idea was a good one, because it would allow the parents to relieve teachers from cafeteria duty. Again, however, even when out-of-the-ordinary solutions were suggested, they were framed within the notion of parent as volunteer for a low status, noninstructional task rather than parent as collaborator in the education of the child.

When communicating expectations to parents that could not readily be met, the staff maintained a subtle advantage in their bargaining for control. As one teacher explained when discussing evening conferences, the staff's willingness to adapt their procedures to meet the parents' circumstances was at least partly contingent upon the parents' willingness to reciprocate by meeting the staff's expectations:

I think I can speak for at least a small group of teachers. Sometimes, even though we're willing to do [evening meetings], you know we work all day, too, and night meetings are really hard. How much of public servants are we? What does that mean? Especially if you don't have homework coming in, and no reinforcement of this or that at home.

Thus, working parents who might not be willing or readily able to provide the support the teachers desire were expected to relinquish their claims on the teachers' time. There was no acknowledgement from the teacher just quoted, or from the rest of the staff, that night meetings (or night work with children) were also difficult for working parents. This position also failed to recognize that parents might resent demands on their time, if they felt that the school neither recognized nor respected their concerns. With the staff defining the circumstances under which they would meet with parents, it was the parents who had to adapt to the school's expectations. This was true, even when those expectations did not take into account the changing realities of the working parents' lives.

Socioeconomic Status
Low-income families were considered by the staff to be less concerned about education than wealthier families were. As Mr. Berry commented:

You know, it's always the poor, poor kids that you're always trying . . . I guess that's just part of the game. The good ones you don't have to spend as much time worrying about.

A teacher echoed the same concern:

We had a lot of trouble this year getting parents to volunteer. Mr. Johnson says its the economy. A lot of other schools, well, I think that we have a rather unique situation. It's a rather poor community.

As another staff member summarized, "There's a world of difference between poor parents and other parents."

Closely tied to income level was the amount of education a parent had completed, and the teachers believed that parents without much formal schooling valued education less than more educated parents:

I think that there's quite a few who don't understand the importance of education and who haven't gone that far themselves.

Some parents don't care anything about school at all, because they have a limited education.

While the staff decried the lack of support from poor and uneducated parents, the inflexibility of the programs perpetuated the stereotypes of the unconcerned parent. Meanwhile, the belief that these parents did not care about education also served the staff by allowing them to take exclusive credit for whatever learning the students did experience:

We have a lot of room for growth, because we have a lot of kids coming in who are doing very poorly, because they are not really prepared, and they have a lot of room to grow. So the teachers come up smelling like roses.

Serving both as the staff's defense for lower test scores and as evidence of what the staff can accomplish in spite of the poor homes, the "growth" of the children of poor parents boosted the self-esteem of the staff, even while these children achieved at levels far below those the staff expected of wealthier children. Were the parents of these children to become more involved, this illusion of success would not be so easily maintained.

Emotive Factors

Finally, the "attitudes" of noninvolved parents were described extensively by the teachers and principals of the school. The staff felt that it understood the attitudes of the parents with whom they had little contact as well as those who were most active in the school. The attitudes of the "no-shows" were explained as being in basic conflict with those of the professionals. This conflict was seen to explain the parents' apparent lack of support. In response to the question, "What's different about those parents who do get involved and those who don't?" teachers responded:

There's a lot of them, that, you know, school's just not important in their lives, and they would just rather leave it up to the teachers. . . . And they just don't understand that how much more their children could get from their parents' attitude being better.

You can tell which parents are going to get involved by looking at their kids a lot of the time. The child seems really interested and involved, and you can almost bet the parents will be too. But we have some children in our room that, whether they're having some real serious problems at home with their families or else their parents really don't ask them about school, don't really seem concerned. And that's the attitude you see at school. It's like they don't really have any motivation.

There are some who are very much interested and some who are just apathetic.

Even while expecting the parents to help the children at home on school work, the "attitudes" of parents were seen as more important than any direct action the parents would take to further the child's learning. A teacher responded to the question, "What are some specific ways that parents help a child to do better in school?" in this way:

A broad answer to that is just to show interest.

(Interviewer: Interest?)

Just by genuine interest in "What did you do today? What did you learn? What did your teacher talk about?"

Other teachers responded:

> Well, their interest in their homework, they want to know how the child is doing.
> They seem really concerned, even when their child is doing real well.

The relegation of parents' responsibility to the realm of "attitudes" intensified the distinction between the professionals who did the "real" work and the parent whose contribution was as an advocate for the teachers and the school. Emotive work with the child was nonspecific and undefinable; it could not infringe upon the tasks over which the staff wished to maintain control. A "good" attitude could then be defined as one which accepted the authority of the school and, conveniently, a "bad" attitude could be blamed for a child's failure. When it was the teachers' perceptions by which parents' attitudes were judged, the legitimacy of the teachers' authority remained unchallenged.

CONCLUSIONS

When parents enter the school, they trespass on territory that teachers defend as their own. The teachers and administrators at Mesner managed this predicament by structuring the opportunities for parent involvement to favor the participation of parents who were most supportive of the staff and their work with the children. Thus, by narrowly defining the bounds within which parents could participate, the staff could criticize those parents who would not or could not work within these bounds.

This view of parent participation at Mesner suggests that the traditional literature on parent involvement offers at best only an incomplete picture of what actually happens when parents are invited to participate in the work of the school. Based on the premise that the problem was simply one of finding the program that would bring the most parents through the school's door in the most efficient manner, these studies have overlooked the formal and informal constraints placed on parents by staff who feared the intrusion on parents into their "professional" domain.

Lightfoot (1978) suggested that a possible solution to these often unarticulated conflicts between parents and teachers would be "making more explicit the spheres over which teachers have ultimate and uncompromising authority and those areas where collaboration with parents could be an educational and creative venture" (p. 42). While this collaboration would be a step beyond the more ritual participation usually proposed, the evidence from Mesner suggests that the obstacles to this collaboration are not explicit. Given that teachers have conflicting interests in nurturing both the support of and independence from parents, programs intended at least superficially to enhance collaboration are confounded by teachers' efforts to keep parents at arms' length. This defensive resistance to parent participation must first be recognized and addressed before collaboration between parents and teachers can occur.

Toward this end, several avenues for further investigation are suggested. First, we should ask why educators prefer control over collaboration, and why, therefore, the resources that parents could offer to the school are viewed as interruptions to the school's work. A possible explanation for teachers' asserting their authority over parents is the erosion of their control over other facets of their jobs. Sykes (1983) has noted that recent policy proposals for increased technical and bureaucratic control of schools gives the implicit message to the public and teachers alike that teachers cannot be trusted. Lightfoot (1978) noted that parents are seen as most threatening when teachers are least sure of their own competence. If policy recommendations such as the recent reform proposals continue to publicly challenge teacher competence, parent involvement programs may be unintentionally sacrificed as teachers become less willing to concede the remnants of their authority and responsibility to parents. In schools such as Mesner, where teachers feel that socioeconomic factors further weaken the control they have over students' learning, teachers might be expected to be even more protective of their authority over their classrooms.

Next, we should ask why educators so readily settle for a stereotypical understanding of the parents of their students. This question is closely related to the first, for the exercise of control over parents is legitimized by the stereotypes that teachers hold of parents, particularly those who are not active in the school. Policy based on these stereotypes becomes a classic example of self-fulfilling prophecy. To the extent that decisions about how far parents can be trusted to work with their own children and how much effort should be expended to reach noninvolved parents are based on shallow and inaccurate information, these policies tend to create outcomes consistent with the original assumptions. Thus, we could further explore the implicit contradiction between educators' claiming to be concerned about involving parents and their failure to take a more active interest in learning why these parents are not now involved.

Finally, given the formal and informal authority that educators have over the structuring of the contacts they have with parents, more positive structures could be sought that would involve parents in improving the achievement of their children without undermining the status of teachers. Parents engage in an often unacknowledged power struggle with educators over poorly defined spheres of responsibility. Research into the concerns of both parents and teachers could lead to the development of collaborative mechanisms that could make the education of the children, rather than the protection of the teachers, the primary consideration. Alliances between parents and teachers take place within the context of power and authority networks of schools. Genuine collaboration is hindered when these underlying issues are neither recognized nor addressed. If the involvement of parents remains a concern of educators, research in the area of parent involvement should be broadened from evaluations of particular programs that now dominate the literature to more comprehensive inquiries into the dynamics that shape these programs.

REFERENCES

Adler, M.J. (1982). *The paideia proposal.* New York: Macmillan.

Becker, H.J., & Epstein, J.L. (1982). Parent involvement: A survey of teacher practices. *The Elementary School Journal, 83*(2), 85–102.

Epstein, J.L., & Becker, H.J. (1982). Teachers' reported practices of parent involvement: Problems and possibilities. *The Elementary School Journal, 83*(2), 104–113.

Epstein, J.L. (1984). School policy and parent involvement: Research results. *Educational Horizons, 62*(2), 70–72.

Goodlad, J.I. (1984). *A place called school.* New York: McGraw-Hill.

Gray, S.T. (1984). How to create a successful school/community partnership. *Phi Delta Kappan, 65*(6), 405–409.

Licata, J.W. (1982). Improving school-community relationships: How receptive are principals, teachers? *NASSP Bulletin, 66*(457), 101–109.

Lightfoot, S.L. (1978). *Worlds apart: Relationships between families and schools.* New York: Basic Books.

Lortie, D.C. (1975). *Schoolteacher.* Chicago: University of Chicago Press.

Moles, O.C. (1982). Synthesis of recent research on participation. *Educational Leadership, 40*(2), 44–47.

National Commission on Excellence in Education. (1983). *A Nation at Risk.* Washington, DC: U.S. Government Printing Office.

Sykes, G. (1983). Contradictions, ironies, and promises unfilled: A contemporary account of the status of teaching. *Phi Delta Kappan, 65*(2), 87–93.

Task Force for Economic Growth. (1983). *Action For Excellence.* Denver, CO: Author.

Twentieth Century Task Force on Federal Elementary and Secondary Education Policy. (1983). *Making the grade.* New York: Twentieth Century Fund.

PART II
THE ORGANIZATION
OF SCHOOLING

The preceding section developed the view of teaching as a social context. This section illustrates that teaching occurs within the larger organization of schools and a school district. These larger organizational entities are confronted with conflicting roles. They must manage both maintenance and change of the organization. This conflict provides a constant tension in the management of schooling. Somehow we must balance these conflicting demands as we pursue effectiveness and therefore excellence in schools.

The three chapters in this section address the role of the larger educational organizations in instructional improvement. These studies illustrate that change is not just a technical problem that can be cured by a change in policy at the central office level. Rather, they suggest that we must consider the images educators, schools, and districts hold about the nature of their work and their effectiveness as we conceptualize strategies for reforming schools.

Whitford examines the implementation of an instructional system that was designed to improve reading in junior high schools. Her description of the implementation of the new program reveals that its meaning varied across interest groups and that changes in the district's organization had unintended effects on the program. Whitford illustrates how social context is important to the success of the program. She suggests that while the program responded to a high-priority problem in the district, it was incompatible with the press for short-term results that was part of the political and organizational context in the school district. Whitford concludes that it may be that educational innovations fail because they are not championed by those with formal authority.

The chapter by Brieschke concerns the implementation—or rather its non-implementation—of a regulatory policy in a large urban school district. Her examination of the impact of implementation of a disciplinary policy on individual, organizational, and macro-organizational levels suggests that we best conceive of implementation as a tentative rather than definitive process. Brieschke demonstrates that resistance to a policy may actually contribute to organizational effectiveness, especially when the resistance is related to unclear, multiple, or changing expectations about the policy and its effects. This chapter examines the range of dynamics at play when a central office policy is both poorly articulated and monitored. Brieschke illustrates how activities at the school-building level are governed by the actors in that building: context, again functioning to shape behavior.

Finally, Dwyer, Smith, Prunty, and Kleine study a single school over time and document a dramatic change in orientation. They view change in schools as a process of fashioning new organizational identities. Their chapter explores the role of the past and of the participants in embodying and reconstructing organizational identity. Kensington, the school studied, was transformed from a new, innovative setting to a rather unexceptional school. The authors' analysis has lessons for those who wish to manage change in the other direction.

These three chapters demonstrate how organizational context affects schooling. What we achieve and desire in schools becomes shaped both by the processes we use to maintain or change the organization and by the contexts in which the schools are imbedded. Thus, change is better understood as a complex sociocultural phenomenon than as a simplistic technical process.

5
Effects of Organizational Context on Program Implementation*

BETTY LOU WHITFORD
University of Louisville

INTRODUCTION

The literature available on how to bring about change in schools is voluminous. While a variety of change models exist, many suggest sequential steps or stages of change based on an image of schools corresponding closely with Weber's classical conception of bureaucracy. The assumption of those who hold this image of organizations is that change can be brought about by following formalized, logical steps that outline tasks, delegate responsibilities down through the organization, and provide guidelines for efficient management.

In recent years, however, this view of change has been subjected to considerable criticism. In part, the criticism is based on questions that arise from the observations that innovations are rarely fully implemented; and when they are, typically in some modified fashion, they seldom produce the intended effects (Sarason, 1971; Schlechty, 1976; Berman & McLaughlin, 1977; Garrou, 1980; Joslin, 1982). A related but more fundamental criticism of the management model of change suggests the need for a more holistic understanding of schools as organizations. For example, in describing how different images of organizations affect efforts to institute change, Firestone and Herriott (1981) observed:

> Past thinking about educational change has been guided by inadequate images of what school districts are like—they are assumed to be much more rational and controllable than is in fact the case. (p. 221)

But how does one begin to understand what organizational images are held by those attempting change? How do those images affect behaviors and events that occur during change efforts? What patterns of behaviors develop or are called into play during attempts to get others to engage in new behaviors and respond to new expectations?

---

*Sincere appreciation is extended to Dr. Phillip C. Schlechty who directed the study on which this chapter is based and first suggested many of the ideas herein. Many thanks also to CMS and the TRICA staff and teachers. Funds from the National Institute of Education supported the research, though the views herein are not necessarily those of NIE and no official endorsement should be inferred.

93

In a large part, the images held of how school systems or school buildings operate are affected by patterns of interaction and the meanings participants attach to behaviors and events. In addition, such understandings and interactions, while becoming patterned over time, are likely to vary depending on the particular context or circumstance in question. Thus, a complex web of structures and understandings exist along with more formalized bureaucratic arrangements. Because formalized arrangements are much more "visible," it is understandable that those interested in change have focused on them. The problem of control referred to by Firestone and Herriott, however, is exacerbated by the dynamic, informal nature of much of what goes on in organizations. Appreciation of these less visible dynamics is necessary to understanding change; indeed, such understandings are crucial to bringing about change more effectively.

This chapter addresses a multiyear effort to implement a junior high reading program in the Charlotte-Mecklenburg Schools, the largest district in North Carolina. The innovation, which came to be known as TRICIA (Teaching Reading in Content Areas), evolved from an in-service session into a complex program including extensive staff development, local and outside funding, and the use of building-based trainers—teachers whose responsibilities involved assisting other teachers in understanding and using project-related materials and techniques.

There are two stories here. The first concerns how a large-scale project evolved and how implementation was attempted. Numerous obstacles were encountered by project participants along the way. Some were overcome; others were not. From the beginning of this research, perceptions differed widely concerning program vitality. "No use in studying TRICIA. It's on the way out." This statement came from a high-level administrator in the school system at the very time that planning was underway by project staff to provide 9 released days and 14 after-school sessions for the training of a new cohort of teachers. A narrative which summarizes the evolution of the program is presented in the first part of the chapter.

The second story is an interpretation of the narrative. It is built, in part, from several broad constructs which organizational theory suggests are salient to understanding change, and partly from categories of phenomena more grounded in the specific setting (Glaser & Strauss, 1967). The categories and explanations that emerged during the study are presented in the second section of the chapter.

The chapter concludes with a discussion of several working hypotheses, or plausible explanations, for why the events that occurred during the attempted change happened as they did. These explanations are then used as the basis for informed speculation about a variety of implications for researchers and practitioners interested in change efforts.

RESEARCH METHODS

The study was conducted over a 2-year period from 1979 to 1981, using extensive interviews, observations, and document review. These techniques were developed in anthropology as a means of understanding unfamiliar cultures. They also provide an especially appropriate and productive way to discover the patterns of interactions, events, and meanings in less unfamiliar contexts. Talking with participants involved in a change effort, observing their work, asking questions which encourage articulation of what they are doing and why—in short, becoming very familiar with the day-to-day operation of a project and a school system can illuminate the substantive complexity of attempts to institute change.

The research on TRICA evolved in conjunction with a more extensive field study which focused on developing a framework for evaluating staff development programs (Schlechty, 1979). That framework includes a group of constructs subsumed by power and authority, and program coordination, status, boundaries, and direction. These "sensitizing constructs" served as the initial source of questions to ask respondents.

Entry for the study was obtained based on contacts and relationships established during the staff development study which began about 7 months prior to the focus on TRICA. Initial interviews with the TRICA staff revealed a complex change effort being introduced through staff development strategies. Because of the complexity, the research team of the larger project decided that TRICA warranted in-depth study, beyond the focus on staff development. Thus, this study of the change process itself emerged.

Data Collection

At least two formal interviews, averaging two hours each, were held with the TRICA initiators. Teachers and administrators at all levels of the system were also interviewed. The formal interviews were generally conducted by two researchers and were audiotaped. Also, there were numerous opportunities to talk informally with TRICA participants and other school system officials in a variety of settings, including a 4-day visit to an out-of-state TRICA site. In addition, a variety of documents were reviewed, including TRICA grant applications, memoranda and training materials, student test score distributions, and school desegregation percentages.

A variety of TRICA-related meetings, attended by project staff, trainers, teachers, outside consultants, and system administrators, were observed. Detailed field notes were taken during these meetings which focused primarily on implementation strategies. Since some of the meetings were held at school sites, they provided additional opportunities to observe interactions among TRICA and building staff, to observe classroom use of TRICA techniques, and to interview participant teachers and principals about the effects of the training and implementation activities in their buildings.

Additional information about the project, the school system, and specific building sites was provided by the staff development research (Schlechty, Crowell, Whitford, Joslin, Vance, Noblit & Burke, 1981) and a companion study of how TRICA was introduced in two buildings (Joslin, 1982). The techniques described here were also used in both of these studies.

Data Organization

Taped interviews and field notes were transcribed onto data analysis protocols. At first, data were organized by source, e.g., TRICA staff, teachers, strategy meetings.

As the study progressed, the protocols were sorted into interpretative catorgories drawn from the sensitizing constructs, emerging grounded categories, and ideas suggested in the literature on planned change. Thus, in operation, the task of data organization increasingly overlapped with interpretation and analysis as the protocols were coded and cross-referenced. During the sorting process, additional questions emerged, some of which required new information, while others were aimed at clarification. Follow-up interviews were held in both cases until no new information was gained. The guiding question here and increasingly during analysis was simply, "What's going on here?"

Data Analysis

As the questions became directed more toward clarification than toward new information, a draft of the study was prepared, containing a narrative and explanations for why things happened the way they did. The explanations were developed around the final set of categories which evolved during organization and interpretation of the data. The draft was reviewed by the staff development research team, the TRICA staff, and others in the school system. Since the research team of the larger study was composed of both university and school-system specialists in social theory, field research methods, administration, curriculum, and instruction, this review provided expert panel judgments of the study. The reviewers were asked to consider accuracy of the narrative and logic of the interpretations. In the one instance when disagreement on fact occurred, additional information was obtained which clarified the disparity. When disagreements on interpretation occurred, these were incorporated into the study as alternative explanations.

THE DEVELOPMENT AND INTRODUCTION OF AN INNOVATION

Issues related to reading instruction have long been a concern in the Charlotte-Mecklenburg Schools (CMS). But in the 1970s, the focus in CMS was on reading test scores in the junior high schools. As in most districts, standardized testing is used extensively in CMS and includes administration of the California Achievement Test and a state competency test. As an official document reveals,

> Systemwide testing in the Charlotte-Mecklenburg Schools over a period of years has consistently revealed a bimodal curve which peaked below the 6th grade and above the 10th grade reading levels. In an effort to meet a school board request, the Program Services Department began its search for a viable program which would help teachers meet the discrepant needs of students in heterogeneous classes. (Charlotte-Mecklenburg Schools, n.d., p.l.)

This concern for students with relatively low reading ability is very closely linked with issues related to desegregation and equity. While physical segregation was remedied through the establishment of a unitary school district in 1972, as in many systems, the effects of a segregated society continue to exist. As Schlechty (1979) reported, on the state mandated competency test, fully 43 percent of the black students failed to perform at the established minimum level as compared to 5 percent of the white student population. The Annual State Wide Testing Program, which uses the California Achievement Test as a primary means of assessment, has yielded similar results. On this test, the average score in reading for white students in the third grade was the fifty-ninth percentile, while the average score for black students was the nineteenth percentile. Language scores were the twenty-first percentile for black students and the fifty-ninth percentile for white students. (pp. 5-6)

One response of the district to such discrepancies is a tuition-free summer school for students who score below the 25th percentile on the California Achievement Test. Given the distribution of scores on these tests, the summer school program is primarily directed toward black students. Embedded in programs of this nature, however, is the possibility that attempts to address the equity issue, as reflected in test scores, may lead to social resegregation of black and white students.

The issue of equity is of particular concern at the junior high level. Busing patterns in the district tend to keep many suburban students in their neighborhood schools for grades K through 3 and to send them to inner-city schools in grades 4 through 6. Many suburban parents have responded to this pattern by leaving their children in public schools for the primary grades, placing them in nonpublic schools for grades 4 through 6, and returning them to public schools for junior and senior high grades. Since junior high then becomes the first time in several years that many students have attended racially mixed classes, many respondents felt that the potential for racial problems at the junior high schools was greater than at other grade levels.

Development of a Program: DART

In this context, the school board in 1974 requested that more attention be given to junior high reading. The first systematic response was called Directed Activities for Thinking and Reasoning, or DART. This program developed as a result of the work and interests of several individuals.

In the system's ESAA (Emergency School Aid Act) office was a resource teacher who had a great deal of interest in reading instruction at the secondary level. Her beliefs about effective strategies for teaching reading in content areas were very compatible with those of a junior high science teacher who, during the 1975-76 school year, designed and conducted a workshop for teachers in her school on content area reading strategies. Later in that school year, the ESAA resource teacher and the science teacher refined the workshop design and conducted several sessions at other junior high schools in the system. During the next school year when the resource teacher left the ESAA office to become resource teacher for secondary reading in the curriculum department, the science teacher was hired as ESAA's resource teacher.

In the spring of 1975, several ESAA staff members attended a national reading conference where they learned of a content area program that was operating in another state. A year later, in the spring of 1976, a consultant from that program was hired to assist the curriculum department in training one teacher from each of the junior highs in content area reading strategies. In the summer of that year, the consultant again came to CMS to conduct a workshop for this same group of teachers, now designated as "lead teachers," and an additional group of three teachers from each involved school.

Thus, after the summer of 1976, teams of teachers with training in content area reading strategies and headed by a lead teacher were in place in the junior high schools. The program was officially given the name DART and a steering committee was established in the central office to direct the program. Active members of the committee were the assistant superintendent for curriculum, the reading specialist, the reading resource teacher (formerly ESAA resource teacher), the ESAA resource teacher (formerly the science teacher), and the English specialist.

Most of the activity in DART took place in workshops conducted by central office specialists and by lead teachers in their schools. The workshops involved training in teaching strategies and the development of materials. DART operated for two school years, 1976–77 and 1977–78, but by the spring of 1978, the steering committee decided, according to official records, that "a more structured program with a more complete delivery system was needed."

Since DART was based partly on the work of Harold Herber of Syracuse University, the steering committee tried to enlist his help for a summer workshop aimed at developing the "more complete delivery system." Based on Herber's recommendation, the system hired a consultant to help design and direct the summer workshop. This workshop and the planning that took place the previous spring were the first efforts in a new content area reading program called TRICA, Teaching Reading in Content Areas. Because ESAA personnel had worked closely with DART, and because of the compatibility of the system's objectives related to desegregation, equity, and junior high reading, ESAA monies were sought and received for the development of the local TRICA program.

Development of a Program: TRICA

Spring and Summer, 1978. In order to develop the more complete delivery system, TRICA planners decided that the initial training should be directed toward teachers who would become part-time TRICA trainers in each junior high school. The plans called for principals to select two teachers, one in language arts or social studies and one in science or math, to attend training sessions during the summer of 1978. The following school year, these teachers would be given two class periods each day in which to function as TRICA trainers.

To familiarize the principals with the purposes of the program and with the selection criteria for potential trainers, the ESAA director and ESAA resource teacher met individually with the 21 junior high principals during the spring of 1978. At the same time, the resource teacher and the outside TRICA consultant began making plans for the summer workshop.

During the summer, the first trainer workshop was held, conducted jointly by the ESAA resource teacher and the TRICA consultant. Twenty teachers from 13 of the junior high schools attended. Many of these teachers had been involved in the earlier DART program, though for some, this workshop was their first experience with content area reading strategies. The content was based on a package of 15 lessons, corresponding videotapes of classrooms, a textbook on content area reading instruction, and a training manual (Herber & Nelson, 1977), or what soon came to constitute phase 1 of training in TRICA.

The concept of trainer is central to what Herber and Nelson called "the multiplier effect." This scheme assumes that practicing classroom teachers are the best trainers of other teachers. In the model, teachers who are proficient in the theory, instructional strategies, and the construction of classroom materials assist other teachers who are less experienced in the approach. At this stage in the development of TRICA in CMS, the designation "trainer" referred to a teacher who worked part time in that capacity and part time as a classroom teacher.

The 1978–79 School Year. The teachers in the summer workshop who continued to work with the program became trainers in their schools in the fall of 1978. Of the 20 teachers who participated in the workshop, 9 did not become trainers. Some left the system and others transferred to high school positions. In other cases, principals decided that they did not want the teachers who had been through the workshop to be out of the classroom for two periods each day. As a result, the first major obstacle to implementation was encountered: Only 8 buildings had trainers on site at the beginning of the 1978–79 school year, while 13 did not.

Originally, the ESAA resource teacher had planned to conduct phase 1 training for other teachers during that school year with the assistance of two trainers in each building. Instead, because of the dislocations previously described, she conducted three separate classes: a second trainer class; phase 1 training for teachers from buildings that had trainers at the beginning of the year; and, the first half of phase 1 for teachers who, by spring semester, had trainers on site as a result of the second trainer class.

The second trainer class met after school, once a week for 4 hours during the fall semester. Even though these teachers were in the process of learning about TRICA, they were designated as trainers at the beginning of the school year and were provided with two periods a day in which to work in that capacity. Their activities as trainers, however, were limited to practicing the strategies with their own classes and developing materials rather than assisting other teachers.

Concurrently with conducting the second trainer class, the resource teacher began phase 1 for teachers from buildings whose trainers had attended the summer workshop. Those trainers attended classes with participant teachers from their buildings throughout the entire school year. The work of these trainers included following up what was introduced during the training sessions led by the resource teacher. They observed participants' classes, had participants observe the trainers' classes, and assisted trainees in the development of materials.

Also during the spring semester, the resource teacher began phase 1 for a second cohort of teachers drawn from buildings whose trainers had completed phase 1 in the fall. These teachers had worked with only half of the 15 lessons of phase 1 by the end of the year.

Thus, during the first year, the project faced several setbacks in the training schedule. Nevertheless, by the end of the year trainers were in place in all of the junior high schools. Selected teachers, usually between four and eight, in buildings whose trainers had completed phase 1 in the fall of 1978, had completed half of phase 1 by the end of the school year. Another group of teachers had completed all of phase 1 by that time.

The 1979–80 School Year. During the next school year, the training format was revised again. The content remained basically unaltered, but the training of a new cohort of teachers took place on 9 released days and 14 after-school sessions. The resource teacher conducted the sessions on the released days, while the trainers ran the afternoon sessions in their individual buildings. When this cohort had completed the first half of phase 1, the cohort from the previous spring who had also finished the first half of phase 1, joined this group. The combined cohort completed phase 1 during the spring of 1980. Partly because of the time lag between the spring of 1979 and the spring of 1980, many of the teachers from the earlier group did not continue the training. Nevertheless, by the end of the year, approximately 200 teachers had completed phase 1 of TRICA training.

Also during this school year, TRICA faced another major obstacle to implementation. In the late fall of 1979, the superintendent decided to abolish the position of assistant superintendent for curriculum. When this happened, the program lost a key central office advocate. Interviews with TRICA trainers and the former assistant superintendent indicated that he was involved in most of the decisions that led to the system's first content area reading program, DART. Also, he was centrally involved in the decision to expand and revise that program which led directly to the introduction of TRICA. Thus, the elimination of that position meant that TRICA lost a vital source of central office support with direct links to key policymakers in the system.

A number of other events also occurred which led many to perceive that the program was in serious jeopardy. One issue concerned released time and payment of stipends. Some months after the dismantling of the department of curriculum, a controversy developed around the provision of released time and the payment of stipends to participating teachers. During this year of the program, ESAA funds were being used to provide substitutes on 9 released days and stipends for 14 after-school sessions. Several consequences dysfunctional to the implementation of TRICA emerged from these practices.

First, despite the fact that teachers were *not* paid stipends on the released days, some in the district believed that they were. Based on this misperception, these individuals began to express concern that such payments constituted "double dipping." Eventually, the protests were discussed at length by the Teacher Advisory Council which met with the superintendent on a monthly basis. While the discussion of double dipping was not limited to TRICA, that program was used extensively as the most visible example of the practice.

Second, some principals felt that the use of released time was working a hardship on them, their faculties, and students. They indicated that the logistics of recruiting appropriate substitutes on so many days presented major problems. Some area superintendents reiterated these views in interviews and in public meetings. In addition, some teachers in the program did not want to go to training sessions on released days. One TRICA teacher put it this way:

> I like the program but it takes so much time. I don't think there is any staff development activity important enough to take me away from my kids.

At about the same time that this issue was gaining attention, a related controversy emerged concerning teacher absenteeism generally. The consequence was that in January, 1980, the superintendent announced that no teacher would be released from class for any reason without his personal approval. This policy was almost immediately modified to permit the TRICA program to continue with the released days for the rest of that year. This exception, it seems, was allowed because the principals by that time had already made provision for substitutes. Because of the protests from some principals about the logistical problems of finding substitutes, earlier in the year the TRICA staff had modified the training format so that only half of the group of teachers from any one school would be released on any particular day. They also set up the training schedule for the entire year so that substitutes could be located and hired with sufficient lead time. The effect on the training program was that the number of workshop sessions necessary to maintain it as planned was doubled. As a result, the ESAA resource teacher voluntarily doubled her work load without any additional compensation.

Again, the issue of released time was not limited to TRICA. However, because of the size and visibility of the program in 21 schools, it seemed to be the center of the controversy. Indeed, some staff development specialists in the system reported that they felt the reason the superintendent had taken such a hard line on released days was because of the perceived excesses in the TRICA program. Since the released-time policy affected the activities of these specialists as well, the situation probably generated additional negative sentiment toward TRICA.

On the other hand, the evidence indicates that the majority of principals did not feel that the released-time controversy was especially important. For example, only five principals reported that released time for TRICA training had caused any problems, and two principals stated that it was only a minor problem, if the principal believed in the efficacy of the program.

Thus, this situation may be a classic example of the squeaky wheel syndrome. However, since the controversy focused on TRICA, regardless of misunderstandings concerning double dipping, the negative attention probably encouraged some to feel that TRICA was operating outside of the mainstream of the legitimate staff development system.

Another controversy that developed during the 1979–80 school year concerned a workshop the TRICA staff wanted to conduct for principals. The purpose of the workshop was to enhance principals' abilities to evaluate TRICA teachers. The workshop was to be held on a weekend and principals were to be paid a stipend for their participation.

Initially, according to some of the TRICA staff, this workshop had the approval of top-level officials. However, when the plan was reviewed by area superintendents, it was rejected on the basis that it might establish an undesirable precedent regarding additional payment for 12 month employees. Since the TRICA staff had no authority to require principals to attend the workshop and could not pay them without line approval, the workshop idea was abandoned. Some of the staff reported that they felt the rejection of this workshop was yet more evidence of the lack of support among area superintendents.

From the perspectives of some area superintendents however, the issue was substantially different. Some reported that they saw the workshop primarily as a way to spend money so that "it wouldn't have to be sent back to Washington" at the end of the year. Whatever the case, by the spring of 1980, there were many administrators who were convinced that TRICA was "more trouble than it's worth."

In light of these controversies and the criticisms of TRICA, the staff attempted to involve administrators more effectively in the program. During the spring of 1980, for example, several area superintendents attended workshops and meetings where TRICA was discussed and techniques were demonstrated. The effects of these meetings on attitudes toward the program are difficult to assess. Two area superintendents reported that the meetings enhanced their respect for TRICA. However, other top level administrators and some principals continued to indicate that they were only vaguely aware of both the program's objectives and training structure.

Thus, during the 1979–80 school year, TRICA was often at the center of controversy and had generated considerable negative sentiment among some influentials, including teacher leaders and administrators. While the TRICA staff tried to increase involvement of administrators in the program, they had mixed success.

Summer, 1980. Another major change took place in the structure of the program during the summer. Because of reduced ESAA funding, there was insufficient money from that source to maintain TRICA as it had operated the previous year. As a result, the program was drastically reduced. All of the building-level trainer positions as well as the position of ESAA resource teacher were abolished. In addition, the number of involved schools was reduced from 21 to 8, 1 school from each of the system's 8 attendance zones, or "feeder areas." Initially, a recommendation was included in the system's budget that, in place of the building trainers, 8 feeder-area trainer positions be funded. However, in the process of budget negotiation, this number was reduced to 4. The former ESAA resource teacher was subsequently assigned to 1 of the 4 area trainer positions.

Paradoxically, while these decisions were being made, the system also accepted an invitation from the original developers of the TRICA approach to become a part of a network of demonstration sites. The nature of the involvement, funded by the U.S. Office of Education, included joining with three other school systems and two universities, to form the Network of Secondary School Demonstrations Centers. The major goal was to "aid interested school districts in learning about an existing program designed to support the teaching of reading in content areas" ("Network of Secondary School Demonstration Centers" n.d.). Selection to participate in this network was perceived by some in the sysem as expert endorsement of the quality of the local TRICA effort. To be sure, this perception was more widespread among advocates of TRICA than among its critics; however, the endorsement seemed to have enhanced the status of the program in CMS, at least among some persons.

However, another controversy soon developed around participation in the network. According to the TRICA developers, one of the characteristics of the network school districts was that each district had

> demonstrated a sustained local commitment to the improvement of reading instruction in content areas. Each school district supported this work through the allocation of committed personnel, professional time and financial backing. ("Network of Secondary School Demonstration Centers" n.d.)

The TRICIA developers believed that such local support was basic to the network, the success of TRICA, and the commitment made to the Office of Education. Thus, the elimination of the building trainer positions, and especially the position of ESAA resource teacher, caused a great deal of tension between the developers and school system officials.

When the developers learned about the reduction in TRICA personnel, they attempted on several occasions to convince school officials to reconsider the decision to reduce the size and scope of the program. In one particularly heated discussion, the network director indicated that the school system might be dropped from the network in light of the reduced commitment. Discussion of the issue continued during the summer and early fall of 1980, but the school system remained a part of the network without any increase in local commitment at that time.

TRICA was also affected during this time by the creation of a new role, that of coordinating teacher (CT). The intent of this role was to have one person in each building in charge of the improvement of curriculum and instruction. The position was roughly analogous to that of a lead teacher with some overtones of an assistant principal for instruction. Since the position was similar in many ways to the TRICA trainer position, its creation was another source of potential conflict.

The CT role was established largely through eliminating a number of staff positions in the central office and in the schools. In fact, over half of these were reading specialist positions which had been operating at the building level but which had direct links to the central office. A substantial number of the individuals who became CTs were former reading specialists. Thus, they were potentially prone to view the role as involving many of the same substantive problems to which the TRICA trainers were oriented. In some schools, this situation created competition, tension, and conflict over resources and responsibilities (Whitford, 1981; Joslin, 1982).

The 1980–81 School Year.   The third year of the TRICA program thus began
with the staff somewhat unsure about the future of the program. While they
actively participated in the network, they also were struggling to become accus-
tomed to the totally new staffing and training structure. While the officially recognized leadership of the program had always resided with the ESAA director, TRICA
was only one program operating from that office. Thus, functionally, much of the
day-to-day responsibility for coordinating the program had been assumed by the
resource teacher with the assistance of several building trainers.

In contrast, during the third year, the full-time program staff only included four
area-level trainers, each of whom was responsible for two officially designated
TRICA sites. Whereas the building trainers had been assigned classroom teaching
responsibilities for part of the school day and were thus on site in the schools every
day, the new area trainers had no regular classroom responsibilities. While they
operated from schools part of the time, they were officially housed in the area
offices and thus were more directly under the supervision of the area superintendents than had been the case in the past.

In addition, training responsibilities changed dramatically. Whereas most of the
training of new participants in TRICA had been the primary responsibility of the
ESAA resource teacher for two years, in 1980–81 training was conducted independently by the four area trainers. Thus, adjustments and accommodations had to
be made within the TRICA staff for sharing leadership and for cooperative planning
of program activities.

To facilitate the new divisions of responsibility, the four trainers, the ESAA
director, and the ESAA evaluator held staff meetings on a weekly basis; thus, time
was allotted for coordination of activities across the eight target schools and for the
planning of network activities. Each area trainer conducted classes after school for
6 teachers in each of the schools; thus, a total of 48 teachers participated in TRICA
training in the project's third year. During the school day, the trainers were often
in the schools to observe and conduct demonstration lessons and to help develop
materials. In addition, trainers held bimonthly sessions, referred to as phase 2
training. These workshops, aimed at refinement of skills, were open to all teachers
who had completed phase 1. The trainers also worked with TRICA teachers in
schools other than the eight target schools on request and as time allowed.

Meanwhile, another development that is critical to understanding the context
in which TRICA was operating was the dissemination of a commercially produced
reading skills management system in the elementary schools. This program was in
direct response to a school board mandate to implement skills management systems
in both reading and math. The reading system eventually adopted by most elementary schools placed heavy emphasis on the identification and assessment of
individual student skill levels and encourage a highly individualized approach to
reading instruction. The reading specialist in the central office repeatedly asserted
in public meetings and in interviews that one of her primary goals was ensuring the
effective implementation of this system.

Prior to the 1980–81 school year, the reading management system did not directly affect TRICA, because it had been used in the early elementary grades and was only gradually being extended to the upper grades as children progressed through school. By the fall of 1980, the system was to be used in all sixth grades, and pressure was building to extend the program into the junior high schools.

Potential conflict between the advocates of TRICA and the supporters of the management system was discussed at several meetings and testified to in many interviews. During a reading workshop in the spring of 1980, for example, an attempt was made to reconcile the intentions of TRICA with those of the skills program. While workshop leaders talked extensively about compatible elements of the two approaches, there is no evidence to indicate that any solutions toward reconciliation were found.

Despite several major obstacles, the system's content area reading program was surviving, though its scope and size had been considerably reduced. Shrinking federal funds took a toll as did the controversies and the lack of willingness or ability of the system to commit local resources to the program. However, during the 1980-81 school year, another series of events suggested that TRICA was beginning to stabilize. By the end of the year, the program was closer to institutional acceptance and central office support than had ever been the case. Or, to paraphrase Mark Twain, reports of its impending death were grossly exaggerated.

Partly in response to the threat of terminating the system's participation in the network and partly because of the advocacy of several area superintendents, the status of TRICA began to change. By the spring semester, the administration had agreed to request local funding for four additional trainer positions for the 1981-82 school year.

A number of planned and fortuitous events occurred during that school year which accounts for TRICA'S enhanced prospects for survival. First, the TRICA staff and teachers, now more attuned to political and organizational realities, hosted another series of meetings for administrators. During the meetings, which were attended by a number of area superintendents, teachers talked at length about what they considered to be the numerous benefits of the program for teaching, learning, and social relations within classrooms. Subsequent interviews with the superintendents revealed that the testimonies of the teachers had considerable effect on swaying their opinions and in gaining their support for the program. As one area superintendent, who had not been very supportive of TRICA in the past, stated:

> Before those meetings, I just didn't know very much about the program. After hearing the enthusiasm, I knew there had to be something good there.

At least three other area superintendents indicated the same sentiment.

Second, as a result of network affiliation, five of the eight area superintendents attended meetings in an out-of-state school district that had also implemented TRICA. Based on observations of some of these meetings, it was clear that top-level officials in the other district were very committed to their TRICA program. Area superintendents subsequently indicated that this commitment positively affected their attitudes toward the CMS program. This support was most clearly demonstrated during a later network meeting held in CMS. During one session, the superintendent publicly endorsed the value of the TRICA program and said that he hoped the program "would continue to do good things for the school children of CMS."

Third, the director of the network visited the school system several times in 1980–81. During these visits, he talked with top-level administrators, principals, and teachers, and observed in classrooms. His presence in the school system caused top-level adminstrators to assess more actively the degree of their commitment than had been the case in the past. For example, in the fall of 1980, the network director continued to discuss the failure of the system to locally fund four area trainer positions. The result was that area superintendents indicated their willingness to request local funding of four additional trainer positions for the 1980–81 school year.

The fourth circumstance which probably enhanced the status of TRICA concerned the distribution of a preliminary research report on staff development in the system. This report indicated that the TRICA training model had significantly and systematically affected teachers' classroom behaviors, at least in some schools. The report was read and commented on by all of the top administrators in the system. Subsequently, the head of the research project was invited by the area superintendents to share his views on how the TRICA training model might be applied more generally to other staff development efforts in the system. The researcher, in an interview for this study, stated:

> The design of the TRICA training model contains many of the elements that are assumed to be most necessary to effective staff development programs, and in fact, there are few staff development programs operating that are logically preferable to the TRICA model. Furthermore, there is considerable evidence that the TRICA training program does foster in teachers a strong commitment to trying to do what the training model suggests. Unfortunately, this model, like many others, still must demonstrate that it can develop the technical capacities suggested by TRICA procedures in students.

Some in the system viewed the discussion of TRICA in the preliminary report and such comments as the one quoted as expert endorsement of the TRICA program itself. As one participant in TRICA stated to the researcher: "Whether you like it or not, you are being forced into the role of an advocate for TRICA." When the researcher responded that his intent was not to advocate TRICA but rather the training model, the respondent said:

> The trainers know that. That's why you are being invited to their workshops. They want to get you to endorse TRICA because they believe that you have the ear of the powers that be.

Summary
Thus, the school system's content area reading program evolved over a number of years through at least three phases. In the beginning, the program was strictly a

local invention, primarily involving short-term workshops. In the second phase, DART, the program had some impetus from outside consultants. During the third stage, TRICA, the program became more clearly identified with an externally developed innovation. Over a period of 3 years, the broad and relatively large-scale intentions of this program were modified by local social and political conditions as well as national funding patterns. However, as of May, 1981, it appeared that the institutional status of TRICA was substantially more secure that it was in May, 1980. It is significant that in a period of fiscal limitations, a budgetary request was made for local funding of four additional trainer positions. While there is little evidence that the program's future was assured, it did manage to survive a series of organizational crises that drastically reduced its size and scope.

GROUNDED INTERPRETATION

The first stages of analysis of data from field research typically involve what Glaser and Strauss (1967) call the constant comparative method. As data are collected, new questions emerge and leads develop and are followed, until no new information is forthcoming. During this process, categories begin to emerge into which the information can be sorted in an attempt to develop explanations for what occurred. A number of such categories emerged during analysis of the data here. No claim is made that these factors are relevant to all change efforts across organizations. Rather, they appear to be especially important to understanding the process of change that occurred related to one such effort in one school system. The categories addressed in this section are: (a) priority of the problem; (b) extent of awareness; (c) power and authority; (d) impermanence; (e) planning and results orientation; (f) organizational flux; (g) position of initators; and (h) decentralization.

Priority of the Problem
While controversy surrounding reading programs had a long history in the district, by 1975, policymakers decided that reading should be given more attention. Bimodal reading scores highly correlated with race, the accountability and basic education movements nationally, and a state-wide emphasis on reading instruction all served to sensitize local educators to the importance of addressing reading instruction. In addition, the emphasis on reading as a priority problem was affected by the belief of many that the failure to address reading problems, especially at the junior high level, was also a failure to respond effectively to desegregation and equity issues.

Prior to 1976, with the exception of ESAA reading labs, there was no formal reading program in the junior high schools. The reading labs were pullout programs; that is, students left regular classes to spend time practicing specific reading skills in small classes taught by a reading specialist. Because of the salience of race in the distribution of scores, most of the students who used the labs were black. Many in the system reported they feared that the reliance on such pullout programs would work against the goals of desegregation. Both DART and TRICA were programs that emphasized teaching reading skills in heterogeneously grouped classes. Thus, the fact that the content area reading program responded to a priority problem in the district accounts in part for its introduction.

Extent of Awareness
Despite the fact that many in the district recognized the problem that TRICA addressed, there was considerably less agreement that TRICA was the best way to address it. It appears that at least a part of the reason for this lack of agreement stems from the fact that few persons beyond the initiators had much knowledge about the program in the early stages of implementation.

As late as the fall of 1980, several area superintendents reported that they had little real understanding of TRICA, until they attended meetings during which teachers testified to the benefits of the program. Even many teachers who became trainers were unaware of the program until after they attended the training workshops. For example, one teacher who later became very committed to TRICA reported the following series of events:

> When I got to school one day, I found a note in my mailbox from the principal—he was fairly new to the school—asking me to attend workshops for TRICA training. I didn't even know how to pronounce it, but I said okay, because he was new and I wanted to be cooperative.

Power and Authority
The system's first content area reading program, DART, was developed by a loose confederation of central office staff who had personal interests in reading instruction. Some of these individuals did not occupy reading positions, and as a result, some felt they were violating the turf of others.

The fact that the assistant superintendent for curriculum officially designated this group as a steering committee did not appear to alter these perceptions. In reviewing the composition of the committee, which included the reading specialist, the English specialist, and the ESAA resource teacher, it is difficult to see an empirical basis for this perception; however, it was a perception that some held. As a result, those involved in initiating TRICA were seen by some as pushing special interests and operating outside rather than within the system's legitimate authority structure.

In addition, most of the steering committee members indicated that they were more sympathetic to content embedded approaches to reading instruction than to the skills approach. However, the elementary reading management system was a skills approach that had been mandated by the school board. Thus, the likelihood was enhanced that the solution selected by the steering committee would be less than congruent with the expectations of key policymakers.

Impermanence
Another factor that contributed to the perception that TRICA was something of a "stepchild" program was the source of funding. From the outset, funding for

TRICA was provided as part of a federal ESAA grant intended to assist the school system with second-generation desegregation problems. The fact that the continuation of these funds in CMS was consistently in doubt fostered the view that ESAA funded programs were temporary and likely to be short-lived. Thus, association with ESAA funds probably reinforced the perception that TRICA not only had been initated from outside the formal authority structure, but also it was likely to be a temporary phenomenon.

TRICA staff, however, believed that the program was unlikely to be effective, unless it were considered a long-range endeavor. For example, one initiator of the program reported:

> TRICA is such a complex program that you can't expect teachers to become fully proficient in the model in less than about three years. Also, it's unrealistic to expect improved test scores until the program has been in place for from three to five years.

Thus, different perceptions regarding the relative impermanence of TRICA may have contributed to some of the barriers to implementation.

Planning and Results Orientation

Top-level administrators in the system were not directly involved in exploring solutions to the problem of junior high reading. This instance of noninvolvement appears to be typical of the staff–line division of labor in most central offices. In CMS, the pattern of planning seemed to be as follows. First, a middle-level staff member would be assigned a problem. This person would then seek out other persons with special skill or interest in the problem and set up a committee to explore solutions. Sometimes these committees represented diverse views and competing interests, but more typically they were selected in a way that assured maximum harmony (Schlechty, et al., 1981). Thus the likelihood of consensus and immediate decisions was enhanced.

Several conditions in the school system reinforced the tendency of leaders of such problem-solving groups to ensure maximum harmony and quick decision-making. First, few public school systems, and CMS is no exception, have clearly identified resources and personnel assigned to long-range planning, especially in curriculum areas. The planning that is done usually results from role overload; that is, planning tasks are added on top of regularly assigned duties. Thus, program planning is often done by middle-level staff and persons from schools who have sufficient interest in the problem to volunteer extra time.

A second condition which enhanced the press to develop solutions quickly is what appeared to be an impatience with the demands of long-range planning. One respondent indicated that others in the system shared her view:

> I don't have time for long-range planning. We're always having to put out brush fires, so there is a lot of pressure to act. Besides, I like to act.

This pressure to act seemed especially intense when the problem had high public visibility or was perceived to be politically important. For example, many respondents indicated a belief that the thrust of the accountability movement, the emphasis on basic skills and related school board mandates, and the sate-wide testing program established the perception that immediate results were expected. Thus, in addition to the perception of TRICA's nonlegitimate initiation and related impermanence, another obstacle seemed to be the incompatibility of TRICA as a long-range program and the perceived expectations for immediate results from all programs that were attempting to improve instruction in basic skills.

A third condition in CMS contributed to the press for immediate action. The superintendent, from his own reports and those of others, was generally results oriented. As he stated,

> Once we know what the problem is, I can't understand why it can't be solved yesterday. I know that this isn't always possible and I'm too impatient, but it seems to me folks in education waste too much time in meetings and retreats. I'm getting tired of retreats. I want to advance!

A wall-hanging in his office had the following inscription:

> There is nothing more difficult to take in hand, or more perilous or more uncertain in its success, than to take the lead in the introduction of a new order of things.
> Niccolo Machiavelli

In pointing to the quote, the superintendent commented:

> When I saw that, I knew that my impatience with the slowness of change had been around for a long time.

The extent to which these conditions affected the implementation of TRICA as a solution to junior high reading problems is not altogether clear. Potential barriers were certainly "in the wings" even in the early stages. By the time TRICA was introduced through ESAA funding, the program had already become identified with individuals who, in the perceptions of some, were operating outside the legitimate authority structure which controlled the system's reading programs. In addition, some of the reading specialists had doubts about the compatibility of TRICA and the school board's reading skills management policy.

Thus, while TRICA responded to a high priority of the school system, the program staff had difficulty in adequately assessing the political context in which the program would have to operate. On the one hand, TRICA was probably more acceptable to junior high teachers than the skills management approach, since those teachers typically saw themselves as content specialists rather than as reading teachers. In addition, the emphasis TRICA placed on group work and interaction among students of diverse backgrounds and skills made the program generally consistent with the intentions of the system to address second generation desegregation effects.

On the other hand, the political environment into which TRICA was initiated argued strongly for a program that promised to produce immediate, measureable results. Since both the developers of TRICA and the local staff did not make such claims for this program, the decision to implement it did involve a number of political risks. However, there is little evidence to indicate that the initiators developed systematic strategies to deal effectively with these problems. Rather, what seems to have happened is that they introduced TRICA largely on the assumption that the strong backing of the assistant superintendent for curriculum and the availability of ESAA funding would ensure the continuation of the program for a time sufficient to demonstrate its long-term benefits.

This assumption caused numerous problems for the program. One of the factors that accounts for some of the difficulties was that initiators, in the early stages, attended more successfully to technical concerns involved in the delivery of training to teachers than to issues related to the organizational context in which the program was to be implemented. Thus, two questions emerged: What were the characteristics of the organizational context, and how did these conditions affect the implementation of TRICA? Among the more important of these characteristics are: (a) organizational flux; (b) position of initators; and (c) decentralization.

Organizational Flux
During the time that TRICA was being introduced, several major changes occured in the administrative structure of the school system. These were (a) the elimination of the office of assistant superintendent for curriculum; (b) the hiring of a new reading specialist; (c) the development of the role of coordinating teacher; and (d) the emergence of a staff development system.

The loss of the assistant superintendent meant TRICA lost a key central office advocate. Another effect was that the TRICA staff had to completely reorder the communication patterns they had developed with those in higher-level positions. When the curriculum department was abolished, the duties of the former assistant superintendent were absorbed by an associate superintendent. In the authority hierarchy, the associate superintendent had been two levels removed from the initiators of TRICA, and in some cases, even three or four levels. Where communication had previously gone through the assistant superintendent, now the TRICA staff had to communicate directly with the associate superintendent.

Those most centrally involved in TRICA encountered difficulties in establishing the same type of interaction they had enjoyed with the assistant superintendent. Several factors account for this difficulty. First, the duties of the associate superintendent included responsibilities in areas other than instructional programs; thus less time was available to discuss TRICA. Second, the TRICA staff had not developed sustained interaction with the associate superintendent, because the link had previously been through the assistant superintendent. Third, and most significantly, many of those central to the development of TRICA had a history of working with the assistant superintendent on problems related to junior high reading. Those experiences had developed patterns of interaction and unstated agreements about the operation of TRICA. As is typical in informal groups, such tacit understandings were infrequently communicated through formal channels. Thus, when the TRICA staff had to communicate directly with the associate superintendent, new modes of response were necessary.

The second instance of organizational flux was the hiring of a new reading specialist during the 1978-79 school year. Since this person came from outside the system, she had not been involved in the introduction of TRICA. In addition, she was employed with the specific expectation that one of her priorities would be the reading skills management system. Her advocacy of the skills program highlighted the debate about appropriate approaches to reading instruction. Once again, a turf issue was barely *sub rosa*. Many felt that the reading specialist legitimately should have more influence on junior high reading or certainly more legitimate control than the federally funded ESAA office.

A third change was the creation of the role of coordinating teacher (CT), a position similar to that of TRICA trainer. System support for the CT position was strong. Ninety-four CT positions were filled during this time, while the number of TRICA trainers was drastically reduced. Also, funding for the trainers came exclusively from temporary, external sources. If this role were to become institutionalized, the initiators needed to consider ways of procuring local support once the external funds were expended. There is little evidence that this issue was addressed. Thus, local funding of the role of CT created a potential barrier to the institutionalization of the role of TRICA trainer at the building level.

A fourth change in the organizational context significant to the operation of TRICA was that at the same time that it was being installed, an elaborate system to encourage and manage staff development generally was emerging under the direction of the assistant superintendent for human resources. TRICA operated totally outside this emerging system, though in many ways, the activities sponsored through TRICA were similar to those officially assigned to the department of human resources. Once again, a condition was created that fostered the perception that TRICA was separate and apart from the central commitments of the school system.

Thus, from the outset, the TRICA staff faced numerous obstacles emanating from larger organizational changes within the school system. While some of the changes were recognizable, emerging phenomena, others came about in a short period of time, making it difficult for the TRICA staff to coordinate and manage the intended training program.

Decentralization and Position of Initiators

Most of the described organizational changes were part of another, more significant change in the structure of the school system. At the beginning of the research project, interviews with administrators revealed much discussion about "decentralization." However, there also seemed to be vague, ambiguous, and in some cases, contradictory understandings of what decentralization meant and what it implied in operation.

On the one hand, some evidence indicated increasing centralization in the district. For example, the mandates concerning reading and math skill management systems were directed from the central office and affected all elementary schools.

At the same time, however, when the feeder areas were established as part of the system's desegregation plan, the official rationale for the concept was that the school system could better serve the needs of particular areas of the district, if it were broken up into smaller administrative units.

Despite these ambiguities, several alterations in administrative and staffing patterns encouraged decentralization *and* the redistribution of authority away from the central office to the feeder areas and school buildings. The establishment of the role of coordinating teacher at the area and school levels and the abolition of the curriculum department were two such moves. A third change concerned staff–line relations. Increasingly, it became policy in the district that central office staff were not to initiate programs at the building level; rather, they were to respond to building- and area-level requests. In support of this policy, staff members were instructed to communicate with building personnel only with approval of their central office superior who would then contact the appropriate area superintendent. The area superintendent would, in turn, communicate with principals and teachers. While many times this policy was followed, at other times it was ignored or bypassed. In operation, staff and line members who had developed informal networks continued to communicate without following official channels. Gradually, these unofficial communication networks became more and more openly acknowledged to the point that, at least in some cases, they were organizationally approved. However, confusion continued to exist surrounding which forms of communication were approved and which were not and under what circumstances. Furthermore, there seemed to be inconsistent and uneven approval across feeder areas and building units.

For the TRICA staff, operating from the central office without the assistant superintendent for curriculum, these new communications arrangements with the areas and buildings created additional barriers to implementation. One of the initiators described the situation this way:

> Organizationally, the program is very complex. It cuts across many areas: reading, content areas, staff development. You have to understand that in this school system, the staff is consultative to the line. All the authority is in the line. We can't initiate things; we have to respond to others. We have money for stipends, but it has to be spent through the line. This doesn't make it impossible for us to work, but these are some problems that have to be overcome. We're learning a lot along the way about how to cope with these things. We get our fingers burned a lot trying to get through the line to the teachers. What we try in one building works great, but in other buildings it doesn't work that way, and we have to learn by trial and error how it *actually* works. Nobody knows how they are supposed to operate. . . . We know that some administrators are supportive but don't know how to express it. They also have to get through the line back to us. It's probably just as difficult to go that way as it is for us to get to them. And the principals have so many demands on their time.

Thus, the organizational position of the TRICA initiators as central office staff enhanced the problems of identifying and overcoming barriers to implementation of the program. For example, initial plans called for the cooperation of principals in the selection of potential trainers and in releasing those teachers from two classes a day. The success of such a strategy seemed to require that at least one of two conditions obtain: (a) that the principals were knowledgeable about and committed to the purpose of the program; or (b) that those in charge of the program had sufficient authority to get principals to reallocate building level resources, including the reassignment of teachers.

Neither of these conditions existed by the time implementation of the program began. Principals were not aware of the program until after the decision had been made to hold the summer workshop designed to put two trainers in each junior high school. In addition, it seems that the TRICA staff acted on assumptions about their authority which were becoming increasingly dubious due to alterations in the authority structure of the school system. Decentralization and new expectations for staff-line relations eroded the power of central office staff to the point that they could no longer rely on their positions to gain compliance from principals.

CONCLUSIONS AND IMPLICATIONS

Using the evidence in this case study, a number of observations about the dynamics of the change process can be made. While these observations are presented as conclusions, they should not be viewed as definitive statements about how change does or does not occur in schools. Rather, they are preliminary, suggestive hunches based on the detailed analysis of one specific effort in one school system.

The first set of observations about the implementation of TRICA concerns the fact that this change effort was not initiated from the "top down" or the "bottom up," but rather came into the organization from the "side." That is, the initiators of the project occupied central office staff positions. As staff, they did not have the authority to direct the work of either low-level or high-level participants in the organization. Without the support of high-level officials, the existing staff-line arrangements made it exceedingly difficult to gain compliance from lower-level participants.

These observations are not new. However, what is somewhat overlooked in the research on change in schools is that those who are most knowledgeable about innovations frequently are not in positions of line authority. Rather, they tend to occupy staff positions as curriculum coordinators, subject matter specialists, or specialists in staff development. These positions probably encourage them to be more attentive to the literature on curriculum and instruction than is the case for line administrators whose assigned tasks are often less directly related to issues of curriculum. Thus, it appears that those who have, or are perceived to have, expert authority in a field where curriculum innovations are attempted are less likely to have legal authority which is assigned to persons in line positions.

These conditions suggest the plausible hypothesis that one of the reasons so many curriculum innovations fail is that those who are most likely to introduce an innovation are also least likely to occupy positions of legal authority in the system.

It is perhaps for this reason that some research (e.g., Goodlad, 1970; Berman & McLaughlin, 1977) suggests that the building unit and the principal are so critical in successful change efforts. In the building, the principal represents the top of the line. When principals initiate change, they are then in a position to coordinate both the legal authority and the expert authority needed to successfully implement an innovation. Beyond the building level, however, staff and line roles are more likely to be differentiated, and those with direct responsibility over curriculum and instruction are less likely than are others to have line authority.

A second set of related observations concerns the distribution of power and authority. The way the innovation was embedded in the power and authority structure of the school system significantly affected the operation of the program. The failure of the program to become integrated into the line structure caused numerous problems, especially in the area of coordination. While these problems were present from the earliest stages of the project, they became more critical as TRICA moved toward full implementation. When project activity took on an identity as a program and began to interact on that basis with other school system subunits, it was perceived by some as a nonlegitimate threat to the decision-making autonomy of those subunits.

These observations suggest the conclusion that change is affected by the degree to which planners and initiators are integrated into the line authority structure of the organization. Not only does degree of integration seem to affect the daily operation of the change effort itself, the same condition seems to affect the likelihood that an innovation will eventually be institutionalized.

In addition, it seems that planning for the *introduction* of an innovation is just as important as planning associated with implementation itself. In this case at least, many of the difficulties experienced in later stages appear to be directly attributable to the fact that planners and initiators were not centrally located in the authority structure, and no plans were developed to gain involvement of line officials in the early stages.

A final conclusion suggested by this study is that, in part at least, the functioning and effects of a change effort can only be understood if one considers the perceptions held regarding the likelihood that support for the innovation will continue in the long run. In this case, with the exception of role overload on the ESAA resource teacher, it seems that abundant resources were available in the short run. Indeed, if anything, the perception of an overabundance of resources caused the project some difficulties. However, there was an equally compelling perception that these resources were temporary and, as is often the case with innovations, many felt "this too shall pass."

Thus, it seems, schools are confronted with a perplexing problem. Experimentalism suggests impermanence, yet for a program to be effective, it needs support sufficient to ensure that those who commit additional energy to it can anticipate long-term as well as short-term rewards. Therefore, one of the conditions that affects change efforts is the degree to which participants perceive that support for an innovation will continue even when nonlocal resources are expended.

Thus, three hypotheses about change efforts are suggested by the study:

1. The position occupied by planners and initiators vis-a-vis the power and authority structure of the school system directly affect the way an implementation effort is carried out, the kinds of barriers that emerge, and the kinds of action that can be taken to overcome these barriers. The position occupied also affects the likelihood that the innovation will be successfully implemented.
2. The more successful a change effort is, the more likely it is that expert authority (e.g., knowledge about a new curriculum) and legal authority (e.g., line authority) are coordinated in a way that supports the intentions of the innovation. Conversely, when expert authority and legal authority are, or are perceived to be, operating independently, the intentions of the innovation are likely to be compromised, and additional barriers to implementation are likely to arise.
3. The impermanence or perceived impermanence of resources to support the change affects the degree to which participants maintain commitment to the innovation; this condition obtains regardless of the adequacy of the resources in the short run.

Implications for Research and Practice

The study suggests that understanding the process of change is dependent on understanding factors in addition to those logically related to the design of training programs, the provision of rewards, and efforts at overcoming resistance to change. In the end, curriculum change, if it is to be fundamental, may require the reallocation of authority as well as the reorientation of individual behaviors and reassignment of resources. Thus, students of change must attend to issues of the distribution of power and authority as well as to issues related to instructional design, the assessment of outcomes, and measurement of consumer satisfaction.

A second implication is that any evaluation of a program that ignores the organizational context in which the change effort occurs is likely to miss the mark. It would be easy, in the case presented here, to attribute the successes and failures of this change effort to the behavior, competence, and personality of individual actors. However, such factors also operated within a context of events that were shaped by the structure of relationships in the school system, the expectations, norms, and traditions of that system, and emerging organizational realities in which the project was embedded.

Practitioners as well as researchers need to carefully consider the organizational and political realities of the schools in which they work. The focus on the logic of instruction and curriculum design tends to distract attention from the "sociologic" of school systems and the interests that are embedded therein (Schlechty & Whitford, 1983). It seems that what is logical from the perspective of a committed initiator frequently appears to be inappropriate from the perspectives of other actors. In school systems as in all organizations, there are many realities and many interests, all of which need to be considered throughout the implementation process. In the broadest sense, the purpose of an innovation is to create a new reality which can be shared by many who prior to the innovation operated in their own distinctive phenomenological worlds. Thus, attention to the concept of multiperspectival realities (Douglas, 1976) is not only essential for researchers, it seems to be a requirement for effective practice as well.

Another implication for practice is that it is important not only to plan well for the implementation of a project but also to consider systematically how an innovation might be introduced in the first place. Decisions about who must be involved in exploring problems and solutions cannot be made any less consciously than those concerning plans for implementing any particular solution. The following suggestions based on the case of TRICA are offered for consideration.

1. Determine the specific nature of the problem and who in the system recognizes or "owns" it.
2. Determine who, in addition to those who presently own the problem, must come to understand that the problem exists.
3. Determine what conditions must be satisfied for those who own the problem to feel that it has been resolved.
4. Develop strategies for making relevant persons aware of the nature of the problem and solicit their views and concerns.
5. Determine which line administrators (or other sources of legal authority) need to be involved to ensure the successful implementation of whatever solution is selected or developed and make plans to involve these persons in problem exploration and early planning stages.
6. Develop an information network to ensure that the planning team will have access to relevant data regarding emerging and potentially competing changes occurring elsewhere in the school system so that these might be taken into account in the early stages.
7. Systematically review information about alternative solutions and evaluate them in terms of conditions suggested in point 3.
8. Develop a systematic and concise method of keeping relevant line administrators (or others with legal authority) updated and informed regarding the progress made in the early stages.

Admittedly, such planning calls for considerable investment "on the front end" of a change effort. However, resources not expended in the early stages are likely to be necessary throughout the project as initiators play "catch-up ball" in efforts to overcome emerging barriers created in part by the lack of effective planning in the first place.

In addition, the work suggested may be viewed by many as nonproductive, since concrete results are rarely forthcoming in the short run. Given fiscal retrenchment, the pressures for accountability, and role overload that planning frequently creates, such effort is contradictory to the traditions and expectations of many school systems. At the same time, overcoming constraints on change involves more than creating a willingness in teachers to engage in new behaviors, a willingness in principals to reward new behaviors, or the addition of tasks to those which already heavily burden the most committed and enthusiastic individuals. Change requires a recognition and appreciation of the complexity of life in classrooms, schools and school systems. Overcoming constraints on change likely involves a restructuring of expectations, rewards and access to policy development. Without such attention, Sarason's view will probably continue to hold: "The more things change, the more they stay the same."

REFERENCES

Berman, P., & McLaughlin, M. (1977). *Federal programs supporting educational change: Vol. 7 Factors affecting implementation and continuation.* Santa Monica, CA: Rand.

Charlotte-Mecklenburg Schools. (no date). TRICA: Historical perspective.

Douglas, J.D. (1976). *Investigative social research.* Beverly Hills, CA: Sage Publications.

Firestone, W., & Herriott, R. (1981). Images of organization and the promotion of educational change. In R.G. Corwin (Ed.), *Research in sociology of education and socialization: Research on educational organizations.* Greenwich, CT: Jai Press.

Garrou, T.M. (1980). *Implementing the "new social studies" curriculum: A case study.* Unpublished doctoral dissertation, University of North Carolina at Chapel Hill.

Glaser, B.G. & Strauss, A.L. (1967). *The discovery of grounded theory: Strategies for qualitative research.* Chicago: Aldine.

Goodlad, J.I., (1970). *The dynamics of educational change.* New York: McGraw-Hill.

Herber, H.L., & Nelson, J. (1977). *Reading across the curriculum: Staff development programs.* Homer, NY: TRICA Consultants.

Joslin, A.W. (1982) *The effects of school context on the implementation of an innovation: A case study.* Unpublished doctoral dissertation, University of North Carolina at Chapel Hill.

"Network of Secondary School Demonstration Centers." (no date). Homer, NY: TRICA Consultants, Inc.

Sarason, S.B. (1971). *The culture of the school and the problem of change.* Boston: Allyn & Bacon.

Schlechty, P.C. (1976). *Teaching and social behavior: Toward an organizational theory of instruction.* Boston: Allyn & Bacon.

Schlechty, P.C. (1979). *A social theory based framework for evaluating staff development programs.* Proposal to the National Institute of Education, University of North Carolina at Chapel Hill.

Schlechty, P.C., & Whitford, B.L. (1983). The organizational context of school systems and the functions of staff development. In G.A. Griffin (Ed.) *Staff development: Eighty-second yearbook of the National Society for the Study of Education (part II).* Chicago: The University of Chicago Press.

Schlechty, P.C., Crowell, D., Whitford, B.L., Joslin, A.W., Vance, V.S., Noblit, G.W., & Burke, W.I. (1981). *The organization and management of staff development in a large city school system: A case study* (Preliminary Report). Chapel Hill, NC: The University of North Carolina at Chapel Hill.

Whitford, B.L. (1981). *Curriculum change and the effects of organizational context: A case study.* Unpublished doctoral dissertation, University of North Carolina at Chapel Hill.

6

A Study of the Implementation of Regulatory Policy In The Urban Elementary School*

PATRICIA A. BRIESCHKE

Chicago Public Schools

There is a tradition of scholarly interest in public policy, particularly in the process of policy adoption and the problems of administrative and judicial behavior. It is common knowledge in bureaucracies that good intentions, high expectations, and a defensible rationale for a new policy may not necessarily lead to its implementation. If the desired change is not implemented in day-to-day routines the policy may produce no measurable effects.

This chapter presents an analytical framework for the study of policy implementation in a large, urban school system which conceptually links interactive processes across three levels of analysis: the individual level of the local worker; the intermediate level of internal organizational structure; and the macro level of the organization as a whole. A central thesis in this work is that an urban school system is most usefully conceptualized as a street-level bureaucracy (Lipsky, 1976) and that one of the primary processes of implementation occurs at the local level of the individual worker. While implementation involves the entire social system of the organization and its environments, it is believed that initial focus on the individual implementer at the local level of service delivery will lead to an investigation of the variables within the analytical levels which influence implementation.

The research reported here explored the fit between this analytical framework and data concerning the implementation processes of a Uniform Discipline Code (UDC) in the elementary schools of the Chicago Public Schools. The study presents a classic case of nonimplementation. It suggests that this successful resistance to a policy may be an act of organizational effectiveness, and that resistance may be related to unclear, multiple, or changing goals on the part of policymakers. Further, the research reported here suggests that the policy implementation process is an inherently tentative process, and that this tentativeness also is linked to policy intention.

*Funded by a Fellowship from the American Association of University Women.

119

LEVELS OF ANALYSIS

Most analytical approaches to social change are not readily adaptable to the requirements of implementation research. Implementation involves a set of processes
spanning at least three levels of analysis. The range of possible influences on these
complex processes includes many variables. While the levels may appear to be
separate structural entities, insofar as they are the pathway to implementation,
they are in fact linked together in mutually contingent interrelationships.

Local Context: The Individual

The first level of analysis involves an examination of process at the micro level
of the individual workers who must incorporate new behaviors into established
routines at the local site. Scheirer (1981) analyzes individual-level variables in
terms of their contribution to role changes required for the implementation of
new programs and includes from the psychological literature three classes of variables: skills, incentives, and cognitive supports. The task is to identify those variables which are related to individual variation in implementation.

Clearly, some form of behavior of individual implementers must be included in
the analysis. The behavior necessary to carry out the new directives, or innovation,
is a logical choice. This may include technical requirements such as in the introduction of a new drug in a medical setting or computers in a classroom. The new
behavior must be integrated into an extant system of behavior—work routines.
A new policy or program may include highly explicit procedures, loosely specified
guidelines, or no behavioral specifications whatsoever. There may be a comfortable
"fit" between the new changes and the old routines. Or individual local workers
may be required to adjust previous routines to incorporate the new ways of doing
things. Integration of the two may require much discretion, by individuals and in
groups. Discretion, in turn, is influenced by workers' beliefs, attitudes, needs, and
perceived choices regarding the new directives. Thus, not only the behavior necessary to carry out the new directives but also the standard operating routines and
the mediating influence of cognitive variables must be included in an analysis of
implementation processes at the level of individual workers. In large, bureaucratic,
client-centered organizations, where routines are necessary to regulate the workload
(Weatherly & Lipsky, 1977), street-level variables—discretionary behavior, ways of
seeing, and work routines—become important components of analysis.

Intermediate Context: The Organizational Subunits

A second level of analysis in the implementation process consists of the internal
structures and processes of the subunits of the organization. At this intermediate
level of implementation, linkages between units become important. Subdivisions
of organizations differ among types of organizations, such as the central bureau,
departments, and local offices of the welfare system, or the central and district
offices and individual schools of the educational system. Subdivisions also include
classrooms within schools. At this level, communication is an important component

—both horizontal and vertical. Information must flow if an organization is to implement a policy or program. How it flows, from whom it flows, and under what conditions it flows may alter implementation processes. Communication between superiors and subordinates, particularly if the former are a source of expertise on an innovative policy or program, is associated with receptivity to implementation in both school systems (Baldridge & Burnham, 1975) and mental hospitals (Fairweather, Sanders, & Tornatzky, 1974). Communication requires the participation of lower-level workers, if not in actual decision-making then at least in the provision of feedback. Weikert and Banet (1976) emphasized the importance of communication as a "bridge" to the source of planned change. In some types of organizations, this connection may be exceedingly tenuous, particularly when directives are passed along through several bureaucratic channels.

The problem of communication processes is compounded by the expectations of supervisors, a second component in this intermediate level of analysis. The importance of supervisors and administrators in the implementation process is well documented (Smith & Keith, 1971; Herriott & Gross, 1979; Gersten & Carnine, 1980). Boundary-spanning and middle-management roles may be important to teach lower-level workers about a new policy, reorienting them, assisting in the development of new routines to incorporate new behaviors, encouraging and securing commitment, and administering sanctions. Supervisors also may encourage or permit negative response to a new policy or innovation. They may make judgments about its worth and influence their staff accordingly. Further, if significant changes in the behavior or techniques of implementers is required, administrators may have to provide technical assistance or instruction, possibly changing the nature of their own supervisory roles.

Decision processes at all levels influence the implementation of policy. However, in large bureaucratic school systems in which policy is implemented by the local teacher, decisions made in the central and district offices may be particularly important to implementation outcomes. Decisions made at the macro level are made in interaction with or in response to the environment and often as a result of political bargaining (Allison, 1971; Williams & Elmore, 1976; Bardach, 1977). These decisions in turn create a situation in which the central office of the organization must respond with further decisions which ideally will lead to desired implementation outcomes at the local level. Evidence that decentralization of decision-making (Hage & Aiken, 1970) or participation of local implementers (Fairweather et al., 1974; Byer & Trice, 1977) facilitates policy implementation is still controversial. Local implementers may or may not be aware or involved in decisions affecting them.

Macro Context: The Organization and its Environment

The macro level of analysis treats the organization as an entity or unit of analysis within an environment of social, political, and cultural influences. Federal, state, and local governments, other organizations, public opinion, the media, and individuals all are components which influence implementation at the macro level.

Often it is at this level that programs and policies are designed and resources are sought (Scheirer, 1981).

Control processes are a component of the macro level of analysis. These processes include not only the mechanisms which the organization uses to control itself and its members, but also the methods used by the environment to control the organization: the political arena, public opinion, legal regulations, etc. At this level, pressure from various groups may radically influence the course of implementation. For example, the Rand study on educational change documented the effects of parental opposition on implementation (Berman & Pauly, 1975). Smith and Keith (1971) reported similar implementation difficulties due to the environmental influence of parental groups.

As a unit of analysis, the organization as a whole in relationship to its environments presents a tangled web of influences which may affect the implementation process to varying degrees. My purpose here is to present the argument that an analysis of implementation must include an overview of the source of the policy initiative and control processes in relation to the larger environment. These components are more than the backdrop for the internal structure, procedures, and routines of the organization.

Table 1 presents an outline of the conceptual framework used in this study in which the three levels of analysis include a set of possible influences on implementation processes in mutually contingent relationships. While some components may prove to be more important than others in influencing the course of implementation, one component by itself, out of context, is not expected to explain variation in implementation outcomes. The framework identifies specific areas subject to analysis during the process of implementation. It is not expected that all components are equal, but that all levels of analysis are necessary.

Table 1. Levels of Analysis for the Study of Policy Implementation in an Educational System

Implementation Levels	Locations	Actors
I. Local Context	School	Teachers
A. Discretionary behavior	Classroom	Principals
B. Ways of seeing	Community	Parents
C. Work routines		Students
II. Intermediate Context	Central office	Board of Education
A. Communication processes	District office	members
B. Expectation structure		Task Force members
C. Decision processes		OEEO members
		District superintendents
III. Macro Context	Justice Department	Judge Shadur
A. Control processes	Community	Leaders of civic groups
B. Environmental processes	organizations	Media workers

In summary, the framework for the study spans three analytical levels. Rather than serve as a single testable model, the framework was intended to be used as a guide or overview of factors to be analyzed when examining applied problems of implementation. Since implementation is contingent upon many organizational and individual factors, it is not predictable in advance. Stages may not necessarily follow one another as expected. This 3-tiered framework portrays implementation as a dynamic system. The analysis involves timetables and deadlines, both self-imposed and those dictated by legislatures and courts. The mutual contingency of the levels means that they do not stand alone; instead, components overlap, and subprocesses influence one another.

The intent of the research was to collect data for the purpose of examining the total set of analytical components surrounding implementation of policy in elementary schools, to analyze emergent patterns of beliefs, ideas, and actions concerning the policy in the school system and relate these patterns to the process of implementation and to establish linkages between and among variables within the analytical framework which already have been empirically supported to varying degrees in the literature.

In this study, the framework was used to guide analysis of implementation of a Uniform Discipline Code (UDC) in the Chicago public schools. The initial focus was on the individual classroom teacher in order to uncover how the discipline policy was implemented at the local level.

THE POLICY

Historically, discipline procedures in the Chicago public schools have been arbitrary, inequitable, and varied according to the racial background of students (see Green, 1981; Hawkins & Rosen, 1981). No uniform standards of discipline have been applied system-wide. Instead, procedures have been left to the discretion of individual principals and teachers at the school level. One of the more severe but common forms of punishment in the Chicago schools—and in many school systems throughout the United States—has been the suspension of students. Suspensions have at least two observable effects: (a) they interrupt the educational process, removing students from the classroom for several days; and (b) they cost the system money from lost days in attendance. Also, there is evidence of disproportionate suspensions of students by race.

There are variations between schools in the number of students suspended in the Chicago system. For example, 1979–80 data show that one school with 100% black student enrollment suspended less than 1% of its students, while another with identical student composition suspended 17.7%. Still another with similar characteristics suspended 34.6% of its students. While a substantial number of student suspensions are thought to be unrelated to the behavior involved, data suggest that suspensions do not covary with race. The Board of Education reasoned that a new policy which ensured the application of fairness, impartiality, and uniformity regarding expected behavior and consequences of infractions could change the course of inequitable disciplinary events.

In April, 1980, the U.S. Department of Justice ruled that a sufficient case existed to warrant filing suit against the school system for violation of the Civil Rights Act of 1964. Negotiations between the Board of Education and the Justice Department resulted in a Consent Decree, a commitment to develop and implement a "system-wide plan to remedy the present effects of past segregation" (p. 3). The second part of the plan, *Educational Components,* consisted of eight components which required attention, one of which was the climate of behavior in the schools. The recommendation on student discipline consisted of one sentence: "The plan shall include provisions to ensure that discipline is administered in a nondiscriminatory manner" (*Consent Decree,* 1980, p. 9).

The Uniform Discipline Code (UDC) went into effect system-wide in September, 1981. (It is important to note that the source of the policy—a federal mandate—was not communicated to the local level.) From public documents (e.g., minutes of the task force which drafted the UDC) and from interviews with central office administrators, it was determined that the multipurpose policy would be used as: an instrument of compliance with a federal mandate; an administrative handle for the central office of the Board of Education to gain control of and establish uniformity of behavior in matters of discipline; a way to encourage a smooth transition and stability of expectations for students in the large-scale movement from school to school generated by the Consent Decree's system-wide student reassignment policies; a way to regain the revenue lost from lost days in attendance due to suspensions; and a method to improve learning environments throughout the system through the reduction of discipline problems.

The Code was the result of an intensive summer of research, writing, and planning, in which a task force devised a rationale for student discipline, outlined a set of recommendations for developing and managing the new policy, and developed strategies for disciplinary practices and procedures. Also included were recommendations for the inservice education of administrators, faculty, and students, the content of which was partially repeated and developed in the implementation plan.

Central office staff considered the new discipline policy a showcase document which both looked good on paper and was expected to alter the climate of the schools. In the fall of 1981, the Justice Department had not yet formally approved the recommendations within the *Student Desegregation Plan for the Chicago Public Schools,* but it instructed the Board to proceed with implementation of the discipline policy and other new policies as if the plan had been approved. The Office of Equal Educational Opportunity approved the Code. Members of the Board of Education were satisfied with the policy. However, during the 1981–82 and 1982–83 schools years, all efforts failed to implement the discipline policy.

In order to understand the reasons why the discipline policy met resistance at the local level and how implementation processes unfolded throughout the study, it is necessary to understand the organization of the Chicago public schools.

THE SETTING

The Chicago public schools is a large, urban system divided into 20 districts with approximately 500 schools (including numerous special categories of elementary schools such as magnet schools, academic centers, classical schools, and community academies), 72 high schools (with one apprentice school, one industrial skills center, and one occupational training center), and 442, 889 students. Racial and ethnic enrollment from 1981 figures include:

Black	269,019	(60.7%)
Hispanic	86,775	(19.6%)
White	76,112	(17.2%)
Asian/Pacific Islander	10,268	(2.3%)
Indian/Alaskan	735	(0.2%)

The school system does not mirror the racial-ethnic breakdown of the city of Chicago: the school system is more minority in character. The 1980 U.S. Census reported that 49.6% of Chicago's population was white, 39.8% was black, 2.5% was American Indian, Asian, and Pacific Islander, and 8.1% was "other." (Hispanics, counted as an ethnic rather than a racial group, were spread among white, black, and "other" racial groups.)

The Chicago public schools are characterized by the same problems of other large urban systems: low achievement; declining enrollment; escalating costs; decreasing operating finances; and school climates which are far from conducive to learning.

The Schools

Two schools were selected for the study: the Rice School, a 100% black school with a student enrollment of 568 from K-8, and the Kent School, a 100% black middle school with a student enrollment of 818 from sixth through eighth grades (names of schools and persons have been changed to ensure confidentiality).

Both the Rice and Kent Schools were racially isolated and had been assigned "specialty programs." (A specialty program is a focus on a special area of study or depth of study offered by one or a few schools and is intended to provide educational enrichment to segregated students.) Each school was located in a district containing 24 schools. During the 1980–81 school year, there was a total of 7,036 suspensions in elementary schools (9,500 in high schools), with an average of 352 per district. The district for Kent School had a total of 443, or 91 more than the average. Within the former district, the average number of suspensions per school was 13, with Rice having a total of 3. Within the latter district, the average number of suspensions per school was 29, with Kent having a total of 37.

During the planning phase, the criterion for selecting schools was the number of disciplinary incidents, based on the number of suspensions in a given year. In time, this criterion proved specious. Number of suspensions in a specific school is not an indicator of problems in that school. For example, during the pilot study of another school in District 7, a suspension rate of 0% was found for 1981, while the school had numerous observed discipline problems and a reputation among principals and the district superintendent as "a bad place" and "a school which runs in spite of the principal." The principal simply categorically refused to suspend students regardless of the seriousness of student behavior: Public records thus listed the school as having few discipline problems.

By reputation, the Rice School was favored by the district superintendent—he considered the principal to be a strong administrator and the school to be well managed. During interviews, the principal, teachers, parents, and students all indicated that the Rice School was a "good" school (i.e., not too many discipline problems and well managed). In some respects, it was not only a neighborhood, but also a "family" school, in that half of the teachers had been teaching at the school for periods ranging from 9 to 22 years—and the principal for 23 years. Children of former students attended the school. Outsiders (children who moved into the district and transferred in, particularly any child from a high-rise housing project) were discouraged from enrolling and were "squeezed" out in one way or another, if they did not voluntarily heed the cues.

The Kent School was not a neighborhood school in the sense of having this history and the involvement of mixed generations. Instead, Kent accepted students from outside the attendance area and had a reputation for being a dumping ground, a school which would accept students unable to "make it" academically or socially at other schools. Usually this meant that they did not fit in socially for one reason or another or that they had been involved in a number of discipline events. With more than half of the building empty and unused, there was a sense of past history, or faded glory, at the school which the long-term teachers (one third of the teachers had been with the school since its inception 11 years previously) reflected in their conversation. The principal was the third in 10 years. In some parts of the building, the school appeared unlived in with boarded windows, broken window blinds, and chairs strewn in hallways, and open, half-empty cardboard boxes containing unused equipment could be found in vacant classrooms.

Gaining access to these two school sites was facilitated both through prior relationship between school staff and members of the university faculty and through initial contact with school principals who were familiarized with the proposed research. In addition to the Rice and Kent School sites, eight other schools from six separate districts were selected for convenience (e.g., easy access based on prior relationship between the schools and university faculty) and were used during the implementation study to provide checks and balances to verify that the particular management of the UDC or the processes observed in Rice and Kent Schools were not isolated events.

The Data
A pilot study of the Rice and Kent Schools was carried out informally to explore attitudes about and behavior surrounding discipline events in the school setting.

Preliminary observations were carried out in four classrooms for 2 months. Informal interviews were conducted with teachers and both principals concerning disciplinary practices, procedures, styles, and attitudes. A protocol was designed for observations to record, then categorize, and later analyze discipline events. The three-part protocol, including Discipline Event Summary Profile, Discipline Event Analysis, and Event Actors Summary was designed as a sorting instrument of teachers' own norms for student behavior and disciplinary styles. Its purpose was to reduce data, code specific items of data selected from field notes, and provide a summary record of information gathered. The protocol was planned to facilitate data collection on lower-level discretion and routinized behavior as they relate to the new regulatory policy.

Following preliminary observations and informal interviews and the construction of the protocol, four teachers were selected, two each from the two schools, on the basis of the frequency of their discipline problems, principals' judgments, and informants' opinions. One teacher in each school had a high incidence and one a low incidence of discipline problems.

Interview Data One major source of information on local-level discretionary behavior, ways of seeing, and routines surrounding disciplinary practices was individual interviews with nearly all of the staff of the two schools studied, including 2 principals; 2 assistant principals; 3 counselors; 73 teachers; 9 teacher aides; 3 security guards, including 1 special investigator; 4 clerical workers; 3 parent volunteers; 2 maintenance engineers; and 1 cleaning woman. Also, 13 parents (9 of whom had children involved in disciplinary procedures) were interviewed, along with 15 students. Outside of the two schools studied, interviews were conducted with 7 high school principals, 8 elementary school principals, 11 classroom teachers, 2 district superintendents, 5 members of the UDC task force, and 14 persons in various positions in the central office of the Board of Education.

The format for most interviews was semi-structured, with standard questions asked of all persons: responses were recorded through note taking. Interviews lasted from a half hour to 2½ hours. Few staff members at the local level refused to be interviewed, but when this did occur, often informal conversation and a little help with some small task such as running off a batch of dittos would gradually lead to completion of most of the interview questions in an informal way.

The initial interview schedule for teachers included some open-ended questions such as a question asking for a general description of a typical day. The major portion of the interview focused on structured-response questions about perceptions of time spent on disciplining, types of discipline problems and methods used in dealing with them, frequency of contact with the administration regarding discipline cases, perceived problems associated with using the UDC, and background variables such as age, years in teaching, years in the Chicago public schools, and years at the particular research school. Assurances of confidentiality were made.

Documentary Data. Records on students' discipline problems completed by the four teachers were examined. Teachers were required to maintain anecdotal records on students whenever an infraction occurred, including the date, the student's behavior, and the action taken by the teacher. These accounts were accumulated in the student's folder and used during parent conferences, in support of a recommendation for suspension, in support of a request for a child study to be conducted, or as evidence of the student's wrongdoing in legal confrontations.

Documentary data were used in the exploration of intermediate and macro-level components of the analytical framework. Information was obtained from numerous documents: the minutes of the Board of Education; the minutes of the UDC Task Force meetings; the Incident Reporting Guide; Elementary and High School Profiles; the Comprehensive Student Assignment Plan, Text and Appendices; the Progress Reports on Implementation of the Student Desegregation Plan: Part I Educational Components and Part II Student Assignment; the School Desegregation Fact Sheet; the Chicago Student Desegregation Plan Summary; the Racial/Ethnic Survey for Students; the Racial/Ethnic Survey for Staff; Test Scores and Selected School Characteristics; Resource Materials of Monitoring Commission for Desegregation Implementation (Amicus Briefs); the Chicago Principals Association Newsletter; the Chicago Teachers Union newspaper; public announcements from the Office of Communication of the Board; and letters from parent groups, educational, and PTA representatives, and local nonprofit community organizations.

Documentary data were used to trace the source, rationale, goal, and planning behind the new policy and to verify some points of controversy which surfaced in interviews and through the media.

Observational Data. While all of the teachers in the two schools were interviewed, only four were selected for observation. Data were obtained on how teachers perceive and manage discipline events, from the initial student-teacher interaction through to follow-up. This information, in part, would be used to explain the behavior of local-level implementers in responding to the UDC. Follow-up of a discipline event might include a parent, counselor, administrator, or another teacher, or it might end simply with an anecdotal note in the student's file.

Twelve 4-hour observations of each of the four teachers were carried out over a period of 5 months (3 months at the end of the 1981–82 school year and 2 months at the beginning of the 1982–83 school year). This gap in time allowed for the possibility that implementation of the UDC might progress. It also allowed for the opportunity to observe the same teachers at different times in the school year and with different classes. Each teacher was accompanied wherever her duties led during an observation period. Thus, observations were carried out in the classroom, the hallways, the teachers' lounge, the lunchroom, the playground, other teachers' classrooms, the gym, the library, the principal's office, and even once in a courtroom. Observations provided data on the relationship between current disciplinary practices and the new policy.

During the course of the study, the initial protocol was adapted for use with observations in order to assess the level of fit between current disciplinary practices and the requirements of the discipline policy. The protocol was used to identify and record: the specific discipline event; the number and identity of actors in the event; the behavior and responses of all actors; any mitigating circumstances cited by the teacher for choosing a particular response; the teacher-student relationship; and the teacher-student perceptions of the event.

Using the standards of the new policy to categorize data quickly revealed the differences between current practices and policy requirements and the changes necessary to implement the new policy at the local level. The observed differences then were used as a basis of discussion for exploring in further interviews with teachers the rationale for certain discipline practices.

METHODS OF ANALYSIS

Interview and documentary data from the second and third analytical levels were examined not only to assess the influence of intermediate and macro-level components of the framework on the implementing behavior of teachers at the school level. These data also shed light on the contribution of each component to the events of implementation. Observation data at the local level were used to examine extant discipline practices and beliefs so as to assess the extent and type of change that would be necessary at this level to implement the policy. The focus of data analysis at the intermediate and macro levels was to develop a case study of the processes surrounding policy adoption and its movement through the organization. Interviews at these levels incorporated open-ended questions on the components believed to be influential in implementation. Content analysis identified repetitive attitudes, ideas, and themes in order to understand the policy adoption process. Content analysis also supported use of the analytical framework for further research on implementation.

RESULTS

A total of 539 discipline events was observed among the four teachers (Table 2). Observed discipline events included all student behavior which resulted in a teacher response which could be classified as disciplinary. Events were informally discussed with teachers following observations in order to record their perceptions of the event and reasons for using the discipline strategies observed. In most cases the disciplinary behavior of the teacher was inconsistent with the behavior prescribed by the UDC. Boys were involved in discipline events more frequently than girls (Table 2). Further, only 79 of the 539 events were recorded (Table 3). The record-keeping system intended for use with the new discipline policy would have required that all events be recorded. Data from observations verified that implementation of the new discipline policy did not occur at the local level. They demonstrated how discipline events are managed behind the classroom door.

Table 2 Summary of Teacher Disciplinary Events by Sex of Student

Behaviors	Teacher 1				Teacher 2				Teacher 3				Teacher 4			
	No. of Events	%	M	F	No. of Events	%	M	F	No. of Events	%	M	F	No. of Events	%	M	F
Verbal reprimands	44	47	30	14	43	41	37	6	95	66	54	41	117	60	69	48
Corporal punishment	23	25	17	6	11	10	11	0	2	1	2	0	5	3	4	1
Parent conference	10	11	8	2	16	15	14	2	20	14	12	8	30	15	19	11
Referral to office	0	0	0	0	4	4	3	1	2	1	0	2	0	0	0	0
Referral to counselor	0	0	0	0	1	0	1	0	6	4	4	2	17	9	14	3
Referral to security guard	0	0	0	0	0	0	0	0	5	4	5	0	8	4	8	0
After-school detention	16	17	13	3	21	20	19	2	0	0	0	0	0	0	0	0
Informal suspensions (3-day deal)	0	0	0	0	10	9	9	1	9	6	7	2	16	8	12	4
Suspension (1–5 days)	0	0	0	0	0	0	0	0	3	2	2	1	1	1	0	1
Suspension (6–10 days)	0	0	0	0	0	0	0	0	1	1	0	1	2	1	1	1
Disciplinary reassignment	1	1	1	0	0	0	0	0	0	0	0	0	0	0	0	0
Total	94		69	25	106		94	12	143		86	57	196		127	69
Percent**		101	74	27		99	89	11		99	60	40		101	65	35

*M = Male, F = Female.
**percentage may not add to 100 due to rounding.

Table 3   Summary of Discipline Events Observed and Recorded

Day	Teacher 1[a] No. Observed Discipline Events	Teacher 1[a] No. Events Recorded in File	Teacher 2[b] No. Observed Discipline Events	Teacher 2[b] No. Events Recorded in File	Teacher 3[c] No. Observed Discipline Events	Teacher 3[c] No. Events Recorded in File	Teacher 4[d] No. Observed Discipline Events	Teacher 4[d] No. Events Recorded in File
1	4	0	7†	0	16†	2	8	1
2	3	0	6	1	9†	0	19††	3
3	6	0	13††	1	5	1	13†	2
4	9	1	5	0	17†	2	22††	5
5	6	2	4	0	13†	3	16††	5
6	11	0	7†	0	10	1	9	2
7	8	1	9	2	11†	2	16††	3
8	9	1	9	0	8	2	20†††	6
9	13	0	11†††	1	15†	4	17††	3
10	9	0	8	0	12†	1	14†	3
11	11	1	15†	3	16†	1	13	4
12	5	0	12†	1	11†	0	29††	8
Totals	94	6 (6%)	106	9 (9%)	196	45 (23%)	143	19 (13%)

[a] Black fifth-grade teacher, 15 years at Rice School.
[b] White teacher, mixed sixth to eighth grades, 11 years at Rice School.
† Each (†) represents one informal, unrecorded suspension of a minimum of three days duration ("three-day deal").
[c] Black sixth-grade teacher, 11 years at Kent School.
[d] White seventh-grade teacher, 10 years at Kent School.

131

It was expected that local-level variables involving the individual teacher would have a particularly strong effect on the implementation process. However, in order for these effects to become apparent the policy would have had to have been passed through organizational channels and presented to the local level together with resources to make implementation possible. Then local-level variables could possibly make a difference. It may also be true that if all processes at the macro and intermediate level of the organization had functioned smoothly and effectively, then there would be little opportunity for discretionary behavior at the local level. The policy would have been planned in such a way that work routines and ways of seeing would have been taken into account and controlled for at the planning stage. However, neither of these outcomes was observed. The new discipline policy mandated a method of discipline without providing the minimum resources necessary to make it possible. A record-keeping system was also mandated, but without communication of information on the system to the local level. Consequently, local-level variables became a moot issue when considered by themselves (Table 4).

Table 4 Effects of Variables Within Levels of the Analytical Framework

Variable	Effect
Local Level	
Discretionary behavior	Entrenched discretionary system, both school-wide and individual, was observed among teachers. *Pro forma* compliance with the unofficial goal of the policy did not require change in discretion.
Ways of seeing	Teachers perceived prevailing discipline practices as necessary to the maintenance of order. Neither principals nor teachers viewed the policy as operable, practical, or applicable, and they did not alter beliefs about students, discipline, or ways of doing things.
Work routines	Disciplinary routines were adapted to the limitations of time and resources. The revised policy required readjustment of two routines—suspensions and record-keeping—but without resources implementation was not possible, and the policy resulted in strengthening the covert disciplinary practices it allegedly intended to change.
Intermediate Level	
Communication process	The policy itself communicated unclear directives because of confused goals. Communication was selective and characterized by gaping holes, evasiveness, long silences, controversy, suspicion, and struggle over power and authority.
Expectations	*Pro forma* compliance was expected by some members of the central office; others expected the remedy of inequity in disciplinary procedures. Principals did not expect teachers to implement the policy but expected the central office to reshape the policy to fit the local level.

Table 4   Effects of Variables Within Levels of the Analytical Framework (continued)

Variable	Effect
Decision processes	The most significant decisions included not addressing the local-level problems of discipline and alleged discrimination, the exclusion of the local level from participation in the planning of the policy and its implementation, and the trading of two control strategies for the opportunity to save money and maintain equilibrium in the system at the local level.
Macro Level Control processes	With minimal legal regulations and guidelines, the Justice Department put control of implementation into the hands of the central office by refusing to interpret its own rulings. The central office traded two control strategies—record-keeping and in-school suspension for the opportunity to save money and maintain equilibrium in the system. The struggle for control over the policy between the central office and the local level brought implementation efforts to a temporary standstill and more than doubled the timeline for the realization of outcomes.
Environmental context	The policy was generated in response to the outer environment rather than the internal local level. Major obstacles to implementation originated in the inner environment. The central office drafted the policy in response to the Justice Department but changed the policy in response to the local level, which threatened to upset the equilibrium of the organization. Principals at the local level used the outer environment (the media) to affect change in the policy from the central office.

In other words, local-level teachers did not implement the policy because (a) they did not perceive it as applicable, and (b) the tools for record-keeping and in-school suspension were not available. By not providing the resources necessary for implementation, central office staff did not appear serious about the policy being implemented at the local level. The reasons for this became clear following investigation of several unexpected events which occurred during the course of the study. Implementation of the discipline policy was characterized by unmet expectations and four major surprises: (a) the policy was not drafted voluntarily in response to local-level problems, as was believed by both the researcher and local-level workers before the study, but was rooted in a federal mandate and larger social issues; (b) nearly an entire academic year after the policy had been "in effect," local-level teachers still were not aware of it; (c) an enormous controversy surrounded the policy—a UDC which seemed so sensible—and involved everyone but local-level teachers, who were expected to implement it; and (d) the disciplining behavior of teachers in schools looked different in practice than all official reports of the incidence of discipline problems.

During the early weeks of this investigation, my research deviated from the initial design. Data collection techniques were adapted to changing conditions and to the pace of implementations as it unfolded. It became apparent that not enough was known about the process of implementation to anticipate its movement. The full meaning of the four surprises became clear only after rigorous study of all three analytical levels over the course of the year.

Surprise 1: The Source of the Discipline Policy

The first surprise which changed the perspective and the dimension of the research was the source of the new discipline policy. The discipline policy had been chosen as a vehicle for the study of implementation, in part, because of its local-level boundaries. By eliminating the distance between policymakers and policy implementers, the study was planned to be unlike other implementation studies reported in the literature in which policy typically originates at the federal level and undergoes many problems as it moves through organizational levels before reaching the local arena. Thus, it was a surprise to learn that the new discipline policy was the result of a federal mandate from the U.S. Justice Department to enhance desegregation and not a local policy which had originated in the central office of the Board of Education in response to problems within the system. Conceivably, the source of the policy might be irrelevant to its implementation. It did not appear incompatible for a policy to address local problems while simultaneously providing required data to legal authorities.

However, in this study of implementation, the policy source created serious problems: (a) it generated doubt about the purpose of the policy; (b) it required the concomitant implementation of a controversial record-keeping system; (c) it created a situation in which following the rules and regulations mandated in the policy identified teachers as incompetent educators (using the logic that one who can manage a class does not have discipline problems); and (d) it necessitated a monitoring system for teachers which invaded privacy and contaminated the issue of discipline policy with questions of teacher evaluation. The entanglements surrounding the source of the policy, among other problems, discouraged implementation at the local level. Thus, a study designed to focus exclusively on teachers at the local level was rendered unimportant, since implementation turned on other actors and larger issues.

Why public documents which discuss the policy did not mention the origin of the policy can only be surmised. It appears reasonable to assume that the instructional committee of the Board of Education, which had the final legal authority in approving and adopting policy, did not want to emphasize the connection between the discipline policy and the federal mandate. Later it was found that teachers, parents, and students also were unaware of the policy's origin. Principals had been informed of its source, but during interviews it appeared that some had not recalled the information.

Surprise 2: Teachers and . . . What Policy?

While the first surprise was potentially important to the course of the study, the second surprise was characterized by mystery. Like the first, this turn of events occurred during informal interviews, but this time with teachers: "What policy? I didn't know we had a new policy. . .," or "Oh yeah, I think I heard about that somewhere, but I don't know anything about it." Most teachers had not seen a copy of the policy. Some had, and among those the responses were as startling: "That's the thing the principal was talking about at the meeting the other day. But we won't be using that here. We have our own ways of handling discipline. . .," or "It's a nice piece of paper but it doesn't apply to us." Twenty-six out of 30 teachers interviewed informally had not heard of the new policy, and those who had were not aware of its applicability to them.

It became necessary to move from the local level to higher levels of the organization to look for an answer to why teachers had not yet heard of a policy which reportedly they had implemented 8 months earlier in May, 1982. In the central office, several administrators explained that the UDC definitely was the official Board of Education policy on discipline and had been since September, 1981. However, copies were not yet available for distribution, because money had not been budgeted for its printing.

An assurance that "everything's under control" was given to me on Friday, May 12, 1982. The following day the Board of Education withdrew the Code from the printer and decided to hold public hearings. Many questions arose. What was the nature of this controversy? What, specifically, was delaying the new policy? Why had it not been communicated to local-level teachers? What feedback, and from whom, precipitated public hearings? According to Board of Education minutes, the Code had already been approved in September, 1981. It was nearly June, and the new policy had, by this time, been "official" for an entire school year, without having been communicated to teachers. So much for public documents.

Some members of the central office expressed an urgency to get the Code printed and distributed under any circumstances. As one member of the task force remarked: "The Judge told us this is a commitment. We have to get something out." Still, others hesitated. One administrator in the central office spoke for himself and others when he said during an interview: "Some say 'let's print it; let's get it out and worry about it later.' But some of us have been begging off and holding back. When they call me up and say 'your Code this and your Code that,' I don't want that. It should be *our* Code, the *system's* Code, *everybody's* Code."

Thus, in attempting to find out why teachers had not yet heard of a policy which reportedly they had implemented months earlier, the third surprise of the study emerged.

Surprise 3: Controversy and the Code

That an enormous controversy could surround the new policy and involve everyone but teachers seemed highly improbable. However, in moving from the central office of the organization back to the local level in an effort to maintain contact with the teachers in the schools and to understand their involvement in the problems surrounding the Code, it became apparent that teachers were quite untouched by the controversy.

The controversy surrounding the UDC originated with a group of high school principals. Repeated interviews with principals elicited negative feedback, resentment, and complaints about specific and substantive issues. There was the issue of imposition of the Code on principals without their representation on the task force which drafted the policy. There was a question about the need for uniformity in handling discipline problems. There was criticism of the "weakness," "inflexibility," "softness," and inability of the Code to "deal with real situations." Principals resented interference by the courts in schools through the discipline policy. They criticized the types of behavior on the part of principals and teachers which the Code was intended to change. They felt that their discretion and decision-making power were being usurped. Others felt that the Code's structuring of discipline situations made it impossible for principals and teachers to take immediate action in serious discipline situations. Others were outraged that the Code mandated that a system of in-school suspension be adopted, but the Board neglected to provide resources—neither ideas, nor personnel, nor money—to devise and implement the system.

The Code was the focus of heated controversy over several months. It was rescinded and revised twice. Public hearings were held. Workshops on the policy were conducted for the general public. One year after the discipline policy supposedly had been implemented, an acceptable version of the Code was printed and sent to schools, staff, and parents. It appeared that the time was right to return to the initial focus of the study—the local-level implementer, the classroom teacher.

In contacting teachers for interviews and observing classrooms in order to develop a comprehensive picture of how the Code was being approached in schools, the findings were startlingly repetitive from site to site. Teachers reported that the Code was a great idea in theory but that it was not practical for use in their schools. It was a document "worth having," but not "worth using." While the study could not follow its intended path, probing with teachers continued, particularly on the use of current disciplinary practices and strategies, their use in particular schools, and the discrepancy between these strategies and the procedures prescribed in the Code. It was hoped that this new area of inquiry would explain some of the resistance to the Code at the local level. Not only were many inconsistencies found during this probing, but also the inconsistencies began to suggest a fourth major surprise of the study.

One of the primary purposes of the new policy was to eliminate an alleged overreliance on student suspension as a method of handling discipline problems. As the chairman of the task force remarked, "The whole business behind this baby is to keep students in school, plain and simple." Yet the revised Code mandated that suspension be carried out for specific discipline events. At the same time, the Office of Equal Educational Opportunity was planning a computerized record-keeping system so that each event, regardless of whether the consequence was suspension, or a parent conference, or something else, would be recorded. With the new monitoring system in effect—and with the perhaps unwitting cooperation of teachers and principals—the Office of Equal Educational Opportunity at any given moment would be able to identify via computer a school, a principal, a teacher, down to the very classroom which was having discipline problems. This detailed, comprehensive monitoring system would be used with the logic discussed by the Board members: Those who record problems obviously are not handling their problems.

It is important to note that the problems potentially addressed by the Code were not necessarily the same problems encountered in schools. Certainly the number of problems recorded had no relation to reality as lived in the schools. Then how were discipline problems being handled in the schools behind classroom doors? If suspensions were not used, then which methods were in use? And why were some schools so insistent on wanting to maintain "our own ways of doing things"?

Surprise 4: The "Three-Day Deal" and Other Dilemmas

In continuing classroom observations, I both observed and recorded an informal, unofficial system of removing students from the environment called "the three-day deal." It was used in situations in which teachers knew that they could not get students formally suspended or did not want to formally suspend a child, but also judged that the student was too much of a disruptive influence to remain in the classroom.

The "three-day deal" (also known as "a brief vacation," "the home remedy," and the "send-him-home-until-his-mama-gets-sick-of-him-cure") was a common, widespread, generally accepted, informal method of managing unruly, disruptive students. The procedure typically consisted of the teacher informing the student that she was excluding him for a few days, writing the informal note, and notifying the office. The principal signed the note; the clerk called the student's home; and the parent was notified that the student was being sent home. Sometimes the security guard would walk the student home.

With the exception of new teachers, nearly all teachers interviewed were aware of a system of informal suspension operating in their schools. The discovery of the "three-day deal" signaled that implementation of the Uniform Discipline Code was probably impossible. The fit between the policy and the situation it was intended to remedy was clearly mismatched. Encountering the first surprise—the source of the discipline policy traced to an unexpected origin—was not only disconcerting but also added a new dimension to the research. Confronting the second surprise—teachers had no knowledge of the policy long after it was "official"—changed the course of the research and initiated a conceptual reassessment of the implementation phenomenon. Uncovering the third surprise—an enormous controversy surrounding the Uniform Discipline Code—expanded the focus of the study and influenced the design of the research while in the field.

These surprises may have presented serious concerns about the ultimate fate of implementation outcomes. However, the fact that a policy was drafted in response to a government mandate, that the primary implementers of the policy were not aware of the policy, and that controversy cast doubt on the rationale and intent behind the Code and the lack of participation of local-level persons in its drafting did not necessarily suggest that the policy would not or could not be implemented. Rather these surprises suggested that the implementation process is far more complex than expected, that the levels of analysis and variables therein are far more equal and interdependent than expected, and that the element of surprise may be a defining characteristic of the implementation process (or, more accurately, that the lack of predictability may suggest our modest understanding of the phenomenon).

The fourth surprise—that the disciplinary behavior of teachers in schools looks different as reported on paper from actual practice—cast doubt on the viability of a policy which did not address reality.

THE GENERIC ORGANIZATION

It is a mistake to begin a case study with a rigid conceptualization. Central questions must be identified beforehand, but during the course of the study dramatically different conceptualizations may arise, leading to other questions. This study began with an organized conceptual framework, but the vehicle for studying implementation was a slippery policy—part of a federal mandate, but not specific in recommendations for implementation. In spite of the fact that the discipline policy emerged in response to a federal mandate, the federal government did not play a role as change agent in its implementation. Indeed, federal actions provided the impetus for change, but the latitude for response was wide. Portrayal of the attempt of a local school system to use a federal mandate to stimulate internal change is closer to reality, but not quite accurate either.

Use of a theoretical framework was intended to guide the study in a particular direction. The focus was exclusively on the classroom teacher, a street-level worker who, theory suggested, would be at the crux of implementation problems and outcomes. Use of such a conceptual framework in this particular study was akin to approaching the field with a cognitive script, or the expectation of a coherent sequence of events (Abelson, 1976). The four surprises encountered during the study made it clear that a tight conceptual framework, which lends itself to truth-making rather than truth-seeking, is not the most productive approach to organizational phenomena, particularly processes about which too little is understood.

Conceptualization of both the policy and the implementation process influenced the research design and consequently created problems as the study unfolded. One problem was the limitation of the case study to four teachers in two elementary schools, an adequate sample for the original intention of analyzing the role of the local-level worker in policy implementation, but a less satisfactory choice as the study moved from the local-level worker to analysis of the larger process of implementation.

Another limitation of the study from the point of view of the larger implementation process was its focus on elementary schools exclusively. This became particularly true when data began to suggest that implementation of the UDC was unfolding differently in high schools. Limitation of the study to four teachers in two all-black elementary schools meant that differences in implementation were not explored in different kinds and levels of schools, and differences in disciplining behavior between black and white teachers toward students of various racial backgrounds—one stated reason for the policy—were not explored. In order to offset the limitation of small sample and to provide a system of checks and balances, eight additional elementary schools were selected informally for monitoring the progress of policy implementation among local teachers in other places throughout the system. Ways of handling discipline were not explored in depth, and observations were not carried out in these other eight schools. Instead, attitudes toward the Code and differences in handling the policy specifically were explored. Interviews were conducted with teachers and administrators in the eight elementary schools to record attitudes toward and use of the policy. Finding that the Code was not used in two schools was not as significant as finding that it was not used in 10 schools.

Since the aim of the study was to depict the process of implementation, and within it the system of perceiving, believing, and evaluating the discipline policy by local-level workers, it was necessary to explore three analytical levels and the conceptual categories used by persons at all three levels to think about and express themselves on discipline and the policy with an everyday relevance. There were difficulties with time and overextension as one researcher worked at multiple levels. Often, there was the overwhelming desire to get everyone—scores of actors at all levels- assembled in one room. In spite of these problems, one advantage of the research design was the confluence of data sources which can increase the reliability of findings and are also necessary in light of the gaps likely to exist and the biases inherent in relying on any one source of information exclusively. Consequently, all propositions in this study were confirmed by at least two or more sources.

The problem of validity is a more difficult concern to address. The study illuminates the role of the street-level bureaucrat in the implementation of policy at the local level, or specifically, the role of the teacher in the implementation of discipline policy. This role proved to be one of discretion as teachers responded to the policy in a way which ensured the status quo of current disciplinary practices. Also to ensure validity, care was taken to distinguish between the researcher's and informants' points of views. At no time were assumptions made about teachers' intentions regarding their observed behavior.

Another consideration in implementation case studies concerns the generalizability of research results. Since every organization and every policy is unique, when an analytical framework of organizational processes is developed from experience in a single organization, the question of generalizability remains open. Were the processes of implementation at three levels of analysis within a large, urban school system unique to that setting, or would the same processes of implementation remain consistent across other urban school systems, or even other types of organizations?

In one sense, large, public service organizations belong to a generic category which presupposes that they have certain elements in common, for example, complexity, hierarchical structure, centralization, bureaucratization, and a local level where service is delivered. Thus, there is reason to believe that the fundamental processes observed in this study may be similar in organizations of the same generic category such as welfare organizations, law enforcement agencies, hospital and medical centers. Whether the local-level worker acting as a street-level bureaucrat affects the policy implementation process in these other organizations remains a hypothetical question.

While this study intended to focus specifically on local-level workers in the implementation of policy, it was necessary to move back and forth between analytical levels in order to gather data to explain findings at the local level. In and of itself, the theory of street-level bureaucracy could not explain the unexpected and surprising series of events without consideration of actions at other organizational levels which had an impact on implementation processes at the local level. What the study clarified is that teachers in this particular case played out the role which policymakers intended for them—not as street-level bureaucrats, but as workers who would maintain the equilibrium in the classrooms by not taking the new policy too seriously.

However, this result appeared to raise more questions than it answered. If the policy was not implemented, yet people at all levels—from the classroom teacher to principals, superintendents and central office staff to the Justice Department—agreed that implementation outcomes were successful, then what level of reality did this agreement address? What actually was the intention behind the discipline policy?

THE TENTATIVE PROCESS AND INTENTIONALITY

When all is said and done, perhaps the most significant question is: What does successful implementation look like? This study analyzed implementation of a policy which the researcher believed was bound to succeed because the need for the policy was so great. Moreover, the policy itself appeared noncontroversial, and its formulation seemed to be in response to local-level problems, eliminating the entangling complications of policies which originate at levels outside the immediate implementing arena. In the course of doing the study, all three of these initial impressions proved false. The outcomes may have been different, if officials had had one unanimous, clear, consistent goal in mind and had been willing to commit enforcement activities to that goal. Different conditions support varying outcomes.

Nonimplementation as Hidden Agenda
The word "implementation" implies that a plan has been carried out and a goal achieved. Implementation outcomes either achieve desired goals or they do not. Sometimes the original goal of a policy changes during the process. And sometimes successful resistance to the policy results in nonimplementation but is never-

theless an act of organizational effectiveness. All policies are not good policies. The act of policymaking itself may have other purposes rather than implementation of its mandate.

In the final analysis, the Justice Department approved nonimplementation of the discipline policy with no criticism, no suggestion for change, and no dissatisfaction. The central office reported that the climate of the schools had improved as expected. Teachers and administrators at the local level, at last, appeared content just to have the policy tucked away in their desk drawers. Apparently, nonimplementation had been successful by many standards. It had achieved something for everyone.

That implementation did, in fact, achieve certain of its goals—not necessarily the stated objectives of the written policy—is not questioned. However, in scrutinizing outcomes of implementation, the importance of intentionality becomes startlingly clear. When policymakers report that, in essence, "we have achieved what we wanted to achieve," the social science observer must move beyond participants' interpretations. Policy statements must be compared with discrepant observations. Yes, there is a saga here about failed implementation. But there is a more important tale of successful nonimplementation.

This study suggests that the most important contribution of an implementation study is not to conclude merely whether implementation outcomes are consistent with stated policy goals, but instead to peel away layers to reduce a policy to its essential purpose. To expose a policy's core—that nucleus of meaning in which all intents and purposes comingle in confusion, contrasts, and conflict—is to provide a substantial basis for explaining the particular configuration of implementation activities and the steps in the process of implementation which are consistent with this nucleus of meaning.

Implementation outcomes may deviate far from the policy's essential purpose. This purpose may be found in the original policy statement. However, such statements are subject to interpretation and revision. Or they may be intended for someone other than implementers, for example an official agency or the federal government. The policy statement may not include the layers of meaning which define the specifics of what the policy is intended to accomplish. This is partly because the specifics of implementation often are not known in advance, but are defined and refined through the implementation process. The point to be made is that implementation outcomes probably are more closely linked to multiple policy intentions than to any other single variable in the implementation process.

This may not hold true in any organization but the one under study, or perhaps within the generic category of public service organizations. Assuming that it does hold true across other organizations—that this link between intentionality and outcomes is an archetypal characteristic of the process of implementation generally—then the implications for implementation begin to emerge.

This is not to say that variables at the local, intermediate, and macro levels of the analytical framework already discussed are not important. Indeed, this study demonstrated the importance of processes at each level of the analytical framework and the interdependence of the variables between levels. What is suggested, instead, is that these variables help to determine the substantive content of policy intention. For example, in the present study the enormous controversy surrounding the policy resulted partly from multiple goals on the part of policymakers. Did they want to satisfy the Justice Department? Did they want to improve the climate of schools? Did they want to establish uniformity in discipline and gain an administrative handle on the unwieldy system? Did they want to assert control over local administrators by dictating policy to control behavior in what principals considered their territory? Did they want to use the policy as a tool of evaluation for local teachers? Did they want to issue a figurehead policy which would look good on paper but not disrupt the balance of disciplining activities in schools? Perhaps most importantly, did they want to attain the goal of the Justice Department's mandate to keep minority students in school? Perhaps one policy was intended to do too much. If policy intentions are mixed, inconsistent, and variable, then outcomes too may be mixed, inconsistent, and variable.

Multiple Goals and the Real World

The Uniform Discipline Code appeared to be a strong, clear, straightforward policy. But the Board of Education declined to provide the resources necessary for its implementation. Consequently, those within the schools, in direct contact with problems at the local level, saw through the facade to the multiple intentions behind the policy and described the Code as "weak" and "ineffective." Indeed, there were far too many goals for local-level implementers to confront realistically, and the policy elicited a wall of anger and resentment. Perhaps the more policymakers hone down the multiple goals of a single policy and merge stated and intended goals, the better the chance for implementation. But how is this done in the real world of administration?

It may require a special skill on the part of policymakers to cope with the multiple intentions behind a single policy. There are many individuals, groups, and organizational levels, each wanting something different from a single policy. For example, the UDC might have been used only to satisfy the Justice Department, as it was. Or it could have been used to establish acceptable procedures for the administration of discipline, thereby satisfying two intentions. These two singular goals might have been accomplished without complications, particularly since the Justice Department had no real interest in the details of implementation and the central office was not restricted by means for achieving ends. The two goals do not conflict. Instead, the policy implementation process was confused and complicated as issues and intentions—all related to the single discipline policy—diverged. As goals proliferated, they began to conflict, and the process of implementation became more and more problematic. In the confusion of multiple intensions, the process of implementation itself appears tentative.

The task of policy analysts interested in achieving a higher degree of successful implementation may be to assess the situation of multiple intentions surrounding a given policy. There may be intentions which are compatible and do not conflict.

They may be intentions which overlap. There may be a minimum which can be achieved for essential interest groups through negotiation and compromise.

The questions, of course, are still complex. Who are the essential groups to satisfy? And how are they identified? Are they necessarily the ones which make the most noise? As these questions are answered, there is still the responsibility to move the organization along one small step in the direction of the desired change, once it has been established that a specific change is desired or necessary— or has been mandated. This may require the reeducation of organizational members in the rationale behind the new policy. Or it may require the use of incentives or sanctions to obtain compliance. There are no easy answers. This study points up some of the problems which may develop when a central office of a large, bureaucratic school system fails to identify the key groups in the implementation process.

In summary, nonimplementation of the Uniform Discipline Code provides an example of the foundering of a policy idea upon the shoals of vague and conflicting goals, inappropriate means, strained communication and undemocratic decision-making, and lack of participation by implementers in the planning process. In another sense, implementation outcomes suggest the tentativeness of and uncertainty associated with policy implementation and the linkages between unstated policy intentions and the final outcomes of nonimplementation. The case provides a study in successful resistance to a policy which may not have been a very good idea to begin with. As one principal observed while nodding and grinning: "When all is said and done, it ain't much different from where we started." Perhaps the important question is: Is it much different from where we wanted to end up?

REFERENCES

Abelson, R.P. (1976). Script processing in attitude formation and decision making. In John S. Carroll & John W. Payne (Eds.), *Cognition and social behavior.* Hillsdale, NJ: Erlbaum.

Allison, G. (1971). *Essence of decision: Explaining the Cuban missile crisis.* Boston: Little, Brown.

Baldridge, J.V., & Burnham, R.A. (1975). Organizational innovation: Individual, organizational and environmental impacts. *Administrative Science Quarterly, 20,* 165–176.

Bardach, E. (1977). *The implementation game: What happens after a bill becomes a law.* Cambridge, MA: MIT Press.

Berman, P., & Pauly, E.W. (1975). *Federal programs supporting educational change, Vol. 2. Factors affecting change agent projects.* Santa Monica CA: Rand Corp.

Beyer, J.M., & Trice, H.M. (1977, Winter). *Organizational structure and the implementation of change within federal sector organizations.* Paper presented at the Academy of Management Annual Meeting, Kissimmee, FL.

Brieschke, P.A. A case study of teacher role enactment in an urban elementary school. *Educational Administration Quarterly,* 1983, 19, 5, 59–83.

Consent Decree (1980, September 24). U.S. Department of Justice and Chicago Board of Education, entered in U.S. District Court for the Northern District of Illinois.

Fairweather, G.W., Sanders, D.H., Tornatsky, L.G., & Harris, R.N., Jr. (1974), *Creating change in mental health organizations.* Elmsford, NY: Pergamon.

Gersten, R., & Carnine, D. (1980, April) *Measuring implementation of the direct instruction model in an urban school district: An observational approach.* Paper presented at the annual meeting of the American Educational Research Association, Boston.

Green, Robert, L. (1981). *Student desegregation plan for the Chicago public schools.* Paper prepared for Chicago Board of Education.

Hage, J., & Aiken, M. (1970). *Social change in complex organizations.* New York: Random House.

Hawkins, J. & Rosen, J. (1981). *Report on student discipline.* Paper prepared for the Chicago Board of Education.

Herriott, R.E., & Gross, N. (Eds.). (1979). *The dynamics of planned educational change.* Berkeley, CA: McCutchan.

Lipsky, M. (1976). Toward a theory of street-level bureaucracy. In W.D. Hawley & M. Lipsky, (Eds.), *Theoretical perspectives on urban politics.* Englewood Cliffs, NJ: Prentice Hall.

Scheirer, M.A. (1981). *Program implementation: The organizational context.* Beverly Hills, CA: Sage.

Smith, L.M., & Keith, P.M. (1971). *Anatomy of educational innovation: An organizational analysis of an elementary school.* New York: Wiley.

Weatherly, R., & Lipsky, M. (1977). Street-level bureaucrats and institutional innovation: Implementing special education reform. *Harvard Educational Review, 47* (2), 171-197.

Weikert, D.P., & Banet, B.A. (1976). Planned variation from the perspective of a model sponsor. In W. Williams & R.F. Elmore (Eds.), *Social program implementation.* New York: Academic Press.

Williams, W., & Elmore, R.F. (Eds.). (1976). *Social program implementation.* New York: Academic Press.

7
Organizational Identity and Complex Change in Schools*

DAVID C. DWYER
Far West Laboratory for Educational Research and Development
LOUIS M. SMITH
Washington University
JOHN J. PRUNTY
Maritz Communication Company
PAUL KLEINE
University of Oklahoma

THE NEED FOR A CONCEPT OF ORGANIZATIONAL IDENTITY

Published accounts of elementary schools rarely communicate that these organizations differ much from one another, that they have any special quality or identity. Many schools do not even have their own name; for institutional purposes, labels like PS 177 appear to suffice. Others are named after nationally prominent figures such as Washington, Jefferson, Lincoln, and Roosevelt. In the latter instance, there may be no indication of which Roosevelt, and no one may care. One school, it seems, is much like another.

This was hardly the case when the new Kensington School first opened its doors. On the contrary, in the modest Milford community dotted with unpretentious schools, Kensington stood out as an unusual example of imaginative architecture and innovative schooling. It represented a special and unique blend of design, people, ideas, and pedagogy that Louis Smith and Pat Keith (1971) described in *Anatomy of Educational Innovation,* a lengthy monograph that related the results of their participant-observation study of the opening of the school in 1964:

> The setting was the Kensington School, a unique architectural structure with open-space laboratory suites, an instructional materials center, and a theatre. . . . The program exemplified the new elementary education of team

*This chapter is based on the project *Innovation and Change in American Education, Kensington Revisited: A fifteen-Year Follow-up of an Innovative Elementary School and Its Faculty,* supported by NIE Grant #G78-0074. The analysis and interpretations represent official policy of neither the National Institute of Education, the Department of Education, nor the Milford School District.

teaching, individualized instruction, and multiaged groups. A broad strategy of innovation—the alternative of grandeur . . . was devised and implemented. The intended outcome was pupil development toward maturity—self-directed, internally motivated, and productive competence. (p. v)

In 1979 we had the opportunity to return to the community of Milford and the Kensington Elementary School and, once again, observe, examine records, and interview faculty about their daily work. In addition, we tracked down the original faculty and interviewed them about their lives and careers since their Kensington experiences. We wanted to understand what had happened to the school and its original staff during our 15-year absence. This fundamental curiosity led us to consider the structure and function of elementary schools; school governance at the building and district levels; the interplay of schools, communities, and state and federal educational organizations; teaching and learning; and the human dynamics of school organizations (Smith, Dwyer, Prunty, & Kleine, 1983).

These two studies of Kensington, made 15 years apart, presented a rare opportunity in the world of social science or educational research; predictions made at the conclusion of the first study could be checked against the actual course of events recorded in the second study. For example, in 1964 we had observed many events and conditions that led us to believe that the innovative plan that the school embodied would encounter obstacles in the years ahead and that the plan would be drastically altered. Incongruities between the community's vision of schools and the Kensington conception, the disharmony engendered by multiple sources of outside pressure on both Kensington and its community, personnel changes, and policy changes within the district all seemed to indicate that Kensington would revert to the "old Milford type." (Smith & Keith, 1971) At that time, we charted our prediction, reproduced here in Figure 1. Thus, from the outset of our return study we anticipated change at Kensington.

Intensively observing a single school at two widely dispersed times seemed like an excellent opportunity to derive a general model of educational organizations and processes of change in such organizations. Our hunch was that we could reveal the parts and dynamics of such a model by comparing the original Kensington with what it had become and tracing its alterations over 15 years.

Abstraction of this sort has great appeal for social scientists. The power of ideal types, unified conceptual schemes derived from empirical reality, is demonstrated by such conceptions as Weber's (1947) bureaucracy, Jahoda's (1958) analysis of positive mental health, or by the centuries-long debate over the concept of liberal education.[1] In education, attempts to form such unified theories have produced a host of models that are useful and interesting for various purposes. (Charters & Jones, 1973; Gowin, 1981; Smith & Geoffrey, 1968) But the paradigm that fits all schools and situations remains undiscovered; the "joints" at which one must cut to dissect schools successfully are yet to be found.

---

[1] The debate lies in the positions of E. Becker (1968); R. Bernstein (1979); E. Nagel (1961); M. Scriven (1959); or P. Hirst (1973); and M. Struthers (1971).

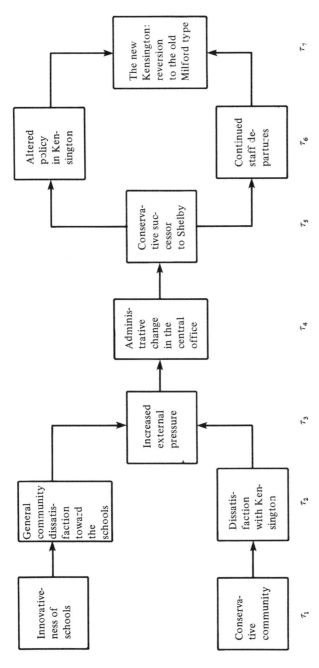

Figure 1. The social context of Kensington's administrative change. From *Anatomy of Educational Innovation* (p. 16) by L. M. Smith and P. Keith, 1971. New York: Wiley. Copyright by John Wiley & Sons, Inc. Reprinted by permission.

There is, perhaps, an important lesson to be learned from the failure to find those analytic joints. That lesson is to look beyond the formal structures and functions in organizations and to realize that organizations are not merely the sums of the arrangements of persons, motives and goals, and technologies, but that they are a good deal more. Intricately woven into their fabrics are their histories, locations, and times, and importantly, the meanings that participants make of all of these elements. Thus, their realities extend beyond the automatic functioning brought about by "inner dynamics or system requirements," as Blumer (1969) has written, and may be better understood by close attention to the meanings derived from the "human factor" that lies behind "structural data," as Berger and Luckmann (1967) have argued. Thus, as our analysis of the Kensington story developed, we became less concerned with deductively arranged nomothetic propositions. Instead, we found ourselves identifying sensitizing concepts, ideas that developed from the immediate and practical world of the teachers, principals, superintendents, parents, and school-board members with whom we worked. We sought to describe the ways in which Kensington had changed during our 15-year absence but, most importantly, we tried to elaborate on the multiple meanings the participants assigned to those changes. We searched for patterns in these meanings and began to label those patterns more abstractly.

As we considered the fact that Kensington had changed from what it had been 15 years earlier, we found that much of our data clustered to create distinct images, *organizational identities,* that helped us understand why and how change had come to Kensington. Far from a theory of organization, these conceptions or metaphors helped organize the physical, functional, and social aspects of the two Kensingtons we came to know so well. We believe that our configuration of the facets of organizational identity, our addition to a growing literature about new metaphors for organizations, helps underscore the roles of "informality," "individual entrepreneur[ship]," and "evolution" as fundamental processes in the lives of organizations. (Peters & Waterman, 1982) These are essential characteristics, evolving from recent theorizing in what Scott (1978) calls the "fourth epoch" of thought about organizations. Before discussing the configuration of Kensington's organizational identities, however, we must digress and briefly describe its saga, informing the reader of the school's relevant who's, why's, where's, when's, and what's.

THE KENSINGTON SAGA

We might begin Kensington's saga by searching for an answer to a simple question: Why did this innovative elementary school appear in Milford at all? Examining records that stretched back to the school district's beginnings revealed that the individuals who committed themselves to the implementation of a creditable school system in Milford were traditionalists at heart who pursued the best of what conservative ideas about education always represent. The appearance of Kensington in Milford was an anomaly that a bit of the district's history can explain. We begin our story, then, in the late 1950s.

In the wake of the Great Depression, World War II, and a tremendous growth in population, a once rural, sleepy Milford was awakened by a boom of housing and school construction. In this context, community members were concerned about the school district's capacity to manage the new pressures generated by the changing times. Within the district's administrative ranks and the board of education, "old hands" were being replaced by younger, more energetic individuals. These shifts generated considerable controversy.

The most significant shift was the hotly contested replacement of Walter Mc-Bride, the man who had been superintendent of the Milford School District for 27 years. This controversy set the occasion for the ripple in the traditional stream of Milford's history that included the designing, building, and staffing of the Kensington School. The debate that raged around the replacement of McBride reached such proportions that resolution was reached only after an outside commission was consulted. In the end, McBride was swept out of office, but the district responded to a rarely considered proposition: Hire a superintendent from outside the district. Action on this recommendation resulted in the hiring of a group of consultants, a contemporary version of the national "old boys network," by the Milford board. This group trained, selected, and controlled the careers and job placements of most of the major superintendencies in the country. Their choices for Milford's chief executive position were bright, young, ambitious, and cosmopolitan men with outstanding qualifications.

A majority of Milford's Board of Education—but not all—welcomed the idea of a new, young, dynamic superintendent to lead the district in a period characterized by growth and optimism in the community as well as in the nation. Eight new schools had been built in Milford during the latter years of McBride's administration, and the country swelled with pride from early space-flight successes and its firm stand against Russia over missiles in Cuba. As the nation's public eagerly anticipated Kennedy's "New Frontier," Milford awaited its new superintendent.

Steven P. Spanman, Ed. D., burst upon the scene ready and willing for a challenge, a young man clearly on the move, a rising star. Interpersonally, he was impressive and charismatic. He was described as "a man who could talk the birds out of the trees." He promised to bring quality, future-oriented education to the boys and girls of Milford. His impact on the small Milford community was nothing less than spectacular. In two short years, he arrived, found fertile soil for his ideas, and proceeded at a blinding pace to commit the district to a million-dollar construction agenda. He entertained national educational figures; placed the district in the national media limelight; involved his teachers in an ambitious and exhausting in-service program; altered the traditional district curriculum; rallied parents to his causes; and, of course, built the Kensington School—the embodiment of his radical and future-oriented ideas about schooling.

Spanman hired Kensington's first principal, Eugene Shelby, also an outsider, and together they planned and implemented a bold educational experiment. Smith and Keith (1971) summarized the progenitors' goals for Kensington as follows:

1. To assist pupils to become fully functioning mature human beings

2. To meet the needs of individual differences by providing a differentiated program
3. To provide the skills, the structures, and the understandings which will enable pupils to identify worthwhile goals for themselves, and to work independently toward their attainment. (p. 32)

At that time, the faculty somewhat whimsically typified Kensington's thrust as developing "fully functioning Freddies" for society's future. Spanman's and Shelby's ideology focused on the individual, and they encouraged the staff to develop an instructional technology that would allow children to reach their self-determined goals through independent means.

Smith and Keith (1971) described the ideal program that Shelby hoped to achieve, one that Kensington's first students did indeed encounter!

> The program was to capture team teaching with all of its varying organizational possibilities—ungradedness, total democratic pupil-teacher decision-making, absence of curriculum guides, and a learner-centered environment. The idea to prevail was primarily that of freedom from staid educational means which, in turn, would unleash both faculty and students from the difficulties of the traditional and move toward an "individualized learning program." (p. 11)

Shelby's effort to realize these ideals is the essential story of Kensington's first two years. His intellect, vision, and personality dominated that effort. But those years were also typified by frustration, conflict, and finally, capitulation. Unable to coalesce his staff around his program or to convince the school's patrons and the larger Milford district about the merit of his plans for the school, Shelby left Kensington halfway through the spring of the school's second year.

Spanman, too, was soon gone. It remains speculation whether he read the handwriting on the wall—the shifting political and economic climate in the district—or whether opportunity knocked fortuitously; but, still only 35 years old, he was provided a face-saving exit. After three years in the district and one year after Kensington was built, he requested a one-year leave of absence from his Milford superintendency to accept an offer to join the prestigious National Foundation, an innovative educational organization. Before the end of that year, Spanman resigned from the district, never returning to Milford but leaving his legacy—Kensington School.

Dr. Ronald George quietly became superintendent of Milford on May 27, 1966. George was an insider; he had taught in Milford for a dozen years, and his appointment as superintendent signaled an important return to the conservative educational values of the McBride era and the beginning of Milford's "back-to-basics" period. The cluster of tighter control and discipline, self-contained classrooms, use of textbooks as curriculum, and assign-study-recitation teaching methods that characterized George's agenda for the schools was also part of the mandate he received from the board at the time of his appointment.

The pace of events in the Milford district slowed in the first part of Dr. George's continuing tenure. Kensington was the last school built in the district. For a while, conflicts over bond issues and tax levies took on a less pressing and emotionally charged quality. The size of the district's student body continued to grow but at a slower rate. And the teaching staff was still riding on the salary increases of previous years. This period coincided with Kensington's golden years under Michael Edwards, the school's second principal.

We were told that Edwards joyfully accepted the challenge of the Kensington principalship; he had been a teacher and principal in the Milford district for 17 years, and boredom had begun to set in. And a challenge he got. He arrived at the school during the last months of Kensington's second year. The teaching staff, aroused by their memories of their departed leader, Shelby, refused to impart any allegiance to Edwards. At the end of that school year, 17 resignations from the Kensington staff were tendered.

When school began in the fall of 1966, a replenished staff greeted the students. Edwards had chosen both beginning and veteran teachers, but most came from within the Milford district. Unlike their earlier counterparts, this group was provincial rather than cosmopolitan, and many remained at the school for many years. The 600 students who entered Kensington in the fall of the school's third year confronted not only this new staff but also a reformed program. One of the staff members recalled that encounter and talked about the changes.

> The kids were not allowed to make as many choices. [In Shelby's era] they were allowed to make choices all day long, and choices in important things such as "Do I want to go to math class today, or do I want to go out and play."
>
> And I can remember talking to [Edwards] about it, and he said, "Oh no, the kids will have class." . . . We said to the kids, "This is the way we're going to do it now, we're all new, and this is what we've decided to do." The amazing part of this is the kids never said—or very seldom said, "But last year, we. . . ." I always found that very amazing.

Modifications in curriculum and instruction appeared to have been carried out swiftly and smoothly. District curriculum guidelines were adhered to more closely; teachers used more direct instructional methods; and students' learning activities were more scheduled and routine and less independent. These alterations endured throughout Edwards's first six years at Kensington.

With these changes came modifications in the building's design: The innovative play shelter, always cold, wet, and windy, was bricked in to become the school's cafeteria and gymnasium; the grandly conceived, but never realized "perception core" simply became the "resource center"; and the school's first interior wall was built in the basic skills area. This wall ended the total openness of Kensington's original design. Overall, however, the school retained its open feel, and visitors interested in its innovative design streamed continuously through the building. Edwards spent much less time with these guests than had his predecessor.

Despite Edwards's propensity for more structure in Kensington's program, he was an innovator in his own right. Though not in the "alternative of grandeur" style of Shelby, Edwards encouraged his staff to try new ideas and to experiment with curriculum. He was supportive of teachers' ideas and also took the initiative in bringing opportunities for change and renewal into the building. One teacher reported, "He was always searching for new things and better ways to do things." Edwards invited guest speakers into the school, arranged for workshops for his staff, and provided opportunities for his teachers to visit other innovative schools and programs.

The first six years of Edwards's tenure were Kensington's "golden years" in the memories of staff and community members. Unfortunately, Edwards's health began to deteriorate at the same time that major alterations in Kensington's community occurred. These contextual factors, particularly demographic shifts in the population of Milford, influenced all aspects of school life within Kensington and the district as a whole.

Beginning about 1964, Milford underwent extensive land development; vestiges of its rural roots all but disappeared. Numerous apartment complexes, shopping malls, subdivisions of small, inexpensive homes, and greatly expanded roads and highways were built. In the middle 1970s, the Milford community was qualified for federal housing support which made the apartment's affordable for minority families who sought better living conditions than those provided in deteriorating areas of the city. Over the next few years, the student population in Milford altered quickly and drastically; Kensington's student body shifted from less than 4% to 60% black.

Kensington's staff was ill-prepared for this rapid transition. Teachers found themselves unable to understand their students' language, distressed over students' behavior, and worn out by the instructional demands placed on them by the large number of underachieving students who suddenly filled their classes. Such perceptions led to drastic alterations in the Kensington program and plant. One teacher recounted:

> In those first years I don't ever remember having a child who read below fifth-grade level, and having them at fifth-grade level was rare. So now, all of a sudden, you had this whole bunch that—you had to revamp your thinking, you know, you couldn't teach them as a whole group. You had to revamp completely.

Another teacher joining this conversation said: "Yeah, that's sort of when the "divisions and all that fell by the wayside." "Divisions" referred to the continuous-progress grouping arrangement used at the original Kensington instead of the more traditional grade-level organization. The first teacher continued:

> And more and more teachers requested walls. That was the first thing they thought—I say they thought, "If I have two walls, one on each side, it will be better."

Thus, the radical shifts in pedagogy and plant that we found on our return to Kensington had begun with the fears of staff who suddenly faced a large number of students they did not understand. Their urgent need to find mechanisms to cope with the new student group drove them back to what was most familiar and to what seemed to offer hope for the most control: self-contained classrooms; structured, basic curriculum; and tight—sometimes coercive—discipline.

During this time of teacher adjustment and changing conditions, Edwards's health worsened. Despite his illness, he insisted that he would see the school through its trying times. He made concession after concession to the clamoring teachers. Interior walls continued to be built. During this difficult period, an appreciative staff closed ranks about their ailing leader. One of those teachers recalled:

> We watched him die is what we really did. We watched the man that used to run up the steps and run down the steps barely able to get up and have a very difficult time getting down. But never did he lose his finesse, his class, his ability to make a decision, or uphold someone, or to tell them they were wrong. . . . And even when he was in the hospital . . . his only desire was to get back to this school, because it was his school, this was his responsibility . . . and all this time we had problems. We had classroom problems, fights, knives, you know, we had problems. So we learned, in essence, to fend for ourselves, to go to different people to get assistance we needed. I spent hours on the phone at night getting parental assistance. . . . We just protected—I don't think central office ever realized for years how sick the man was.[2]

Shortly after Edwards's death, in appreciation of his dedication the community and district renamed the school the Michael Edwards Elementary School.[3]

Kensington's next principal was William Hawkins. He was preceded by one of Kensington's teachers, a woman appointed "teacher in charge," who many of the staff felt should have been given the principalship. As Hawkins, however, commented later:

> There are no woman principals in Milford, as I'm sure you're aware. There was one a long time ago . . . and she was relieved of her position. . . . There's not been a woman principal in this district since that time.

He recalled his view of the Kensington situation when he first arrived at the school.

> The first morning I come into school, out in front on the circle out here and up on the hill, there must have been 150 kids playing right out in the streets where the cars were coming in. So I decided something had to be done quick. I called the director of elementary education to come over, and he came over that morning and we walked around the building and broke up three fights the first time around.

---

[2] This assertion was strongly contested by a central office administrator, a "best friend." His contention was: "How do you handle a situation where a longtime, dedicated, and creative administrator doesn't want to give up, yet you know he is terminally ill?" He felt that there was no "good" solution.

[3] For clarity, we will continue to call the school Kensington.

I suspended three children, I think, that first week. And things began to cool a little bit. Every time I would call a parent, practically, their theory was "You've got to use a paddle up there at that school," and I hadn't been used to doing that. So I tried to break up the situation, and I began discipline and to control without it. But after a while, I finally decided that that was the way you had to do it.

Hawkins's administration of Kensington School was complicated by a host of factors that were beyond his control. The transiency of the school's newer families, for example, increased the turnover rate of pupils at the school. This problem reached a peak during the 1978–79 school year when 49 students enrolled after the beginning of the first semester and 102 left, a fluctuation of fully one third of that year's student body. In addition, the enrollment for the first time of Vietnamese children added the problem of non-English-speaking students to Kensington's agenda. Furthermore, the school's need for special education for handicapped, learning-disabled, and underachieving children continued to rise. Matters were worsened because, for 10 years, the district had been unable to pass a tax levy to increase school funds. Hawkins saw little opportunity to respond to the multiple needs of his school.

Despite Hawkins's frustration with and concern for the school and its students, he did not believe he could turn the school around. He was near the end of his career when we returned to Kensington, and like Edwards, his predecessor, Hawkins suffered debilitating health problems; he retired after a very brief tenure as Kensington's principal.

Dr. Jonas Wales, Kensington's current leader, assumed the principalship in 1979. He arrived at a time when the faculty was fatigued by their long struggle in a troubled school that had been without strong administrative support for eight years. He brought with him experience as an elementary school principal, solid connections with Superintendent George's conservative central office administration, and his own traditional views about education. The staff eagerly responded to his back-to-basics and law-and-order campaign. As a result, all remnants of Kensington's auspicious and innovative beginning gave way to traditional textbook curriculums, self-contained classrooms, paper-and-pencil instruction, and strict discipline.

Thus, after 15 years, Kensington had reverted to the "old Milford type." In our telling of Kensington's saga, we have accounted for the school's unusual appearance in an otherwise conservative district. We have introduced the major actors, superintendents and principals, and discussed their roles in the implementation of Kensington's grand plan and steady march toward the Milford mean. Finally, we mentioned many of the contextual issues that intruded on Kensington, influencing its origination as well as its culmination. We will return, now, to Kensington's organizational identities, 1964 and 1979. We believe these constellations of meanings are helpful in understanding the process of complex change in school organizations.

ELEMENTS IN THE CONFIGURATION
OF ORGANIZATIONAL IDENTITY

A great deal happened at Kensington and in its community between 1964 and 1979, and our brief saga relates many of the most crucial events that affected the school during that 15-year period. As we mentioned earlier, we were aware immediately that the Kensington to which we returned in 1979 was not the same school we first studied in 1964—somehow its *identity* had changed. This intuitive and metaphorical application of a construct borrowed from psychologists opened us to the notion that schools are constellations of special circumstances and unique individuals; although schools nominally share similar purposes and structures, they are different from one another in important ways. Similarly, as the story of Kensington illustrates, schools do change over time. As their contexts and memberships shift, their constellations are altered; new identities emerge. We believe the concept of *organizational identity* heightens awareness of the individualistic and dynamic nature of schools as organizations.

If an organization has an identity—a sum of parts that one can readily sense—what lies within that configuration? Just as theorists in psychology have attempted to discern the elements that typify individuals' identities—patterns of traits, motives, and schemas—we have found elements within the Kensington identities that can be compared from time to time during the school's history (McClellan, 1951). Comparing the alterations within these elements reveals much about the process of change that drove Kensington's radical shift in identity from 1964 to 1979. Understanding that complex shift is, after all, what we set out to accomplish. Thus, we explore several facets of Kensington's organizational identity: building, past as legacy, participants, program, and facades.

The Building

We were somewhat surprised at the ease with which a building could be changed—set in concrete or not. Significant modifications in Kensington's structure demostrated that school buildings, like other parts of an organization's identity, embody meanings and change over time. As individuals with authority came into association with Kensington and as their ideas, values, and purposes differed, the building was altered, reflecting successive beliefs and goals.

Since 1966, in Milford and probably in most school districts, the community, the school board, and the superintendent have shared a conservative and traditional philosophy of education. By this we mean that they were concerned with discipline, basic skills, and a recitation and textbook-based instructional style. In most, instances, any variation in the school day would be permitted only when those modifications furthered traditional tenets of schooling. At the district level, this traditionalism included the beliefs that education should be cost effective, that programs at all schools in Milford should be uniform, and that available resources should be dispersed equitably among buildings. This conservative view of schooling intruded at Kensington, a building that had been constructed to support a phioloso-phy of openness, creativity, and individualism.

On our return to the school, some of the obvious changes in the building in-cluded the erection of a flimsy principal's office in the center of a large central area that was once the open administrative suite; the conversion of the open play shelter to a lunchroom and gymnasium; the removal of a large aquarium; the addition of vandal screens and barbed wire; the transformation of the audiovisual nerve center to a remedial reading classroom; and, of course, the appearance of walls throughout the interior of the building.

With all of the advantages of hindsight, some changes appear to have been the result of poor planning on the part of Kensington's designers. The necessity of ringing the building roof with barbed wire, for example, might have been avoided by designing a building facade without the lattices that enticed students to climb to the roof. And the outdoor play shelter, now bricked in and serving as lunchroom and gymnasium, seems an improbable conception in a geographical area given to cold, wet, and windy winters. In an early planning meeting, however, the mere suggestion of a more conservative plan to construct a multiuse room rather than the covered play shelter had met sarcastic resistance; the cry "multiuseless room" had defeated the less flamboyant notion. It seems that practicality did not guide such decisions about Kensington's original design. Instead, a vision of a new education drove the planning of the school's progenitors.

In the years that followed, as the economic and political climate changed in the district and as old-guard administrators returned to power, that vision changed. As a consequence, this building that had symbolized Spanman's conception of the future of education was altered to resemble more closely buildings of the "old Mil-ford type" and to support a more traditional form of instruction. The construction of the enclosed principal office provided a place for private conferences with parents and obstreperous or frightened children in an era of tight discipline. Lux-uries like the "acting tower" and rear-view projection screen were simply aban-doned, fragments of another era and a debunked vision. Lastly, more than any other change, the construction of walls throughout the building signaled the end of Spanman's dream. Their erection occurred during the transition of the school's student population. The staff worried about how they would cope with their new charges. Their response was almost uniform: build walls, regain control, and Prin-cipal Michael Edwards had bowed reluctantly to those demands.

Thus, the very architecture of an educational vision and the bricks, mortar, and plaster that had brought it to life had been changed. A tangible part of Kensington's first identity had evolved into something recognizably different. The importance of those modifications to the more traditionally oriented men and women who came to Kensington over the years is underscored by the fact that Kensington's recon-struction was accomplished during years of difficulties with tax levies, tight budgets, and resource limitations.

The Past as Legacy

An aspect of the organization called Kensington that struck us in the original study was the liability of its newness. When the school opened its doors for the first time, it had no traditions, no set procedures, no history. In our first report on the school, we stated:

> School personnel, probably like people in general, usually do not appreciate what it means to have a history. To possess a past is to have a social structure or "sets of alternative actions, or tendencies to act in certain ways . . . and the constraints that specify or limit these alternative actions. . . ." A major part of an origin of an organization centers on generating or building these sets of alternatives and the constraints that define them. (Smith & Keith, 1971, pp. 81–82)

The past as legacy, then, develops as people within an organization go about their business, day to day, year to year. Traditions had developed at Kensington over time, and many of these were important to the staff. The school's annual Halloween party, for example, would probably continue to be held each year despite the present principal's reservations about its merit.

More central to a school's formal mission are its standard operating procedures. Here, too, Kensington had accumulated its share. By the time Principal Wales came on the scene, much of the Kensington faculty had worked together for a long time. They had struggled through periods of hardship in the absence of a strong leader. They had evolved their own ways and means. Part of Wales's success with the faculty stemmed from the way in which he fit into those patterns. Rather than disrupt the established Kensington operating procedures, Wales supported and strengthened them. He provided a line of authority for the teachers that stretched right to the superintendent and board of education. The opening days of his administration proceeded smoothly, because he followed the staff's lead. As we watched, we had the feeling that the school was virtually running itself. Thus, a sense of history can provide continuity for an organization, and that continuity can strengthen the organization's purpose—two valuable assets in the uncertain environment that surrounded Kensington as Wales assumed his post.

There is another aspect of the past and its legacy: reputation. Deserved or otherwise, reputation accrues as an organization evolves, as agents and clients pass through it, and as persons tell, retell, and interpret events associated with the group. This aspect of an organization may not always be beneficial. In Kensington's case, reputation developed from the notoriety the school achieved at its outset. For example, faculty members who had been at Kensington since its third year said that they still received remarks about the "favorite-son status" attributed to the original building and faculty, references to what many in the district had considered lavish and wasteful spending at the school. Apparently, some members of Milford's staff still carried a grudge.

Another faculty member related that she had decided to join the Kensington faculty only after an opportunity to teach at the school during a summer session had presented itself. Previously, she had been put off by the school's open, unstructured, anything-goes reputation. The summer job dispelled the myth for her, and she happily transferred to the school shortly after. The point is that reputations linger and affect decisions and actions in organizations long after the bases for those reputations have dissipated. Part of a school, it seems, is what it once was.

This phenomenon occurred within the school as well. Michael Edwards, the school's second principal and the one who remained for 10 years, became the standard by which subsequent Kensington principals were judged. Our records contain comments from central office staff indicating efforts to give succeeding principals a chance in the school: "Yes, Mr. Edwards was special, but. . . ." Similarly, teachers' perceptions of earlier students—their racial and economic background and academic performance—was the mark against which contemporary student groups at the school were measured. The past lingers in the present, sometimes making life more difficult for new actors in old settings.

The past contributes to organizational identity. As an organization proceeds about its business, its past accrues. Some of it hangs on with surprising tenacity and potential to shape the future. Perhaps this view of the past is most important in an action or policy framework in which one can determine where an organization has been, where it is, and where it is most likely to go. As persuasion and consensus building seem to proceed most often within a historical context, knowledge of that context seems an important tool for any leader.

Stars, Heroes, and Troopers: The Interpersonal Culture[4]

Organizational identity is a composite. We have discussed two parts thus far: Kensington's building and the school's past. Another major facet of the school's identity was and continues to be its staff. Four principals, dozens of teachers and instructional specialists, and a bevy of secretaries, aides, nurses, cooks, and custodial staff have, for 15 years, strived to help children—each person in his or her own way. Sometimes their approaches differed markedly. Sometimes, as in 1979, their attitudes toward working with children have been relatively uniform. Regardless of attitudinal differences, however, Kensington's organizational identity has always been shaped by its stars, heroes, and troopers.

Stars and Heroes. From the very beginning of our association with Kensington, we were struck with the ideological or cultlike quality of the organization. These terms apply to groups—religious or secular—with strong, if not excessive, devotion to an individual or ideal. That impression of the organization's past remains strong and has been developed into a major analytical theme in the overall study.

---

[4] To us, these terms connote several kinds of esteem. Some of the Kensington staff who reacted to an earlier draft of this paper saw the latter as pejorative. One individual at the school commented wryly and compared "stars" to shooting stars that blaze brightly for a brief moment before disappearing forever.

Cults develop around strong, charismatic leaders—the group's stars or heroes. Spanman and Shelby were the leaders in the Kensington saga who moved Milford parents and the board to an emotional pitch that permitted the implementation of a radical educational innovation in a conservative community. Edwards was the revered, long-term principal of the school, the man whose name the school bears today. Although each was a prominent actor in the Kensington story, each is remembered differently, and the impact each man had on the organization differed greatly.

Spanman and Shelby were the stars in the Kensington story. Their roles were large and dramatic for a short period of time. Today, however, Shelby is little remembered and rarely discussed at the school. Spanman's contributions are discussed but not felt. In the district office, reactions to Spanman varied from strongly negative ("The mess we were left with, including the ridiculous building, the Kensington School") to strongly positive ("the most exciting years in my . . . decades in the district"). The predominant memory, however, is one of ambivalence—admiration for Spanman's intellect and energy combined with skepticism about his ideas and their relevance for a community like Milford.

The hero, of course, was Michael Edwards, principal of the school for 10 years, remembered as the man who died in office, the man who never stopped trying to help his students and staff. Edwards's heroism in the collective memory of Kensington's staff did not result from total success, from achieving the ideals the school represented. In fact, he was the man who relented to the wishes of his staff and watched wall after wall built to divide the inner space of the school. He was admired, rather, for his mettle, his determination to keep trying. His most lasting contribution to Kensington was the memory of a better time at the school, a memory that sustains teachers today by providing a sense of direction and purpose.

Kensington's stars created the emotional fervor that characterized the school when we met the first faculty, but in retrospect, that pitch was short-lived. Edwards's leadership, on the other hand, sustained the school for a decade. The emotional character of the school changed with his guidance; true belief gave way to professional respect. With his passing, cults and ideologies at Kensington also died.

Troopers. Leaders unquestionably influence the identities of organizations, but by virtue of numbers alone, staffs can also have significant impact on the idiosyncratic nature of organizations. When the staff consists of persons who perform their duties largely unobserved by administrators or by one another, its power to shape an organization grows. When, as in Kensington's case, strong leadership is absent for a period of time, we must look to the staff as a potent contributor to organizational identity.

The 1979 Kensington staff was comprised of many experienced teachers, half of whom had been hired by Michael Edwards in 1966. Another fourth of the staff joined the group during Edwards's tenure. This group of old hands was dispersed across grade levels at the school. Many of the teachers were good friends outside the school context. Some had taught for a time with Milford's superintendent at another elementary school. Several of this group carried informal administrative responsibilities at the school in addition to their regular classroom tasks. In our view, this is a formidable set of credentials that would allow an informal faculty social system to gain a great deal of influence over the proceedings of an organization. It was an aspect of Kensington that an alert administrator needed to understand. As we indicated earlier, it was an aspect that Wales recognized and supported rather than bucked.

One daily occurrence at the school provided a mechanism for the maintenance of the staff's collegiality and like-mindedness. This routine event was the morning coffee klatch, when the faculty gathered in the staff lounge above the resource center. Over the years we observed in the building, various arrangements had been made by the teachers for sharing the cost and work of morning coffee. A refrigerator had been added that permitted noncoffee drinkers to have milk, juice, and soda accessible.

A number of teachers regularly arrived early with their newspapers, handwork, or catalogues of clothing, crafts, or teaching materials. Some entered with students' assignments still to be graded, a task they accomplished casually over their morning drink and cake. But it was the quality of their conversation that made the time so special. Their chatter was folksy and familial. The majority of their conversations, though, centered on their students and their classrooms. From kindergarten to sixth grade, in regular class, music, or P.E., the foibles, the problems, the triumphs of these teachers with their students were exchanged in light banter.

The significance of the morning coffee klatch was that it provided a time when the staff could gather, could share experiences that normally occurred behind closed doors, could add meaning to their lives through comparison and parable. This is the stuff from which community is ultimately built—shared experience with significant others that leads to the formation of norms and builds organizational identity.

The development and maintenance of this kind of community within an organization has many implications. The morning gatherers meld. The formation of such a group within a school faculty means that the members are no longer entirely individuals or an aggregate of individuals. They evolve group perspectives and procedures as well as means to socialize newcomers to the organization and to sanction activities and attitudes. At their best, such groups can act as stablizers in difficult times in schools. (Metz, 1981). At their worst, they become significant barriers to creative change and innovation in educational organizations (Hargreaves, 1975). In many schools, it is the one setting where "democracy" prevails.

Gatherings such as the early morning coffee klatch—freely attended, without agenda, with open discussion, with people speaking their minds about the mundane and the significant—are social mechanisms of considerable importance. They are of vital interest for those who seek to understand, lead, or change schools, as well as for those who wish to build meaning into their day-to-day professional activities, careers, and personal lives.

One last reflection grows from the consideration of the teacher group at Kensington in 1979. These teachers' expressions and acts in many instances revealed an affinity for a reasonably identifiable cluster of beliefs, values, and customs that we associate with a rural way of life. This cultural aspect of the teacher group has changed over years at Kensington and has variously meshed or conflicted with leader and student cultures. We have charted this plurality of cultures at Kensington at three points in its history: (a) Shelby's beginning year, 1964; (b) the midst of Edwards's golden years, 1970; and (c) the first year of Wales's tenure, 1979 (see Figure 2). A comparison of the principals finds that the "cultures" they embodied— the constellation of beliefs, values, and norms that they represent—differed in each instance (Jackson, 1960). We have described the first man as white, cosmopolitan, and innovative; Edwards, by comparison, was white, suburban, and moderate in his approach to education and educational change. Lastly, Wales is presented as white, rural, conservative, and local.

At the same three points, we found the first teachers to be predominantly white, innovative and creative, cosmopolitan, and true believers. The second group was white, traditionalist, localist, and of rural origin. The second and third groups were similar (the same individuals made up more than half of each group), but they differed dramatically from the earliest group of teachers we encounted at the school.

	1964	1970	1979
Principal	White Innovative	White Urban/suburban Moderate	White Rural Conservative Localist
Teachers	White Creative Innovative Cosmopolitan True Believers Lower-middle-class but upwardly mobile	White Traditional Conservative Localist Rural origin Lower-middle-class	White Conservative Rural Traditional

Pupils
and Their
Families
	White
	Conservative
	Traditional
	Localist
	Lower-middle-class
	  in origin and goals
		White
		Traditional
		Conservative
		Localist
			Majority
			  Black
			  Urban
			  Transient
			Minority
			  White
			  Upper-lower to
			    lower-middle-class
			  Traditional
			  Conservative
			  Localist
			Small Vietnamese
			  group

Figure 2 The cultures of the Kensington School.

Finally, the chart shows the student cultures at the school changing drastically over the 15 years. At the first point, students represented a white, conservative, localist, lower-middle-class population. At the second point, they appeared much the same: white, conservative, localist, and lower middle class. But by the beginning of Wales's tenure, the majority of the student group was black, urban, and transient. One distinct minority in the school was comprised of white, conservative, upper-lower-class and lower-middle-class students. Another very small, but distinct group comprised Asian children, recently arrived Vietnamese.

The point of drawing these comparisons is to note that congruency between leader, teacher, and student cultures existed only in Edwards's era. The greatest incongruency among groups has occurred most recently, and those differences are increasing. It seems that this cultural plurality complicates the task of educating Kensington's youngsters. We commented at one point on the distinctly different languages used at the school on our return: a black student dialect that teachers found difficult to comprehend; a rural white idiom that could be confusing to untuned urban and Asian ears; and Vietnamese—no adult in the school had any understanding of the language or the culture. This problem, and we believe it is a significant problem for educators, transcends Kensington's boundaries. For example, in a recent study of principals' activities, one school was encountered in which 16 languages and 26 dialects were spoken as primary languages by families within the student group (Dwyer, Lee, Rowan, & Bossert, 1983). The problem at Kensington pales by comparison. Yet the dilemma of cultural and linguistic pluralities in schools remains an enigma for educators who work on the opposite side of these barriers from their students—particularly in a period when basics are being stressed and the teaching of standard English is a common and a primary objective of instruction in many schools.

In sum, organizational identity is greatly affected by those who participate in organizations. At Kensington, the stars, heroes, and troopers all made their contributions over the years as they interacted among themselves and with their students. In the long run at Kensington, it seems that it was the long-term staff members who contributed the most to the school's nature and who were responsible for what continuity there has been in that setting.

The Instructional Program

Perhaps the least distinctive component of Kensington's organizational identity in 1979 was its instructional program. Reviewing our notes about the school's classrooms and the activities within them stirred memories of other elementary schools in which we had worked, particularly Washington Elementary School, an unremarkable inner-city school, whose classroom dynamics were studied by Smith and Geoffrey (1968). This very fact, however, is extraordinary from the perspective of change; in 15 years Kensington's innovative instructional program had reverted to the "old Milford type," the antithesis of what the school was to have represented.

A chart, created by Principal Shelby early in the school's history, had been designed to illustrate what Kensington was to have accomplished. That same chart, reproduced as Figure 3, ironically captures the school's programmatic reversal. Originally, it listed a series of from-to statements. Reversing the "from" and the "to" columns accurately portrays the kind of program we found at the school in 1979, marking Kensington's steady drift over the years.

We have already reported the staff's perceptions of a changing student body—lower-ability students; less interested students; children of broken and transient homes; children with less respect for authority and with little self-control—of changing economic and political climates, of faltering leadership at the school, and of the reemergence of the community's fundamental conservatism to explain the direction of the school's pedagogical U-turn. In the remainder of this section, we wish to comment further on some of the changes we found on our return trip.

The Shift in Goals and Objectives. "I'll try to get you ready for junior high." This comment, expressed by a sixth-grade teacher addressing his students on the first day of school, aptly represented the more immediate, practical, "realistic" goals held for students by Kensington's 1979 faculty. Talk of developing "fully functioning Freddy" was completely gone.

This narrower conception of schooling—getting the student ready for the next grade level—assumes a rational, hierarchical arrangement of distinct bits of knowledge that can be progressively imparted to students as they wind their way through the K-12 organizational structure. This frees a teacher from feeling solely responsible for students' development, since he or she is only one cog in a complex, multilevel education system. Within this arrangement, the integration of acquired skills and knowledge is largely left to the student. It is an opposing view to the holistic vision that guided Spanman, Shelby, and the original faculty. John Dewey (1916) discussed such views of education as related to opposing views of childhood. The 1979 Kensington staff would see childhood as a readiness phase for adulthood. The

From	To
Passive, reactive pupils	Active, initiating pupils
Pupil followership	Pupil leadership
Restriction of pupils	Freedom for pupils
External discipline	Self-discipline
External motivation	Self-motivation
Group activities	Individual activities
Restricting pupil interaction	Encouraging pupil interaction
Teacher responsibility for teaching	Pupil responsibility for learning
Teacher planning	Teacher-pupil planning
Teacher evaluation	Teacher-pupil evaluation
Teacher as a dispenser of knowledge	Teacher as catalyst for inquiry
Teacher as controller of pupils	Teacher as organizer for learning
Identical roles for teachers	Differentiated roles for teachers
Closed, rigid social climate	Open, flexible social climate

Figure 3. The institutional plan's redefinition of teacher pupil roles. From Anatomy of Educational Innovation (p. 34) by L.M. Smith and P. Keith, 1971. New York: Wiley. Copyright by John Wiley & Sons, Inc. Reprinted by Permission.

original faculty would tend to view childhood as a convenient nomenclature for one portion of the continuous experience of life. The purpose of schooling varies between these conceptions. For the first, school is a mechanism for preparation, for doing something in the remote future. In the latter, schools exist to provide places for children to perform their life's work, experiencing.

The Shifts in Staff Organization and Specialization. When Kensington received its first students, the staff was organized differently from most schools. Grades 1 and 2 were combined into the Basic Skills Division, and 4, 5, and 6 constituted the Independent Study Division. Three teachers shared the third-grade students in a program called Transition that readied students for the independent and individualized program they would begin the following year. Grade levels were not emphasized in this arrangement. Instead, the plan called for students to master skills at their own rates, independent of their ages and of the rates of their cohorts. In the Basic Skills Division and Transition program, teachers tended to function in similar ways and were each responsible for a variety of instructional contents. In the Independent Study Division, on the other hand, teachers functioned as subject matter specialists and met with students as the students required their services. In all levels, the teaching staff was bolstered by numerous aides who were needed to monitor the independent progress of students.

In 1979 we found that this organization had shifted to a traditional, self-contained classroom pattern. The special needs of students were serviced by a number of remedial specialists who operated on a pullout basis, that is, students were removed from their regular classes for brief periods of specialized instruction. In the classrooms of older students, some informal departmentalizing occurred; one teacher offered all the science, another offered math instruction, another social studies, and so forth.

On our return, it was the complex program of remediation that was most strikingly different. Learning-disability classes, remedial reading, speech therapy, individual and group counseling with parents and students, and special language classes for the few Vietnamese children who attended the school competed for time, space, and resources. Public Law 94-142 was responsible for much of this proliferation, and the district and county had added their own special education initiatives.

Classroom teachers fretted over the trade-off between the benefits of these services for individual students and the disruptions the programs created for regular classroom instruction. The principal openly admitted that the necessary coordination required to gain the maximum benefit of the multiple programs was too complex for him to develop an organized plan. Instead, teachers bargained their priorities with one another in the fairest and most meaningful way that they could. Too, Dr. Wales placed a great deal of faith in the classroom teacher's ability to adapt to the special needs of his or her students. He worried over the time students spent outside those homeroom environments. His skepticism affected the teachers and frustrated some of the specialists.

In many ways, the integration of these multiple remedial programs into the predominantly self-contained classroom pattern that typified Kensington in 1979 produced an organization that was every bit as complex as the 1964 individualized approach had been; complicated scheduling and the coordination of curriculum and instruction between teachers were still required. In our earlier analysis of Kensington's efforts at team teaching, we raised a number of thorny issues about unintended consequences of instructional programs that required a good deal of coordination. At Kensington in 1979, in a traditional instructional setting of self-contained classrooms, we were surprised to find that our caveats remained germane. In 1964, we raised these issues as points of departure for further research. We reiterate those here, in the belief that they actually address a broader array of educational contexts than we suspected in 1964. They deserve serious consideration in any schooling situation where coordination, decision making, resource allocation, and specialization are at issue (Smith & Keith, 1971).

1. Teaming requires the most sophisticated form of interdependence, what Thompson (1967) calls reciprocal, and the most difficult kind of coordination, mutual adjustment. This coordination is very time-consuming and expensive in communication and decision making. Organizations and individuals with limited resources (time and energy) must divert them from other activities, for example, on occasion productive effort such as teaching, itself.

2. As various hierarchical levels of decision making are introduced (for example, teaming), decision-making freedom at the lowest level (teacher-pupil) is constrained. For those who speak of "democracy" in the classroom, teaming raises serious incompatibilities.

3. Unless individual skills are unique in kind or highly developed in degree, teaming as reciprocal interdependence will be higher in cost than it is productive of benefits.

4. As teams increase in size, from two to more than two [teachers], for example, seven, these effects are magnified.

5. Because of faddism and emotionalism instead of analysis in professional education, the new elementary education that offers team teaching to the practitioner contains mutual incompatible elements leading to latent and unanticipated negative consequences–dysfunctions. (p. 234)

Shifts in Instructional Materials. It was immediately apparent on our return that instructional materials had also changed. Fishing poles had given way to textbooks that kids could call their very own and to ditto sheets, lots and lots of ditto sheets.

The transition to textbooks began in Edward's era, and teachers reported that the change was readily accepted by the students. A first impression on the first day of school in 1979 was that the textbooks provided continuity in the instructional program from grade to grade; despite new teachers and classrooms, students began their work with little hesitation and few questions or comments.

When teachers agree with the scope, content, and sequence of activities in textbooks and when the texts match the ability level of the students using them, presumably results can be very positive. The 1979 staff, however, commented on several occasions that these conditions were not always congruent; yet the adoption of the text series preempted much of their prerogative to make adjustments.

In brief, the use of textbooks has a host of consequences. Some seem instructionally beneficial and others seem problematic. In an earlier analysis of a textbook-based instructional program, we commented on a number of these consequences. That same analysis is relevant to Kensington and is included here as Figure 4.

One way in which Kensington's staff was able to modify or supplement the school's textbook program was through the use of ditto work sheets. This type of seat work was ubiguitous at the school. Teachers listed the following reasons for the common use of dittos:

1. Need for repetition in the practice of basic skills;
2. Need for a way to occupy students while working with individuals in other groups;
3. Relative inexpense of materials;
4. Availability and ease of production;
5. Congruence with back-to-basic mode of instruction; and
6. Classroom control

The staff did not address potentially negative consequences such as student boredom, incompatibility with textbook objectives, or students' inability to relate these discrete activities to larger learning objectives.

Like the return to partitioned classrooms, the progressive use of texts and dittos at Kensington seemed another response to the staff's need for control, their perception of the needs of the new student body, and the influence from the back-to-basics surge in schools. In addition, the district's renewed conservative thrust and economic difficulties gave momentum to the instructional shift. These themes emerge again and again as we think about the changes in Kensington's organizational identity.

Facades and Realities: "What You See Is What You Get"

This cliché, "What you see is what you get," summarizes for us much of our feeling about today's Kensington Elementary School. It also captures another important way in which the school has changed and one final element of the configuration we are calling organizational identity.

In 1964, we suggested that different realities existed at Kensington, and we discussed them in terms of facades, doctrines, and day-to-day activities.[5] In common-sense language, we were trying to distinguish among what was talked about, what

---

[5] "Reality" even when used in quotations carries implications of the sort suggested by Kurosawa's (1969) *Roshomon* or Durrell's (1960) *The Alexandria Quartet*. For the moment, we would define reality as that part of the social world about which substantial intersubjective agreement exists among observers and participants.

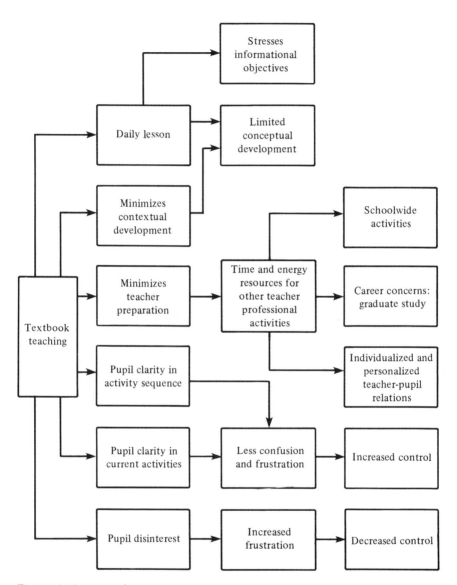

Figure 4. Impact of textbook teaching on aspects of classroom and school social structure and processes. From *The Complexities of an Urban Classroom.* (p. 183) by L.M. Smith and W. Geoffrey, 1968, New York: Holt. Copyright 1968 by Holt, Rinehart & Winston, Inc. Reprinted by permission.

existed in writing, and what occurred in the behavioral and social realms at Kensington. Our point was that there were substantial gaps among these versions of reality and that those gaps led to both anticipated and unanticipated consequences for the early Kensington.

As our heading suggests, these gaps have narrowed at today's Kensington to the point of being nonexistent. In general, this convergence seems desirable. The complex task of educating children seems easier when the multiple groups that participate in the enterprise share a common knowledge about events in the school.

The convergence of realities is particularly useful when an organization's goal is stability and when the system is nearing some form of equilibrium. When change is desired or new visions are pursued, however, differeing realities may serve a purpose. The innovator can argue that the system has greater potential and is not living up to its aspirations. In this sense we recall a familiar line from Browning that was popular around Kensington in its earliest days: "A man's reach should exceed his grasp or what's a heaven for?" Contrasting this passage with the "What-you-see-is-what-you-get" cliché crystallizes the differences in this final aspect of Kensington's organizational identity in 1964 and in 1979.

CONCLUSION

As we have described, the Kensington envisioned by Spanman and Shelby is gone. For better or for worse, the once innovative elementary school has been physically and programmatically altered to offer more traditional educational fare. The major purpose of this essay has been to argue for the importance of a concept such as organizational identity for theorists and practitioners who want to talk with increased clarity and potency about schooling and about innovation and change in schooling. The data are from an intensive case study of the Kensington Elementary School at two points in time: first reported in 1971 in *Anatomy of Educational Innovation* and then in 1979 in *Kensington Revisited: A 15-Year Follow-up of an Innovative Elementary School and Its Faculty.*

Although we had anticipated change at Kensington, the magnitude and complexity of that change after 15 years exceeded our expectations. Increasingly, as our study and analysis progressed, we found a warm and human story filled with hopes and despairs. We came to understand this organization's overall change as the consequence of the interactions of a large cast of characters who sought to adapt to shifting economic, political, and demographic conditions within an increasingly complex educational system.[6] We found that individual entrepreneurship, personal conviction, friendships, and serendipity explained much more of Kensington's change than did rational decision-making, bureaucratic fiat, or pedogogical and organizational expertise.

---

[6] We explore this complexity of the Kensington story in Smith, Prunty, and Dwyer (1981).

In order to preserve aspects of this story that were more personalistic and contextual, we turned to elements from the Kensington experience that captured the many alterations that brought about the overall change in the school's "nature," "complexion," or "feel." We called the constellation of those elements organizational identity. We suggested that the physical structure that houses an organization is a significant aspect of its organizational identity; the design and ultimate uses of a structure may embody the values and goals of the people who work within it. We explained that an organization's past is carried on through reputation and evolved operating procedures and that this history affects the present. We discussed the importance of individuals in organizations and their impact on organizational identity. Our conclusion is that those individuals who remain the longest and attend to the more routine details of a group's work may have the greatest influence on the group's identity. We further discussed a shift in the nature of Kensington's work, in both process and content, and how that shift made the organization distinctly different from what it once had been. Finally, we commented on the convergence of realities at Kensington that had also contributed to the school's organizational identity.

Thus we find the organization, Kensington School, to be distinct from other elementary schools. In the beginning, it was different by virtue of its innovative structure and program. In 1979, Kensington remained unique. Although its edifice and program were much more similar to other elementary schools in Milford and the nation, its identity had evolved through its own staff and patrons' responses to, and interactions about, policies, politics, personal agendas, and a host of chance events. We suspect that in order to understand the process of complex change in any school or organization, learning about the evolution of its organizational identity would bring one much closer to that understanding.

REFERENCES

Becker, E. (1968). *The structure of evil.* New York: Free Press.

Berger, P., & Luckman, P. (1967). *The social construction of reality: A treatise in the sociology of knowledge.* New York: Anchor Books.

Bernstein, R. (1979). *The restructuring of social and political theory.* Philadelphia PA: University of Pennsylvania Press.

Blumer, H. (1969). *Symbolic interactionism: Perspective and method.* Englewood Cliffs, NJ: Prentice Hall.

Charters, W.W., & Jones, J.E. (1973). On the risk of appraising non-events in program evaluation, *Educational Researcher, 2,* 5–7.

Dewey, J. (1916). *Democracy and education* New York: MacMillan.

Durrell, L. (1960). *The Alexandrian Quartet.* New York: Dutton.

Dwyer, D., Lee, G., Rowan, B., & Bossert, S. (1983). *Five principals in action: Perspectives on structional management.* San Francisco CA: Far West Laboratory for Educational Research and Development.

Gowin, B. (1981). *On educating.* Ithaca, NY: Cornell University Press.

Hargreaves, D. (1975). *Interpersonal relations and education.* London: Routledge & Kegan Paul.

Hirst, P. (1973). The nature and scope of educational theory: Reply to D. O'Connor. In G. Langfield & D. O'Connor (Eds.), *New Essays in the Philosophy of Education.* London: Routledge & Kegan Paul.

Jackson, J. (1960). Structural characteristics of norms. In N.B. Henry (Ed.). *The dynamics of instructional groups.* Chicago: University of Chicago Press.

Jahoda, M. (1958). *Current concepts of positive mental health.* New York: Basic Books.

Kurosawa, A. (1969). *Roshomon.* New York: Grove.

McClellan, D. (1951). *Personality.* New York: Dryden Press.

Metz, M. (1981). The closing of the Andrew Jackson elementary school: Magnets in school system organization and politics. In S. Bacharach (Ed.), *Organizational behavior in schools and school districts.* New York: Praeger.

Nagel, E. (1961). *The structure of science.* New York: Harcourt, Brace, Jovanovich.

Peters, T., & Waterman, R. (1982). *In search of excellence: Lessons from America's best-run companies.* New York: Harper & Row.

Scott, W.R. (1978). Theoretical perspectives. In M. Meyers, (ed.), *Environments and organizations,* San Francisco: Jossey Bass.

Scriven, M. (1959). Truisms as the grounds for historical explanations. In P. Gardner (Ed.), *Theories of history.* New York: Free Press.

Smith, L. M., Dwyer, D., Prunty, J., & Kleine, P. (1983). *Innovation and change in American education, Kensington revisited: A fifteen year follow-up of an innovative elementary school and its faculty.* Washington, DC: The National Institute of Education.

Smith, L.M., & Geoffrey, W. (1968). *The complexities of an urban classroom.* New York: Holt.

Smith, L.M., & Keith, P. (1971). *Anatomy of educational innovation.* New York: Wiley.

Smith, L.M., Prunty, J., & Dwyer, D. (1981). A longitudinal nested systems model of innovation and change in schooling. In (S. Bacharach (Ed.), *Organizational behavior in schools and school districts.* New York: Praeger.

Thompson, J.D., (1967). *Organizations in action.* New York: McGraw Hill.

Struthers, M. (1971). Educational theory: A critical discussion of the O'Connor-Hirst debate. *Scottish Educational Review, 4,* 71–78.

Weber, M. (1947). *The theory of social and economic organization.* Oxford, England: Oxford University Press.

PART III
FOCUSING ON EFFECTIVE SCHOOLS

Interest in effective schools is currently high at the national, state, and district levels. Two factors have contributed most to this recent surge in interest. First, the recent publication of a spate of national reports generally lamenting the poor condition of education has spurred the Reagan administration to sponsor a set of schooling reforms that focus on stiffening graduation requirements and extending the time students are in schools. This call to raise standards has an intuitive appeal and has found its way into the recent legislation of a majority of states. Second, the research-based efforts of Brookover, Beady, Flood, Schweitzer & Wisenbaker (1979), Edmonds (1979), and Rutter, Maugham, Mortimer, Ousten & Smith, (1979) to both identify and describe the characteristics of schools that surpass expectations with respect to student achievement have caught the attention of practitioners nationwide. Many school districts have taken the lists of characteristics generated by these researchers and incorporated them into school improvement projects in an effort to create their own effective schools.

Unfortunately, this extended attention on the need to create more effective schools has not resulted in anything approaching a consensus about either the form or substance of school improvement. The 30 or so national reports, for example, have serious limitations as a reform agenda for creating effective schools, because they offer no single definition of an effective school. Moreover, with the exception of Boyer (1983), Goodlad (1984), and Sizer (1984), none of the reports, and thus the reforms they advocate, is based on analysis of data collected from schools. Consequently, the reforms are little more than simplistic and ungrounded solutions to complex problems. Elementary and junior high schools are largely ignored in the reports. The high school is seen as the locus of the problem and therefore the schooling level requiring reform.

The effective schools research is flawed, because it too fails to offer a single definition of an effective school. Perhaps more importantly, however, it fails to detail what schools currently identified as effective did to become effective and what they presently do to remain effective. Moreover, this research suggests a "one best model" approach to school improvement, i.e., transport the effective schools practices to less than effective schools. While the majority of this research focuses on high-achieving elementary schools, it has little to say about effective junior high and high schools. Missing from the current national debate on creating effective schools are data that illuminate (a) how the key components of schools identified as effective actually function within the social context in which the school is located, and (b) how effective elementary and secondary schools may differ. The four chapters in this section address this omission.

Sizemore (chap. 8) details the key organizational factors important to producing high achievement in three predominantly black elementary schools. Pushing beyond the existing research on effective schools, which she suggests is short on descriptive detail about process, Sizemore compares three schools by focusing on (a) organizational goals; (b) the relationship between the school, parents, community, and central administration; (c) school climate; (d) interractional patterns between principals, teachers, and students; and (e) instructional routines. In illustrating different paths to effectiveness, Sizemore details the importance of characteristics of the local school setting to the development of goals and organizational procedures.

Next Noblit examines the degree of fidelity to the middle school ideology as an indicator of effectiveness. Three unusually effective middle schools in different communities are compared. Noblit details considerable variation between the schools and concludes that following the middle school formula is not the key to effectiveness. Instrumental to both the form and substance of the three schools was the past history of the schools and the current belief system of the local board and superintendent.

In Chapter 10, Pink details the key elements of an effective junior high school. Using a case study approach, Pink emphasizes the importance of (a) people; (b) curriculum; (c) governance; and (d) the relationship between school, parents, and central administration, to school effectiveness. His research highlights the importance of the localized school community, i.e., school, parents, central administration, in reaching the educational goals developed by the community. On the issue of creating effective schools, Pink concludes that it is not so important to attempt to transport *how* things are done from school to school as it is to focus on *what* is done. In short, schools would have greater success in becoming more effective by focusing on key improvement components and working *within* the constraints of the local setting than by attempting to superimpose on schools an improvement model that disregards the local context.

Finally, Garibaldi describes the similarities and dissimilarities of eight effective high schools. What emerges from his analysis is (a) the importance of several key components to effectiveness (e.g., strong and diverse curricula, highly able and committed staff, orderly academic climate, effective leadership); as well as (b) the range of ways in which each of these components can be successfully operationalized. These differences, Garibaldi argues, are in great part a function of the social context in which schools are grounded (e.g., they vary in size and geographic location as well as in race and social-class composition). Again, the message is that while there are important components of schooling that must be addressed if high schools are to become more effective, the "one model" approach to school improvement appears misguided.

REFERENCES

Boyer, E. (1983). *High School: A report on secondary education in America.* Princeton, NJ: Carnegie Foundation for the Advancement of Teaching.

Brookover, W., Beady, C., Flood, P., Schweitzer, J., & Wisenbaker, J. (1979). *School social systems and student achievement: Schools can make a difference.* New York: Praeger.

Edmonds, R. (1979). Effective schools for the urban poor. *Educational Leadership, 37,* 15–27.

Goodlad, J.I. (1984). *A place called school.* New York: McGraw Hill.

Rutter, M., Maugham, B., Mortimer, P., Ousten, J., & Smith, A. (1979). *Fifteen thousand hours: Secondary schools and their effects on children.* Cambridge: Harvard University Press.

Sizer, T.R., (1984). *Horace's compromise: The dilemma of the American high school.* Boston: Houghton Mifflin.

8

The Effective African American
Elementary School*

BARBARA A. SIZEMORE
University of Pittsburgh

The effective African American school is an abashing anomaly in the public school system and not the result of ordinary organizational routines. In fact, such a school forces the system to explain the existence of ineffective African American schools. It also raises questions about standard operating procedures (SOPs) and policies which allow such ineffective schools to operate. The National Institute of Education (NIE) funded this study in School Year (SY) 1979-1980. The study had two objectives: (a) to determine organizational factors important to producing high achievement (scores at or above the national and/or local mean on a standardized test in reading and mathematics achieved by a majority of the students) in three predominantly African American elementary schools, A, B, and C (K-5); and (b) to identify any differences between these high-achieving schools.

Allison's (1971) Organizational Process Model (OPM) revealed the schools' desired ends (goals) and priorities and determined to what extent the schools' outputs approximated these goals. The underlying assumption of the OPM was that governmental behavior could be understood less as a result of deliberate choice than as outputs of large organizations functioning according to complex routines coordinated through SOPs. Additionally, unsought consequences of established routines, SOPs, repertoires, and random behavior (means) were examined and analyzed to ascertain whether or not they were satisfactory, unimportant, or trivial. If the routine achieved the goals, it was considered functional. If it did not, it was classified as dysfunctional.

This study viewed the generation of standardized test scores in reading and mathematics at or above the national and/or local norms by a majority of African American poor students in a school as effective performance. The researchers fully understood however, that this attainment was not the sole criterion for quality education. Indeed, we felt that standardized tests were culturally biased and often presented precepts and concepts alien to the culture of the African American student

---

*Funds from the National Institute of Education (NIE-G-80-0006) supported this research. The views expressed here are not necessarily those of NIE, and no official endorsement should be inferred. Readers interested in a more extended report of this study should see Sizemore, Brossard, and Harrigan (1983).

175

(Hale, 1982; Hilliard, 1976; Stodolsky & Lesser, 1967). However, because of the chronic failure of most schools servicing these clients to teach them how to read and to compute, and considering that the study schools were accomplishing these goals better than most, we accepted test scores as the criterion. Nor did we mean to imply that the attainment of the national and/or local norms by more than 50% of the students was an indicator of excellence or the best that African American students could do. We simply recognized that the African American schools accomplishing this feat were doing more than the majority of such schools.

The effective schools chosen for this study were grounded in this multidimensional concept: Effective schools result from the routines in place at a given time. These routines were created by the school actors who had developed a consensus around high achievement as a goal. This consensus was influenced by a strong, aggressive, "take charge" leader who developed routines which led toward the adopted goal. School actors deferred to this strong leader because they were obligated by his/her assumption of responsibilities which furthered the means to the goal. This multidimensional concept is reinforced by research findings.[1]

This research on effective schools focused on strong leadership but failed to speak to the routines and daily activities of the leader and staff. Studies pointed to the importance of individual buildings but did not explain how their operation made a difference. Goals, consensus, control, and coordination as well as the characteristics of staff and principal were stressed in various works; however, much of the research called for more examination of the factors influencing the origin of the climate of instruction, the buildings where this climate occurred, and the activities of the staff and principal.

In short, there was the need to: (a) secure more data on the activities and routines of the principals and teachers; (b) determine their goals, attitudes, expectations, and characteristics; (c) explore their relationship with parents, community, and the central office administration; (d) characterize the climate of the school, the interaction patterns between teachers and principal, among teachers, teachers and students; (e) describe the discipline procedures and instructional routines; and (f) link all of these phenomena with outcomes, usually the elevation of achievement and the establishment of discipline. Since we were concerned with outcomes, we sought a theoretical frame which would provide a lens for such a focus and a methodology which would permit accurate and detailed description.

Throughout this chapter the unhyphenated name, African American, has been used to identify the black population, previously called Negro, colored, and black. African Americans have called themselves many names since their ancestors were torn from their tribal moorings in Africa and deprived of their histories. The hyphen is not used to emphasize this rupture. African Americans are not connected. The African Americans' change of name reflects their enlightenment over the centu-

---

[1] See, for example, the work of Brookover (1978), Brookover (1979), Edmonds (1979, 1981), Edmonds and Frederickson (1979), Hoover (1978), Lezotte and Passalacqua (1978), and Weber (1971).

ries about the " double-consciousness" introduced by W.E.B. Du Bois in *The Souls of Black Folk* in 1903. [2] Therefore, African American is used in this article to illuminate the meaning of the contradictions of this double-consciousness.

This chapter will: (a) explain the research paradigm; (b) describe the context and setting of the study; (c) discuss the outcomes produced by the study schools; (d) present the differences between the study schools; (e) detail the organizational goals; (f) describe the routines observed in teaching, administration, supervision, and coordination; and (g) make policy recommendations.

THE RESEARCH PARADIGM

OPM emphasized organizational output and was to discern the behaviors the organizational components exhibited in the implementation process in terms of outcomes delivered by routines, scenarios, and processes. A *routine* is a series of repetitive activities which are related to a goal such as high achievement in reading. A *scenario* is a series of routines, and a *process* is a series of scenarios. OPM permitted the study of the organizational routines, scenarios, and processes (SOPs) which produced high achievement. OPM was operationalized through nonparticipant observation supplemented by interviews, questionnaires, documents, school board minutes, reports, and records used to describe the SOPs of the school, and the beliefs and behavior of the school actors. This work is called *ethnography*.

Each school in this study represented a general style of life for the culture exhibited by the actors in the environment. *Ethnography* is the task of describing these cultures exemplified by the knowledge the school actors used to generate and interpret their social behavior. This involves both the investigators' points of view as well as the actors' points of view (Singleton, 1967; Spradley & McCurdy, 1972). *Culture* is defined here as the complex whole which includes knowledge, beliefs, art, morals, law, custom, and any other capabilities and habits acquired by persons

---

[2] Du Bois (1903/1967): discussed the double-consciousness in this way:

After the Egyptian and Indian, the Greek and the Roman, the Teuton and Mongolian, the Negro is a sort of seventh son, born with a veil, and gifted with second sight in this American world–a world which yields him no true self-consciousness, but only lets him see himself through revelation of the other world. It is a peculiar sensation, this double-consciousness, this sense of always looking at one's self through the eyes of others, of measuring one's soul by the tape of a world that looks on in amused contempt and pity. One ever feels his twoness–an American, a Negro; two souls, two thoughts, two unreconciled strivings; two warring ideals in one dark body, whose dogged strength alone keeps it from being torn asunder.

The history of the American Negro is the history of this strife–this longing to attain self-conscious manhood, to merge his double self into a better and truer self. In this merging he wishes neither of the older selves to be lost. He would not Africanize America, for America has too much to teach the world and Africa. He would not bleach his Negro soul in a flood of white Americanism, for he knows that Negro blood has a message for the world. He simply wishes to make it possible for a man to be both a Negro and an American without being cursed and spit upon by his fellows, without having the doors of Opportunity closed roughly in his face. (pp. 16-17)

as a member of society (Wallace, 1970). Semistructured interviews were conducted with the teachers and principals to determine their characteristics, goals, and priorities. Parent questionnaires were also constructed and distributed, but the return on these was good for only one school, School A. The structure of the schools was studied: the roles, informal and formal organization, routines, programs, and priorities. In addition, goals stated by the principals in their interviews were codified. Using suggested categories from Firestone and Herriott's (1980) matrix on goal selection, priority, and consensus, an instrument was developed to determine the degree and kind of agreement existing among the teachers' goal choices and priorities and those of the principals. This instrument was called the professional staff questionnaire (PSQ). These data were all cross-checked with observations. Our intent was to use the steps in Glaser and Strauss's (1967) intensive field study approach called the Constant Comparative Method of Qualitative Analysis (CCMQA) to gather, categorize, and codify the data for the ethnography.

Each principal was observed in his/her office for two school weeks (10 days). Each classroom teacher in each school was observed 5 days (Monday through Friday) from December 1, 1979, through June 13, 1980. During July, August, and September, 1980, each researcher read the observations from the three schools and formulated questions to be included in the principals' interview schedule administered in November and December, 1980. The PSQ was composed of 310 statements taken from the principals' goal responses in the principals' interviews. It was administered to the teachers to determine the goals of the school, the teachers' priorities, and the routines which implemented these goals. These 310 statements were categorized under five scales: achievement, administration and supervision, discipline, teaching and teacher autonomy, and parent and community relations.[3]

These scales were further coded into subscales. First, the respondents were asked to prioritize their goals using the five scales as indicators. Second, they were asked to agree or disagree with a statement and to show the intensity with which they felt this agreement or disagreement. A large number failed to respond on the intensity scales on many items; therefore, these data were not used. The data which were reported were indications of teacher goal priorities and teacher agreement or disagreement with the 310 goal statements of the five scales which appeared in the instrument. This agreement or disagreement was then used as an index of consensus. Consensus was defined as unanimity of opinion in either direction. Reported percentages represented the relative frequency or the percentage of the number of respondents in a school who responded in one direction; however, in Table 1 the reported percentages represent the percentage of the number of scale items which received a level of consensus between 60% and 100%. Low consensus was set at 60 to 69%. Middle consensus was set at 70 to 89%, and high consensus was set between 90 and 100%.

---

[3] The Professional Staff Questionnaire scales were divided into a number of subscales. *Parent Community Relationships:*(a) to improve parent involvement; (b) to improve parent-school communication and relations; (c) to work on joint school-community projects to improve

Table 1. Percentage of Scale Items Reflecting Teacher Consensus
On the Five Scales of the PSQ for Schools A, B, and C

School A		School B		School C	
Scale	%	Scale	%	Scale	%
ACH	75	ACH	66	ACH	89
DIS	71	TTA	59	TTA	83
AS	66	PCR	58	PCR	72
TTA	59	DIS	55	AS	72
PCR	52	AS	36	DIS	70

ACH = Achievement; AS = Administration and Supervision; DIS = Discipline; PCR = Parent and Community Relations; TTA = Teaching and Teacher Autonomy

As expected, the highest level of consensus occurred in all three schools on the achievement scale. The investigators predicted that achievement goals would have the highest priority in the high-achieving schools. Also predicted was the ranking of the schools. School C was expected to show higher consensus than School A which was expected to show higher than School B. This occurred; and School B was predicted to have a higher level of consensus between teaching and teacher autonomy than School A which was expected to rank higher than School C. This did not occur. Nor did the prediction that the ranking for all schools would be: (a) achievement, (b) discipline; and (c) administration and supervision (see Table 1). We predicted that discipline would be the second most important goal for the teachers in the study schools. In examining the results, we considered that the level of consensus among the teachers in School C on this scale was nearly the same as the level of

schooling outcomes; and (d) to create a feeling of family within the school and community. *Teaching and Teacher Autonomy:* (a) to have inputs into decision-making; (b) to determine one's own curriculum; (c) to set rules for administration and supervision; (d) to determine teacher-pupil relationships; and (e) to improve teacher relationships. *Administration and Supervision:* (a) to communicate with parents and the community in order to improve relations; (b) to monitor progress of students in reading, mathematics, and writing; (c) to monitor teaching progress and evaluate teaching performance; (d) to identify problem areas in discipline and to improve student discipline; (e) to identify problem areas in teaching and to support the teacher; (f) to adjust the curriculum to meet the needs of the students; (g) to complete paperwork such as recording test scores, central office reports, and such; (h) to make decisions about the school and to coordinate school routines; (i) to be a student advocate; (j) to communicate with teachers and staff; (k) to ensure everyone's safety in the school; (l) to prepare schedules in a fair manner accounting for teacher comfort and expertise and student needs and characteristics; and (m) to improve relations between teachers and students. *Achievement:* (a) to improve basic skills in reading and mathematics; (b) to reinforce basic skills in reading and mathematics; (c) to cover other required courses; (d) to supplement required basic skills achievement; (e) to learn about black history, culture, and literature; and (f) to elevate achievement scores on the MAT. *Discipline:* (a) to achieve compliance and obedience to school rules; (b) to improve study skills; (c) to improve social skills; (d) to improve attendance and punctuality; and (e) to monitor and correct one's own behavior.

teachers at School A on the same scale, although the ranking was different. Consensus percentages on the last three scales for School C approximate the percentages of the first two scales for School A. School B is the different school.

In order to categorize all incidents, all observations were read by each investigator. Each categorized the descriptions by school history, size, enrollment, organization, and structure; classroom size, enrollment, organization, and structure; student characteristics; teacher characteristics, consensus, and goals; principal characteristics and goals; goals, both formal and informal, actor-specific and subject-specific; activities, functional and dysfunctional; and processes, functional and dysfunctional. Two types of organization were coded, vertical, concerned with the placement of students in groups from entry to exit; and horizontal, concerned with the placement of students in groups for teachers to teach; accelerated, average and low. Two tiers of horizontal grouping appeared: (a) students were separated into groups by reading skill mastery achievement using scores from criterion referenced tests forming three kinds of classes; and (b) students within these classes were grouped according to their progress and advancement.

Structure was defined as the presence of rules, regulations and directives and the dominance of routines for their execution enforced by a hierarchical authority. Classrooms in this study were classified as high, flexible, and loose according to the amount of structure observed in the organization and operation of their routines, scenarios, and processes. In highly structured classrooms, a unilateral teacher-student relationship prevailed. The teacher's authority was constantly recognized and rarely challenged or questioned. Students generally played a passive role in these classrooms. Orders were given and followed. In the flexibly structured classrooms the teacher had a different style of management to attain goals. The school rules provided the basic structure for the operation of the classroom, but adjustments were made to maximize goal attainment. These classrooms were firm but pliable. The teacher's authority was recognized and the teacher-student boundaries were clear. But the teacher shared a participatory relationship with the student. In the loosely structured classroom settings the absence of a clearly defined authority was apparent. Students were constantly asking for consistent boundaries and testing the teacher. Teachers spent a great deal of time trying to assert their authority, and students constantly tried to push back the boundaries. Keeping the students occupied with a task was a technique frequently used to get compliance. It usually failed.

THE CENTRE CITY SCHOOL SYSTEM (CCSS)
AND THE STUDY SCHOOLS

The CCSS had 21 schools which were 70% or more African American in the years 1976–1979 and 22 during the 1979–1980 school year. School rankings were determined by how many times a majority of the students in each grade scored at or above grade level in reading and mathematics on the Metropolitan Achievement

Tests (MAT) during the spring testing (posttest) during the 5-year period commencing spring 1975. There are five testing checkpoints in K-5 schools, one for each grade in reading and one for each grade in mathematics. Any K-5 school which is at grade level in reading and mathematics in every grade would have a perfect score of 10 for each school year and 50 for the 5-year period. Three schools were selected: School A, B, and C, all of which were 89% or more African American and 50% or more poor. The highest-ranking school was School C with 46 points. School A had 31 points and School B had 23 points.[4] Two other schools ranked higher than School B. One was excluded because it was only 75% African American, and another was excluded because of its recent emergence into this top group and an uncertainty about the stability of its performance. When the principals of these three schools were approached about being included in the study, two were enthusiastic about their participation and the third was reluctant. The latter felt that we would create community and/or central office intervention in the affairs of the school, thereby disturbing its serenity, solidarity, and success. The two enthusiasts thought the study would bring them long overdue recognition and acclaim.

The Organization of the CCSS

The CCSS was divided into 71 elementary and 24 secondary schools during SY 1979-1980. Of these there were 10 middle and 14 high schools. Additionally, there were two Occupational and Vocational Training Exploratory Centers (OVT) and four special schools. The elementary schools were of four kinds: K-3, K-5, K-6, and K-8. During SY 1979-1980 the system was unified. All elementary schools were made K-5, and all children in grades 6-8 attended middle schools accommodating those grades. This was a part of the desegregation plan implemented in September, 1980. Under this plan School A was desegregated. There were 23,634 African American students in the CCSS in 1979, a decline in African American enrollment. The African American membership decreased by 5,098, or 18%, between 1969 and 1979. The total school population declined from 72,722 to 43,795, or 33%, between 1973 and 1979. African American students constituted 52% of the students population in 1980.

Students were placed in groups in classrooms by chronological age. These groups were called grades. The pupil-teacher ratio in elementary schools was determined by counting the number of pupils in grades 1-6 and 1-8 (excluding students in special education which includes Educable Mentally Retarded or EMR, Learning Disabilities or LD, Brain Injured or BI, Socially and Emotionally Disturbed or SED, and The Scholars Center for the gifted and talented, and classes for students who failed such as Project Pass) and dividing by the number of teachers (excluding teachers of special education and of classes for children who failed). The computation of the average class size in elementary schools did not include sections in classes for chil-

---

[4] School B should not have been chosen for this study since it did not achieve 50% of the time as was the criterion (25). It had, however, been in the top group for five years.

dren who failed, kindergarten, special education, and remediation classes provided by Title I or Chapter I programs funded under the Elementary and Secondary Act (ESEA) of 1965. The average class size was computed by summing the total number of students in each academic section and dividing by the total number of academic sections. The city-wide average for pupil-teacher ratio was 18.7:1 and 22.3 for class size. Schools A, B, and C had pupil-teacher ratios of 18.8, 16.6, and 18.8, respectively, and average class sizes of 21.4, 20.3, and 22.3, respectively. The city-wide average for general fund expenditure for the school was $1565.62. This did not include the cost of plant maintenance and operation. Poverty data in the CCSS was obtained from requests for free and reduced lunch fees. Although these data were not completely reliable, coupled with the census reports on the socio-economic status (SES) of the area, School A, B, and C were classified as low-income schools with 74, 57, and 92% of students receiving reduced or free lunch. School B and C were 100% African American during SY 1979-1980, and School A was 89.35% African American.

The CCSS was organized in a hierarchical line from the 9-member Board of Public Education (BPE) elected from nine school districts to serve 4-year terms on a staggered basis with four being elected at one time and five at another. There were six whites and three African Americans on the BPE during the study year. The three African Americans were all males and all had doctorates; two were professors at the local university and one a minister. Of the six whites, five were female and one, male.

The superintendent of schools during the study year was an insider having worked in the CCSS as assistant superintendent. He was appointed on November 20, 1973, and served until August, 1980. He was very wary of our original study proposal which sought to compare high-achieving predominantly African American schools with low-achieving ones and did not approve it. He thought all schools showed growth if not achievement. Under the superintendent was a deputy superintendent to whom three assistant superintendents and a director of educational program development reported. The deputy and two of the assistant superintendents were African American. Principals reported to the assistant superintendents, elementary, middle, and high schools. The main help for school principals was the instructional supervisor who worked directly with school teachers. Supervisors were considered ineffective by principals because their assignments were too large, and although teachers said that the supervisors were willing to provide services and were helpful whenever they did so, most of those interviewed considered the supervisors' contribution to high achievement as minimal.

Teachers were represented by the Centre City Federation of Teachers (FOT), and the building representative was the agent of the union in any work location, functional division, or group. Every school had an FOT representative and the BPE-FOT agreement stipulated that the principal should meet at least once a month, if requested, with the FOT building committee to discuss professional concerns and recommendations; such meetings were to be held at mutually agreeable times. The BPE-FOT agreements limited the principals' control over recruitment and transfer of teachers. Many factors such as teacher seniority and longevity were constraints. Teachers were evaluated twice a year by principals, and the process of firing a teacher was initiated by the building principal. But, it took two consecutive unsatisfactory ratings sometimes given by two different principals, since teachers rated unsatisfactory had the right to transfer. Principals rarely rated teachers unsatisfactory in the CCSS before 1980.

The BPE majority developed board policy which was interpreted by the superintendent who directed the deputy superintendent, who, in turn directed those under him. But little monitoring or supervision seemed to occur in a consistent way to accomplish system goals and philosophies as stated for public consumption. What monitoring or supervision there was seemed to protect jobs and parochial interests and privileges. Ineffective and incompetent personnel were often retained, relatives were frequently employed, and instruction and high achievement became secondary concerns, especially in African American and poor schools.

ACHIEVEMENT AND GROWTH: THE OUTCOMES

Because the evaluation of principals was cursory, compliance with system goals was uneven across schools. In 1978, the superintendent of the CCSS set forth the following goals for SY 1979-1980: (a) greater achievement in fundamentals . . . reading and mathematics . . . as measured by national standards; (b) improved student attendance; (c) improved cumulative school holding power; and (d) improved standards of student conduct. These goals had been the same since September, 1976, and, although they were not established as the formal goals in 1980, attemps to effect improvements in each were to continue to be an inherent part of the instructional program. The assistant superintendent in charge of elementary schools added two process goals for all elementary schools: (a) a positive warm teaching climate; and (b) the creation of a positive relationship between home and school. A new superintendent was hired in August, 1980, however, and different goals were established for the future.

When reviewing the draft copy of the final report of the study, the School B principal said that her school should be presented as an effective school since high growth had been attained 85% of the time during the 5-year period preceding the study and the year of the study. She said that a school where the majority of the students entered with low base-line scores should not be expected to reach the National norms in achievement at the same rate as a school where the majority of the students entered with high base-line scores. Achievement was often displaced by growth in many African American and/or poor schools as a high-priority goal. Principals judged the effectiveness of their students' progress by however many months' growth in achievement had occurred between the October and May standardized test scores. Where students had maintained 7 to 9 months growth, progress was deemed acceptable although the achievement scores remained low (see Table 2). The numbers in the table represent the number of grades where achievement was high (equaled or exceeded the city or national norms) and growth was high (equaled

Table 2. Achievement and Growth: SY 1975-1976 through 1979-1980

	School	N of Grades	% of Grades	N of Grades	% of Grades
HIGH	A	0	0	22	55
ACHIEVEMENT	B	1	2.5	12	30
	C	1	2.5	35	87.5
	A	0	0	18	45
	B	5	12.5	22	55
	C	0	0	4	10

LOW	GROWTH	HIGH

or exceeded the city or national norms) or where they were both low or where one was high and the other low. The horizontal axis represents growth with the left end showing low growth and the right end, high. The vertical axis represents a-chievement with the bottom showing the low achievement and the top end, high. The test used was the MAT. Grade 1 was excluded since there were no growth norms for this grade, because the MAT was not administered to students in kindergarten. School A was a K-6 school in SY 1975-1976 and Schools B and C were K-7. Only scores for Grades 2, 3, 4, and 5 were used. The total number of times a grade score appeared, therefore, was 40. Each school produced two scores for each grade, a total of 8 times 5 years, or 40. Twenty-two times out of 40, School A accumulated scores which were high in achievement, or 55% of the time, while high growth occurred 100% of the time (40 times out of 40). For School B, high a-chievement occurred 13 times out of 40, or 32.5% of the time, while high growth occurred 34 times out of 40 or 85% of the time. At School C high achievement occurred 36 times out of 40, or 90% of the time, while high growth occurred 39 times out of 40, or 97% of the time.

This important finding reveals the necessity of looking at growth through achievement. It is not enough to say that a school is effective, if only high growth occurs unaccompanied by high student achievement. Although high growth is necessary to reach any set achievement goal, it is not sufficient. Normal growth expectations must be exceeded when students' base-line achievement levels are too low. In School B, the output was low achievement in reading and high achievement in mathematics with high growth in both. Yet, the high growth in reading was not high enough to yield high achievement. Growth rates had to be increased in order to bring students who were below the national norms up to that standard.

In Table 2, School B had one grade high in achievement but low in growth. In other words, the mean score for the grade was at or above the city or national norm for that grade in that subject, but the growth norms for that grade were below the norm. There were five grades low in achievement and growth. Twelve grades were high in achievement and high in growth and 22 were low in achievement and high in growth. For School B, 2.5% of the grades were high in achievement and low in growth; 12.5% were low in both; 30% were high in both; and 55% were high in growth and low in achievement. Fifteen percent of the grades at School B were low in growth; 85% were high in growth; 32.5% of the grades at School B were high in achievement and 67.5% were low in achievement.

In Schools A and C, routines were operationalized to increase growth rates. These routines: (a) institutionalized high expectations; (b) increased time for instruction; (c) provided differential treatments for individual variation; and (d) emphasized conceptual development when pacing lagged. Study skill mastery instruction consisted of one to one teacher-student interactions sometimes called direct instruction; but this was not practiced as stimulus-response behavior characteristic of Bereiter-Englemann's (1966) process.[5] Here students were given information by lecture or demonstration, or both. Then students demonstrated their understanding by application. Teachers gave immediate feedback, and students corrected their mistakes. A variety of activities were pursued until students mastered the skill and/or concept. Differential treatments involved grouping students according to skill mastery, providing more difficult work for those who were advanced, and easier and more concentrated work for those who lagged behind. Students in the middle progressed along the expected curriculum. Students who lagged behind also received additional instruction in concept development. The assumption was made that they lagged behind because their understanding of the conceptual framework undergirding the skill to be learned was faulty. All treatments were buttressed with homework.

The effect of attendance on high growth and high achievement was obvious. Missing a month by absence meant that these students had to grow 7 months after only 5 months instruction (between pretest and posttest or from October to May, minus vacation). Students commencing 3 months behind had to make 10 month's growth after only 5 months of instruction. Slow students who were absent compromised their chances of reaching high achievement. The lowest-achieving school, School B, had the highest student absentee rate (see Table 3, column 5). The lowest absentee rate was held by School A which was the highest-achieving school during SY 1979-1980: School A was the only study school with an attendance program. Twenty-three percent of School A students, 36% of School B students, and 25% of School C students were absent in excess of 11 days during the study year.

At Schools B and C attendance and achievement groups negatively correlated for some groups and positively correlated for others. High absenteeism among the higher-achieving classes in grades 1, 2, and 3 eroded the high growth gains made

---

[5] Bereiter and Englemann's (1966) process of direct instruction is derived from behavior modification theory. It is a verbal didactic curriculum model with emphasis on teacher–child interaction and a de-emphasis on child–child interaction and child–material interaction. The theoretical orientation holds that learning, which is defined as changes in behavior, can be most efficiently induced through instruction involving repetition of associations between teacher's stimulations and the child's responses. Although direct instruction was employed at Schools A and C, more child–material interaction was employed than is dictated by Bereiter and Englemann. Moreover, skill mastery instruction involved more concept development and more consideration of the African American culture and language.

Table 3. SY 1979–1980 School Differences

	1	2	3	4	5	6	7
School	Average total teaching experience (N of years)	Total N of teachers	N of Black teachers	N of Male teachers	Average N of student absences per school year (in days)	% of students transferred in and out (1979–1980)	Student enrollment (June, 1980)
A	10.2	26	5	3	4.5	16	368
B	7.2	18	5	6	7.6	57	197
C	16	18	9	2	6.8	32	327

	8	9	10	11	12	13	14	15
School	Tenure of principal (N of years)	Style of principal	N of external programs	N of K-5 teachers[a]	N of SS teachers[a,b]	N of SE teachers[a,c]	N of teachers with M.A. degrees[a]	N of teachers with ME[a,d]
A	12	Authoritarian	2	12	6	3	6	13
B	3	Collegial	6	10	6	2	6	2
C	12	Authoritarian	3	12	4	2	6	5

[a] The number cited in these columns represents the number out of those reponding to the PSQ.
[b] SS means special subject.
[c] SE means special education.
[d] ME means M.A. equivalency; one teacher at School C had a doctorate.

there; and, conversely, high absenteeism among the lower-achieving students in grades 4 and 5 made it difficult to catch up. High achievement at School C was maintained to some degree in spite of this condition by its intense instructional regimen, its militant time expansion prerogatives, its persistent pursuit of skill mastery and its highly controlled, centrally coordinated environment.

Generally, at Schools A and C, high achievement and high growth were the result of three factors: (a) goal consensus among the school and community actors; (b) high expections for student achievement by the school actors; and (c) choices of functional routines which yielded high achievement. The outputs of high growth and high achievement resulted from the principals' basic decisions which generated consensus among the teachers and the community around achievement as the highest priority goal. This stimulated teachers to choose functional routines. While these schools were high-achieving according to the definition used in this study and compared to other predominantly African American and poor elementary schools in the CCSS, there were some differences between them (see Tables 3 and 4).

Table 4. Percent of Students At or Above Grade Level in the Basal Readers and on the MAT by School and Grade

School	Basal Reader (June, 1980)	MAT (May, 1980) Reading	Math
A			
Grade:			
1	63	71	75
2	52	74	70
3	35	70	50
4	25	79	86
5	34	73	77
B			
Grade:			
1	.3	71	80
2	0	54	59
3	.2	38	70
4	31	37	52
5	25	31	37.5
C			
Grade:			
1	49	75	98
2	26	93	93
3	22	63	83
4	16	38	63
5	11	48	70

SCHOOL DIFFERENCES

In Table 3 the study schools are compared on 15 criteria. School B differs from Schools A and C on the following: (a) faculty mobility and experience; (b) number of male teachers; (c) students mobility; (d) student enrollment; (e) student SES; (f) student absenteeism; (g) principal's tenure and style; (h) the number of extra programs in the school; (i) the number of K-5 teachers and the number of teachers with a master's equivalency; and (j) the structure of the classrooms. There were more loosely structured classrooms at School B, which was the only school with split grade assignments in one classroom. School C was alone in the use of departmentalization where students passed in classes to different teachers for subjects such as reading, mathematics, language arts, social studies, and science. Most students passed in classes to different teachers for the special subjects, music, art, library, and physical education in all three schools, and some passing occurred by informal arrangements at School B.

Unlike the other principals, the principal of School B who was in her third year as principal neither grew up in Centre City nor was she educated in its public schools. Although she was less authoritarian she depended on central office more for assistance and problem resolution. She had no formal vehicle for parental and community involvement outside of the regular PTA, parent representatives of Title I, or Headstart. School A had a parent advisory program and School C had a "School C Family" consisting of teachers, students, and parents of conforming and achieving students.

Finally, School A was the only school practicing student advocacy where students had the right to grieve over teacher practices. School B, additionally, had a school board member as a parent of three children in Grades 2, 3, and 4 during the study year; the vice president of the FOT taught third- and fourth-grade reading; and the relative of one of the high officials in the CCSS taught third- and fourth-grade mathematics.

ORGANIZATIONAL GOALS

Organizational actors in the OPM face situations where decisions have already been made and their choices are confined by these previous actions. However, in the cases of Schools A and C, the leaders counteracted many decisions which had been made prior to their appointments regarding goals, instruction, curriculum, coordination, and control. Sometimes they worked within constraints and sometimes they simply ignored them. First, each principal believed that the African American poor student could learn and that high achievement in reading and mathematics in an African American poor school was possible. Next, Schools A and C principals were willing to take the risks necessary for the selection of high achievement as a high priority goal. Third, as a protection against sanctions from their superiors, principals engendered loyalty from their faculties by their hierarchical independence or willingness to disagree with their superiors and by their tendency to obligate their teachers to them through the assumption of student discipline and parental conflict. Because of this loyalty, teachers accepted their principals' rigorous monitoring of their teaching and student progress in reading and mathematics (Blau & Scott, 1962). Lastly, Schools A and C principals chose functional routines for goal achievement. These seemed best accomplished by moderately authoritarian approaches, using selective sanctions in a flexibly structured environment where there was staff and student stability.

In School A, the principal made a conscious decision to make the school a part of the community. He saw the principal as an educator responsible to the community's needs and best interests. He disagreed with the superintendent about the interpretation of his community's goal priorities. He was open and candid about this disagreement and his goal priorities. His first priority was to build a strong healthy self-image in his students. Second, he wanted them to acquire academic skills and knowledge. Third, he wanted his students to learn to cooperate with others, and, lastly, to transfer those skills acquired to the community. He spent a great deal of time pursuing these goals. He extended the school program into the community; he was a part of the community and concerned about its development, because he believed that whatever affected the community would affect the school. This extended-family concept was based on the assumption that parents should be knowledgeable about the school and equipped to evaluate what happens there. School A parents were always welcome and parental involvement was solicited. Guidelines for this participation were mutually developed and respect was generously reciprocated. Many claimed that the parents abdicated their responsibilities to the principal who enjoyed widespread respect and deference. The School A principal was an African American male in his late forties, a native of Centre City who attended the CCSS, having spent some time in special education classes by error as a retardate. He earned his doctorate in education from the local university, came up from the teaching ranks in the CCSS to be an assistant principal, and, finally, principal of School A.

The highly authoritarian principal of School C disagreed with the superintendent on goal priorities also, but she did not openly state this disagreement. Rather, she incorporated his goal relating to parent participation as a high priority, but did not establish any effective routines for its operationalization. She held on to her high-priority goal of high achievement in reading and mathematics. She believed that some of her parents could not make their children behave in school well enough to progress at the expected rate; therefore, she usurped some parental prerogatives, earning their animosity. Furthermore, she disagreed with her superiors on instructional methods and routines. When confronted about these disagreements or parental complaints, she relied on her established record of high achievement for support from her School C Family and her board representative. Her advanced learners' parents served as a buffer against both central office and community opposition, and the high structure of the school was a protection against any uncertainty within School C's technological core.[6]

In School C unsolicited parental cooperation was unwelcome and discouraged. Because of the inability of some parents to discipline their children, the School C principal isolated her school from the community, creating the School C Family which was a substitute for the community. Within this buffer spanning mechanism, she substituted the School C Family's values for the community's values. The School C principal was an African American female in her early fifties, who was a native of Centre City, having attended the CCSS and earned both of her degrees from the local university. She, too, had come up from the teaching ranks, served as an assistant principal, and had been principal of School C for 12 years.

The principal of School B valued teacher professionalism and believed in delegating her authority to the teachers. Yet, in this school, there was an unresolved conflict between the teachers and the principal over the management of discipline and parental conflict. Teachers attempted to recruit parents to assume the responsibility for the discipline in School B, once it was clear that the principal was not going to do it. School B operated on two principles: collegiality and specialization. The goals were developed by negotiation and bargaining with the faculty and were not different from those of the superintendent. Although the principal stated that high achievement in reading was a high-priority goal, she displaced it with high growth and traded off the former for the latter. Her goals were also affected by her steady reliance on system-approved external sources for supervision and altered by the needs of these sources. The School B principal was an African American female in her middle forties. She was a native of a small mill town near Centre City and was educated in its schools. She earned her doctorate in education from the local university. She had come up through the teaching ranks, served as assistant principal, and had been principal of School B for the past 3 years.

The personal interests and seniority of the principals also affected their goal priorities. The willingness of the Schools A and C principals to buck the system and to deviate from the low-achieving norm for African American schools was reinforced by their disinterest in promotion in the school system. Having accepted the possibility that they would not receive a promotion if they failed to cooperate with central office personnel by working within the system's rules and regulations, Schools A and C principals showed no hesitation in questioning central office

---

[6] Thompson (1967) viewed the organization in terms of technology, domain, structure and task environment. The chief problem was dealing with uncertainty through the utilization of norms of rationality. For Thompson, instructional action derived from man's expected outcomes and his beliefs about cause and effect relationships. Technology or technical rationality was a means to the production of these outcomes by actions based on his beliefs. On the other hand, organizational rationality was the combination of technological activities, plus inputs and outputs. Organizational rationality faced constraints, contingencies and variables in the total environment in which it was located. In schools, the technology was teaching.

practices. These principals were loosely coupled with central office and tightly coupled with their faculties. The loosely coupled view of organizations stresses the autonomy of the individual actor in the system and the absence of centralized control of behavior, especially with regard to instruction (Weick, 1976). In contrast to Schools A and C, the School B principal was tightly coupled with central office. She followed the system's rules, even when they were dysfunctional. School B data reflect a school hierarchically dependent on central office direction and supervision although professing to practice collegiality.

DISCIPLINE, COORDINATION, AND CONTROL

The principals of Schools A and C were firm overseers, strictly monitoring reading and mathematics achievement and teaching performance in their schools. They observed and visited classrooms daily. At 9:00 a.m. they "did the rounds." They walked or looked into every classroom to observe student and teacher conduct. Teachers and students were confronted, if noncompliance with school rules or poor performance in school tasks was noted. At School B, the principal's visitation and observation schedule was erratic; and, when it did occur, it was announced. None of these principals used dominance or sheer authoritarianism to force teacher compliance. Schools A and C principals looked inward to the resources of their own faculties and staffs for problem solving and obligated their teachers to them by assuming responsibility for both discipline enforcement throughout the school and parental coordination and control. At School A, the principal was in contact with students throughout the school day. The emphasis on student advocacy permitted students to confer with him continuously, bringing him their concerns, complaints, and grievances. This provided the principal with a useful source of information about school business, teacher conduct, and community affairs. The School C principal obligated her teachers additionally by assuming responsibility for meeting with irate parents or those whose concerns created confrontations and conflicts with teachers.

On the other hand, the School B principal mainly looked outward to the system-approved external agencies, resources, and support networks. She was lax or erratic in oversight, monitoring, and teacher evaluation although she used the union representative for reading administration and permitted specialization by teachers in their perceived areas of expertise, when they requested this. These requests emanated from teachers and rarely were initiated by the principal. Having surrendered her decision-making prerogatives to teacher negotiation, she was often rendered ineffective. She used neither obligation nor dominance. She relied instead on teacher professionalism to force compliance and performance and expected, in exchange, for them to handle all discipline cases and parental conflicts. She entered only when an emergency or crisis arose.

Principals at Schools A and C saw themselves as disciplinarians in their respective schools. In these schools, the principals established routines for the acceptance and resolution of discipline cases. At School A the principal developed the Socratic Counseling Program, composed of routines which engaged students in self-analysis to change their own behavior. For the School C principal, an authoritarian routine emerged, characterized by rewards and punishment. Denial of attendance at student-preferred classes in special subjects, denial of privileges at lunchroom, and dismissal, isolation, verbal harrassment, and reprimands were all modes of punishment permitted at School C. Jobs as monitors and school leaders, excursions to movies, plays, and other forms of entertainment, and school parties were forms of rewards. At both schools, A and C, there were well-known routines for rule violators, and each student knew that the office was a place of serious endeavor where, more than likely, one would have much more work assigned than would be given in the classroom. At School B, a trip to the office often meant a holiday from class work. Some teachers used the office merely for isolation purposes, sending their students to it, and later picking them up without any intervention by the principal. In classrooms where chronic discipline problems existed, teachers consumed much instructional time handling these situations.

At Schools A and C, the principals interacted heavily with the students. The School A principal invested the greatest amount of time in this interaction. He talked with the children during all outdoor recesses, on arrival and departure to and from school, during lunch periods, and in his office. One benefit of this high interaction between students and principals at Schools A and C was the opportunity it afforded the principals to communicate their high expectations to each student. Both principals learned to know the students well from these interactions, which also helped them to be more familiar with the student's pacing and progress characteristics.

Both principals conferred with their teachers about student performance and behavior, and teacher in-service training was provided when needed at Schools A and C. Both were interested in developing the highest potential for each student. Constant searches for processes to do this were considered with individual teachers and ancillary staff. To accomplish this, School A opted for self-contained classrooms throughout the school's organization. School C chose departmentalization, used a supplementary reading series, and grouped children for the teaching of mathematics in the intermediate grades in order to satisfy the perceived needs for increased growth rates among advanced and slow learners. School C administered its own placement tests for transfer students, not relying on the placement recommendations of sending schools. Moreover, it was the only school where the teachers agreed that skills were retaught whenever students did not pass the unit or level mastery tests in reading and/or mathematics. In an attempt to operationalize this routine, the principal chose to use the Title I reading teacher as a reading clinician, even though the position had been abolished by the central administration. School A implemented (a) the Parent Advisory Committee Program to teach parents how to observe classrooms and make decisions about their children's futures; (b) an attendance program which established a routine for the treatment of chronic absenteeism by counseling parents and students together; (c) a Principal Monitoring

Program for keeping abreast of teacher and student performance and progress; and (d) a Socratic Counseling Program which has already been discussed.

In both schools, A and C, the office was the place for the coordination of the school's business. It fostered complementary interactions to reach clear targets. Coordination demanded sustained supervision and monitoring. Both Schools A and C principals developed several routines for coordination and control: (a) daily rounds in the morning to determine classroom operation and control; (b) official business executed in the office, i.e., ordering supplies, conferring with the principal or the school clerk, getting the mail or messages, signing in and out, admitting all visitors to the school through the office; (c) specified routines for referring students to the principal; (d) prompt handling of student and teacher discipline problems; (e) school memoranda and bulletins distributed regularly; (f) consistent monitoring of student achievement and teacher performance. (g) specific placement routines for student pacing and progress; (h) specific routines for parent involvement and visitation; (i) specific routines for teacher evaluation; and (j) well-developed networks for teacher help and assistance. By contrast, the School B principal developed only the last 2 items. In addition, School B had a school newspaper which was sent home bimonthly. Further, the School B office was a place of social gathering for the faculty. Staff and faculty engaged in informal chatter, frequently lasting 2 to 12 minutes, in some cases, this lasted a whole period. Propriety disappeared, and the disruption of secretarial work was common.

In Schools A and C, teachers telephoned the principal of their intended absences, and the principals called for substitutes. This forced the teachers to inform and explain their reasons for absence directly to the principals. In School B, this task was delegated to the school clerk. In Schools A and C, a constant principal presence and the direct involvement of the principal in the affairs of the schools increased their sense of what was happening and the amount of information which they obtained. These principals received information first. Teachers and staff were directed to keep them informed. Censure and sanctions resulted, if this rule went unobserved. In School B, information often came to the principal last.

TEACHERS AND TEACHING

There were 26 teachers at School A, 21 white and 5 African American, 23 women and 3 men, one of whom was African American (see Table 3). Sixty-six percent of the teachers had been teaching 10 years or more. The largest cohort of these teachers was graduated from college between 1965 and 1969 ($33\frac{1}{3}\%$). More than 50% of these teachers received their bachelor's degrees from public institutions of higher education in the study state.

There were 18 teachers at School B, 13 white and 5 African American, 12 women and 6 men, two of whom were African American. Two teachers taught in the Elementary Scholars' Center, one white woman and one African American man. Of the 16 remaining teachers, 10 were regular K-5 teachers, and 6 were special subject teachers. The typical full-time classroom teacher had spent the bulk of his/her teaching career at School B, whereas special subject teachers had not. On the average, intermediate teachers had been at the school three times longer than primary teachers. At the lower level, one out of every two rooms had inexperienced teachers. At the higher level, a student was guaranteed an experienced teacher. For full-time teachers, three simple trends prevailed:

1. African Americans, regardless of sex, were primary, special subject, or satellite teachers (teachers in programs such as special education, Day Care, Headstart, etc.).
2. Both full-time white men handled intermediate grades. Most full-time white women taught primary grades and, for whites, the school displayed sex bias in assignment patterns. For African Americans, assignment biases placed them at the primary grades.
3. Correspondingly, white men were underrepresented in special subjects and overrepresented in intermediate teaching. Fifty-six percent of the teachers had been graduated from college between 1970 and 1974.

There were 18 teachers at School C, 12 classroom, 4 special subject, and 2 special education. There were 9 white teachers and 9 African Americans. All except two were women. One male teacher was African American; he taught a special subject. Eight of the 12 classroom teachers were white. The white male teacher was a classroom teacher. Of the 6 special education and special subject teachers, 5 were African American. Two teachers did not respond to the questionnaire: Both were African Americans, one man and one woman. They both taught special subjects. Over half of the reporting teachers acquired their bachelor's degrees during the 5-year period commencing 1965. Over three fourths acquired these degrees from institutions of higher education in the state, half of them in public institutions. The principal had a master's degree. There was only one probationary teacher, a third-grade teacher, in the school. All other teachers had extensive experience in the grade or subject taught.

What teachers did in the classroom with the students was ultimately the important factor in the elevation of achievement in predominently African American schools. Teachers were loyal to the principals of Schools A and C and showed higher consensus. This consensus was translated into a general theme of reinforcement and reteaching for skill mastery in reading and mathematics and the necessity for discipline defined as routinized behavior developed by the students in compliance with this highest priority. As a consequence, School C was characterized by tight coordination and strict control and practiced consistency in a highly structured environment, which seemed to be required more in a divided community. Teachers operationalized this structure with two dominant modes of enforcement: strictly and sternly, and affectionately and considerately. The latter mode seemed to be more successful in reaching the goals for both types of classes, accelerated and low achieving.

At School C, regimentation, rote, and drill techniques presented the typical teaching style. Class discussions were kept at a minimum. The severity of this style was modified somewhat since more than half of the teachers showed affection to their children with fond hugs and pats when they did well on academic tasks. They also rewarded students with parties, goodies, and stars when praises for excellence were warranted. School C teachers demanded obedience without qualification, and students there did not have the principal's open permission to complain about teachers and other staff; yet the affectionate, considerate teachers allowed their students to state their sides of disputes. Moreover, students laughed with their teachers in class over funny incidents. In fact, in the Early Learning Skills (ELS) division which was highly structured, students formed small instructional groups where the teachers or teacher's assistant conducted concept development sessions informally in circles on the floor encouraging creative and different interpretations of phenomena.[7] But, beyond a doubt, School C was a regimented, controlled school.

At School A, most of the classrooms reflected the flexible style of the principal. Teachers and students adapted to change easily, and students were encouraged to express different opinions. There were only two loosely structured classrooms at School A. Of the 10 regular division grades at School B half were loosely structured and half were flexible. Loose structure was not tolerated for long in School C. There were two loosely structured classrooms at School C during SY 1979–1980. Only one of these was a regular classroom; the other was a special subject. By SY 1981–1982, however, both teachers had moved, one by transfer and the other through retirement.

By contrast, there were no highly structured classrooms at School B. Student achievement was low in each of the loosely structured classrooms, except one, an accelerated group. Constant movement, chatter, distraction, occasional fights, physical and verbal sanctions, high noise level with most students off-task, characterized three of the four loosely structured classrooms. Fifteen undistracted minutes would be an unusually orderly event in one of these classes. Often the centerpiece of disorganization was one student whose educational requirements, social and emotional developmental stages, and incorrect placement in the grade ignited such a volatile context. Teachers caught in this predicament called out for help, but the spirit of professionalism could not solve this problem. This failure affected the flexible classroom teachers' morale.

At Schools A and C, teachers were conscious of the ethnic background, history, and culture of their students. They regularly used materials reflecting this background on the bulletin boards and in their lessons. This was a year-round endeavor strongly approved by the principals. At School B one first-grade teacher assumed the responsibility for generating this ethos among the teachers and often became very frustrated at the perceived lack of cooperation of her faculty and principal. Generally, teachers felt that the emphasis on black history, literature, and culture helped to maintain a positive self-image in their students.

---

[7] Early Learning Skills (ELS) was a classroom for 16 students who were deemed unready for first grade after 1 year of kindergarten.

Teachers at School C were the most cooperative with one another, and School B teachers were the least. At all three schools there were cliques of teachers who worked together more than with others. At all three schools there were loners. The tightest network of support was at School C where the teachers had worked together as a unit longer; the least effective was at School B. At both Schools A and C, all of the teachers were responsible for all of the students. At School B, most teachers were responsible only for their own classes. Teachers at School C were the most consistent about the use of preparation, in-service, and special-subject class time for tutoring, small group instruction, remediation, and compensatory work. Teachers at School A relied also on the principal for extra teaching time. School B teachers made use only of in-service training time. At all three schools teachers stole time from special subjects, social studies, and science for remediation, reteaching, and reinforcement in reading and mathematics.

In all three schools teachers were generally present and prompt, although there were variations at School B. Some teachers were persistently tardy, and others regularly left early, especially on payday Fridays. Teachers kept meticulous lesson plans, which were carefully followed at Schools A and C. Veteran teachers often did not have lesson plans at School B, and a few seemed unprepared on some days. Over all, what seemed the most important effect on teachers was (a) the climate of the school, (b) the presence of the principal, and (c) the ability of teachers to devote the majority of their time in school to instruction. Wherever these three conditions were present along with high expectations for student achievement, positive and functional routines were established, and goal consensus occurred. This consensus was important to the total creation of a positive school climate.

Teaching Reading

In all three schools there was consensus about the importance and priority of achievement goals, especially in reading and mathematics. Students were placed in groups according to reading achievement in the basal readers. Reading was taught in the morning in all three schools except for one class, a fourth grade, at School C. Mathematics was taught in the afternoon except for one class, a fifth grade, at School A. With the exception of School C, whole group instruction was used to teach mathematics.

The dominant mode of teaching reading at all schools was the persistent pursuit of the lessons as outlined in the teacher's guide. First, the concepts of the story were outlined with examples, and children were familiarized with the basic theme of the story. Then vocabulary was developed, and the words taught. Phonics lessons followed to teach children word attack skills. Then the story was read orally and silently, after which workbook exercises were assigned, explained, and demonstrated by means of both teacher and student activities. Students then worked on seatwork. Teachers usually began with their fastest groups. These groups also were permitted to choose activities and work on independent activities more frequently than slower groups. Slower groups, by contrast, generally received more skill mastery instruction in all schools.

In Schools A and C, each reading group received the maximum amount of time in skill mastery instruction. The exception was one fifth grade at School A where the teacher was new, and the fourth and fifth grades at School C where departmentalization required movement at specific times and prevented teacher manipulation of schedules. At School B, some reading groups did not receive skill mastery instruction at all because of disciplinary problems. The tendency to take the slowest groups last thereby penalized the students least able to tolerate neglect when there was insufficient time for all groups to receive instruction. Moreover, in School B the least experienced teachers in the lower grades received the slower groups for instruction thereby doubling the penalty.

Each child was taken through each activity and skill category, whether she/he needed the instruction or not. Each child was also tested with each unit and level test. No attempt was made by teachers to use the MAT achievement test scores to make teaching decisions. In one case at School A where the observer noted that one student had scored significantly higher in reading on the MAT than his basal reader placement warranted, the principal ordered the child tested with the basal-reader-level test immediately. The teacher thought that every child needed to do every activity and take every test consecutively in spite of the MAT score. This practice was reflected in the percent of students who performed at the norms in reading but who were behind the norms in the basal reader (see Table 4). School A came closest in the first grade to parity where 63% of the children finished the first-grade readers, and 71% reached the national and/or city norms in reading. Nowhere else did this occur. This could be due to the freedom of teachers at School A to: (a) send reading books and workbooks home for completion; and (b) permit students to take level and unit tests before they had completed units and levels when other indicators revealed mastery of skills.

The integration of the Title I programs into the school's regular instructional schedule often posed a problem. Students could miss the regular instruction to go to these classes. At School A, for instance, Title I mathematics classes were held in the afternoon, when most of the mathematics instruction occurred. At School C, Title I reading was held in the morning, when most of the reading instruction was programmed. Teachers arranged their groups to include these students: This was another factor which led to teaching the slower groups last.

Persistently slow learners required more reinforcement and reteaching; consequently, teachers stole time from other subjects in order to achieve reading skill mastery. At all three schools, teachers usually stole time from music, art, physical education, social studies, and science to satisfy this need. At Schools A and C this practice was approved by the principals. At Schools A and C, teachers often used preparation and in-service time for student tutoring, disciplinary counseling, and reinforcement instruction to small groups. More often than not, teachers of slower reading groups detained them after school hours to explain homework necessary for reinforcement. The decline in the number of students at grade level in reading at the fourth grade level in School C was probably due to departmentalization and its restriction on the manipulation of class time. These routines, although functional in reading, did deprive the students of their special subjects, social studies, and science. This did not occur as often at School B, probably because the union official supervised compliance with the union agreement. This disparate use of preparation time by teachers in Schools A and C compared to those in School B indicated that reconsideration should be made of this special allocation of time in the school schedule. Most teachers in the high-achieving schools seemed to need that time for small group instruction or tutoring whereas teachers in the low-achieving school squandered it.

Reading seemed to require more one-to-one interaction in teaching than mathematics did. The grouping requirement demanded more time in the schedule in order to create more instances for face-to-face relationships. Under the grouping mandate, for three groups to receive the minimum of 8 periods of instruction a week, 180 minutes of school time had to be allocated for reading each day alone. Reading occurred then from 8:40 a.m. until 11:40 a.m. each school day. Schools A and C teachers devoted considerably more time than this. Also, curriculum changes in the third grade mandated other subject time allocations. The School A principal opted for self-contained classrooms for these reasons.

Obviously, classroom management skills were required to conduct what one School C teacher described as her "three-ring circus reading program." The teacher conducted one activity while children were executing other activities. She had to know how to keep order, answer questions, carry on a lesson, pace, and progress all at the same time. Inexperienced teachers were confused often by these many demands on them. Without the assistance of the principal to help with severe discipline problems, their survival was questionable, and learning could not take place.

Teaching Mathematics

Mathematics had a higher priority in School B than in the other two schools because of the goals of the Teachers' Corps program established there. Improving mathematics was its main objective. Every grade in Schools A and C reached the Centre City or national norm in mathematics, and every grade except the fifth arrived there in School B. Mathematics was taught by whole group instruction usually in the afternoon in every school except School C. In the fourth and fifth grades at School C, students were placed in three groups in each of the four classes.

The regular textbook was used to teach the concepts and skills in mathematics. Instruction generally involved lecture–demonstration activities by both teacher and students in a variety of forms using seatwork, board work, homework and independent games. In method, the student-centered explanation of steps for problem solving worked. The copious exercise format produced skill mastery. Yet, the ceilings on expected achievement were alarmingly low on word problems at School B. By not tackling this issue, the staff discouraged and suppressed a possible achievement path.

Teachers at School C spent more time on the development of concepts and understanding of the meaning of numbers, place value, and infinity than those at the other two schools. More demonstrations of meaning were incorporated into lessons, and more attempts were made to relate these concepts to the everyday lives of the children: Popsicle sticks were used as counters, and children made place value pockets in art class. Emphasis on reading encouraged the use of word problems in vocabulary development. Moreover, School C was the only school where students were grouped for mathematics instruction. In the departmentalized program for grades 4 and 5, students were taught mathematics by one teacher who grouped his classes in accelerated, average, and slow groups. Students could move from one group to another by skill mastery testing. Although the lecture-demonstration, pretest, posttest operation was used, more independent scat-work and chalkboard activities were characteristic of the instruction than in the other schools. Students tutored each other, and there were more face-to-face relationships.

Teachers at School A followed the student-centered, copious exercise format previously described. The principal's intervention with students who were not performing well encouraged them to do better. This response to a student who had failed a mathematics test illustrates the point: "Do you know that your ancestors built the pyramids, man? They were the greatest mathematicians in the world." This principal also spent a great deal of time teaching students about mathematics, whenever they were sent to the office for incomplete work.

Special Subjects

In all three schools, special subjects were considered of secondary importance in the instructional program. This relegated them to an inferior symbolic universe and did irreparable harm to student motivation and teacher inspiration in these areas. Generally, these teachers accepted their plight and agreed that the teaching of reading and mathematics was more important. Yet, they knew that creativity was central to humanism and that such experiences should be provided.

The need for more time for more reinforcement and reteaching forced teachers to use special subject time for this purpose. Unless other options are available to teachers trying to deal with this disadvantage, this undesirable practice will continue. Some thought should be given to the design of such options. Moreover, school systems should rethink the imposition of additional programs on already overburdened time schedules in schools heavily populated with African American and poor children.

Special Education

In all three schools there was a reluctance to place students in special education, especially the EMR and LD/BI divisions. High expectations were held by the teachers for the students' performances. In all three schools the teachers felt that their children could and would achieve and reach the national norms on the MAT in reading and mathematics. These expectations precluded special education placement, until teachers and the principal were certain beyond a doubt that the child was irretrievable by them from that classification.

The Essential Functional Teaching Routines

The organizational outputs of excessive high growth and high achievement resulted from routines, scenarios, and processes in place at that time in these predominantly African American elementary schools. The following teaching routines were most important in maintaining these anomalies:

- The implementation of a horizontal organization based on some kind of reading skill mastery grouping determined by criterion referenced tests, with no more than three reading groups per class within which arrangement grouping and re-grouping for mathematics is permitted.
- The use of self-contained classrooms modified by some kind of nongrading and team teaching as the norm.
- The presence of flexible structure or high structure moderated by affection and consideration.
- The expansion of the school day by the use of preparation, inservice, special subject, social studies, and science periods for tutoring and small group instruction for students who need reinforcement and reteaching.
- An accurate diagnosis of student skill mastery placement.
- The constant monitoring of student pacing and progress and the holding of conferences with the principal over stubborn cases.
- The reteaching and reinforcement of concepts and skills in a consistent manner.
- The provision of intense concept development instruction to increase growth rates which yield high achievement.
- The use of materials which prove functional for elevating achievement when these are not approved by the board of education, especially in the area of phonics, black history, culture, and literature, and mathematical word problems.
- The denial of student placement in EMR/LD divisions, unless all strategies for regular learning have been exhausted.
- The use of teacher expertise and knowledge for problem solving.

REFLECTIONS

The high-achieving African American elementary school was an anomaly in the CCSS and not the result of ordinary organizational routines. It forced the system to explain the existence of low-achieving African American schools and raised questions about standard operating procedures and policies which allowed such schools to operate. This study revealed the antecedent conditions contributing to the origin of these anomalies and the essential functional routines which produced high achievement and high growth. Since some of these routines such as the use of teacher in-service time and the stealing of class time from science and other subjects are undesirable, the implications of these findings for public policy are important.

Superintendents and boards of education need to consider several policy and/or administrative changes in order to test what will create and maintain high-achieving schools for African American poor students using the previously cited routines.

1. Designate student achievement as one of the most important criteria on which teacher and principal performance will be judged. Consider growth rates sufficient when they result in high achievement over a given period of time.
2. Lengthen the school day in schools where the population demands reinforcement, repetition, and reteaching; pay staff accordingly, and improve student attendance.
3. Require evidence that teachers can teach reading and mathematics before hiring or that principals provide proof of this ability during the probationary period, using student achievement as the basic criterion in cases where probationary teachers receive satisfactory marks or better.
4. Establish routines which stress skill mastery determined by criterion-referenced tests; provide differential treatments for individual variation, and emphasize conceptual development.
5. Provide probationary periods for principals and decentralize more authority at the building level for veterans, but monitor these principals' performances in elevating achievement.
6. Place research teams in schools which are high achieving in hopes of increasing our knowledge base.
7. Recruit and hire more teachers and principals who believe that African American poor students can learn; make this a requirement for working in African American and poor schools.
8. Monitor more stringently the selection and purchase of textbooks and educational materials for cultural bias and selected emphases for deviant populations such as in phonics, linguistics, word problems and ethnic history and culture.
9. Monitor the proliferation of programs in schools which service African American and poor student populations. Where these programs are desirable, principals should be given assistant principals to deal with their administration and supervision.

REFERENCES

Allison, G.T. (1971). *Essence of decision: Explaining the Cuban missile crisis.* Boston, MA: Little, Brown.

Bereiter, G., & Englemann, S. (1966). *Teaching disadvantaged children in the preschool.* Englewood Cliffs, NJ: Prentice Hall.

Blau, P.M., & Scott, W.R. (1962). *Formal organizations.* New York: Chandler.

Brookover, W.B., Schweitzer, J., Schneider, J.M., Beady, C., Flood, P.K., & Wisenbaker, J.M. (1978). Elementary school climate and school achievement. *American Educational Research Journal, 15,* 552–565.

Brookover, W.B., Schweitzer, J., Schneider, J.M., Beady, C., Flood, P.K., & Wisenbaker, J.M. (1979). *School social systems and student achievement: Schools can make a difference.* New York: Praeger.

Du Bois, W.E.B. (1967). *The souls of black folk.* Greenwich, CT: Fawcett. (Original work published in 1903)

Edmonds, R.R. (1979). Some schools work and more can. *Social Policy, 9,* 28–32.

Edmonds, R.R. (1981, October 27). *Testimony before the House of Representatives Subcommittee on Elementary, Secondary, and Vocational Education.* Washington, DC.

Edmonds, R.R., & Frederickson, J.F. (1979). *Search for effective schools: The identification and analysis of city schools that are instructionally effective for poor children.* New York: Office of Educational Evaluation, New York City Public Schools. (Eric Document Reproduction Service No. 170 396)

Firestone, W.A., & Herriott, R.E. (1980). *Images of the school: An exploration of the school organization of elementary, junior high and high schools.* Philadelphia, PA: Field Studies, Research for Better Schools.

Glaser, B.G., & Strauss, A. (1967). *The discovery of grounded theory.* Chicago, IL: Alpine.

Hale, J. (1982). *Black children: Their roots, culture and learning styles.* Provo, UT: Brigham Young University Press.

Hilliard, A. (1976). Alternatives to IQ testing: An approach to the identification of gifted minority children. Final report to the California State Department of Education. Sacramento, CA: State Department of Education.

Hoover, M.P. (1978). Characteristics of black schools at grade level: A description. *Reading Teacher, 31,* 757-762.

Leiter, J. (1981). Perceived teacher autonomy and the meaning of organizational control. *The Sociology Quarterly, 22,* 26.

Lezotte, L., & Passalacqua, J. (1978). Individual school buildings: Accounting for differences in measured pupil performance. *Urban Education, 13,* 283-293.

Singleton, J. (1967). *Nichu: A Japanese School.* New York: Holt, Rinehart and Winston.

Sizemore, B.A., Brossard, C.A., & Harrigan, B. (1983). *An abashing anomaly: The high achieving predominantly black elementary school.* Washington, DC: NIE (NIE-G-80-0006).

Spradley, J.P., & McCurdy, D.W. (1972). *The cultural experience: Ethnography in complex society.* Chicago, IL: Science Research Associates.

Stodolsky, S.S., & Lesser, G.S. (1967). Learning patterns in the disadvantaged. *Harvard Educational Review, 37,* 546-593.

Thompson, J.D. (1967). *Organizations in action.* New York: McGraw-Hill.

Wallace, A.F.C. (1970). *Culture and personality.* New York: Random House.

Weber, G. (1971). *Inner city children can be taught to read: Four successful schools.* Occasional paper No. 18. Washington, DC: Council for Basic Education.

Weick, K.E. (1976). Educational organizations as loosely coupled systems. *Administrative Science Quarterly, 21,* 1-19.

9
Ideological Purity and Variety in Effective Middle Schools

GEORGE W. NOBLIT

University of North Carolina at Chapel Hill

To many of us the middle school movement seems to be a recent development. However, the movement has been around for most of this century. Philosophically its ideas seem almost timeless, but it is an application of liberal ideals for improved schools. It is appropriate to view the current middle school movement as a second attempt. Many of the ideas and indeed even some of the proponents were part of the movement early in this century to expand secondary education that resulted in the creation of junior high schools. Liberal ideals were frequently used to justify such innovations, even as they were subjugated to the bureaucratic ideas that were popular in that age and used by school administrators to define and legitimize their emerging role (Tyack & Hansot, 1980). The first attempt of this middle school movement saw liberal ideals lost to bureaucratic imperative.

The second attempt of the middle school movement began in the 1960s as a reaction to an inconsistency between what junior high schools had been assumed to be and how they actually functioned (Alexander, Williams, Compton, Hines & Prescott, 1968; Alexander & George, 1981). In particular, junior high schools had ceased to embody liberal ideas. They were frequently "junior" high schools: They mimicked the bureaucratic high schools in organization, instruction, and intent. To educators and scholars, research on human development was clear about the inappropriateness of this: Early adolescence was a period of psychological, social, and physical transition that warranted a responsive educational program. As Grooms (1967) wrote:

> Middle school programs directed toward the individual student are tailored to fit a period in the student's life when change is rapid. The student develops from the period of total reliance upon the parents for psychic support to a situation where an adult, external to the home, can furnish much assurance. The changed personal need of the student dovetails uniquely into the student-counselor relationship peculiar to the middle school. The student's need to discover his own capabilities, to understand better who he is, finds expression in opportunities to pursue independent study, to participate in group endeavors, and to fulfill creative desire in the fine and practical arts. The middle school affords a more effective transition to the high school with its specialized curriculum and often more impersonal organizational structure. (p. 8)

The middle school seems well grounded in research on early adolescence (Lipset, 1977) and in a substantive critique of traditional secondary education. However, good ideas are not usually sufficient in themselves to change things: Concerted action in accordance with those ideas is also necessary. Certainly that is the case with middle schools. The proponents turned to activism and created a modest social movement that has had a dramatic impact. In large part, the movement has been effective. The number of middle schools has increased dramatically to approximately 5,000 (Alexander & George, 1981), and as systems replace worn-out school plants they have planned buildings that embody at least some of the precepts of the middle school ideology.

IDEOLOGY AND SOCIAL MOVEMENTS

Successful social movements are not anarchies in which anything goes. Rather they use beliefs to provide direction and social control. Thus, the middle school movement also has a middle school ideology in that the beliefs are: (a) widely shared by the proponents; (b) systematically interconnected; (c) central to what the movement is about, and; (d) have influence on behavior (Geuss, 1981, p. 10). By using the term "ideology" I am not being pejorative. Ideology also has a positive sense in that it is "something *to be* constructed, created, or invented . . ." that "enables the agents effectively to satisfy some of their needs and desires" (Geuss, 1981, p. 23). Thus at least to some extent, it was the positive ideology of middle schools that has led to middle schools becoming a reality. Without an ideology the movement could have lost its integrity and/or its ability to accomplish what it set out to achieve.

However, ideologies control only the members of social movements. Typically, social movements expand their control by creating converts and expanding the ranks of believers. The ideology itself also has some independent effect in that, as it becomes known to nonmembers, they can be informed by it, even if they do not become full converts. It is also possible that nonmembers—by being aware of the ideology and the social movement—can view it as something to be used to satisfy rather different ends from that of the movement. This seems to happen in the case of junior high schools. On the other hand, desegregation and the demographic shifts that resulted from combining black and white students were major impetuses to putting middle school ideas into practice (Noblit, 1982). Some districts have been forced by sheer demography to adopt a 5-3-4 grade structure that middle school proponents argue is developmentally correct for early adolescents. For these districts, the middle school ideology is a convenient rationale for the shift in grade structure, but this does not mean that the ideology will in fact be put into effect in these middle schools.

In education, we are always searching for innovations that are transferable from one setting to another, yet also remain predictable in form and function. This is a rigorous standard that is rarely achieved. In large part this is because we have ignored the positive role that ideology serves in keeping a social movement or educational innovation "pure," while we have transported technical innovations into schools that do not share the ideology. A compelling ideology provides guidelines for what ought to be and also what ought not to be. In the case of middle schools, it is apparent that they are a rather popular innovation, but it is not clear whether all the schools called middle schools are ideologically pure or that it is the ideology itself that determines the school's effectiveness. However, the movement does recognize that it needs to defend the ideology and to use it to critique misapplications. Alexander and George (1981) state:

> Although the middle school movement of the 1960s and 1970s has encompassed the development of some 5000 middle school units, these schools do not uniformly exhibit the characteristics educators have come to agree upon as essential for effective education in the middle of a child's school career. Perhaps the movement has been a bandwagon; the reasons for establishing the schools at times has been primarily social, economic and/or political rather than educational. We ... call attention to the gap between the consensus-based characteristics of middle schools and the actual practice. (p. iv)

It is apparent that the current effort of the middle school movement is promoting some purity in ideology and practice. Certainly this seems desirable. But this also assumes that we know that it is the ideology that makes middle schools effective and not other factors. I will address this issue by analyzing three middle schools selected as unusually effective by the Secondary School Recognition Project of the National Commission on Excellence in Education. A comparison of these three schools will reveal to what degree they embody the middle school ideology in practice.

It would seem that if we are to believe that the middle school ideology and movement is an inprovement over the junior high school, it would be necessary for the three middle schools to each embody the middle school ideology in practice. Further, if they vary from the ideology in systematic ways and yet have still been recognized as unusually effective, then the ideology itself may need to be reconsidered. In short, this analysis has significant implications for the middle school movement that needs to be explored, precisely because it examines the basic assumption that it is the middle school ideology that makes a middle school exemplary (Alexander & George, 1981).

THE MIDDLE SCHOOL IDEOLOGY

We must not assume that an ideology does not have some variation. It must, if the movement is to have an internal vitality. It is not enough to have a common enemy, traditional secondary education, for that largely provides for an agreement on what ought not to be. A positive ideology that leads to a creation like the middle school emerges from the debates of proponents concerning what ought to be. Yet in 20+ years of the middle school movement some agreement on ideology has been welded. The literature is in agreement on some basic points (cf. Alexander et al., 1968; Alexander & George, 1981; Grooms, 1967; Stradley, 1971). In general, the middle school is transitional in that it moves students from the self-contained class-room of primary schools to the multiple-classroom curricula of high schools, as well as from dependence to self-determination in learning and decision-making. The ideology suggests that this parallel transition is accomplished by an integrated program of balanced curricula, a variety of instructional strategies, guidance, student involvement, facilitative school organization, and appropriate facilities that many junior high schools no longer achieve.

The middle school curricula should balance personal development, skills for continued learning, and organized knowledge; provide for continuity between grade levels and among teachers at a single grade level; be flexible enough to respond to student needs; and provide for individualization. According to the ideology, instruction in the middle school should employ discovery and inquiry methods as well as didactic approaches. It should also involve teaming, either as interdisciplinary teams responsible for specific cohorts of students or as team teaching. Guidance should be either individual or group, but focused on developing self-determination, decision-making skills, and values, and involve both the regular classroom activities as well as the guidance counselors. The organization of the middle school, according to the ideology, should move from self-contained classrooms to a departmentalized structure over the grades within the school, provide an opportunity for subject and interdisciplinary teaming and planning, and provide for flexible grade assignment through nongraded, multigraded, or continuous progression structures. Finally, the middle school ideology also proposes that the school facilities and plant provide for both total school population activities and space for student team activities as well as specialized facilities for the arts, music, media center, and health and physical education. In general, the ideology favors flexible space that can be used for a range of activities whenever possible, so that the plant does not determine the program.

This, then, is the rudiment of the middle school ideology. It is guided by a concern for responding to the needs of the students even as it prepares them for the high school experience. My concern here is whether it is a reasonable assumption that ideological purity is responsible for the effectiveness of the middle school.

THE STUDY

To address these questions, I will use data from the Secondary School Recognition Project that also provided the data for the chapters by Garibaldi and Pink. I visited five middle schools in the south and mid-Atlantic states that were semifinalists. Of these, three were selected by the Secondary School Recognition Project of the National Commission on Excellence in Education as finalists. The process of selection included a nomination by the chief state school officer, completion of an elaborate application, review by a panel of educational experts, selection of semifinalists, visits to the schools by a researcher resulting in a case study protocol submitted to the panel of experts, and selection as a finalist by the panel. The selection was rigorous and broad-based.

After receiving questionnaire data that led to the schools' selection as semifinalists, I visited each school for one day, talked with central office officials, the principal and administrative staff, teachers, guidance counselors, parents and students, and toured and observed school activities. I took running notes and later completed the protocol for the Secondary School Recognition Project. The data for this chapter were drawn from all three sources: the application data submitted by school, my field notes, and the protocol.

In what follows, I will present and discuss case studies of the three finalist schools. It must be remembered, however, that these schools were not identified using criteria drawn up by middle school proponents but rather were identified as effective schools (that happened to be middle schools) by using a broad range of criteria (see the Garibaldi chapter in this volume). The difference may seem to be subtle, but it is not. It may be that some of these schools are effective according to the criteria of the Secondary School Recognition Project but cannot be appropriately termed middle schools. If this turns out to be the case, then we must consider if close adherence to the middle school ideology is the primary factor in creating a school that is effective.

Three middle schools will be discussed: Shelbytown, Verne, and Promised Valley. These three schools are truly exemplary from test scores to student activities; from curriculum to building maintenance; from the people involved to the support they were given. Yet each school was somewhat different, as we shall see.

SHELBYTOWN MIDDLE SCHOOL

Shelbytown Middle School has 605 students in grades 6, 7, and 8 (16% black, and 23% on free lunches), 26 teachers, and 1 aide. It serves a small southern town that has become a desirable place to live because of its proximity to, yet distance from a nearby large city. Residents see themselves as having the best of both worlds. Commuting is possible, but in general it is a self-contained community that views itself as conservative, religious, and family oriented. Yet Shelbytown Middle is not conservative. In fact, it is an open school, and when it was built in 1974 members of the community believed that the school system had gone "too far." Parents of school-age children were wary and watched the school closely after it opened. The former principal, they argued, justified their worst fears about open schools being unmanageable. Now, however, parents openly admit that the school is more than they could ever have hoped, and although the openness still seems strange to them, they are unabashed in their praise of the school, the new principal, and the staff. The parents are especially grateful that Shelbytown Middle is "concerned about the child" and focuses on developing the "whole" student through community and local business involvement, parent participation, strong discipline, an empathic approach to problems, a quality staff, a focus on basics, and open communication. The parents and other community members agreed that "they're (the school) supporting the community and we have to support them." At Shelbytown Middle, "open" seems to mean that there are no walls between classrooms and between the school and community.

There is no doubt that the staff has worked hard to make the open plan school operable. The staff was actively involved in planning the school's program from the beginning. The faculty "worked up the schedule," designed a grade-level team concept for planning and coordination, and "accepted constructive criticism." They said that the early years were difficult because they "had to change a reputation we didn't earn:" The community simply did not trust the open school concept and consequently the school. They now say they are "happy with the school, but not the content." The teachers describe the school as "supportive," "child-centered," "warm," and "flexible." There has been little staff turnover even though relations are quite intensive, given the communication and cooperation required to implement the open school concept. Two staff members reported having transferred because of this intensity but transferred back after comparing the school to others. The teachers argued that all their efforts have come together after one of their staff, Mrs. Collier, was promoted to be the new principal three years ago. To them, an open school especially required a common orientation for principal, staff, and students, and theirs revolved around open communication, constructive criticism, praise, and trust.

The teachers believe they have discovered an highly effective instructional system. It starts with "teaching by example" in that the rules and expectations are similar for staff and students while also being clear and explicit so that the "kids know what is expected of them." Teaching by example covers three areas: "responsibility, citizenship, and academics," and the staff argues that the open plan of the school requires more responsibility and citizenship among staff and students to function successfully than do self-contained classrooms. The school also has an educational philosophy displayed in the school's lobby: "If a student can't learn the way we teach him, we must teach the way he can learn." As a result, teaching assignments, curricula, and the instructional methods are "constantly changed" to better meet the needs of the students. For example, direct instruction is bolstered by laboratories in reading and math that use computers, and science classes extend their laboratories into the community by using field trips. Further, the school is organized by grade-level teams with a cohort of students assigned to a team of teachers for all their academic subjects in heterogeneous classrooms. Scheduling a common planning period for each teacher team by assigning all the team's students to band, art, physical education, remedial education, and other cocurricular subjects enables close communication and supervision of students as well as team planning and coordination. The coordination that results is quite extensive. For example, science teachers report testing English skills, enabling considerable "cross-communication."

Coordination and communication across teams is enabled by: (a) subject area meetings where curricula are reviewed based upon standardized test results; (b) weekly meetings between team leaders and the principal; (c) the principal's encouragement to talk things over with her; (d) the principal's "consensus-building;" (e) the selection of two or three themes for total school attention annually and the rewriting of academic curricula by "lead" planners to support the themes; (f) surveying students for input annually; (g) guidance staff teaching study skills three days a week for sixth-grade students with "brushups" for the seventh and eighth graders; (h) scheduling remedial classes and laboratories so that students are not pulled from their academic subjects; and (i) interim grade reports to the parents so the student can improve before the end of the marking period. The community focus of the school also provides opportunities for a cooperation and communication as well as teaching citizenship. For example, members of the local business community teach short courses in economics for the students, and the science classes have designed a new park for the town.

The students respond well to all this effort. They "love" the school and its variety of teaching approaches. While it is "comfortable," it is also "challenging" and "exciting." They say that much is expected of them: homework, responsibility to get school work completed, and respect of others. Nevertheless, they perceive the school doing all it can to ensure that students succeed and also contribute. The students realize the open plan can be noisy and distracting at times but argue that the teachers overcome it not only by making school work a challenge ("You have to think about it, not just do it"), but also fair and "well explained." Grading, the students say, is based on completion as well as quality of work; they say that effort is also praised ("I try hard" awards, for example). The student council is active in charity and community service as well as school initiatives (talent show, May Day activities, etc.), and see themselves as the "voice of the school." The students are not only enthusiastic, they rarely misbehave (2 suspensions in 1982-83), they have high attendance (96% in 1982-83), and achieve at high levels (match or exceed state and national norms on California Achievement Test in all areas).

There is little doubt that to the community, parents, teachers, students, or Secondary School Recognition Project, Shelbytown Middle is an exemplary school, but the question does remain: How close is it to the middle school ideology? Shelbytown does focus on transition. Sixth-grade classes are held in self-contained classrooms, and teachers explain that this helps students to adjust to the open plan and learn the necessary norms of responsibility and citizenship that make the open plan successful. Further, the guidance staff teaches sixth graders study skills to prepare them for the later grades and reinforces these skills in the seventh and eighth grades. Shelbytown also has the integrated program promoted by the middle school ideology: a balanced curriculum, variety of teaching methods, supportive use of guidance services, a facilitative organizational structure, and flexible facilities. The exception to the ideology is in the area of grade structure. While Shelbytown Middle uses the team concept to enable more responsiveness to students, it typically assigns students to a grade for a year and uses gifted and talented and remedial programs to accommodate the wider range of abilities, even though all basics are heterogeneously grouped. With this exception, Shelbytown Middle departs from the middle school ideology largely by adding to it an open school plan and using the middle school ideology to promote a transition to more self-determination and responsibility for both the high school and the open middle school itself.

VERNE MIDDLE SCHOOL

Verne Middle School has 633 students in grades 6, 7, and 8 (34% black, and 41% on subsidized lunch programs), 29 teachers, and 3 teacher aides in an older, well-kept classroom building. Verne Middle serves a pie-slice-shaped piece of a medium-sized southern city in order to achieve its racial balance and contribute to the overall desegregation plan. School desegregation was the focus of considerable turmoil in the city and led both to a loss of faith in the school system and to a loss in enrollments when blacks and whites put their students in private schools. However, this pattern is now changing, and whites and blacks are returning to the public schools. Verne Middle School has played an active role in increasing community faith in the schools, and community members and school system officials all note that Verne Middle "attracts" students from the private schools. The overall enrollment for the district, however, continues to decrease, consistent with national trends in school enrollment. This continues to affect Verne Middle, even though it is able to attract students. In 1982-83, enrollment dropped sufficiently so that it was no longer possible to schedule grade-level "clusters" in which a cohort of students was assigned to a grade-level team of teachers. As a result, the organization of the school has been changed. In grades 6 and 7, grade level is the unit of organization for teachers and, as much as is possible, each grade has a common planning period. In grade 8, teachers are organized by departments, and, again, as much as is possible, each department shares a common planning period.

Competition is emphasized at Verne, but the staff is aware that competition is not an end in itself. As Mr. Vinton, the principal, put it: "We use competition constructively around here." To that end, the school organizes activities around the homeroom by fostering competitions in attendance and the number qualifying for the honor roll each marking period. Further, a student must audition for drama and thus compete to qualify for the class (which is a "related subject" in the curriculum). Homogeneous grouping is extensively used. In general, the school deemphasizes clubs in an effort to sponsor school-wide and school-relevant competitions related to service and achievement. The school as a unit also competes rather successfully: It won the state award for excellence in 1981-82 as well as being selected by the Secondary School Recognition Project. Another example is that 60% of Verne students who qualify for a system-wide honors program that requires them to attend classes in a different building elect to stay at Verne and in their regular classrooms. From these competitions, the school has generated "a lot of pride," and the school reinforces this pride by recognizing achievement and giving awards. Parents, staff, and students all agree that Verne Middle is a winner and that they are proud to be a part of it.

The teachers and principal alike ascribe the achievements at Verne to the "powerful faculty." The teachers are recognized as experts in their academic areas as well as in teaching methods. The teachers also compete and have won district and state-wide awards for outstanding educators and as innovative teachers. The teachers set high standards in the school and carefully monitor new teachers, the curriculum, and student assignments. The principal reinforces these standards by expending considerable effort in personnel selection ("the most important job I have") and helping the faculty to set goals and achieve them. The faculty maintains that they "get to decide things that are important to us" via their faculty council and that, in consultation with the principal, "every request is listened to and, if not actualized (approved by the principal), it is for a good reason." The faculty curriculum committee advises the faculty on schoolwide issues, and most instructional issues are resolved by grade-level teams and departments during their common planning periods.

The teacher's emphasis on instruction is heralded by the use of a range of instructional techniques with a special emphasis on activities such as field trips and projects. The principal does not let other concerns interfere in these activities. Classroom interruptions are not allowed, and discipline is strict (60 suspensions during 1981-82) but fair (the principal is seen by all as "a great detective"). The principal's recognized public relations skills also protect the school from unwarranted intervention, while still fostering an active PTA that focuses on student activities. In fact, one gets the sense that this school actively manages its environment rather than being subject to it. The teachers are active on the Citizen's Advisory Committee and the School District Steering Committee. The student council is active in local charities and causes. And parents are used extensively as volunteers.

The school uses its resources well to facilitate the operation of the school. Guidance staff members conduct periodic group guidance activities in language arts classes and also run an extensive individual counseling program. The testing program which they manage is used as feedback to the teachers. Remedial programs function as both part of the homogeneous grouping plan and as elective courses from which students select their "related arts."

The students interpret these efforts as making Verne Middle the "best" school in the state. To them, the teachers "make it interesting" and "put fun into learning." They also describe the school as "friendly," "warm," "exciting," and "welcoming." The students recognize that there are "high expectations" for them and report homework assignments averaging over an hour per evening. Nevertheless, they report that teachers give "plenty of help" with assignments, diligently remind students of deadlines, and do not assign unreasonable tasks. The students also volunteered that they are expected to behave like "young adults" and are expected to be responsible for themselves and the school. As noted, the student council concentrates on community service and student activities and report that they have open access to the principal on matters of school policy. The students "love" their teachters, have 96% daily attendance, and exceed state norms on the state's minimum competency testing program.

Again there is a little doubt that to the community, parents, teachers, students and the Secondary School Recognition Project, Verne Middle is a good school, but it is quite unlike Shelbytown Middle. It also seems to vary from the middle school ideology on several key points. Because of enrollment decline, Verne middle has altered its organization so that less emphasis is placed on teaming. However, the school did seem to use middle school ideology concerning transition as a guiding principle in this reorganization. The student now moves from grade-level coordination (although not specific teacher teams assigned to cohorts) to departmental coordination by the eighth grade. The student's transition to self-determination and independence seems to be left to the competition that characterizes Verne Middle and is not as evidenced in a balanced curriculum. That is, the curriculum emphasizes traditional academics over personal development and skills for continued learning, and guidance and student involvement do not seem designed for the student's developmental transition. Nevertheless, consistent with the instructional focus of Verne, a wide variety of instructional techniques are used by a recognized, talented staff with considerable success. Homogeneous grouping for instruction, however, is not part of a nongraded, multigraded, or continuous progression structure as required by the middle school ideology. Students are both in traditional grade structures and homogeneous groups within grades. No doubt, homogeneous grouping may be altered during the course of the year, but there was no evidence that this was a school policy, suggesting that flexibility in response to student needs is actually reduced further. Finally, Verne Middle is an aged building. There is some flexible space, one large multipurpose room, and separate rooms for music, arts, and vocational courses, but individual classrooms predominate in the building. Verne Middle School, then, has some departures from the middle school ideology. In general, it may be seen more as a traditional school that has incorporated parts of the middle school ideology than an integral middle school.

PROMISED VALLEY MIDDLE SCHOOL

Promised Valley Middle School serves 756 students in grades 6, 7, and 8 (20% black, and 29% low-income) with 48 teachers and 15 aides, in a school plant that was modified and expanded 10 years ago on an open plan. Promised Valley Middle is a rural school and, because of the county's limited recreational and community service facilities, it has become the site for community activities. Community organization banquets, County Board of Supervisors, the school board, the recreation leagues—all use the building and grounds regularly with the active encouragement of the principal. The taxpayers enthusiastically support this orientation and see it as evidence of the school's sound management.

Like Shelbytown Middle, the open plan was greeted with concern by parents and community 10 years ago. However, as the school stabilized and modified both the open plan (to a flexible wall system) and demonstrated a responsiveness to the children and the community, the school earned a now-positive reputation that is the envy of neighboring school systems. Now Promised Valley Middle attracts out-of-district students.

In a conservative rural county, Promised Valley Middle has a reputation for good management and entrepreneurship. Like Shelbytown, Promised Valley has actively sought to support the community in ways that benefit the school. The school recognized the need for school facilities that could also serve the needs of the community. It organized the PTA to raise funds for specific projects (playing fields, amphitheater, etc.) and lobbied county government and the school system, until they agreed to match PTA funds for capital improvements. In the end, Promised Valley was also given a staff position for "community services" to facilitate its services. The community cites the principal both as a man who has "the organizational skills to make anything work" and who has carefully developed the school into a model for others to emulate.

Management at Promised Valley Middle means involvement and coordination. The school has an elaborate management structure that allows many leadership roles for teachers. For administrative coordination, each grade level has a unit leader that is responsible for budgeting, vertical communication and feedback between the administration and teachers. Grade-level coordination is achieved by each grade level having multiple teacher teams each led by a team leader. Curriculum coordination is achieved by having subject area teams led by a master teacher who is responsible for (a) the major curriculum writing; (b) lead planning for each subject area; and (c) coordinating annual schoolwide "themes" for study. The school day is scheduled so that all teachers have a 45-minute planning period before students arrive as well as another planning period during the day. Having these two periods means that day-to-day instruction can be planned and that teachers can also meet in grade level, teacher teams, and subject area teams at least once weekly. The administration meets with the unit teachers, master teachers, and team leaders each week. Management at Promised Valley is focused on coordination, communication, planning, and "prevention" of problems. Over the years, the school has continually improved its organizational systems. The master schedule is now designed around the needs of individual students as the first priority. It is written and rewritten each year to achieve this priority. This has led to an additional program for students who are not responding well to the "unstructured" school, to an in-school suspension program (14 out-of-school; 38 in-school suspensions during 1981–82), the replacement of the teacher evaluation form with a teacher-planned professional development system, and a mastery learning curriculum written by the master teachers with an emphasis on higher-order skills is now near completion.

The school schedule creates homogeneous classrooms that are multigraded in seventh and eighth grades; this also allows for assessment and reassignment (over 100 changes reported in 1982–83). Sixth grade functions like a "school within a school" with self-contained classes for the academic subjects and selection of electives from a range of "exploratory" subjects. A careers course is offered by the guidance department as one of the exploratories, together with vocational education, agriculture, art, music, and Latin.

Prevention at Promised Valley also means giving those who are involved in the activity the responsibility for designing and implementing it. The teachers have designed the professional development system and the curricula. The students have been given the responsibility for their own behavior. Students who obey the three school rules ("Be at the right place, at the right time, and do the right thing") earn the privilege of spending time in their grade-level lounge. Further, vandalism prompted the principal to give each grade-level student council its portion of the repair budget (each grade level has its own area) and to allow them to determine how to spend what was left over after any vandalism had been repaired. Vandalism has all but ceased. Feedback is also a vital part of prevention, and parents and students are surveyed annually for it. Day-to-day feedback is direct as teachers meet to plan their instruction and respond to individual student needs.

Finally, Promised Valley rewards its people. Each student receives some award at the completion of each year. The teachers are given some sort of treat at the end of every week (e.g., an ice cream social). The roles of unit leader, team leader, and master teachers have small stipends. Every opportunity it taken to recognize people's contributions and the school's accomplishments.

Such emphasis on management has brought considerable rewards. Teachers and students believe they have a meaningful role in decision-making and cite instances of changes they have initiated. Teachers see the school as "one big family" that "interacts very well." To them, all this management has enabled the school to be "child-centered," "friendly," "extremely supportive," "orderly," and characterized by "cooperative relationships." The students say the school "looks at each person individually," has a "comfortable atmosphere," plenty of "encouragement," and is "challenging" in that it "keeps you busy—at your level." Ninety-five percent of the students attend daily, exceed state requirements in skill competency, and score above the 50th percentile nationally on the composite scale of reading, math, and language arts.

Promised Valley seems to live up to its name as well as most of the middle school ideology. It has a building that was adapted to fit the middle school ideology. The classroom walls are flexible and movable, multipurposive areas enable a range of exploratory courses, and electives have specialized areas and equipment, if it is required. The school is organized so that students move from self-contained classrooms to departmentalized classrooms over the three years, provides for considerable team planning, and uses homogeneous grouping quite flexibly in a multi-graded structure. The curricula itself is in the process of being transformed into a mastery learning system with an emphasis on higher-order skills. However, even with the exploratories and electives, it appears that personal development and skills for continued learning are decidedly secondary to academic skills. Certainly, opportunities are there, but in a school that is so skillfully managed, the lack of integration is noticeable.

IDEOLOGY AND VARIETY

The three middle schools selected by the Secondary School Recognition Project as finalists are exceptional schools according to their standards and to me. The case studies only reflect part of the total story of each school. Yet, even though they were selected as being among the most effective schools in the country, each varied in some ways from the middle school ideology that was their genesis and justification. In part, the variety was due to the larger context of each school. Shelbytown and Promised Valley were built to be open schools in conservative communities, and both had to demonstrate in some way that they were not fads. Shelbytown expended its effort to make its openness a meaningful context for middle school education which could serve the community; finally, the community believed in them. Sadly, despite the success of the open school, the superintendent of Shelbytown's district is planning to erect permanent walls in the school. Promised Valley worked more directly on integrating themselves into the community and moved away from the open school plan, but within the middle school ideology, it moved from open space to flexible space. Promised Valley lost in this transition the balanced curriculum that Shelbytown found was necessary to make the open school function smoothly and successfully. Verne Middle's context was also defined in part by its building. Flexible space was not planned for the classroom areas, and the school simply had to use classrooms as they came. That constraint, however, also played into Verne Middle's more traditional focus on academics and competition. Classrooms could compete as units and in rather traditional ways.

This pattern of results is both interesting and provocative. It certainly seems that the middle school ideology is most vulnerable in the area of the balanced curriculum and multigraded structure—the two areas that are the province of educators to design. Further, it appears that the only case that achieved a balanced curriculum was because the results were necessary for the school's open plan to work; and the only case that achieved a multigraded structure did not achieve a balanced curricula. It may be that educators are simply not prepared sufficiently to overcome a bias toward defining curricula as skill-based, established knowledge that comes in annual programs, unless the situation requires them to do so, as it did at Shelbytown. While the middle school ideology is sufficiently powerful to achieve most of its goals in practice, the creation of balanced curriculum and multigraded structures still lags behind.

The middle school ideology is powerful regarding the notion of transition, especially in terms of the school's organization. Educators are seemingly adept at this. Again, however, transition in terms of personal development and self-determination is less fully achieved. Further, the flexibility issue in responding to the students is somewhat confounded. It seems apparent in the more traditional-classroom, academics-oriented school like Verne that flexibility is difficult to achieve. Promised Valley overcame that inflexibility with an elaborate management system and multigraded, homogeneous grouping. Shelbytown used heterogeneous grouping within each teaching team, with classes having multiple, but more flexible grouping. The issue seems to be more involved than the literature suggests. In a rather structured school, flexibility requires a lot of effort on management, while in an open school the effort is contained at the instructional level by responding to multiple levels of performance within each class. Thus, while it is clear that Verne does not achieve the flexibility required in the middle school ideology, it is not clear which of the other two approaches is more consistent with the ideology.

It does appear, however, that a lack of ideological purity does not negate a middle school being regarded as effective. In the case of Verne Middle, the school is not sufficiently similar to the ideology to be regarded as middle school in other than name only. Further, it is also apparent that the middle school can more easily accommodate other child-centered embellishments or movements such as open education than more traditional emphases. The middle school movement is certainly humanistic and would seem to need to guard against enrichments from more traditional teacher-centered innovations, if it is to be seen as accounting for the effectiveness of such schools.

The middle school ideology also has underestimated the importance of the community's response. Humanistic innovations have to prove themselves, and the ideology gives little guidance on how they may be achieved. Each of the three schools chose different paths: Verne accepted a traditional role in the community and proceeded to otherwise reduce community control; Promised Valley compromised somewhat, but organized to overcome the effects of the compromise and actively sold itself to the community; Shelbytown held to its ideology, and, through hard work, proved itself to the community. In some ways, Verne took the easy way and lost key elements of middle school ideology. Promised Valley and Shelbytown were more courageous and more fully achieved the middle school ideology in practice.

It is apparent, then, that the middle school ideology, as an ideology in the positive sense of enabling the creation of something, is lacking in some key ways. It underestimates the effect of community, gives little guidance on accommodation of more traditional approaches, and does not alone seem to convince educators that a curriculum should be multigraded and balanced between personal development, skills for continued learning, and established knowledge. Nevertheless, the ideology does not seem to require absolute purity in implementation, because it more easily accommodates humanistic modifications and innovations than traditional ones.

It is also evident that the middle school ideology is not *fully* determining of the effectiveness of schools for early adolescents. The case of Verne Middle points out that another means to achieving the status of being unusually effective can be in an emphasis on traditional academics. Further research must determine if a "pure" middle school is more likely to be effective than an "impure" one and which elements of the middle school ideology seem to contribute most to this effectiveness. The first issue assesses the value of the middle school movement, while the second can give guidance as to what cannot be compromised. Without such research, it appears that effectiveness need not be seen as consonant with strict adherence to a "pure" middle school ideology.

Ideological studies such as this one can give guidance to the middle school movement as to issues it may need to address, but the movement itself must create the positive ideology that makes middle schools uniquely effective innovations. This study suggests some ideas which the movement may wish to incorporate into the ideology, but also leaves unresolved whether the ideology is the primary factor in the effectiveness of the middle school.

Certainly, the middle school movement is no passing fancy. It has a long history and is firmly entrenched as the major humanistic movement in secondary education. But it also may be that the cases presented here indicate that the essential element of a successful middle school is the honest belief by participants that what they are doing is well worthwhile and not that they conform to the middle school ideology. In practice, it may be that these two are related in that an ideology may help school participants come to such a state of belief.

REFERENCES

Alexander, W., Williams, E., Compton, M., Hines, V., & Prescott, D. (1968). *The emergent middle school*. New York: Holt, Rinehart, & Winston.

Alexander, W., & George, P. (1981). *The exemplary middle school*. New York: Holt, Rinehart, & Winston.

Geuss, R. (1981). *The idea of a critical theory*. New York: Cambridge University Press.

Grooms, M.A. (1967). *Perspectives on the middle school*. Columbus, OH: Charles Merrill.

Lipset, J. (1977). *Growing up forgotten*. Lexington, MA: Heath.

Noblit, G.W. (1982). School desegregation, legitimacy, and middle schools. *American Middle School Education 5*, 13-18.

Stradley, W.E. (1971). *A practical guide to the middle school*. New York: Center for Applied Research in Education.

Tyack, P., & Hansot, E. (1980). From social movement to professional management. *American Journal of Education, 88*(3), 291-319.

10
In Search of Exemplary Junior High Schools: A Case Study*

WILLIAM T. PINK
National College of Education

Presently, there is much interest at the national, state, and local school levels in improving the quality of public schooling. A central focus of this current interest has been the perceived need for America to regain its economic edge internationally. In substantial part, this widespread interest in improving schools has been created and sustained by extended media attention given to the "gloom and doom" pronouncement made in several recent commissions and reports suggesting that schools, especially high schools, are in urgent need of resusitation to prevent their imminent death (e.g., Boyer, 1983; Goodlad, 1984; National Commission on Excellence in Education, 1983, henceforth referred to as the National Commission; Sizer, 1984; Twentieth Century Fund, 1983). One of the reports, *A Nation at Risk,* gloomily states that education is "being eroded by a rising tide of mediocrity that threatens our very future as a nation and a people" (National Commission, 1983).

While these reports have certainly sparked debate, perhaps their most serious limitation is that their extended lists of reforms offer no single, unified, or unifying vision for better schools. By ignoring both the cost of the proposed reforms as well as the strategies for implementing the reforms, the reports gloss over the complexities of changing organizations as unique as schools. These limitations notwithstanding, many states have rushed to mandate reforms detailed in the reports (e.g., lengthening the school year and raising graduation requirements). It would seem, however, that for all this media coverage, we are no nearer a blueprint for improving schools after publication of these reports than we were before they were released.

DISCOVERING EFFECTIVE SCHOOLS

A second closely related reform idea for improving schools is also enjoying both media coverage and popularity with practitioners. This approach is based on effective schools research. This work has identified components of schools where scores on standardized tests are significantly above the levels predicted by student charac-

---

*The research reported in this chapter was supported by the U.S. Department of Education. However, no endorsement by the Department should be inferred. I want to thank Kathryn M. Borman and George W. Noblit for comments on earlier drafts.

teristics such as social class and race. The common-sense features of the components of effective schools identified by researchers like Brookover, Beady, Flood, Schweitzer, & Wisenbaker (1979), Edmonds (1979), and Rutter, Maugham, Mortimore, Ousten, & Smith (1979) have resonated so strongly with educators that there has been a widespread attempt to use these components to guide districtwide improvement programs. Many districts, for example, have begun school improvement projects designed to raise student achievement in basic skills grounded in the five effective schools components "discovered" and popularized by Edmonds (1979), i.e., strong leadership by the principal, a climate of high expectations, an orderly atmosphere, and an emphasis on the acquisition of basic skills with frequent monitoring of student progress (Clark & McCarthy, 1983; McCormack-Larkin & Kritek, 1982; New York Department of Education, 1974; Project SHAL, 1982).

While a single definition of an effective school remains elusive as do the means of making less effective schools more effective, there is general agreement among both researchers and practitioners that raising student achievement should be the major objective of school improvement programs (Edmonds, 1982; Fullan, 1982; McKenzie, 1983; Miles, 1983; Pink, 1983; Purkey & Smith, 1983; Rowan, Bossert, & Dwyer, 1983). Effective schools research has called into question the position popularized by Coleman, Campbell, Hobson, McPartland, Mood, Weinfeld, & York (1966), Jencks, Smith, Ackland, Bane, Cohen, Gintis, Heyns, & Michelson (1972), and Jensen (1969), which argued that student achievement was more a function of factors such as social class and race than school-level factors. This recent work, by contrast, suggests that emphasizing key components of schools can be a productive strategy for raising student academic achievement (e.g., Brookover et al., 1978; Clark & McCarthy, 1983; Edmonds, 1979; McCormack-Larkin & Kritek, 1982; Rutter et al., 1979; Weber, 1971).

DIVERGENT VIEWS OF SCHOOL IMPROVEMENT:
THE REPORTS AND THE EFFECTIVE SCHOOLS LITERATURE

The authors of the national reports and the authors of the effective schools literature hold quite different views concerning the best way to improve schools. The effective schools movement grew out of the desire to identify and publicize urban elementary schools that effectively teach the required curriculum to students of the economically less fortunate who traditionally have performed poorly in school. By contrast, the majority of recent reports focus on the need to improve high school education of children of the economically more fortunate who traditionally perform relatively well in school. The major proponents of effective schools are primarily concerned with social class and race equity at both the classroom and school levels (e.g., improving the access to learning opportunities for lower-class and minority students as well as raising the learning rate of students performing in the bottom quartile on standardized tests). The primary concern expressed in most of the recent reports, however, is to attain educational excellence by upgrading the quality of schooling for the better performing students (e.g., cutting electives, narrowing the curriculum, extending the number of units needed to graduate).

In recent months, these two opposed lines of argumentation, the "equity" and "excellence" positions, have become political issues. Pursuing "equity," defined as ensuring that students from differing class and ethnic groups enjoy (a) equal access to opportunities to learn, *and* (b) similar rates of achievement when compared with the majority, is argued by some to be attainable only at the expense of the "most able" students. By contrast, it is also argued that pursuing excellence only for the elite is gained at the expense of the majority. Currently, however, we find ourselves debating the cost benefits of an equity versus excellence strategy for school improvement without sufficient attention being given to defining these terms to ensure that we are all talking about the same thing, detailing the long-term educational consequences of pursuing one strategy or the other, or considering if it is possible to achieve excellence without first ensuring equity.

LIMITATIONS OF THE REPORTS AND EFFECTIVE SCHOOLS LITERATURE FOR SCHOOL IMPROVEMENT

The equity and excellence views are grounded in different ideological perspectives. Central to the debate are the taken-for-granted assumptions about the educability and differential learning rates of students labeled and subsequently categorized as "least able" and "most able" (Coles, 1978; Pink, 1984; Pink & Leibert, in press; Rist, 1970). While some argue for a common core curriculum for *all* students, others argue that students with different measured abilities should be provided different curricular experiences. As a result of these different conceptions of education, many of the reforms proposed in the recent national reports are contradictory. For example, several reports suggest expanding the school day, year, and graduation requirements (e.g., National Commission, 1983), while others suggest reducing the years in school and the number of subjects taught (e.g., Goodlad, 1984).

A second serious limitation of these reports for guiding school improvement is that the reforms they propose are neither based on systematic observations of schools nor on asking people working in schools how to improve schools. Moreover, many of the suggested reforms are aimed more at system-wide change than at the more critical classroom- and building-level factors. Thus, it is not clear how they would improve the quality of education in schools. The recommendation to raise graduation requirements, for example, says nothing about what should be taught or how it should be taught in these new courses. Moreover, little, if anything, is said in the reports about how requiring more of the same is related to creating more effective schools. Is more of the same necessarily better? Pink and Leibert (in press) argue in another context, teaching reading in urban elementary schools, that without restructuring the classroom instruction for reading, urban students will continue to do poorly in tests of reading achievement, independent of the amount of time devoted to the teaching of reading.

While the recent research of both Goodlad (1984) and Sizer (1984) overcomes many of the limitations of the reports, even this work has shortcomings. The combination of small samples and a limited observational framework reduces their authority to talk about reforms to improve *all* schools. Finally, with the exception of Goodlad (1984), these reports ignore both the elementary and junior high schools.

The effective schools research also has serious conceptual and methodological flaws which limit its utility for guiding school improvement. Consequently, the rush we have seen by school districts to mandate school improvement based on the effective schools research is, I believe, a mistake. The most serious limitation of this literature is the lack of a single definition of an effective school and standardized instrumentation for measuring the components identified as important (McKenzie, 1983; Pink, 1983; Purkey & Smith, 1983; Rowan et al., 1983). Second, an over-dependence on correlational data, almost to the exclusion of longitudinal and observational data, does not permit a discussion of how the identified components of effective schools are related to each other within the social context of the school, or how the identified components were initially developed and presently maintained in the targeted schools. Third, the effective schools literature does not address how the identified components can be transported from school to school, so they can be used to improve schools currently less than effective. While these questions are addressed, although not resolved, in research that has focused on change in organizations (e.g., Fullan, 1982; Huberman & Miles, 1984; Joyce & Showers, 1980; Miles, 1983; Sarason, 1971), this change literature has not been, to date, incorporated into the effective schools literature. Finally, most of the effective schools research has focused on identifying components related to improving reading and mathematics achievement in urban elementary schools. This research, therefore, is questionable as a basis for improving secondary schools whether they are located in urban, suburban, or rural areas (see Farrar, Neufeld, & Miles, 1984; Firestone & Herriott, 1982).

In sum, both the reports detailing a national agenda for reforming schools and the effective schools research have serious limitations for helping us understand schools in general and the junior high school in particular.

THE FEDERAL ROLE IN IDENTIFYING EDUCATIONAL EXCELLENCE

One federal effort designed to bring some clarity to the issue of school effectiveness at the secondary level was launched in January, 1983, by Secretary of Education, Terrel Bell. It was called the Secondary Education Recognition Study. In political terms, this initiative can be viewed as a counter to the negative picture of education that was painted by the then soon-to-be-released National Commission on Excellence in Education's (1983) report entitled *A Nation at Risk*. Simple in design, this initiative proposed to identify a national sample of secondary schools considered, by reputation, to be "good schools." Once identified, descriptive details of these schools could then be disseminated as a basis for school improvement nationally. Thus, it was conceptualized as a way of publicly recognizing what is working well in public schools.

In March, 1983, chief state school officers were invited by Secretary Bell to nominate a maximum of five junior high and five senior high schools that they considered exemplary. The approximately 400 schools nominated by 42 states and the District of Columbia then completed an extensive questionnaire which was to be used by a prestigious nonfederal review panel as the basis for initial screening. At this initial review, in April, 1983, panelists used this self-reported data to classify schools into an "out" category or an "in" category. Schools in the latter category were to move forward to a second, more intensive stage of screening and receive a site visit. Data were requested from the nominated schools over an extended range of "attributes of success" and "indicators of success" suggested by the literature to be associated with effective schools (see Garibaldi's chapter for details of these factors). Approximately one half, or 200, of the nominated junior and senior high schools were selected to receive site visits.

It was at this point that I was contracted as a researcher with school-based qualitative experience to conduct a series of site visits to nominated junior high schools that had survived the first round of review panel screening. Each site visitor went into the field with an 11-page protocol designed by the project staff. The protocol contained several questions to be asked of teachers, students, special service personnel, parents, principals, and superintendents as well as questions about the formal instructional setting, the informal settings, and the physical facilities. This standard protocol served both to structure the site visits and generate comparable cross-site data. I visited six junior high schools in three states during May and June, 1983. The schools differed in size (473 to 1268 students), location (rural to urban/suburban), racial composition (99.25% to 80% white), economic level (0.5% to 31% of the students receiving free lunch), and age groupings (sixth- through ninth-grade schools and seventh- and eighth-grade schools).

I spent one day in each of the six schools. Written reports of my visits formed the basis for a second review by the review panel. Site researchers met with review panelists over a 2-day period to discuss the merits of each school on a site-by-site basis (June, 1983). Finally, in September, 1983, 152 schools, including all six junior highs that I visited, received awards for exemplifying excellence.

THE CONSTRUCTION OF A CASE STUDY

When writing up my field notes for the six junior high schools I visited, I was struck by the many similarities among them. While none of them was involved in a district-wide effective schools project and while they differed on a number of factors, i.e., size, location, and clientele served, I frequently found it difficult to distinguish between the six sites. They had common goals (e.g., to provide a caring child-centered, yet demanding and structured education that would enhance cognitive, emotional, and physical growth), and had discovered remarkably similar ways of achieving these goals. It was then that I realized that presenting a single composite school would be the best way to answer the question: What are the key elements of a junior high school that is reaching for excellence?

The Birth of Exemplar Junior High School

What follows is a description of a fictitious school that I have named Exemplar Junior High. I will breathe life into Exemplar by describing the "best practices" I saw during my visits to the six nominated schools. I am not presenting this description of Exemplar to suggest that this is *the* model for all junior high schools to emulate. However, I am offering Exemplar as an illustration of exemplary school practice in action in the expectation that both researchers and practitioners will find something worthy of debate and study as they work toward improving junior high schools.

Perhaps the most intriguing aspect of this analysis of Exemplar is the fact that it illustrates the critical importance of factors not usually identified in the effective schools literature. Whereas this literature frequently stresses the importance of five school-level characteristics for improving student achievement (e.g., strong leadership, a climate of high expectations, an orderly 'atmosphere, an emphasis on basic skills, and frequently monitored student progress; see Edmonds, 1979), the study of Exemplar reveals the importance of the people, the curriculum, the governance structure, shared goals, and the interrelationship between the school, parents, and central office. The importance of a shared desire to become a better school, coupled with a widespread dissatisfaction with poor student performance, is clearly illustrated. Thus, this detailed examination of what makes Exemplar such a successful school moves us beyond the rather restrictive view of urban elementary schools provided by the effective schools literature.

Methods and Procedures

The methods for gathering data were standardized across six sites. I preplanned my day in each of the schools with the principal. I emphasized that I was interested in seeing a "typical day in the life of the school." Happily, I wasn't subjected to a single "staged" event. I talked with similar groups, observed similar events, and enjoyed similar blocks of unstructured time in each school. More specifically, site visits usually began around 6:30 a.m. with breakfast with the key school site administrators. We were back in the building by 7:45 a.m. From this point on I was engaged in the following activities:

1. Semistructured interviews with groups of teachers, administrators, parents and central office staff. Basic questions for each group were generated by the standard protocol and data furnished by the school and used for initial screening by the review panel.
2. Unstructured interviews with purposeful samples of students, teachers, administrators, parents, central office staff, and janitors.
3. Observations of a variety of events and locations, i.e., before school, classrooms, corridors, lunch room, teachers' lounge, extracurricular activities, and the school grounds.

I usually left the building by 7:00 p.m. and then met with school and central office staff informally until 9:30 or 10:00 p.m. Throughout this time I kept running notes and tape-recorded some conversations; these were later worked up into transcripted narrative prior to analysis.

Three additional data sources proved invaluable to my understanding of these schools as social systems:

1. School and district documents were collected for subsequent analysis (e.g., handbooks, course syllabi, newsletters, study guides, reports for disciplinary referrals, suspension, vandalism, etc.)
2. Written responses were solicited to questions either unaddressed or inadequately addressed during my site visit.
3. Telephone contact was made with the site administrators for clarification and/ or amplification of material in hand and my interpretation of practice and policy.

In bringing Exemplar to life, I will describe the following eight key components that appear to work together to make the school so effective: (a) the building; (b) the people; (c) the program; (d) the extracurricular activities; (e) the governance structure; (f) the school-central office connection; (g) the school-community connection; and (h) the glue that holds the entire enterprise together. What follows is a description of a fictitious school. By using pieces of the puzzle from each school that I visited, I will construct a composite "picture" of a very vital and dynamic school that is intent on providing the best possible education for all students.

EXEMPLAR JUNIOR HIGH SCHOOL: TOWARD UNDERSTANDING EFFECTIVE SCHOOLING

We need to understand the social setting of schools before we can begin to make sense of the key factors that make that school a success. For example, a procedure that works well in school A might be very ineffective if transported to school B: We are learning that specifying and understanding the context of schooling is equally as important as the process of schooling in determining the effectiveness of a school (Fullan, 1982; Miles, 1983; Pink & Leibert, in press; Purkey & Smith, 1983; Sarason, 1971). Thus, even before arriving at Exemplar Junior High School, I had learned from the questionnaire that it was one of two junior high schools in an urban district of approximately 10,000 students. A large state university was the major industry of the city. The school housed 840 students in grades 7, 8, and 9: The student body was 80% white, 12% black, 8% Hispanic, and .9% Asian. Fourteen percent of the students received free or partly subsidized lunch (a majority being children of typically low-paid students at the university). The school had 45 full-time and 10 part-time teachers, 2 administrators, 3 counselors, 1 librarian, 5 teacher aides, and 7 clerical staff.

1. The Building: Undistinguished, Respected, Inviting

When first arriving at the school I was eager to see if anything distinguished it from other school buildings. Exemplar, physically, is anything but distinguished. The school is a large two-story brick and glass building built in 1959: From the front, the school appears to be a single-story building. Exemplar is none too attractive either in design or color: Pink and blue panels adorn the front of the school. While beginning to show its age, nevertheless the exterior shows no signs of abuse: I saw no graffiti or broken windows. Several other buildings, including the gymnasium and craft shops, sit adjacent to the main building and to the rear. The front of the building has recently been relandscaped with grassed areas, bushes, shrubs, and trees: I later learned that this work was the result of Project Green, an activity sponsored by the Parent-Student-Teacher (PST) Organization, and only coincidentally finished two days before my visit. An expansive area marked out for football, soccer, and baseball is adjacent and to the west end of the school building. All of this area is clear of trash; it presents a cared for, yet well-used appearance. On the far west end of these impressive school grounds are several public tennis courts and an Olympic-size swimming pool; both are used regularly by students.

On first entering the building, I sensed an ambiance of warmth, orderliness, and purposefulness; this ambiance was manifest in a numer of ways. Students, for example, can enter the building prior to school to (a) visit a teacher in a classroom for assistance; (b) go to a "study hall" to complete homework or receive help from student "monitors" or "duty" teachers; or (c) simply visit with each other in the central locker area. During this time students were not only very task oriented but also well behaved. I saw very little noisy horseplay during my visit; rather students were very respectful of each other. When moving around the building, for example, students were very quiet in those areas where others were studying. Abuses of the early-entry privilege lead to a loss of the privilege: Administrators, teachers, and students supervised it carefully.

I was also struck by the cleanliness and attractiveness of the interior of the school. Several areas appeared newly painted (last year, I was later informed), and student concern for the facility was much in evidence; I could find no signs of abuse, even after I had conducted my own tour of the building some time after my official tour. A wide variety of student work was highly visible in every hallway, including colorful murals linking awkward corners of long corridors. In the main entranceway of the building was a large free-standing circular glass cabinet that housed examples of student work in ceramics, costume design, and jewelry. Elsewhere in the building I found examples of student work in mathematics, science, and social studies. It was evident that the central focus of this school was the student.

The corridors and classrooms were uncarpeted. Recently renovated library and counselor and administrator suites were carpeted, well lighted, and filled with professionally framed and juried student artwork. These areas were furnished in earth tones. Upholstered chairs and large potted plants contributed to projecting an ambiance of warmth and professionalism. While the classrooms were traditional in design and most teachers functioned in their self-contained rooms, these rooms were well lighted, colorful, and filled with student work. As a visitor, I immediately felt welcome and safe in this building. It was evident that the school's activities were directed toward student learning and that the school took pride in showcasing student work.

2. The People: Students, Teachers, Administrators

It didn't take long to understand that it was the people at Exemplar who were critical in making it an excellent school. Given clear and agreed-upon organizational goals, it is the people in the organization, the students, teachers, administrators, who make the school "work" so effectively. Stated simply, Exemplar has very self-consciously developed a caring, almost familylike, setting that is designed to support each person, both in times of success and difficulty. This isn't to say that the cast of characters was unique and that the best features of Exemplar can therefore never be replicated. Rather, I am suggesting that Exemplar was fashioned to its present state by emphasizing (a) the importance of learning; (b) the exploratory nature of the junior high school program; and (c) the importance of providing a caring, structured, and nurturing environment.

Students: Involved, Responsible, Enthusiastic, Committed. Perhaps the most striking thing about the students at Exemplar is the relaxed and confident way they interact with adults. Whether talking to me in groups or individually, students in all grades and types of classes from special education to Algebra II seemed happy, highly motivated, animated, and opinionated. They enjoy school for a number of reasons (e.g., "It's as fun as you make it . . . getting involved is the key. . .."; "A good place to be social. . .."; "Teachers really care about me, and they make it (school) fun. . .."; and "Summers get boring, I like to be involved. . ..") and are articulate in explaining why Exemplar, for them, is a "good school":

- It's the people. . . . Teachers really care about students and give everyone help. . . . Teachers try hard to be human. . . . They are always there when you need them. . . . They make school fun"
- Teachers are always ready to talk about all kinds of stuff . . . before school . . ., after school . . ., they make you work, but they're fair.
- We don't have cliques here like my other school. . . . Here, lots of kids are involved, it's fun here.
- We have great classes. . . . I did film making, now I'm taking science fiction writing.
- Class isn't boring. . . . Teachers really try to make it interesting. . . . You work as hard as you want. . . . I always have time to socialize (in class) and still get my work done. . . . Teachers understand we're kids.
- "The Student Representative Association gets us involved in running our school. . . . The principals are great in helping us get started. . . . We do

everything, like writing the agenda. . . . Mr. _____ talked to me for two hours after school on Tuesday about the Exchange Day (ninth graders spend a day at the other junior high school).

- Our music program won State this year. . . . I'm in the band and orchestra.
- We love sports, even girls get to play. . . . Several sports don't cut, that's just great. . . . I get to play every game.
- Homeroom is neat. . . . Mrs. _____ had us over for a cookout. . . . We're like family.

Themes of fairness, honesty, and concern continually surfaced as I talked with students about the teachers and administrators at Exemplar. Students flipped between serious statements about the quality of the education they received (the majority stressed the need to maintain options for college) and displays of exhuberance over the fun they had with teachers during "Crazy Days."

Students thought that the expectations the school had for them were fair. They liked the fact that the school rules were uniformly enforced, but noted that teachers varied in the amount of work they required. Students displayed enjoyment in talking to the "federal visitor" and took obvious delight in naming the "easiest teachers." The school used a contract grading system that permitted students to negotiate the course workloads with each of their teachers; several students, however, said they had considerable pressure from their parents to contract only for A.s. The school does not have a formal homework policy, but students indicated that every teacher assigned from 20 minutes to 2 hours of homework. Even ninth-grade students who had contracted for A grades in science and advanced mathematics classes felt the expectations to be both reasonable and manageable. Only students involved in several sports or music activities indicated that sometimes the homework was too much to complete. Despite being very busy, at no time did students at Exemplar portray the school as being too academically focused: They continually emphasized the fact that teachers made learning fun.

Students projected a strong sense of personal efficacy. Moreover, they were perceived by both teachers and administrators as capable of making reasoned decisions. Consequently, they played a very active role in the governance structure of the school. Students said, "It's easy to get something changed (at Exemplar)." The formal mechanism for getting things decided or changed is the Student Representative Association. One student is elected from each homeroom to sit on the Association. Officers are subsequently elected by the members of the Association: A girl and boy serve as joint presidents. This group meets weekly with the two principals. They not only own the concession rights to a pop machine, but are engaged in several other fund-raising activities throughout the year. They have actively plowed much of this wealth back into the school by furnishing new landscaping, scholarships for summer camps, and new equipment (e.g., band uniforms, gymnastics equipment, and computer software) as well as by providing food and clothing for a local shelter. Students are proud of the fact that the Association is frequently used by the principal as a "sounding board" for proposed changes in school policy such as revision of the disciplinary code and modifications to the student handbook. The joint presidents of the Association sit on the Parent-Student-Teacher Advisory Board with full voting rights.

Students praised the availability of the principal and the counselors as an informal mechanism for voicing concerns. The principal usually greeted students at their lockers in the morning, made it a practice to attend every sporting, social, and cultural event, and maintained a 24-hour "open door" accessibility. Administrators and counselors were characterized as "good listeners" and "people who care about me" Beyond the infrequent story of blocked aspirations—students recounted the fact that they could not order in pizza for lunch or leave the campus for lunch and study hall—students at Exemplar project a picture of satisfied involvement in decision-making about the things which most affect their lives in the school.

Teachers: Caring, Professional, Accomplished, Critical, Team players, Tireless. Exemplar enjoys a very energetic, professional, yet warm and caring staff. From talking to them and watching them work in different settings, it is clear that they are a close-knit group who are very concerned about the students. Teachers said, "This faculty cares for each other. . . , supports each other," and "we focus our energies on providing the best education possible."

Teacher turnover is low; people seem not to want to leave Exemplar. Only seven teachers have been in the school less than three years. Eighty-four percent have M.A. degrees, and all the teachers had attended either workshops or full-semester courses during the last academic year. Several were pursuing advanced degrees. Scholarship was a priority for Exemplar teachers. Several teachers had authored books or professional papers, won juried competitions in the performing or fine arts, or were active in leadership positions in state and regional professional organizations. Simply put, they were proud to be professionals and valued the fact that they were treated like professionals by the administration of the district.

Curious about the level of harmony in the building, I asked teachers why they liked the school so much and how it had come to be such a supportive place to work. Without much hesitation, the majority of teachers named the department chairs and principal as most instrumental in creating both a climate and a system to monitor and improve classroom instruction. It seems that about four years ago the principal had been initiated into the Madeline Hunter model of teaching and had subsequently "strongly suggested" that all teachers adopt it. Extensive staff development in the seven steps in lesson design was provided, and both the department chairs and principal monitored and evaluated teachers on their use of the Madeline Hunter technique. Since that time, teachers saw instruction "become the principal focus of the school," and the Hunter model provide a common language for teachers to "talk and plan for teaching."

Teachers were very quick to point up the rather unique setting they enjoyed for instructional improvement. They detailed the connection between (a) the Hunter teaching model in which "we have all had training"; (b) the arrangements for peer observation of classroom teaching, coaching, and feedback which the faculty "designed *with* the administration" (their emphasis); and (c) the weekly staff development activities which a faculty committee "coordinates *with* the district staff development coordinator" (their emphasis). This school-wide emphasis on good classroom teaching at Exemplar focuses much of the faculties energy on self-improvement. The quality of classroom instruction is, in large part, the result of this match between the interest of the faculty and administration in instructional improvement and the organization of the school and district-level resources to support instructional improvement.

As teachers saw it, the principal was so committed to the Hunter model and aggressive in promoting the idea of continued staff "self renewal," that teachers "either got very excited about continued professional development . . ., or they left." The result of this focused effort to improve instruction is a very cohesive faculty working toward the realization of a "good school." The importance of common goals which serve to unify the efforts of all the actors in a building cannot be over emphasized. Teachers showed much agreement in detailing what made Exemplar a "good school":

- We have great kids. . . . They think of this as their school. . . . (They) work hard but have fun in everything they do from academics to orchestra.
- Our staff is fantastic. . . . (They are) professional and really care about students.
- The administration is super. . . . Dr. _____ (the principal) is tough, but so supportive of anything we want to try. . . . (Interviewer: Describe him.) He's a leader, strong, encouraging, supportive, fair . . ., has good listening skills.
- The counselors are very active here . . . teaching classes. . . . They give us information about students (family separation or divorce) . . . that helps us understand our kids better.
- We don't have discipline problems. . . . The kids police themselves. . . . The student code . . . and the counselors help a lot. . . . Dope, alcohol, or smoking is not a problem here.
- The parents really support the school. . . . We have 10 to 12 helping in the building right now. . . . Our PST Advisory Board is always helping us do something new.

The teachers at Exemplar simply enjoyed coming to school: They saw it both as a place that was professionally rewarding and a place where they could be with people they enjoyed. Several teachers said this was the first school in which they had taught that they could describe in these terms. The school district fostered high morale by supporting faculty interest in scholarship and professional development. For example, the district provided (a) release time and travel support to attend professional meetings; (b) sabbaticals for advanced study; and (c) summer stipends for either independent research or curriculum development. The district also utilized an early-release plan for students that provided two hours each week for structured staff development activities. In addition to acknowledging district-level support for self-improvement, teachers were highly appreciative of the several ways they were recognized for doing a good job. Most frequently mentioned were: (a) written comments from the principal following activities, even observed classroom presentations; (b) visits or phone calls from parents just to say "thanks"; (c) articles about teachers featured in a monthly newsletter sponsored by the PST Board; (d) commendations from the superintendent; (e) departments spotlighted at monthly parent meetings; (f) books and similar artifacts prominently displayed in the school; and (g) invitations to make presentations at professional meetings and in-service days. Teachers at Exemplar were happy, competent, energetic, and concerned about their students. They had worked collaboratively over a number of years to create a school ambiance that nurtured these important characteristics.

Administrators: Visible, Instructionally Focused, Principled, Motivational. The principal and assistant principal, both male, received high praise from teachers for making Exemplar a good school. They have been at Exemplar five and three years, respectively. While different in style, they work very well together. The principal has a take-charge, aggressive, yet engaging personality. The assistant principal, by contrast, has a more subdued "counselor orientation" when dealing with people and events. The superintendent told me they were intentionally teamed to "help straighten out (Exemplar)," but I am not sure that he realized what a strong and efficient team he was creating.

The principal is in his middle forties. He has been a principal for 10 years and earned a doctorate in educational administration 5 years ago. He is very professional in his approach to improving Exemplar. An avid reader, circulating all kinds of material throughout his staff, he is thoroughly committed to self-improvement. Armed with a vision of the "good school" and some well-conceptualized ideas concerning how to realize it, the principal at Exemplar "works all the time to make my staff happy and effective." He is certainly the building leader: He has high visibility to teachers "on the firing line." Much of his day is spent in classrooms observing teachers teach and students learn. He comments to both teachers *and* students about their performances. A good social studies teacher, a fact substantiated by teachers, the superintendent, and the principal himself, he enjoys visiting the rooms to "get the thrill of performing." When in classrooms he frequently asks students: (a) "What are you doing?" (b) "What are you learning?" (c) "Why are you learning it?" and (d) "What has this to do with _____?" Both he and his teachers work hard at making the classroom experience for students more than an exercise in memorization for an upcoming examination: Teachers in all kinds of classes emphasize understanding and integrative thinking. The principal cites the widespread use of the Hunter technique of "checking for understanding" as being instrumental in helping teachers focus more on "monitoring what students grasp from period to period."

The assistant principal, in his middle thirties, is on his first administrative assignment: He is a mathematician by training, and his last position was as counselor in the high school. He manages the day-to-day business of the school, thus allowing the principal the freedom to be "out of the office almost all day," if he needs to be. The principal is extremely active in the community: He devotes much of his energies to church, Rotarian, and youth club activities. Thus, he knows and is known by many families with students at Exemplar. He sees such familiarity as a plus in relating to students "in real terms." He has a very genuine interest in getting to know each student (he has yet to lose his annual wager with a counselor that he will know every student's name before Christmas) and how they are progressing through school: By working closely with the three counselors (who each take an entering class every fourth year and follow them through until graduation), the principal monitors students experiencing difficulties. As problems surface, behavioral, emotional or academic, the principal works with the counselor, student, teacher, and parents to find a solution that all parties can agree with. He is tireless in working to make the school a place that students find both challenging and fun.

This concern about making Exemplar a good place to be also fuels the principal's relationship with teachers. While widely acknowledged as demanding regarding classroom performance, he works hard at maintaining a climate that provides opportunities for experimentation and improvement. For example, (a) a teacher committee plans for and coordinates staff development activities within the building twice each month; (b) teacher-initiated plans for teaming in social studies were tried out in the first semester; and (c) a teacher-developed plan for "writing across the curriculum" was piloted this year. Teachers praise his open, democratic, yet demanding leadership style, while citing his arrival as marking the beginning of changes critical to "shaping the school into its present form."

Finally, the principal's responses to the question, "What makes Exemplar a good school?" are strikingly similar to teacher perceptions:

- A strong instructional program based on the Madeline Hunter model. All new and probationary teachers must take the training . . . most others have opted to take.
- Exceptional receptiveness of staff to professional growth.
- Strong kids. . ., well-behaved, and highly involved in all kinds of activities. . . . Just a super group of young people.
- A sound curriculum that emphasizes doing the basics well . . . (and) providing many elective options that facilitate the exploratory phase of education.
- Constant high expectations. . . . There's a congruance between home and school. . . . Students level themselves in most (subjects) . . . . There is an emphasis on doing your very best.
- We emphasize a caring philosophy. . . . Some days (each month) all staff wear "We Care" buttons to emphasize our family concern.
- Our department organization manages decision-making. . . . We have professionalized faculty involvement in management. . . . They love it.
- Teachers are constantly involved in upgrading the curriculum. . . . They want our students to learn. . . . We get calls from the high school to slow down, we're teaching their material . . . , especially in mathematics and science.

It is significant that teachers and the principal see the same factors as contributing to making Exemplar a good school. This means that they are working in concert to further improve these key factors. As we shall see later, this collaboration for school improvement is further enhanced because the parents share a similar view of school improvement.

While it is clear that the principal has been and is an important figure in moving Exemplar in five short years from a very ordinary to an excellent school, he credits the hard work and dedication of the staff. The key to improvement, he suggests, was decentralizing decision-making to the departments and "keeping everybody honest" by insisting on "nothing but an excellent school." He is convinced that when he moves on, his successor will be able to maintain excellence by utilizing the enthusiasm and varied competencies of the faculty to continue challenging students "to be the very best that they can be." The principal believes in public education and takes every opportunity to take his message about success to any group in the community: It is interesting that he does not see himself at the center of this success story.

3. The Program: Instruction, Curriculum, Discipline

The program was identified almost as frequently as the people as a major reason for Exemplar being a "good school." In different ways, students, teachers, administrators, central office staff, and parents all sang the praises of the teaching and curriculum at Exemplar. Both the principal and superintendent, for example, saw the recent improvements at Exemplar, beginning with the arrival of this principal, as a direct function of (a) using the Madeline Hunter model to focus attention on instruction; (b) involving all faculty in curriculum development activities,; and (c) tightening down the management of discipline.

Instruction: Structured, Responsive, Consistent, Monitored, Challenging. As already noted, Exemplar's principal had "adopted" the Madeline Hunter model for instruction and included elements of clinical supervision in his routine monitoring of faculty performance. Teachers enthusiastically endorse this model of teaching. They like both the structure it provides them in designing lesson plans and the structure it provides to their evaluation of instructional performance. The key is that the principal does not demand slavish attendance to the "seven steps of lesson design" but instead encourages teachers to use the model as a foundation to improve their own instructional style. Thus, I found teachers using very different classroom arrangements. For example, while one teacher engages in direct, whole-class instruction, another uses cross-ability group projects as the *main* presentational model. This "freedom to experiment and be one's own person" was highly valued by teachers; yet it existed within a setting that was controlled by the expectations of the principal.

Students at Exemplar were given a number of aids designed to maximize learning. At the beginning of each new class, each student receives a detailed course syllabus. This syllabus lays out (a) the weekly units, required readings, and study questions; (b) the test schedule; (c) sample test questions; (d) supplemental readings; (e) the requirements for contracting for A, B, and C grades; and (f) the relationship between courses offered at Exemplar, the high school courses, and the entrance requirements for different universities and occupations. Students also reveive a package of materials outlining good study habits, time management, and methods of receiving assistance. In addition, the counselors teach short courses which focus on succeeding in school. Part of this experience involves participation in small group interactions designed to help manage stress in adolescence. All of these aids clarify the school's expectations for students, make the classes less threatening, and show the relationship between "the junior high experience and the rest of their lives." A serendipitous outcome of this exercise was that it served to clarify for all teachers the general philosophy and specific objectives of Exemplar. The principal saw the school "coming together" as a result of asking, "How (does) each course we offer relate to our expectations for students?" It would seem that requiring teachers to "write down what we want to do in each class" improved not only the quality of classroom instruction, but also the general instructional program of the school.

It is evident that instructional improvement is a carefully planned event at Exemplar. In place, for example, is a rather sophisticated system for monitoring the classroom performance of teachers. The first element of this system is that department chairs function somewhat like "resource teachers" by routinely monitoring instruction. They teach 5 periods in an 8-period day, receiving 2 periods each day to complete their administrative responsibilities. They make routine and unannounced visits to the classrooms. They provide formative feedback to teachers. They play no role, however, in evaluative data collection that could be used to make decisions about tenure. The second element in the monitoring system is peer review. Within each department, teachers observe each other teach three times each year. Again, informal feedback is given to the observed teacher in a one-on-one conference setting: This feedback plays no part in formal evaluation. Teachers can request additional visits from both within and outside their departments. The third element is the principal review, described previously. Teachers expect to see the principal in their classroom. He arrives unannounced and will usually offer both written and oral feedback. It should be emphasized that none of these activities is related to the formal evaluation of teachers which is conducted by the principal. By contrast, this formal evaluation activity constitutes contractually required, prearranged visitations and lengthy written comments on standardized forms. Teachers, chairs, and the principal praised this open system of monitoring classroom instruction. They all thought it worked well. Teachers pointed up the advantages of knowing what was expected and receiving "continuous feedback" about their classroom performance. The involvement of so many actors in instructional improvement served to accentuate the importance of good instruction at Exemplar. Moreover, the principal's close involvement served to make him highly visible to teachers in an area they valued most highly. Teachers respected his skills as a teacher as well as a building leader.

Closely tied to this system of monitoring the quality of classroom instruction was the staff development program. Topics for weekly staff development meetings frequently focus on issues surfacing from the routine observations of teachers, chairs, and principal. Moreover, teachers requiring additional help can receive assistance from the instructional staff in the central office as well as district support to attend workshops and courses. The emphasis in the school is on professional development: The principal named three teachers who had voluntarily left Exemplar in the last two years as a result of the increased focus on superior instruction. The outcome of this school-wide emphasis on instruction is a school that prides itself on its good teaching. As the principal is fond of saying, "Nothing creates success like success."

Exemplar does not track students. Classes are selected through consultation between student, counselor, and parent. All teachers employ a contract grading system. I was somewhat dubious of this set of procedures. I expected to see students either grouping themselves into "fast and slow" classes or teachers grouping students within their classrooms into "fast" and "slower" groups. Much to my surprise, I found predominantly mixed-ability classes, and teachers employing multiple learning strategies with either whole-class or mixed-ability groupings. This emphasis on teaching, testing, and reteaching," I later learned, had been a continuing theme of staff development throughout the last two years. I was also impressed by (a) the range of different learning materials that teachers had in their rooms; (b) the wide use made of "learning centers" in the library/resource center for group projects; and (c) the systematic way parents and other community resource persons were used to support and supplement the day-to-day program. Teachers at Exemplar had recognized that learning was sometimes troublesome for junior high students. Consequently, they had set about creating an environment and a set of learning experiences to accomodate all students. It was evident in watching students in classrooms that teachers had succeeded in creating effective ways to help students learn and have fun while doing it.

Curriculum: Articulated, Current, Varied, Evaluated. The administrators and teachers at Exemplar placed a high priority on maintaining a curriculum that was both current and met the diverse needs of students. They saw this as an important activity in making Exemplar a "good school." An emphasis placed at the department level on developing both materials and instructional strategies was critical in maximizing the learning of every student in the building. Time was available each week for teachers to produce learning materials for use in classrooms as well as for discussions concerning "how to reach" students showing the unmistakable "signs of stress." Teachers in all departments worked closely with counselors to "monitor the school experience" of every student. Counselors taught classes, for example, as well as worked with teachers to help provide tutoring for students experiencing problems in keeping up with their school work. Counselors credited the principal as being the individual who drives the teachers "not to give up (academically and personally) on any student." Teachers at Exemplar actively demonstrate a personal responsibility for their students, both as persons and as learners; teachers said how important the homeroom was for "getting to know students . . . , and letting them get to know you as a person." Students benefited during these developmentally difficult years from the stability generated from this quasi-family setting.

At a more mechanistic level, teachers are continuously involved in curriculum revision on at least two levels. First, at the district level each subject area is revised on a 3-year cycle. Several teachers from the two junior high buildings serve on these committees: Recommendations are made to the associate superintendent for instruction by April of each year. There is also a standing districtwide committee at the junior high level that serves to align the curriculum "across subjects and between the two junior high schools." The product of these revision committees is "curriculum guides that are better than State guides" to maintain a challenge to students in all subjects. Second, all teachers meet in a standing committee within their respective departments at Exemplar to develop specific improvements on a course-by-course basis. This involvement serves to focus the department on the importance of content to good instructional practice. In addition, considerable planning is done across departmental lines. In recent months, for example, a team of English and social studies teachers have collaborated on developing an elective course on filmmaking while teachers in several departments have been working throughout the year to develop a detailed plan for "writing across the curriculum" initiative. This latter activity was also supported by the district through the award of some summer stipends to four teachers.

The result of all this attention to curriculum development is a constantly "changing and relevant" curriculum. While the principal actively encourages innovation and experimentation, the teachers enjoy the opportunity to "plan on school time" (to) "change things that didn't work." Parents are also highly appreciative of this kind of teacher activity (e.g., "My son's into computers. . . . They have really challenged him here," and "Kelly flunked English last semester. . . . I made her retake . . . from Mrs. Ross. It was a completely different class. . . . She loved it."). Moreover, this systematic focus on curriculum development serves to provide a forum in which students with special needs, especially Chapter I and special education eligible students, for example, are seen as equally important as other students at Exemplar. The relationship between regular classroom teachers and "special needs" teachers, for example, is strengthened by this interdepartmental focus: The counselors, functioning as brokers for each student, coordinate with all teachers the development of the program on a student-by-student basis. This schoolwide communication system focusing on learning outcomes ensures that no student "falls between the cracks." The principal sees "instruction and ongoing curriculum improvement" as the two most important tasks teachers perform.

Discipline: Uniformly Endorsed, Consistent, Fair, Swift. Prior to the arrival of the present principal, Exemplar had "a discipline problem." The superintendent volunteered that he "selected Dr. _____ as principal in the hope that he would clean things up." He did. Teachers characterized the old Exemplar:

- He was ineffective. . . . Discipline was the teacher's business.
- Kids would smoke over behind the gym.

- Parents would complain to me. I told them to go see (the previous principal).
- You never saw a teacher in the halls during passing. . . . Hell, you would get trampled under foot.

In turning Exemplar around, the present principal worked simultaneously on both the content and process of discipline. He created the present highly efficient and widely supported set of rules and procedures by adopting a school-wide plan for. developing a discipline code and by insisting that students take responsibility for their own behavior. On assuming the principalship, he distributed the discipline code to all the students and teachers and insisted that "they follow it to the letter." The code had the provision that the principal would deal with "anything serious," so he personnally policed the halls at key times, such as before and after school, as well as the known "trouble spots." By dealing "swiftly and perhaps harshly" with problems during his first three or four months in the building, things slowly began to improve. "Students and teachers got the message" that the principal cared about the orderly running of the school and would call in the police, if necessary.

Finding too much of his time devoted to discipline, at the expense of his first love, instruction, the principal gradually developed the present system. It took him three years until he "stopped worrying about maintaining order." While some things about the present system remain unchanged, others are very different. Teachers are still held accountable for maintaining discipline in their own classrooms: Classroom management has been a longtime focus of staff development activities. However, students causing classroom disruptions that cannot be dealt with by the teacher are now referred to the office. The principal has made it clear that class time is for teaching and that teachers are not to waste their limited instructional time on discipline. Perhaps the biggest change in the system is what happens to students on reaching the office. The assistant principal, now in charge of discipline, convenes a staffing panel comprising himself, two teachers, and the student's counselor to hear the case of students referred to the office. The parents are usually involved, either when the infraction warrants suspension or after repeated offenses. The outcome of the initial hearing is a "Behavior Contract" signed by both student and teacher. This contract is monitored by teachers and the counselor. It is subsequently reviewed by the panel. Over a 5-year period, this system has reduced the yearly suspension rate from 80 (1977–78) to 3 (1982–83), and the office referral rate from "hundreds" (1977–78) to 36 (1982–83). Students see this process as fair. The emphasis on the nonadversarial proceedings, providing students an opportunity to present their case, sits well with students. The assistant principal uses this time to develop the students' "sense of responsibility for their actions" as well as their ability to engage in both critical thinking and problem-solving activity. He engages referred students, for example, in a discussion of hypothetical disruptive acts to activities they want to accomplish: In this way he shows students the value of deferring some short-term needs to a longer-term goal. Thus, visits to the office become learning experiences rather than merely punitive.

The principal credits the teachers with working hard to enforce the disciplinary code. He also makes the connection between improving the instructional competence of the staff via adoption of the Madeline Hunter model and the improved classroom management skills of teachers. Teachers, however, praised both principals for working hard to involve teachers in decision-making through the staffing panel and for personally enforcing the rules with "the most difficult kids." Students, by contrast, note that the turnaround in discipline at Exemplar is due in part to their involvement in revising the discipline code and the student handbook as well as the recent campaign of the PST Board to publicize the "health problems (of) using dope and booze." It is true that the norms of the student subculture have changed somewhat over a 5-year period and that we cannot therefore attribute the impressive reduction in disciplinary problems solely to the operation of the new discipline code and procedures. Nevertheless, it is evident that Exemplar has systematically developed a monitoring system that involves all the actors in the process and functions in a way that provides opportunities for all the actors to change their behavior. The key to success would seem to be (a) the uniform enforcement by teachers *and* students of the published code, and (b) the swift, yet fair, administration of a "negotiated punishment" that the student understands is related to his or her behavior.

4. The Extracurricular Activities: Varied, Fun, Well Supported

The extracurricular activities at Exemplar were seen as important by students as opportunities "to have fun" and "to be with your friends." Students ranked these activities right behind teachers as the reason why Exemplar is a "good school." Teachers saw them as an opportunity to extend the "relationship between teachers and students." While the principal and parents characterize them as opportunities for students to "work hard. . ., learn responsibility, and have fun."

I was impressed with the range of activities offered each semester, and the high percentage of students who were active. The most popular activities in terms of number involved were music, drama, computers, and sports. Approximately 95% of the students at Exemplar were in at least one activity per semester, and fully 65% were engaged in music-related activity. The school boasted two different bands, two orchestras, and several chamber ensembles. The eighth- and ninth-grade orchestra has competed successfully at the state level for the last two years. Several recent graduates had matriculated with offers of full scholarships to more than one university.

While the school offered a range of extracurricular activities similar to that found in most junior high schools, Exemplar was distinguished by the extended use made of the expertise of the community. The orchestra would frequently practice before school and be joined by parents and university faculty providing a "master class" experience. Similarly, several parents came to school at 7 a.m. to give assistance to the computer club. Students also enjoyed the expertise of local artists, frequently parents who routinely gave time after school to assist with developing printing, painting, sculpting, and jewelry-making skills. These extra-curricular experiences provided both varied and rich learning experiences for students. The principal stressed the importance of letting "students explore," "try new things," and not be afraid of doing things "they don't excel in."

The principal saw extracurricular activities as a vital element in his plan to improve Exemplar for two major reasons. First, they provide opportunities for students and teachers "to learn about each other as individuals"; in changing their roles, they change the way they can relate to each other. Second, they provide opportunities to bring the "community into the school (in) significant ways": It is evident that parents learn about the school and the staff through this kind of contact. The willingness to open up the school to the community, viewed by the principal as the most effective way to make Exemplar "more responsive to the people who pay the bills," is a key element in creating a good school. Both the parents and administrators emphasized how much respect they gained for each other by working cooperatively on school-based projects. Each saw the contributions made by parents as improving the quality of the schooling experience for students.

5. The Governance Structure: Democratic, Participatory, Decentralized

"The way we are involved in decision-making" was frequently singled out by teachers as a contributing factor in making Exemplar such a successful school. Teachers appreciated the professional way they were treated by the principal. Several commented that they worked that much harder knowing that their views mattered. The key for them was being involved in making policy in the areas of school rules, curriculum, and staff development.

The development of a governance system based on notions of participatory democracy had been and was a continuing high priority for the principal. Since arriving at Exemplar, he had worked on "decentralizing decision-making to the department level" and providing opportunities for teachers to "resolve things that are bugging them." To achieve this, the principal has given over responsibility for key activities such as making schedules, budgeting, and developing curriculum to the department chairs. Chairs meet twice each month with the principal. Departments meet once per month: Minutes of the chairs' meetings are routinely circulated to all teachers. The entire faculty meets only four times each year. While still retaining a veto, the principal is convinced that involving all faculty in making decisions has been a critical element in the improvement of Exemplar: He reasons that teachers are just as responsible as he is for "generating solutions to problems." He specifically noted that this rule-making system has served to "defuse negativism" while providing a forum for the "professional discussion of issues." Also, by maintaining an open door policy for teachers and working quickly to resolve any issue that teachers perceive endangers their ability to teach well, the principal has nurtured the development of a climate in which teachers feel they are important. Teachers are quick to point to their involvement in decision-making as a major reason for the low teacher turnover since the arrival of the present principal. By requiring teachers to "formalize gripes by documenting them (on a) standard form," the principal has managed to reduce the amount of time spent dealing with "silly non-issues."

The same level of openness and participation are enjoyed by teachers in the areas of curriculum and staff development. Again, the principal has initiated and energetically maintained a system that draws all teachers, via the departmental structure, into decision-making roles. This is not to say that there is never tension or disagreement. Teachers, however, value the opportunity to plan their own lives. The principal is held in considerable esteem for being willing to act swiftly, responsibly, and with compassion in implementing decisions reached through this faculty governance system. The system appears to be so successful, because the principal engages the faculty as equals in resolving the critically important questions regarding the education of the students. He does not take every decision to the faculty or hold up making decisions until he has a consensus. His strongest attribute, according to many teachers, is his ability to make reasoned decisions and "help everyone learn to live with the consequences."

6. The School–Central Office Connection: Collaboration, Facilitation, Support

Teachers, administrators, and central office staff frequently listed the fine working relationship between the school and the central office when asked to give a short list of key factors that made Exemplar a good school. Teachers commented most frequently on their level of involvement in decision-making and the interest the superintendent had in instruction. Both the principal and superintendent highlighted the freedom the school enjoyed to "chart its own course." It is evident that both the teachers and administrators at Exemplar enjoyed the full confidence of the superintendent. It is also evident that the interest shown by the superintendent in Exemplar's effort at improvement is a key factor contributing to the seriousness with which the administrators and teachers engage in school improvement.

The superintendent has occupied his present position for 10 years: He was hired into the district as superintendent with a reputation for "making a (school) system cost efficient." He is a tall, well-dressed, articulate but low-key person in his early fifties. While openly admitting that he has a "good track record (for) getting the management (of the district) humming," he is intensely interested in both curriculum and instruction. One of his first actions on arriving in the district was to move principals he thought "incapable of leading school improvement." His philosophy on school improvement is disarmingly simple: "I hire the best (principals) and get out of their way."

As a new superintendent he moved quickly to decentralize decision-making to the building level. He also set about trimming his own central office staff; he presently functions with an associate superintendent and three other top-line administrators responsible for instruction and curriculum. His preference for a "bottom-up administration" is formalized through the monthly meetings of the cabinet. This cabinet is a standing policy-making committee comprising all the principals in the district: 13 elementary, 2 junior high, and 1 high school principal.

It is in this setting that the superintendent works directly with his hand-picked leaders of the district; he refers to it as his "brain trust."

The superintendent credits the principal for turning Exemplar around, simply making it "the best damn school I have" as well as for taking the leadership role in making the cabinet "(such) a worthwhile and productive committee." In looking so consistently to Exemplar's principal for counsel, the superintendent has projected high expectations on both the principal and his staff. Both the principal and staff characterize this special relationship as an opportunity to improve themselves and the school rather than as a burden to be endured. To his credit, the superintendent does not appear to give special consideration to Exemplar: If anything, he appears to enjoy making it "as tough (for them) as any other school." Thus, while he openly acknowledges Exemplar to be the best school in the district, he also praises other schools when it is appropriate.

The superintendent spends "at least two days a week in schools." He sees this as an important way to "understand the district (and its) problems and successes." He usually spends one unannounced day in each school, arriving before the students in the morning and leaving when they do in the evening. Referred to as "walking-a-school," he routinely includes both playground and lunch duty in his schedule. He recognizes that "doing *everything* that my staff does . . . doesn't hurt the image." Both the teachers and the students at Exemplar commented on the visibility, interest, and knowledge of the superintendent. They like the way he is always ready to listen to their concerns and get things changed. By acknowledging that the playground and lunchrooms are sites where he gains much informal feedback, he is emphasizing the importance of a healthy school ambiance to learning. These visits also provide him with an opportunity to assess "up close and personal" the effectiveness of the administrators in each building. During these visits he has seen programmatic changes at Exemplar such as the procedures for enforcing the disciplinary code, the writing-across-the-curriculum proposal, and the use made of the PST board for school improvement that he has requested become agenda items for the cabinet. Several of these initiatives generated at the school level have subsequently become institutionalized as district policy.

The key to the success of this school-central office relationship is the support provided by the central office for the school-based initiatives. Undergirding this support is a climate of self-criticism and improvement. Simply put, the superintendent has charged the building leadership to improve schools: With limited central office directives, the schools are held accountable for generating their own school improvement plans. Exemplar has enjoyed exceptionally good relationships and support from the central office, because it has been highly successful in improving itself by employing both sound management and creative instructional techniques. As the superintendent is quick to point out, almost all the schools in the district are "getting the idea (and) moving forward," but Exemplar "is our flagship (school)."

7. The School-Community Connection: Partnership, Ownership, Resources, Respect

Parent members of the PST board, 11 women and 4 men, are high-energy people who are knowledgeable and very articulate about the current status of education both nationally and locally. All, for example, had read *A Nation at Risk* (National Commission, 1983), and several were actively lobbying for a change in the state funding formula for education. Not only did they have high expectations for the school, but they were willing to invest "whatever it takes" to help the school deliver on these expectations. Such a positive and cooperative concern about the quality of education their children received meshed nicely with the principal's ever-present optimistic "We Can" attitude. It seems that this joint enthusiasm and willingness to go to any lengths to succeed had been an important catalyst in igniting Exemplar to develop itself into a good school. The parents characterized their relationship to Exemplar as one of joint ownership. They see the school as being the school of the community and their role as helping to facilitate a good educational experience for their kids.

The majority of board members were professionally trained women who had chosen not to work outside the home at this time. They brought to the school not only high levels of expertise in organization and management, but also an ability to be in the building whenever the need was greatest. Thus, Exemplar enjoyed not only the individual skills of many parents, but also the expertise that the board could recruit from the wider community. The principal saw the parent group "as the second most important resource (after) my staff." He had an excellent working relationship with the PST group: He worked closely with the chairperson and the school board member who also sat on the PST board. He, in return, was held in extremely high regard by members of the PST board. Responses to the question "What makes Exemplar a good school?" reveal the depth of understanding board members have about the various key elements of a good school:

- Teachers and administrators (here) like students. . . . Students feel good about themselves."
- The teachers are excellent. . . . Kids have fun, but there's an emphasis on self discipline.
- Dr. _____ (the principal) is the best thing to happen (to Exemplar). The kids love him. . . . I know he will always level with me. . . . (He is) a good listener and a man of action. . . . He even returns my phone calls.
- We (the parents) are encouraged to get involved in the school. . . . Our board is always recruiting volunteers to sell supplies, tutor, host coffees, and chaperone dances. . . . Our parents always come through. . . . (They) enjoy being in the school.
- (Exemplar) offers a wide range of interesting courses and activities. . . . Also, they do a good job helping kids move from elementary and later into high school. . . . The counselors are a great help.
- Teachers put in long hours. . . . I really appreciate the music director, she

is fantastic. . . . The tour the orchestra took to Europe last year was beautiful.

- This school gets results. . . . My son is learning both French and Spanish. . . . I can't keep him off the computer . . . . He is getting an excellent foundation for high school and college.
- I have two children here. . . . My seventh grader (a boy) is having trouble reading. . . . I love the special help he is getting. . . . Julie (another Board member) is tutoring him twice a week in his English class.
- The PST board plays an important part in making (Exemplar) a good school. . . . We help make policy and get people involved in helping out. . . . I think it's important to help. I know the teachers and students appreciate what we do.

It is evident from their comments that the board members are very supportive of the teachers and administrators at Exemplar. They are quick to point to the arrival of the present principal as marking the beginning of the turnaround at Exemplar. They voiced some fears about uncontrolled drinking and smoking during the previous administration and said that at the time several families had talked about putting their children in private schools for the junior high years. Now, however, they see Exemplar as a healthy, happy, familylike environment where they feel comfortable sending their children. They credit the principal for bringing about such a change by maintaining a "24-hour availability" and working to resolve the concerns of parents about the safety of students. Board members also saw a congruence between their own aspirations for their children, and the "We Can" philosophy projected by the school. To illustrate this point, the story was told to me of a board member, not present at the meeting, who had "turned down a sizable promotion in another city" after visiting the junior high schools in that community. He returned to tell everyone how fortunate they were to have Exemplar, which he viewed as an "extension of the family."

The PST board comprises 15 parents elected from the 7 feeder elementary schools; 1 parent is elected "at large." Two students from the Student Representative Association, 2 elected teachers, and the 2 principals complete the board. It meets formally once per month during the day. The board is chaired by a parent, and meetings are open to all parents. While the membership is dominated by parents, its charter indicates that it will work with the principal "to maximize the learning opportunities for every child." This board and the variety of expertise it mobilizes is important for the maintenance of the current program at Exemplar. The board is active in three general areas. First, the principal uses the board "as a sounding board for certain policy decisions." While the principal sees this as a good way to get "quick feedback from a cross section of the community," he also understands the "PR payoff" from involving parents in this way. Parents on the board are confident that they can provide good feedback when called upon to do so ("We changed some reporting codes on grade cards"), but point out that they frequently provide feedback before it is asked for! Moreover, they see that they serve an equally important role by preventing misinformation from circulating throughout the community—"We act as a rumor mill." Second, the board mobilizes volunteer help for the school. The range of activities they are involved with is somewhat remarkable. For example, they provide (a) aides for classrooms; (b) tutors for areas such as reading, mathematics, and languages; (c) resource persons for extracurricular activities; (d) sponsors for staff appreciation days and dinners; (e) hosts for new-parent coffees and open house; (f) chaperones for dances and school-sponsored trips; (g) staff to sell supplies; and (h) expertise in sponsoring drug awareness week and food drives for shelters. Third, they function as fund raisers for all kinds of projects at Exemplar that simply could not be offered from district funds. They are involved in printing the student handbook and the monthly PST newsletter, buying art work for display in the school, dispensing scholarships for summer courses, providing transportation for all varsity sports, furnishing landscaping, buying band uniforms and sheet music, and sponsoring the orchestra's trip to Europe. In raising several thousand dollars each year, they also supplement the instructional program by purchasing such things as library books, classroom materials, and software materials for use in a number of areas using computer-assisted instruction.

Beyond this obvious help the board provides to improve the educational climate at Exemplar, the principal also highlights the "two-way communication and trust" that such working together provides. He credits the PST board for working hard to make Exemplar more accessible to all parents. As illustration of this involvement, he pointed out that the board first suggested involving parents in the routine monitoring of the "Behavior Contract" developed by the staffing panel following a disciplinary hearing. Parents also first suggested changes in the reporting of grades. They also helped develop the "Exemplar-gram," a communication sent by teachers to parents to report on "good things done by students": This could highlight classroom work, extracurricular activities, or citizenship. The point the principal was emphasizing is that by opening up the school in this way, the school becomes more sensitive to the needs of the parents at the same time the parents are learning more about the methods and procedures used by the school. Thus, what we find at Exemplar is a congruence between the expectations the community has of the school and the goals of the school. Inasmuch as Exemplar is delivering on these expectations, the community is more than willing to invest itself in supporting the school. So interwoven is the school with the community that I doubt if the school could be as successful as it is without this level of community involvement and support. As one board member stated, "This community can only be as good as its schools."

8. The Glue That Holds the School Together:
Vision, Dedication, Expectations, Aspirations

Trying to define the glue that holds together the key elements of the school is a difficult task. As any good cabinet maker will attest, the glue usually cannot be seen in a finely crafted item: It almost seems as if the joints are held by an invisible hand. Moreover, the ingredients for a craftman's glue are frequently closely guarded secrets. Exemplar has the look and feel or superior craftsmanship. After several years of shaping and polishing, the various elements detailed above seem to fit naturally to form the whole, the school. But on closer inspection, it become apparent (a) that there is a glue which holds the school together, and (b) that this glue is an important part of the finished product. Let me attempt to separate out the several ingredients in this glue.

First, it is apparent that the major actors at Exemplar share a common vision of a good school. This vision, shared by teachers, administrators, and the majority of parents, includes a view of the school as it ought to be as well as a view of the means for achieving it. Such general agreement on the philosophy, goals, and school improvement strategies generates not only "can do" feelings of optimism, but also relationships that are cooperative and collaborative rather than antagonistic and adversarial. Consequently, the implementation of changes in either the form or substance of any element of the school (e.g., school rules or instructional strategies) becomes a relatively simple, rather than more customary complex, task. Proposed changes at Exemplar are judged on common criteria: The utility of present practice is assessed against the shared view teachers, administrators, and parents hold of what they want the school to become. It is this vision that drives Exemplar to constantly strive to achieve excellence.

Second, teachers and administrators at Exemplar have developed a healthy self-critical attitude about their performance. They want feedback from students and peers on their effectiveness in the classroom. Thus, not only do the teachers routinely solicit student and peer evaluations for their classes, but administrators routinely seek out feedback from students, teachers, and parents on their performance. Such a willingness to receive criticism helps create feelings of trust and cooperation: Teachers "have no fear of evaluation"; they see evaluation as a means of "improving the product."

Third, the teachers and administrators at Exemplar seem ever willing to work on improving themselves and the school. In talking with them they never seem satisfied to maintain what they have: "Doing things better" was a frequently expressed sentiment. They were eager, for example, to take the evaluation data on their classroom performance and work on self-improvement: Many teachers as well as the principals were anxious to receive a copy of my report, anticipating that it would contain a detailing of "things we can improve on." This desire for perfection was nurtured both by the parents and the central office. Parents encouraged the quest for excellence by projecting onto the school their own high aspirations for success in the world of work: They also provided fiscal and personnel support for activities that the district could not provide. The central office was equally supportive of Exemplar's improvement efforts, because it created an example for other schools to emulate: The central office also provided some incentive for innovation and self-improvement in the form of summer stipends, travel support, and in-service contracts.

Fourth, teachers and administrators at Exemplar project a sense of importance of purpose in their relationships with students and each other. From talking with them and watching them interact with students in a variety of settings, it is evident that they take seriously the charge to educate students, while also helping them become better citizens. This is done at Exemplar without losing sight of the fact that junior high students also need to have fun. Exemplar is organized to maximize both the time available for learning (e.g., there is a strict enforcement of the 3-minute passing time between classes, and announcements are only made before the first class) as well as the enjoyment of learning (e.g., many teachers employ team competitions as a learning device). It is interesting to see how the students have internalized this value system. For example, the students currently maintain a buddy system that pairs an A student with a student having trouble with excessive tardies or absences: This program is currently oversubscribed by A students wishing to adopt a "troubled student." The A student not only helps the errant student get to classes on time by telephoning in the morning and providing an escort during the day, but may also engage in tutoring material lost due to absences. In the meeting I observed, the appeal from the A student to the not-A student hinged on the need to "get with it" so as not "to lower the class mean" (classes are in competition to win trips to places of interest) or to jeopardize later opportunities to "go to college."

Fifth, we cannot overlook the importance of the personal drive and enthusiasm of the principal and the dedication and professionalism of the teachers. Teachers have a great trust in each other. They enjoy each other as friends and display much comraderie while working at Exemplar. There is a nice match between the principal's enthusiasm for improvement and the teachers' desire to engage in professional development.

The principal appears to be the key ingredient of the glue, if only because he is the most visible in the school and is frequently its prime spokesman outside of the school. Of greater importance, however, suggest a majority of teachers *and* the principal, is the organizational mechanism that is in place which involves all teachers in decision-making i.e., the decentralized governance system which emphasizes the departmental decision-making structure. It would appear to be the cohesiveness of the staff on issues such as philosophy, goals, and improvement strategies which outweighs the importance of the principal in making Exemplar effective.

Finally, Exemplar enjoys a match between the aspirations of the community and the goals of the school. Parents want a school which provides (a) a sound educational preparation for high school and "a good university"; (b) a happy and nurturing environment for both emotional and physical development; and (c) an enriching mix of cultural and artistic activities. Inasmuch as Exemplar provides this, the community works tirelessly *with* the school to provide every opportunity to maximize their children's success.

In sum, it may well be that this glue is invisible to the casual viewer of Exemplar. However, the shared vision, the continual self-criticism and striving for excellence, the sense of importance of the mission, the enthusiasm of the principal combined with the professionalism of the teachers, and the congruence of community aspirations and schooling outcomes are real. Moreover, they are critical ingredients in the glue which holds Exemplar together as a school. These elements serve to facilitate the development of the seven components detailed earlier: Without this glue, Exemplar would be less than the sum of its components.

SOME FINAL REFLECTIONS ON EXEMPLAR AND ITS TRANSFERABILITY

I began this chapter by suggesting that school reform was ill-served (a) by focusing only on the improvement proposals advocated in many of the recent national reports, or (b) by rushing to implement in every school in the nation the school improvement model emerging from a less-than-careful analysis of the effective schools research. I argued that school reform was ill-served in the first case, because most of the improvement proposals were not grounded in research on schools, and in the second case, because the effective schools model was derived from limited research on basic skills acquisition in urban elementary schools, In short, I concluded that we need to proceed cautiously, because we simply do not yet know enough about how to create effective schools in different settings (e.g., in elementary, junior high, or senior high schools, or in schools varying in size) to be talking in anything approaching authoritative terms about a blueprint for school change.

Next I developed the idea of describing Exemplar Junior High School, a composite school comprising parts of the 6 exemplary junior high schools I observed as a site visitor in the Secondary School Recognition Program sponsored by the U.S. Department of Education. Cross-site analysis of a large body of data revealed a consistent pattern across all 6 schools. Eight components of these schools formed the framework for describing how and why this fictionalized school named Exemplar achieved excellence. In detailing the building, the people, the program, the extracurricular activities, the governance structure, the school-central office connection, the school-community connection, and the glue that holds the school together, I tried to bring the school to life to describe both the form and substance of these elements which function in concert to make Exemplar so outstanding.

While I have been careful to suggest that Exemplar should not be seen as *the* model for improving all junior high schools, the question we must now answer is "In what way is Exemplar useful in guiding school improvement at the junior high school level?" In looking beyond Exemplar as an idealized quick-fix model for creating an effective school, it becomes evident that Exemplar is important for several reasons. First, Exemplar is a composite of several excellent schools which have developed themselves over an extended period of time independently of districtwide mandates to become more effective by using the popular model of effective schools (see Brookover et al., 1979; Edmonds, 1979). This emphasis on self-improvement at the building level signals, I suspect, that Exemplar may well be representative of junior high schools throughout the country.

Second, Exemplar illustrates that components not emphasized in the existing school effectiveness literature are important to school improvement. Whereas this literature highlights the importance of factors such as strong leadership from the principal, a climate of high expectation, an orderly atmosphere, and an emphasis on basic skill acquisition with frequently monitored student progress, the analysis of Exemplar revealed the importance of factors such as interpersonal relationships, a professionally oriented faculty, curriculum innovation, a consistent instructional strategy, the governance structure, extracurricular activities, the relationship between school, community, and central office, and a shared vision of the "good school." This difference signals a need to reexamine the original literature using an expanded conceptual frame. It also suggests that there are important qualitative differences between elementary and junior high schools that will necessitate somewhat different approaches to school improvement (see Farrar et al., 1984; Firestone & Herriott, 1982).

The data from Exemplar are more supportive of the range of effective school components identified by Rutter et al. (1979) than those identified by Edmonds (1979). Edmonds generated his list of five components of effective schools by observing American urban elementary schools that did a good job of teaching the basic skills to all students. Rutter and his colleagues by contrast, identified eight key components from their research comparing British urban secondary schools with "good" and "bad" records of success in national examinations. While these two lists of key effective school components are similar, Rutter et al. note the increased complexity of secondary schools and detail the importance of (a) an emphasis on clear instructional goals; (b) consistent teaching strategies; (c) participatory governance; (d) high interaction between staff and students based on mutual respect; and what they call (e) a positive ethos for success. Clearly, Exemplar is more like Rutter's effective secondary schools than Edmonds's effective elementary schools.

Third, this description of Exemplar is important, because it details what people in schools do to bring about school improvement. By contrast, the majority of effective schools literature generates either (a) lists of components of effective schools while ignoring both how people behave within the components as well as how these components interact (e.g., Edmonds, 1979), or (b) descriptions of how people act within single components, such as leadership provided by the principal, again giving no sense of how these components interact and how actions in one component have implications for other components (e.g., Bossert, Dwyer, Rowan, & Lee, 1982; Dwyer, Lee, Rowan, & Bossert, 1983; Morris, Crowson, Hurwitz, & Porter-Gehrie, 1981).

Fourth, Exemplar illustrates how individual school improvement can be achieved by focusing attention on key components within the social context in which the school is located. By this I mean that *how* things were done at Exemplar was in large part a function of the attributes of the specific people in the building and the characteristics of the wider community. Thus we can predict that *how* things are done in other junior high schools is likely to be different from how they were done at Exemplar (e.g., there might be a different kind of parental support system in less affluent communities or a different school governance structure given teachers with varying views on decision-making). The point to be emphasized here, however, is not that the elements for making junior high schools more effective are likely to be different from school to school dependent on the social context, but rather that the social context of a specific school is likely to dictate a variety of ways of making these same elements effective.

Finally, Exemplar is a useful model for school improvement, because it provides a focus for discussion by teachers, administrators, and parents as they develop school specific plans for self-renewal. By extending the effective schools literature into the junior high school, Exemplar also provides a focus for further research in *both* elementary and secondary schools.

REFERENCES

Bossert, S., Dwyer, D.C., Rowan, B., & Lee, G.V. (1982). The instructional management role of the principal. *Educational Administration Quarterly, 18,* 34–64.

Boyer, E. (1983). *High school: A report on secondary education in America.* Princeton, NJ: Carnegie Foundation for the Advancement of Teaching.

Brookover, W.B., Beady, C., Flood, P., Schweitzer, J., & Wisenbaker, J. (1979). *School social systems and student achievement: Schools can make a difference.* New York: Praeger.

Clark, T.A., & McCarthy, D.P. (1983). School improvement in New York City: The evolution of a project. *Educational Researcher, 12,* 12–24.

Coleman, J.S., Campbell, E., Hobson, C., McPartland, J., Mood, A., Weinfeld, F., & York, R. (1966). *Equality of educational opportunity.* Washington, DC: U.S. Government Printing Office.

Coles, G.S. (1978). The learning disabilities test battery: Empirical and social issues. *Harvard Educational Review, 48,* 313–340.

Cuban, L. (1984). Transforming the frog into a prince: Effective schools research, policy and practice at the district level. *Harvard Educational Review, 54,* 129–151.

Dwyer, D., Lee, G.V., Rowan, B., & Bossert, S. (1983). *Five principals in action: Perspectives on instructional management.* San Francisco: Far West Laboratory.

Edmonds, R. (1979). Effective schools for the urban poor. *Educational Leadership, 37,* 15–27.

Edmonds, R. (1982). Programs of school improvement: An overview. *Educational Leadership, 40,* 4–11.

Farrar, E., Neufeld, B., & Miles, M.B. (1984). Effective schools programs in high schools: Social promotion or movement by merit? *Phi Delta Kappan, 65,* 701–706.

Firestone, W.A., & Herriott, R.D. (1982). Prescriptions for effective elementary schools don't fit secondary schools. *Educational Leadership, 40,* 51–53.

Fullan, M. (1982). *The meaning of educational change.* New York: Teachers College Press.

Goodlad, J.I. (1984). *A place called school.* New York: McGraw Hill.

Huberman, M., & Miles, M. (1984). *Innovation up close: How school improvement works.* New York: Plenum.

Jencks, C., Smith, M., Ackland, H., Bane, M.J., Cohen, D., Gintis, H., Heyns, B., & Michelson, S. (1972). *Inequality: A reassessment of the effects of family and schooling in America.* New York: Basic Books.

Jensen, A. (1969). How much can we boost I.Q. and scholastic achievement? *Harvard Educational Review, 39,* 1–123.

Joyce, B., & Showers, B. (1980). Improving inservice training: The message from research. *Educational Leadership, 37,* 379–385.

McCormack-Larkin, M., & Kritek, W.J. (1982). Milwaukee's project RISE. *Educational Leadership, 40,* 16–21.

McKenzie, D.E., (1983). Research for school improvement: An appraisal of some recent trends. *Educational Researcher, 12,* 5–17.

Miles, M.B. (1983). Unraveling the mystery of institutionalization. *Educational Leadership, 41,* 14–19.

Morris, V., C., Crowson, R.L., Hurwitz, E., & Porter-Gehrie, C. (1981). *The urban principal.* Chicago: University of Chicago Press.

National Commission on Excellence in Education (1983). *A nation at risk: The imperative for education reform.* Washington, DC: U.S. department of Education.

New York State Department of Education.(1974). Reading achievement related to the educational and environmental conditions in 12 New York City elementary schools. Albany, NY: Division of Education.

Pink, W.T. (1983, November). *Translating the literature on effective schools into practice: Some words of caution.* Paper presented at the American Educational Studies Association Annual Meeting, Milwaukee, WI.

Pink, W.T. (1984). Creating effective schools. *The Educational Forum, 49,* 91–107.

Pink, W.T., & Leibert, R.E. (In press). Reading in the elementary school: Some observations and a proposal for reform. *The Elementary School Journal.*

Pink, W.T., & Wallace, D.K. (1984). Creating effective urban elementary schools: A case study of the implementation of planned change. *Urban Education, 19,* 273–315.

Project SHAL. (1982). An educational intervention project for the development of more effective schools. St. Louis, MO: St. Louis Public Schools.

Purkey, S.C., & Smith, M.S. (1983). Effective schools: A review. *The Elementary School Journal, 83,* 427–452.

Rist, R. (1970). Social class and teacher expectations: The self-fulfilling prophesy in ghetto education. *Harvard Educational Review, 49,* 411–451.

Rowan, B., Bossert, S., & Dwyer, D. (1983). Research on effective schools: A cautionary note. *Educational Researcher, 12,* 24–31.

Rutter, M., Maugham, B., Montimore, P., Ousten, J., & Smith, A. (1979). *Fifteen thousand hours: Secondary schools and their effects on children.* Cambridge, MA: Harvard University Press.

Sarason, S.B. (1971). *The culture of the school and the problems of change.* Boston: Allyn & Bacon.

Sizer, T.R. (1984). *Horace's compromise: The dilemma of the American high school.* Boston: Houghton Mifflin.

Twentieth Century Fund Task Force on Federal Elementary and Secondary Educational Policy (1983). *Making the grade.* New York:

Weber, G. (1971). *Inner-city children can be taught to read: Four successful schools.* Washington, DC: Council for Basic Education.

11
Effective High Schools

ANTOINE M. GARIBALDI
Xavier University of Louisiana

Since the publication of the report by the National Commission on Excellence in Education (NCEE) in April, 1983, a great deal of attention has been devoted to the "mediocre" quality of American education, both public and private. An exhaustive litany of problems and deficiencies have been cited (e.g., poor facilities, inadequate and inferior educational materials, insufficient state, local, and federal revenues, an attenuated potpourri of academic subjects in secondary schools, lack of discipline, incompetent teachers). But, while many immediate solutions have been presented, few of them are either sound and radical enough to abate these problems mentioned or strong enough to hold back the "rising tide of mediocrity" which the report mentions ever so often.

The proposals include a range of reforms: emphasizing literacy processes in reading and writing; incorporating study skills courses into the curricula; strengthening curriculum content; encouraging teachers to make better use of classroom time, to organize students by academic achievement, and to use rigorous (and more) textbooks in the academic disciplines; encouraging schools of education to ensure that teacher education candidates are as competent in the academic subjects as they are in methods and education courses; and increasing parental involvement in all schools. The most popular response to these proposals taken by many state departments of education and local school districts has been to increase minimum graduation requirements for students. As of May, 1984, 48 states were considering new high school graduation requirements, and 35 had already approved changes (U.S. Department of Education, 1984). However, to believe that an increase in the amount and type of courses for secondary students will produce more well-rounded and competent students is fallacious. More does not always necessarily mean better.

Simultaneous with the release of the NCEE report came a barage of related findings from other federal, state, and private commissions (e.g., National Science Board Commission, 1983; Twentieth Century Fund, 1983) that also gave American education, particularly public schools, a low grade for their efforts. Moreover, recent books and monographs by educators such as Goodlad (1984), Boyer (1983), Ravitch (1983), and Sizer (1984) also provide both reflections of the history of public education in this country and suggestions for reform. All of these action agendas spring both from declining test scores by high school students on national achievement and aptitude tests over the last 25 years as well as the perception of American citizens that public (and private) education is not meeting the expectations they hold for the academic and social training of children.

This chapter is not a theoretical discussion of the aforementioned issues, but rather (a) a description of eight high schools which consider themselves "excellent" and effective; and (b) a discussion of the critical elements which seem to make them that way. These eight high schools describe themselves as institutions that have identified their deficiencies and worked diligently to ameliorate them. It is clear that no one solution such as curriculum reform will remedy the problems that American education faces. It is hoped that educators will learn from the examples reported in this chapter. We must remember, however, that it is difficult to generalize from this small sample of schools, because more than 13 million young people attend 16,000 public high schools in this country.

SELECTION CRITERIA FOR EFFECTIVE SECONDARY SCHOOLS

Data for this chapter come from eight site visits to high schools in four states that were conducted for the Department of Education's Secondary School Recognition Program. Begun during the 1982–83 academic year, the purpose of this program was to recognize junior and senior high schools that were doing "an unusually effective job of educating students." Great care was taken by government officials to note that these were not necessarily the "best schools" in America, because it would be impossible to evaluate all secondary schools that considered themselves excellent in a short span of one year. Additionally, states could only nominate five junior high/middle and five senior high schools during the first year of the competition. Nevertheless, the schools that were screened to receive a site visit were quite diverse in terms of geographic location, school size, type of community (urban, suburban, and rural), grade levels served, staff size, and physical facilities. A profile of all the high schools which received site visits in the spring of 1983 showed that: 21% were rural, 50% were suburban; 20% were mixed; 28% of the schools had a minority enrollment of 25% or more; 18% had a sizable group of recent immigrants; 17% had 25% or more students from low-income families; and enrollments ranged from 91 to 3,666 students.

Nomination Forms
Very specific criteria were used to "evaluate" school programs (based on the nomination forms submitted by each school). The nomination forms provided information on: the school's staff and student body; the school's instructional goals, programs, policies, and practices; graduation requirements; remedial and advanced programs; homework policies; student rewards and incentives; attendance and discipline (including suspension and expulsion rates); cocurricular activities; teacher evaluation processes and their involvement in curriculum decisions, staff development, etc.; administrative leadership; community support; monitoring of student progress; student achievement scores; and many other items. These 20-page forms were then "evaluated" by 18-member panels of nongovernment experts (school teachers, state, and local school board members, parents, principals, researchers, education policy analysts, and others). There were two separate panels: one for

junior high/middle schools and another for senior high schools. Each panel consisted of 18 members.

Panelists "judged" the overall quality of each school on 14 attributes and 7 indicators of success using each school's nomination form to make that determination. The 14 attributes of success were:

1. Clear academic goals
2. High expectations for students
3. Order and discipline
4. Rewards and incentives for students
5. Regular and frequent monitoring of student success
6. Opportunities for meaningful student responsibility and participation
7. Teacher efficacy
8. Rewards and incentives for teachers
9. Concentration on academic learning time
10. Positive school climate
11. Administrative leadership
12. Well-articulated curriculum
13. Evaluation for instructional improvement
14. Community support and involvement

The 7 indicators of success were:

1. Student performance on standardized achievement tests
2. Student performance on minimum competency tests
3. Percentages of students who go on to postsecondary education or training, who enlist in the military, or who are successful at finding jobs
4. Numbers of students who receive scholarships or other awards
5. Student dropout rates, daily student and teacher attendance rates, rates of suspensions and other exclusions
6. Awards or recognition for outstanding school programs and teaching
7. Student awards in academic, vocational, or other school-related competitions such as science fairs, essay contests, or industrial arts competitions.

The nomination forms, as described earlier, were quite comprehensive and included detailed information for review panels to obtain a sense of a school's accomplishments and/or improvements. These data assisted panelists to determine whether the school should receive a site visit or be excluded from further competition.

Site Visits
The site visits were designed to collect more information on the school through a day-long observation of a normal school day. These visits were not intended to be complete evaluations. However, the observers, most of whom were university faculty and administrators knowledgeable about school processes, were charged with collecting information that could amplify certain activities or school processes

noted in the nomination form, but perhaps not fully comprehensible to the review panel members.

The site visitors were the key linkages between the schools nominated and the review panel. The site visitors returned detailed reports on what they observed. They reported on their interviews with students, teachers, special service personnel (special education teachers, remedial teachers, counselors, librarians, teacher aides, cafeteria and janitorial staff, and others), parents and community members, administrators and the district superintendent. Representative groups of each of these categories were consulted primarily to provide their perceptions of the school, especially regarding the interaction of students with teachers and administrators. Each impression provided a collective collage of the school, and despite the fact that the visits lasted for only one day, it was possible to sketch a picture of each of the schools represented.

The remainder of this chapter focuses on a description of the schools and the impressions of the interviewed groups about their schools. The information is presented in aggregate fashion primarily to preserve anonymity of the schools and also to amplify several commonalities and differences of the eight schools. Each of these eight high schools was subsequently recognized by the panel to receive an award.

EIGHT EFFECTIVE HIGH SCHOOLS

Overview

Close inspection of Table 1 reveals both the diversity and commonalities of the eight schools visited. Three of the schools were in urban areas, four were suburban, and one rural. District sizes ranged from slightly more than 3,000 students to a high of 56,000. Six of the schools served students in grades 9 through 12, while two served students in grades 10 through 12. School student bodies averaged slightly more than 1,300 with a range of 1,157 to 1,538. Ethnic composition of the students in the schools varied considerably, although the majority were predominantly white. (Only three schools had minority enrollments exceeding 40%, and two had minority enrollments of less than 4%.)

Each school had an average of almost four administrators for the students served and an average of 67 full-time teachers and approximately 3 part-time teachers. Teacher aides were not common in most of the schools, and full-time social workers and security officers were nonexistent. Almost every school had two librarians.

Minimum graduation requirements were fairly consistent among the eight schools, despite the fact that they were in four states. Approximately 4 years of English, a little more than 2 years of mathematics, 2½ years of social studies, and about 2 years of science were required for graduation.

The information on students after graduation varied considerably among the eight schools. On average, 64% of the graduates enrolled in 4-year colleges or universities (with a range of 45% to 96%); an average of almost 10% enrolled in community colleges; almost 7% were in vocational schools; close to 20% worked part time or full time; and an average of about 3% enlisted in the military.

Table 1. Characteristics of Eight Exemplary High Schools Visited for Secondary School Recognition Program

Characteristics	Schools								Averages
	1	2	3	4	5	6	7	8	
Type of school	Urban	Urban	Suburban	Rural	Urban	Suburban	Suburban	Suburban	
District size	46,310	12,024	23,199	11,397	47,628	3,161	56,109	53,995	
Grade levels served	9–12	10–12	9–12	9–12	9–12	9–12	10–12	9–12	
N of students in school	1,538	1,230	1,432	1,157	1,221	1,212	1,491	1,184	1308.25
Administrators	3	4	4	3	4	5	5	3	3.9
Ethnic composition (%)									
White	57	96.6	97.8	62	45.1	82.5	79	78	
Black	43	.5	0.76	33	50	15	11	17	
Other	0.85	1	1.25	5	7	2.5	10	5	
Teachers (FT/PT)[a]	71/6	72/3	70/2	62	74/4	86	73/1	57/8	66.9/3
Teacher aides (FT/PT)	4	1	1	2/1	2	5	3/2	0	2.25/.38
Library staff	2	2	2	2	1	2	2	2	1.9
Social workers	1	2	0	0	0	0	0	0	
Security officers	part-time	0	1	0	2 part-time	2	0	0	
Food service staff (FT/PT)	12	6	17	13	1/10	10/4	11/5	10	10/2.38
Clerical	7	7	6	4	10	18	9	4	8.5
Counselors (FT/PT)	3	4	4/0	2/0	4	6	3	3	3.6

Graduation requirements (minimum; in yrs.)							
English	4	4	3	4	4	3	4	3.75
Math	3	1	2	3	2	2	3	2.375
Social studies	2.5	2	2	2.5	3	3	2.5	2.5
Science	2	1	1	2	2	2	2	1.75
Graduates:								
Enrolled in a 4-yr. college (%)	65	55	60	67	50	76.8	45	96	64.3
Enrolled in a community college (%)	1	25	2	12	20	11.9	2	2.5	9.5
Enrolled in a vocational school (%)	8	7	2	16	10	2.1	11	.5	7.0
Found full time employment (%)	7	5	23	3	10	4.5	0	1	6.8
Found part-time employment (%)	10	0	27	10	5	3.1	23		13.2
Enlisted in the military (%)	6	8	3	2	5	1.6	1 student		3.0

aFT = full-time; PT = part-time.

255

Teachers

Teachers were interviewed both in groups and individually. They were asked a series of questions regarding their perceptions of their school's quality, atmosphere, their role in planning and curriculum development, the extent of communication among faculty and administrators, and whether they believed their efforts were recognized and appreciated at their respective schools. The responses to these questions were extremely consistent across all schools. Their places of work were described as pleasant environments with a relaxed atmosphere and where the goals and rules of the school were well-articulated. The key to this consensus of opinion, however, is best explained by the low turnover rate in almost all of the schools. In at least four of the schools, the average length of stay for 90% of the faculty was 15 years, with many teachers having spent considerably more than 20 years.

Another key factor that contributed to the positive descriptions of the school milieu is best typified by the constant acknowledgment of the work of the principal—whom faculty often described as instructional leaders as well as good and sensitive managers. Five of the principals had taught at their respective schools before assuming the leadership role, and, interestingly, four of the principals had also previously served as counselors. Four of the eight principals were female. Understanding the role of the faculty and the problems of students was noted often by teachers and students as essential ingredients to an effectively managed high school. At those schools where the principal had previously served as a teacher, the faculty believed that these administrators understood their daily problems of teaching and planning as well as handling "difficult" students. At one of the schools where the principal had served as a counselor, students said that the administrator "was easy to talk to, because he had been a counselor and director of student activities." They felt that he understood their problems and could offer realistic solutions to make school more enjoyable for them.

While most teachers felt that there was never enough time for planning and developing curricula, all believed that they had a meaningful role in school decision-making, both with respect to school policies and the instructional program. Most were very comfortable with the fact that students oftentimes made recommendations for new courses. These requests were implemented if there were enough students interested in taking the courses. Schools which had an assistant principal for academics believed that the process of course scheduling and development was even better managed than schools without such an administrator.

Though it is somewhat trite to say that teachers receive their satisfaction and greatest rewards from seeing students learn and seeing them go on to successful careers, that statement perhaps epitomizes the feelings of those teachers interviewed. Although one school has had a merit pay plan in effect since 1953, the majority of the teachers reported that having students come back to the school after they graduate to thank them for their secondary preparation was appreciated. Teacher appreciation days and secret-pal activities established by the students were commonplace in almost all of the schools. The supportive efforts of the administrators, parents, and the community appeared to heighten morale among the teachers in recognition of their caring and sensitive attention to students.

Students

Students were also interviewed in groups. However, numerous opportunities were also available for asking them questions individually while touring the building or observing extracurricular activities. The students were asked to provide their perception of the school in terms of academics and interrelationships with other students, faculty, and administrators; they were asked what they did not like about the school, whether they believed they knew what was expected of them in terms of academic work as well as whether those expectations were realistic; and finally, they were asked whether they believed they had a meaningful role in influencing school programs or policies.

The students interviewed were representative of the schools' student bodies, even though the samples were usually less than 30. Some were student government representatives, others athletes, others very active in extracurricular activities, and some not very involved in the total school program. On the whole, however, they were quite positive about the school atmosphere, usually had high praise for teachers and administrators, and admitted that the competitive nature of the academic requirements sometimes created personal pressures and tensions that they would have preferred not dealing with, even though they recognized that this would be good preparation for their later careers. The school atmospheres were characterized as "friendly" places with a good deal of school spirit and as environments where teachers were "down to earth" and not "high and mighty." Students were candid in their responses, even comfortable with noting that they occasionally took "easy" courses in which a bare minimum was expected. Most students liked the kinds and types of relationships they had with teachers and administrators and intimated their recognition of the extent of caring that teachers showed toward students.

In a few instances, it was difficult for students to identify what they did not like about school beyond the standard reply of "the food." However, numerous points did surface. For example, some students expressed their displeasure with rigorous grading for advanced placement courses, others noted dress codes (e.g., Why can't boys wear shorts when girls can wear miniskirts?); the outmoded facilities were also mentioned by a few, and some complained about students who habitually broke school rules (e.g., smoking in lavatories).

Students believed that school rules were well-articulated and understood by most students. Similarly, the expectations of most teachers' courses were understood, and the amount of daily homework usually varied depending upon course or the teacher. On the average, students indicated that they did from one to two hours of homework per weekday evening. Those students taking several advanced placement or honors courses said it was not unusual to do five or six hours of homework per evening. Students prefaced some of their comments by saying that the amount of homework they did was usually a choice made by them, since they were fully aware of what courses demanded more outside work.

Finally, the majority of students interviewed expressed positive sentiments for their principals. When they were asked whether they felt they had a role or opportunity to influence school policies or programs, the majority of the responses suggested that students were actively involved in making recommendations for new courses, but that their role in changing school practices was quite limited. Only two of the eight schools provided formal opportunities for students to participate in school decision-making. One of the schools had approximately 10 standing committees (e.g., administrative/faculty communications, guidance and counseling, faculty affairs, student affairs, public affairs, staff development, discipline and attendance, scholarship committee, board of control, etc.), and at least one student sat on each committee. Another school had a Student Congress which had four committees: curriculum, privileges, special programs, and elections. Students who served on these committees met regularly with the principal and assistant principal to discuss school policies or student-generated issues. While most schools did not have such formal mechanisms for student involvement in school decision-making, the student government was the primary mechanism by which student concerns were conveyed to the faculty and administration. Student councils appeared to be engaged more in planning activities than changing school policies.

Special Service Personnel

Counselors, special education teachers, remedial teachers, and aides were not numerous at the schools, but when present, their roles appeared to be well-integrated into the school program. Counselors at the schools spent at least 80% of their time with students. Special education and remedial teachers acknowledged that the amount and kinds of cooperation they obtained from regular teachers facilitated their work with students. Parents, too, were quite cooperative with teachers and counselors. The implementation of a regular academic monitoring system by the principals helped parents know how their children were performing in their classes. The cooperation was important but, even more, auxiliary personnel were considered and treated as regular staff. The work of the counselors was organized and, despite the large case loads, these individuals had an opportunity to meet with their students on a regular basis. Teachers also sought out counselors and the special service personnel when problems arose in their classes with particular students.

Parents/Community

Parents were proud of the schools their children attended and provided considerable support to teachers and administrators: Some were amazed at how free students seemed to be with calling teachers at home; others were pleased that their children had many opportunities to participate in school clubs and cocurricular activities; and still others were pleased with the number of activities going on in the schools. They constantly made reference to the staff as a group of "caring" and "friendly" individuals who "love kids." Items such as knowing all students by name and the positive attitude of the school were very important to parents since they recognized how easy it was for their child to get lost in a large student body. Parent-teacher associations were nonexistent at almost all of the schools, but parents still felt they were able to make contributions in a variety of ways. Some of the examples they cited were: fund-raising activities for athletics, academic, or cultural clubs; serving as volunteers during the school day to assist teachers as aides or operating the mimeograph machine in the principal's office; and preparing the school newsletter for parents of the students. Booster clubs are quite popular at most of the schools, and two schools raised $50,000 and $60,000, respectively, so their bands could play in parades. Community support was also evident in scholarships given to graduates, adopt-a-school programs with businesses, internships for students interested in technical careers, and sponsorships of school activities. Rural schools appeared to reap the most benefits from their communities as local citizens expressed the pride and concern they had for local educational institutions. In almost all schools, parents mentioned that it was easy for them to contact any staff member. They felt that the "early warning system" of monitoring academic progress at the end of six or nine weeks gave their children ample time to improve their grades and a chance for parents to more closely monitor homework.

CONCLUSION

These eight schools, despite their differences in size, geographical location, and student body, share many more commonalities than differences. The commonalities are those critical ingredients which make each of them exemplary and unusually effective secondary schools. In reading the site-visit reports of these schools it is difficult to tell that these are suburban, urban, and rural comprehensive (two were magnet) high schools serving diverse student bodies in four states. Similarly, one might presume that the school sites have luxurious school campuses. But that, too, is not the case. Two of the school plants are 50 years old, while the other two are about 20 years old. All are well-maintained. Clearly, it is not the building which makes a school effective, but rather the learning that permeates throughout the school environment.

Commonalities

There were several similarities among the eight schools: (a) graduation requirements at the schools exceeded their state minimum requirements; (b) staff turnover rates were exceptionally low and most teachers had been at their schools for several years; (c) schools were orderly and teachers obtained their greatest rewards from seemingly insignificant signs of appreciation; (d) discipline in the schools was exemplary and both students and teachers had very low absentee rates; (e) the leadership of principals was noteworthy and teachers were complimentary of the supportive efforts of administrators; and (f) students were heavily involved in a wide selection of cocurricular activities. Parents were quite contented with the expectations of the school and felt that their children were able to meet the school's academic challenges. This motivation on the part of students and the schools' high expectations for achievement are critical ingredients to the success of any school.

What Makes a School Effective?

After reviewing and visiting the eight secondary schools discussed thus far, this writer (who also spent three years as a secondary administrator in the mid-1970s) came away from this experience with the following criteria for making schools effective: sound and diverse curricula; highly able and committed staff; good (but not oppressive) discipline; an orderly academic climate; effective school adminis- trative leadership; functional involvement of parents; numerous and diverse cocur- ricular activities; and students who are motivated and have high expectations for themselves.

Since secondary schools serve so many different types of students, both in terms of socioeconomic status and ability levels, it seems imperative that the variety and depth of the curriculum prepare students not only for college or vocational train- ing, but also for the world of work which many young people will enter immediate- ly after graduation. The eight schools visited had advanced placement, honors, and remedial courses, as well as a range of elective courses which faculty believed were important to liberally educating their students. As Table 1 clearly demonstrates, all secondary graduates do not enter college after their 12 years of education. And since only about 30, 18, and 5% of all high school graduates go on to 4-year col- leges, 2-year colleges, and vocational or technical schools, respectively, secondary staff must offer diverse courses to meet the needs of all students and to ensure that their "life chances" are filled with hope and optimism (National Center for Educa- tional Statistics, 1984).

School effectiveness can be achieved, it would seem, by having an administra- tor who (a) recognizes and understands student and faculty needs; (b) delegates responsibilities (to students and faculty); (c) participates in the school's instruc- tional decision-making processes; (d) carefully screens, selects, and evaluates staff; and, lastly but most importantly, (e) projects the belief that all students can learn and achieve their potential. Leadership is essential to the productivity of any organizational unit. Selecting a principal who can convey a positive attitude and reinforce it by example and involvement is an important aspect of school im- provement. Finally, it should be noted that all of these criteria are attainable, and at hardly any additional cost to local school districts. These data suggest that organizational changes will improve schools—not necessarily more money to do more of the same thing.

REFERENCES

Boyer, Ernest L. (1983). *High school: A report on secondary education in America.* New York: Harper & Row.

Goodlad, John. (1984). *A place called school.* New York: McGraw Hill.

National Center for Education Statistics. (1984). College attendance after high school. *NCES Statistical Highlight.* Washingtin, DC: U.S. Department of Education.

National Commission on Excellence in Education. (1983). *A nation at risk: The imperative for educational reform.* Washington, DC: U.S. Government Printing Office.

National Science Board Commission on Precollege Education in Mathematics, Science, and Technology. (1983). *Educating Americans for the 21st century.* Washington, DC: National Science Foundation.

Ravitch, D. (1983). *The troubled crusade: American education 1945-1980.* New York: Basic Books.

Sizer, Theodore, R. (1984). *Horace's compromise: The dilemma of the American high school.* Boston: Houghton Mifflin.

Twentieth Century Fund. (1983). *Making the grade.* Report of the Twentieth Century Fund on Federal Elementary and Secondary Education Policy. New York: Author.

U.S. Department of Education. (1984). *The nation responds: Recent efforts to improve education.* Washington, DC: U.S. Government Printing Office.

PART IV
MOVING FROM SCHOOL
TO WORK

The transition of youth from school to the work force has been characterized as both inevitable and problematic. While there are organizational similarities between schools and work places, youth are nevertheless confronted with transferring school learning into the world of work. Finding a job, learning about the job, and holding a job become important activities for young workers. Because so little is known about *how* youth become workers in contrast to how many youth become workers in different kinds of jobs, the three chapters in this section are important contributions to our knowledge.

Borman (chap. 12) draws similarities between the people-processing functions of schools and the workplace. She notes the presence of formal and informal mechanisms in both settings which serve to "indoctrinate the students or workplace recruit into the organization's routine." Employing a cultural transmission model, Borman examines the informal processes at work in a range of job sites which serve to assist young workers fit into a job. Learning the pace of work is her focus. Borman argues that opportunities for social learning is the key. Success in fitting into a job is seen as a function of the characteristics of the work setting and of the individual worker. Borman finds that the opportunities for learning differ across a range of job sites. Young women are found to experience the most difficulties due to the limited opportunities for social interaction in the jobs they typically hold.

In Chapter 13, Reisman explores the authority relationship between young workers and their managers. Drawing comparisons between the workplace and schools, she details the notion of authority as vested in the position versus the notion of authority as negotiated in the setting. Reisman argues that young workers must learn to contain their spontaneous behavior and to understand the varied ways authority operates at the work site. While she notes negotiation between workers and managers, Reisman concludes that termination is usually seen by management as the result of the young workers' "failure to respect the rules and comply with practices."

In the final chapter, Wolcott questions the validity of the assumption that "after school comes work." He presents a case study of a young man struggling to establish identity and security outside of the school–work nexus. Wolcott examines the frequently poor connection between schooling and finding and holding a job. By detailing *how* a young male attempts to resolve marginality resulting from choosing to remain outside the conventional path of school-to-work, Wolcott brings into sharp focus the limitations of our culture to provide career alternatives.

12
Fitting Into a Job:
Learning the Pace of Work*

KATHRYN M. BORMAN
University of Cincinnati

Schools and workplaces as social organizations are negotiating environments in which one set of individuals (teachers/trainers) attempts to shape the behavior, skills, and attitudes of another set (students/new workers) (Van Maanen, 1976). This view emphasizes the importance of social interaction or negotiation in achieving membership in these organizational settings.

As agencies of cultural transmission, schools and workplaces have several features in common. Both attempt to establish control over inexperienced members of the group but are less successful with some individuals than with others in achieving compliance with organizational goals and standards. Schools suffer the loss of disaffected students who leave school for a variety of reasons. Workplaces apparently have difficulty retaining young workers who constitute the disproportionately largest group of job leavers in the society (Buros, Kin, Santos, & Shapiro, 1983).

Both schools and workplaces inculcate specific skills viewed from the organization's perspective as appropriate for handling the task at hand. These skills are related to the governing technologies in each organization. In the school, *formal* descriptions of the curriculum include reference to literacy and computing skills at particular grade levels. In the workplace, training manuals list skills and abilities associated with degrees of proficiency in performing specific tasks such as processing statements in a bank, turning an elbow in a sheet metal shop, or even shelving stock in a super market.

Finally, both have unofficial but highly important *informal* programs designed to indoctrinate the student or workplace recruit into the organization's routine. In schools these programs are referred to as "citizenship training," cooperative learning, career education, and the like. They exist alongside and complement the "hidden curriculum," that system of values and behaviors which ensures that things move along on schedule and with minimal difficulty. In workplaces similar programs are spoken of as "induction," "orientation," "initiation," or "breaking-in" (Israeli, 1977, p. 135). Lessons learned from these unofficial agendas in both the

*The research reported here was supported by a grant from the National Institute of Education (NIE-G-83-0005) through the National Center for Research in Vocational Education at The Ohio State University.

school and the workplace probably carry over from these settings and affect interaction in the family, community, and other institutions and thus assume considerable importance in the daily lives of individuals.

The primary purpose of this chapter is to analyze informal learning processes in
the workplace by providing illustrations of one dimension of cultural transmission,
learning the pace of work. The pace of work refers to what Donald Roy (1959-60)
in his study of worker relations in a machine shop setting called "a patterned combination of horseplay, serious conversation, and frequent sharing of food and drink
to reduce the monotony of simple, repetitive operations to the point where a regular
schedule of the long workday became bearable" (p. 166). Roy, who worked as a die
cutter during his research, initially developed a series of mental games and later
became a partner in the ritualized verbal exchanges of his co-workers. Roy's accommodation to the pace of work took a developmental course over 2 or 3 months'
time. At first he concocted a series of games in which he mentally manipulated the
shapes and colors of the plastic and leather dies. Later he used breaks such as scrap-
ing the block, going to the lavatory, or getting a drink of water to vary the routine.
Finally, when he had developed some rapport with his co-workers, Roy entered the
complex rituals of "banana time," "fish time," and "Coke time" to regulate the
pace of work. He discovered that conversation during these events had a thematic
quality; jokes about one worker's relationship with his wife and another's status as
the father-in-law of a professor enforced a pecking order among the workers. His
workplace relationships had evolved into an easy, but highly structured, interactional
system. After 3 months Roy was well integrated into the machine shop culture.

Learning the pace of work requires the novice worker to gain an understanding
of at least three highly complex and interrelated components of work place culture:
(a) management culture; (b) work culture, and (c) task technology. In a later section, I will focus primarily on the second of these, work culture, although I will also
consider management culture. An analysis of task technology, the "nuts and bolts"
of processing bank statements, repairing air conditioners, and the like, is beyond
the scope of this discussion.

My major interest is in illustrating the different patterns of *social* learning available to young workers in different job settings. I will argue that along with characteristics of the job setting, characteristics of young workers, particularly gender,
profoundly affect these patterns. Young women seem particularly handicapped by
virtue of their more circumscribed opportunities for social interaction of any kind
in clerical and routine service jobs which they typically hold.

The data for this analysis are drawn from a longitudinal study of young workers
who were observed in their first full-time jobs after leaving high school.

MANAGEMENT CULTURE AND WORK CULTURE

In work settings, groups of co-workers collaborate to control the pace of work,
despite the existence of a hierarchy of authority that invests management with the
right to establish rules governing the work process (see Reisman, this volume).

Although there is an identifiable management culture, it remains relatively remote from the daily lives of ordinary workers.

Management culture stresses efficiency and effectiveness in getting the work accomplished in line with the formal authority structure of the workplace. The manager of a sheet metal shop, a job setting in the author's longitudinal study of young workers, stressed the importance of both technical skills and informal work rules in his assessment of a new employee's productivity:

> The key to working in our sheet metal shop is can a student count, and can a student follow instructions? . . . When they are instructed to get four pieces of a certain type of metal, they should be able to go and know where the right metal is, and get it. They should know how to cut it and do what is necessary for that piece of metal.

Although the emphasis is upon productivity, management may recognize that there are constraints on effective performance. In the case of the sheet metal shop, the manager allowed that not only was the work "tedious," "repetitive," and "very boring," but that in his role as supervisor, he typically does not "ever really make it completely clear what we expect from them." Thus, although managers may acknowledge difficulties inherent in negotiating new work roles for young employees, managers appear to hold very closely to an ideology that stresses productive output in line with legitimate demands flowing from a distant but authoritative source. By not making expectations for job performance particularly clear, management tacitly transfers the task of breaking in new workers to their co-workers and line supervisors. Thus, new workers become initiated in a *work* culture rather than a *management* culture.

Work culture is less visible to the observer than management culture, which is often broadcast in the form of slogans and prescriptive memoranda and is thus submitted down the line in written, codified form. Moreover, the new worker is likely to see workplace culture initially as barren in contents except for the technology involved in doing the job: for example, cutting sheet metal forms in the shop, batch processing overdraft statements in the bank, or taking inventory in the appliance repair shop. Cultural learning probably occurs in ways analogous to two intriguing metaphors, namely Harry Wolcott's (1982) recognition that all learners, like the child acquiring language, engage in *active* participation in the learning process to take on what Wolcott, citing Geertz, terms the "informal logic of actual life" and David Moore's (1983) image of scaffolding, a process by which the learner and trainers, i.e., co-workers and line supervisors, *together* construct a framework to which learners gradually add more and more bits to complete an increasingly elaborated, complex structure of workplace knowledge. The important dimensions of the learning process stressed in these metaphors are *active* participation and *negotiated* construction of workplace knowledge. Thus, the interactional nature of cultural transmission is fundamental to learning the work culture.

In considering the culture of work, it is important to clarify what is meant by the concept. *Work culture* can be defined as a "relatively autonomous sphere of action on the job, a realm of informal, customary values and rules which mediate the formal authority structure of the workplace and distance the workers from its impact" (Benson, 1978, p. 41, quoted in Apple, 1982). Work culture is not only a buffer against management culture, it constitutes a relatively autonomous "sphere of action" constructed by the activity of the workers.

Michael Apple persuasively argues that work culture is bolstered by norms that develop in specific work sites in various organizations. These norms provide workers with considerable autonomy and control. The institutionalization of banana time, peach time, Coke time, and other breaks in the clicking room allowed Donald Roy and his co-workers to manage the pace of their work. The significance of these brief breaks throughout the day became apparent when an altercation between two of the men temporarily shattered the social harmony and the pace of work in the clicking room. The breaks as well as the banter that accompanied them no longer occurred. Workers, fatigued and irritable, left their jobs physically exhausted and angry. Moreover, production declined as less work was accomplished, despite an unremittingly constant pace of work. Later, when harmonious relations had been restored, the pace of work once again became synchronous with the physical and psychological capacities of the workers. The important point here is that workers, not managers, regulated the flow of production.

In the longitudinal study, we observed an analogous case in a hospital setting. Workers whom we observed in the hospital cafeteria discussed the possibility of not accepting an order from staff in Labor and Delivery who habitually placed orders just as food service staff were in the process of turning off the grill, closing work stations, and cleaning up late in their evening shift. Although we did not observe them carrying out this threat, their conversation illustrates that these workers were clearly aware of the power they had to regulate the flow of their own work.

THE LONGITUDINAL FIELD STUDY OF ADOLESCENT WORKERS

Given the existence of a work culture, the question arises as to which aspects of the culture seem especially crucial in mediating management's norms of productivity and authority. In examining the initiation of new, inexperienced young workers into the cultural stream of the workplace, what evidence do we have that work norms are in fact gradually being acquired, particularly with respect to learning the pace of work? Correspondingly, what evidence is there to suggest that these norms are acquired in the context of a work culture as opposed to a management culture?

In order to answer these and other, related questions, my colleague Jane Reisman and her team in Columbus and I and my team in Cincinnati spent approximately 12 months conducting fieldwork in several work sites where we observed the processes by which youth become workers in these settings. The study focused on young people between the ages of 17 and 22 who had left school in order to find a job. Most of the 25 youth were high school graduates, all of whom were working part time or full time at entry-level jobs and were not currently in school.

The work sites were varied and eventually included approximately 90 different settings over a representative range of industrial sectors (Borman & Reisman, in press). The four sites to be considered here include two major banks, one in each city; an appliance repair and sales shop; and a fastener factory, the world's largest producer of industrial staples. These particular sites and the experiences of the young workers within them were selected for analysis here, because they readily provide contrasting and comparative pictures of cultural transmission. There is also sufficient documentation in these cases of processes of workplace learning, because in each case we were able to remain in the setting for at least 9 months. In no case did we spend less than 20 hours of observation at the workplace, and in one case field notes included more than 50 hours of observational time.

Observational accounts began with the first day the new worker was on the job or on the day closest in time to that day. The bulk of the data to be analyzed here is in the form of field notes taken during work-site observations. These field notes were later transcribed, typed, and analyzed. Additional data sources include work history interviews, current events interviews conducted periodically during the course of the study, and life history interviews conducted toward the end of the study.

These settings and the unfolding lives of the young workers within them were, as mentioned previously, particularly rich in comparative and contrasting detail as is clear from the four sets of analyses which follow. The analyses are organized as individual case studies. In a following section, I draw out themes and questions that seem important to consider regarding the contents of workplace learning, particularly with reference to learning the pace of work.

Betty: Customer Inquiry Representative, Midland Bank

Betty began her part-time job at the downtown headquarters of a major bank by attending an orientation for new employees hired throughout the firm. The orientation began at 9:00 a.m. after all new workers had been photographed and fingerprinted for the bank's personnel files. The orientation was designed to provide a picture of the bank's employee benefits program; organizational structure; and evaluation, promotion, and reward schemes. During the course of this presentation, new workers learned whom they should regard as their trainers and supervisors. Indeed, the organization's structure was portrayed primarily in terms of the individuals who were in charge of various of the bank's units. The trainer flashed a slide picturing the "key people" comprising the staff in Betty's unit, the customer inquiry department, and remarked, "Listen to Jeanne (the department supervisor)—smart lady—you'll learn a lot from her." In this manner, the organization's view of the process of learning and cultural transmission on the job was made explicit to the new recruits.

In explaining the salary structure for employees in the bank, the orientations officer stated, "In considering your grade level and hourly rate, we compare job responsibilities, not just job titles." She went on to display a transparency showing the range of salaries available to hourly personnel and others employed at the bank, saying, "You can't pay the teller as much as you would a manager because he or she has a college education, manages 25–50 employees, and has more responsibility." Thus, the lines between ordinary workers such as Betty and managers such as

Jeanne were made explicit both with respect to function (trainers and managers with more responsibility than ordinary workers) and wages (trainers and managers with regular, higher salaries than part-time and hourly ordinary workers).

The evaluation process was described as "the way you rise up the payroll scale." The categories for evaluation included job knowledge, "how well you know and understand your job"; quality of work; quantity of work; dependability; resourcefulness; attitude and cooperation with co-workers; and customer relations including not only "how well you get along with customers," but also "how well you dress." New employees were told that they would be given a rating of 1–5 on each of the dimensions and an overall rating. During their initial 30 to 90 days on the job, they would not be eligible for a salary increase but would be subject to termination, if they failed to maintain at least a rating of 2 on all dimensions. Each of the rating categories was then referenced with a statement regarding the probability for a pay increase associated with each of the rating categories.

At another orientation meeting later the same day, Betty met with her two immediate supervisors, Nancy and Vera. During this session involving only those new workers hired in the customer inquiry department, Nancy and Vera reviewed policies covering salaries and procedures. Time sheets, procedures for taking sick leave, the salary schedule, and training procedures were all described. Attendance, including policies governing tardiness, absences, and breaks, received most of the attention in the supervisors' remarks. Workers were told they would be continued on probation beyond the usual 6-month period, if they were late or absent more than four times during the initial 6-month period.

The rest of the meeting focused on how new workers would be affected by the training period. Each day over a 3-week period, new cusomter reps were told that they would be quizzed on aspects of the bank's policies and procedures including methods for taking sick days as well as procedures for handling customer queries. Quizzes would be administered following a period for study and review of assigned material. Trainees were expected to achieve a score of 85% or better on the quizzes. The first day's quiz, for example, covered their knowledge of the organization's key people. Trainees were given time on the job to review and study for these quizzes; however, they were also instructed to take about 1½ hours at home to review and consolidate their understanding of the material.

The final piece of information given to these new workers during their initial department meeting concerned the "star system," the computerized monitoring device used by the bank to supervise and regulate the flow of work. This system provided information to assist managers in scheduling Betty and her co-workers to cover periods of greater or lesser volumes of work during the course of the day. The major task handled by Betty and her co-workers in their jobs as customer reps was to answer incoming calls from customers who typically wished to find out the balance in a checking or savings account, determine the reason for an overdraft charge, or make a stop payment on a check. The bank's computing system recorded the number of telephone calls handled during the course of the work day by individual employees, the length of each call, the number and length of pauses in individual conversations with customers, and the like. Based on previously analyzed similar information, supervisors in Betty's department developed performance criteria for employees which they used to determine performance standards covering the pace of work. The new workers were told that reps were expected to handle 26 calls per hour.

Midland Bank provided the most highly detailed picture of its expectations for new employees of any business in the study. Moreover, it had certainly the most sophisticated technology imaginable in place to monitor the pace of work. A month after she had been hired, Betty was perceived by her immediate supervisors as doing well, primarily because of her skill in handling difficult customers. Frequently Betty and other customer reps received angry calls from customers whose plastic cards had disappeared into the bank's automated check-cashing machines or whose accounts had been assessed an unfamiliar charge by the bank. According to Betty's supervisor, her "quality of service" in these cases was exceptionally good.

The pace of work, particularly the volume of telephone calls handled each hour by Betty and the other reps, was expected to increase over the first 6 months of employment. Vera put it this way:

> We have a requirement of 22–26 calls an hour. They [the reps] start out anywhere from 15–18 the first month, then they go up to 19–20. So it's not something we expect immediately. We give them a good 6 months to really get ahead, because the more confidence they get, naturally, the more times they are plugged in. . . . They are going to get these calls promptly. If they know the job and naturally, gradually, once they learn everything, it (i.e., the pace of work) will pick up.

Calls were distributed among the five or six reps on the floor by an automated distributor. During their first 6 months on the job, Betty and her new co-workers were monitored on a regular basis by any one of three immediate supervisors who, through the bank's computerized star system, could, undetected by the rep, listen in on telephone conversations whenever they wished. According to one of these supervisors:

> In monitoring, we pick up different things such as the type of call, her answer to the call, the content of a call, the timing, her voice, tone, the service she gives. Then we have what we call a miscellaneous (category) such as using correct procedures.

In addition to providing accurate accounting information and the like, "correct procedures" included other components such as gaining proper identification from the customer before providing information and maintaining an "appropriate" number of conversational pauses, as described by Betty's supervisor:

> We as a bank naturally are confidential so we don't give out information (to just anyone). Customers have to identify their account, and our branches have to give a code that we set up, or we don't give them any information at all. Also we monitor outgoing calls—whether they are personal or business.

After hang-up time, we also put on (the rating sheet) whether they are filling out forms, if there is unnecessary talk, or if they are just idle.

Although Betty was perceived by all three supervisors as "exceptional" after little more than one month on the job, they only mentioned her skill with irate customers and her ability to handle the technical details of the job as indicators of her "exceptional" skills. Further, they were reluctant to give her an overall rating of anything over 3, indicating performance was "acceptable." This they explained by saying that Betty was still asking questions of her supervisors when certain issues came up.

At her telephone where she spent her day, Betty had access to a computerized fund of customer account information. However, when the computer was "down" as it usually was for some part of each work day, Betty was forced to use microfiche cards. Microfiche data was typically incomplete and frequently did not provide the most recent account activity. Thus, information regarding such things as overdrawn accounts and stop payments could not be accurately provided during the time the computer was not working. Reps, including Betty, were cautioned not to tell customers that the computer was unavailable, lest customers develop a lack of confidence in the bank. A frequently occurring theme in Betty's occasional asides to her co-workers concerned the difficulties of handling customer queries and problems with the insufficient information provided by the fiche. Thus, not only did the bank's computer system exert tremendous influence on the manner in which Betty's performance was evaluated, it was also critical in regulating the pace of her work. More calls could be processed when Betty was obliged to respond, "Our activity files are unavailable now, can you call back in an hour?"—the usual request made of a customer, if the computer was down.

Betty's work was tightly regulated by the technology of her job. Her breaks were taken at 4-hour intervals, and she was given a 45-minute break for lunch. Although their telephone activity was constantly monitored, Betty and her co-workers were allowed some measure of control over the pace of work. Customers' reps could simply unplug their telephones to avoid incoming customer queries. They could "cover" their "unplugged time" by taking more time than might be necessary in filing reports, stuffing envelopes, and handling other paper work. Betty, however, was never observed pulling the plug on incoming calls.

After 2 months on the job Betty was not only bored with her work, but she was also extremely upset about what she regarded as the bank's rigid enforcement of rules regarding absences and lateness. After 90 days, Betty had reported in ill once and had been 3 minutes late to work on two different occasions which placed her on a list to be "counseled" by her supervisors. For Betty, being an employee of the bank was like being back in school. Although she expected the bank to be conservative, she did not expect her supervisors to be strict and distrustful:

Employees are assigned to seats at work like in school. Employees are not permitted to receive personal telephone calls . . . , and (telephone) lines are . . . monitored.

Not only were calls regulated, but behavior in the office could also be scrutinized by supervisors who had placed specially ordered glass panels on their office door to allow them a clear view of office floor activity. Betty quit her job at Midland after 9 months as a customer rep.

Miriam: Bookkeeping Clerk, River City Bank

Miriam would have preferred secretarial work to the position she was given part time in the bookkeeping department at River City Bank. During the 7 months she was employed by the bank her tasks remained essentially the same, processing and filing the following sets of documents: overdraft notices; checks and statements; deposit and withdrawal slips; and statements for personal accounts and occasionally for business accounts.

Miriam's department in the bank was responsible not only for processing monthly statements but also for handling customer queries. Miriam worked in the same department as River City Bank's customer reps, but on the periphery at a work table facing away from the computer stations where the reps worked. Unlike Betty, Miriam received no initial training designed to acquaint her with the bank's structures and policies. Instead, training for her tasks occurred on an ad hoc basis as the nature of the particular bookkeeping chore changed. The pace of work in her case was highly dependent upon the monthly cycle followed by the bank in issuing statements to its customers.

By not having received either an orientation to the bank or written materials explaining bank policies, after a full 2 weeks on the job Miriam was still unaware of such procedures as whom to notify in case of lateness or sickness or even of the whereabouts of the employee lavatory. She remained equally mystified about such issues as evaluation and the extent to which it was permissible for employees to use conversation to regulate the pace of work. She suspected after 2 weeks of work that conversation was not regarded positively: "They don't like you to talk here. Whenever Sharon (a co-worker) comes back to work at the files, we talk a little, and Margo (the supervisor) comes over and gives us more work."

Although the atmosphere in Miriam's department seemed gradually to lighten and spontaneous conversations to increase among the workers, these conversations rarely involved Miriam, primarily because of her location at the periphery of the work area. Also, as a part-time worker, Miriam was expected to put in five hours of work between 10:30 a.m. and 3:30 p.m. without a break. Interactions most frequently involved customer reps who sat side by side at their repsective telephones with computer screens in front of them, much like Midland Bank where Betty worked.

Miriam's isolation was an important aspect of her strategy for regulating the pace of work in the bookkeeping department. She used mental games such as timing her successive performances of a particular task to regulate the pace of work in much the same way that Roy had done in the early stages of his work as a die cutter. Another aspect of her job that contributed to this method was the decreasing amount of time spent in conference with her immediate supervisor. By the second month on the job, training which had taken up 12-15 hours of her 35-hour work week had dropped to 5 hours per week. By the third month, direct instruction on the job had completely fallen off. Without regular training sessions built into her day and with no official breaks scheduled to punctuate the flow of work, Miriam became increasingly isolated from the flow of activity around her.

During her third month at the bank, a new clerk with similar job responsibilities was hired. Miriam and Donna became friends, riding to work together on the bus and "sneaking" occasional conversations together over a filing cabinet at work. It was at this time that Miriam began to be seriously concerned with locating another job. When a representative of her employees' group, the American Banking Institute (ABI), discussed the set of course offerings sponsored by the ABI for office workers, Miriam expressed interest and took a brochure. The brochure presented information on two types of courses, all of them offered as seminars after business hours from 6:30 to 9:30 p.m. Under the "Functional Courses" category were courses in consumer bankrtupcy, branch management operations, loan interviewing, selling bank services, and new deposit instruments. Under the heading "Banking Support Courses" were courses on fund bank data processing, preparing for supervision, and microcomputers in banking. After looking over these materials, Miriam remarked: "I don't see anything here about typing," and put the brochure aside. Of course, she was correct; all the courses assumed an interest in pursuing a managerial position within the banking industry. Miriam, although frequently asked, typically declined to take extra hours when additional clerical help was needed to get business statements out at the first of the month. Miriam was put out by the bank's policy regarding overtime: "They expect you to stay overtime, don't pay you any extra, and don't even give you a break." Instead, Miriam went home every day to practice her typing: "I've got to keep my skills up."

The poor rapport between Miriam and her supervisor was obvious from the first observation made at the bank. During a 15-minute training session her supervisor did not once establish eye contact and never referred to Miriam by name, something that Miriam herself commented upon during the course of an observation some time later.

Relationships with her various supervisors did not improve during the course of Miriam's employment. Each side viewed the other with suspicion. Miriam's reluctance to work overtime was taken as evidence of her lack of interest in her job. Since she occasionally gave babysitting responsibilities as an excuse, it was even assumed that she had an out-of-wedlock child at home. Miriam had no idea of what the bank expected of its employees: "It seems they want you to smile and talk to them a lot. What would I have to talk about with *them*? I come here to do my job." Establishing supportive relationships with her supervisors was impossible for Miriam, given her lack of experience and the chilly atmosphere of her department.

Miriam quit her job at the bank to take a job on the assembly line at the major toy manufacturing plant where her mother worked. She reported that she was much happier in this job, primarily because "they let you talk to the person you're working with."

Don: Repairment, A-1 Appliance Service Company

According to Bill, one of A-1's two owners, the summer of 1983 was the hottest since 1954. The shop's workload during the summer months was staggering. The back room was continually crammed with as many as 50 air conditioners stacked eight high around the room's periphery. The shop's work area was a 10 X 10 ft. space in which the men work on the machines. There was a stationary work bench along one wall and a table in the middle. Each man had a work cart, the hulk of an ancient dishwasher on which the disabled unit was placed and wheeled around to the work bench, table, acid bath, and the tank of freon near the table. A man might work on a single unit for a full morning or might complete repairs in a few minutes. During October, the amount of work awaiting the attention of the men was considerably reduced. During the last weeks in October, the men began to bring up stoves, refrigerators, and washing machines from the basement storage area. These appliances were overhauled and moved to the salesroom at the front of the store where they were available to customers who walked in off the street. Repairing these machines constituted the shop's bread and butter during the fall, winter, and spring when few air conditioners were brought into the shop for repairs.

Although the volume of work in the shop during the peak days of July and August was considerably greater than in October, the pace of work established by the employees remained fairly constant. What changed over time was the contents of the banter that punctuated the pace of work, although the pace of work itself remained the same. During the summer tempers often appeared to be barely under control. In the fall, after two of the men had been replaced, the tone was far more relaxed. It is difficult to say with absolute certainty that it was primarily the shift in personnel and not the reduced workload that influenced the social interaction. However, the equilibrium in the pace of work observed in the summer appeared to extend into the fall. Unlike the men in D.F. Roy's die manufacturing shop, the men in the appliance shop did not have a ritualized banana time, although Coke time, coffee time, and cigarette time regulated the flow of production. The conversation that punctuated the work flow had a thematic content, i.e., the same conversations recurred and appeared to both reinforce individual worker identities and to maintain the hierarchical order of the shop. Pete, the new employee, although a participant in the interaction, infrequently initiated conversation. Nonetheless, his opinions and reactions were often explicitly sought. Recurrent conversational topics include relationships with women, preferences in music, and chatter about sports.

Pete's initiation into the work culture of the appliance shop was eased by his relationship with Roy, his brother and parts manager who was influential in getting him the job. In contrast to Don who was also hired during the summer but who was subsequently fired, Pete's interactions with his co-workers appeared to develop smoothly and rapidly. He was quickly absorbed in the pace of work and actively contributed to its maintenance after less than a month on the job.

To provide a picture of the pace of work in the shop and the differential relationships of the new employees (Pete and Don) to their co-workers, I have relied upon extensive excerpts from field notes taken during two different observations. In each case, the period of time is approximately 20 minutes during the day's work. Each observational period followed a major break in the pace of work. In the first episode, Pete had just finished lunch, which on that day was a sandwich hurriedly eaten in the shop.

Pete puts on his apron and leaves the shop briefly before coming back and approaching Tom, the supervisor's brother. Tom's brother has left the room to assist Don, the other new worker who is repairing air conditioners in the show room, since the shop is too crowded to accommodate a fourth air conditioner and cart. Pete asks Tom a question and, although, he is on the telephone near the stationary work bench, he responds, saying, "Heat it up—in the tubes. See if it flows better." At the work table Pete says, "You get better at it." Tom concludes his conversation on the phone and walks over to Pete saying, "Let me show you." At this point, Bob, one of the store owners, walks into the room and says, "Tom, whenever you're ready, pick up the fan motors." Tom replies, "I just talked to them about it." As Don and Tom's brother Frank, the shop supervisor, walk in with a large air conditioner, the lights begin to flicker, indicating that a fuse is faltering. Don is told to set the circuit. As he leaves, Tom asks, "Do you know where they are?" Don replies, "Yeh," and leaves.

Meantime, Pete is working on the coils of his air conditioner with an arc torch. Don returns and says, "This hasn't been a good day at all." Tom says, "I didn't say a word." He moves to Pete, looks at the air conditioner he is repairing, and says, "Beautiful." Frank moves to assist first Don and then Tom and asks Tom if he has heard about the fan motors. Tom replies, "They don't know if they have them. The computer says they have two." Frank returns to assist Don while Pete adjusts two gauges on the wall. Pete pauses, then turns to Don, and asks, "Do you turn these counterclockwise?" Don hesitates for a moment and then answers, "Yes." Tom moves closer to Pete at that moment, and Pete repeats his question: "Do you turn these counterclockwise?" Tom says "Yes," and Pete continues to adjust the dials.

The lights dim, and Tom says, "I think the air conditioner blew the fuses." Frank, working with Don, says to him, "It kicked in right away, didn't it?" Don replies, "In a few seconds." Pete lights a cigarette, continues to work on his air conditioner, and asks Frank about regulating the freon he is injecting in the unit: "That thing got to be running when I pump that in?" Frank says, "Yeah. About 20 ounces." Frank looks over Pete's shoulder as he continues to adjust the dials. Tom also watches and begins to tinker with the dials. Pete explains to Tom what he is doing, while Tom watches and holds his hand in front of the unit as if to test the flow and temperature of the air. As Tom leaves, Pete says, "I think I found a leak." Both Don and Tom approach to look. Tom disagrees, and Pete explains. Tom looks relieved and says, "I thought you said 'It wasn't really a leak.'" At that moment a spray of freon explodes from the machine. Don shouts at Pete, "I never saw you move so fast!" Pete says, "It didn't scare me as much as it did the other day." Bob, the owner, enters and asks, "Anybody not doing anything? There are bulbs out downstairs." No one responds. Just then a man moves a washer into the shop through the side door. (8/8/83).

At first glance, the pace of work seems unremitting and the division of labor among the men fairly equitable. After all, Pete, Don, Frank, and Tom were *all* engaged in repairing air conditioning units during this 20-minute period. However, upon close examination of the events observed during this episode, several things become clear. First, directives from Bob, one of the shop owners, were not acted upon. Recall that Bob first told Tom that he could pick up the fan motors whenever he was ready. Tom chose to put off the errand and, in fact, did not attend to the task for several hours. Bob later mentioned to no one in particular that light bulbs in the basement needed replacing. This statement did not even draw a response.

The men were in charge of the pace of work in that they regulated the flow of their efforts. Although each man was a participant in this effort, a pecking order among the four workers was clear. Frank and Tom supervised and monitored the work of the two new employees. However, Don and Pete were accorded differential praise for their work. Pete's work was acknowledged, when Tom approvingly said "Beautiful" as he passed Pete's cart. Pete's efforts were encouraged. Tom said, "You get better at it," and provided unrequested assistance. In contrast, Don was given the job of resetting the fuses which were faltering because Pete's machine was pulling considerable amperage. The authority of Don's response to Pete was questioned when Pete, apparently discounting the veracity of Don's observation, immediately turned to Tom and raised the same question about the dials. Pete took a cigarette break, Don who also smokes, did not. And, finally, when Pete let loose a jet of freon into the shop, an amateurish mistake that we did not observe any other worker make, Don commented on the error, but was the only person who does so. Thus, although the pace of work was managed by all the men, it appeared to be managed to benefit Frank, Tom, and Pete at Don's expense.

In October, 2 months after Don was fired, the shop atmosphere was far less tense, though the pace of work remained the same. The following 20-minute portion of field notes, taken during an October workday, begins as Pete returns from running an errand for Virgil, Bob's partner and co-owner of the shop. He walked down the street to have 3 Xerox copies made since the shop does not have its own duplicating machine.

Pete had returned to the kerosene bath in which he has been working all morning. Kerosene has been poured into a refrigerator crisping tray. Pete has been cleaning the plates and parts of a washing machine transmission and continues this job which consists of bathing the parts, placing them in a vise to file them after wiping off excess kerosene, using an air hose that emits a highly compressed stream of air to remove particles, bathing the plates in oil after placing several other pieces back on the plates, and putting the two plates back together with the transmissions's contents encased inside.

Pete looks up from the vise where he has placed the transmission plates and says, "I need some oil. He looks around and asks, "Where's that oil at, Frank?" Frank asks, "What did you do with the pump, Gary?" Gary points, and as he gestures, says, "Right here."

Meantime Frank is assisting a new worker, Sam, in taking apart a large Tappan range. Gary asks, "What did you do with my nice clean, clean . . . what do you call it? . . . throw rug?" Fred points in the direction of the far end of the back room. Gary gets the rug, places it in front of the washing machine he is repairing, and sits down cross-legged to face the machine. Virgil comes back and looks at the stove that Sam and Frank are repairing, doesn't say anything, and leaves. Pete is filing the transmission plate while Gary is pounding the bottom of the washer. Frank leaves while the new worker removes burners from the top of the Tappan. Pete shuts off the machine and adjusts the transmission plate in the vise. Pete asks Gary a question, and Gary assists, saying, "You put the shaft here . . . two pumps, two circuits." Gary assists Pete in rigging up the oil cylinders, which begin to ooze an oil substance on the top of the plate.

Fred returns from the lavatory and walks to the Tappan. Frank turns to Gary and says, "Go upstairs and bring (word unclear). Gary says, "Need a ball and t-bearing." Frank, now inspecting Pete's work, says, "They don't leak that way," and removes one of the plates. Gary asks, "We got any balls in stock?" Frank says, "Sure." Gary replies, "T-bearings?.. Frank says, "Yeah, upstairs." Gary responds, "You hope," as he goes into the loft to fetch the parts.

Frank has now turned his attention from the stove to the transmission Pete is repairing. Frank says, "Put this ((here)). I'll back off (word unclear)." Pete continues the work on his own, while Frank returns to the Tappan briefly before leaving the room. As Gary decends from the loft he remarks, "Oh, Pete, Sherrie liked that joke." Pete replies, "Brenda didn't, huh?" Gary says, "I'm glad she was sick 'cos she woulda chewed me up." Gary adds, "Her sister's different." Pete says, "Like me, huh?" Gary says, "Not everyone's a druggie," and chuckles as he turns to the new employee and says, "You can turn this on." Gary backs off from the Tappan, saying, "Boy . . . lots of grease . . . wash it with kerosene, wash it in water—about 70°—hot, soapy water." Sam responds, but his remark is unintelligible. Gary says, "They said it checked out OK." Sam says, "They replaced the valve." Gary says, "See if they want you to clean 'em up." (Starts mimicking a radio jingle): "Only 15 minutes from downtown."

Gary returns to his washing machine as Frank returns to assist Pete. When the job is finished, Frank leaves the room. Bob and Virgil enter the shop. Sam, the new employee, looks up from the Tappan, and says, "Bob." Bob replies, "Yes, Sir." The new employee says something unintelligible about the range. Bob responds, "We had this out; it didn't work. I told Frank to check the thermostat, check the gas valve." Sam says, "It opens up (word unclear)." Bob replies, "Let him play with it. If we get too many people involved, no one will know what we're talking about."

Bob and Virgil leave, and the new employee fiddles with the Tappan's timer, which begins to buzz. Frank returns, and he and Sam continue to work on the Tappan. (10/21/83)

During this 20-minute interval, Gary and Frank's roles as mediators of management norms seem particularly clear. Their roles were really complementary. Gary was the boisterous fun-loving cut-up who later that morning described "a nice little scuffle" he had seen at a bar that previous evening, concluding his narrative by saying, "The bouncers drug the guy out by his throat . . . be a really nice bar, if they got Frank Sinatra off the juke box." However, Gary was also a respected mechanic who provided assistance to both Sam, the new worker, and Pete, who was still learning the intricacies of repair work on a variety of machines.

Frank, who was married, coached soccer, and also held a job as a city firefighter, was the shop authority. Although the new employee requested Bob's advice on repairing the Tappan when Bob and Virgil chanced to come near his work station, Bob deferred to Frank who was temporarily out of the shop.

In the appliance shop, workers appeared to have developed a relatively stable work culture that emphasized norms of cooperation and reciprocity among members of the shops core of repairmen. Gary later complained that the shop "is for the birds . . . I don't get to sit down or drive." As a road man, Gary had considerable autonomy and could enjoy the pleasures of driving around the city free from any close contact with or supervision from co-workers. Nonetheless, while in the shop, Gary smoothly participated in and maintained the pace of work.

Jerry: Materials Handler, Slade, Inc.
Slade, Inc., the factory where Jerry was employed closely approximated Roy's (1959) and Burawoy's (1979) machine shop setting. The work was divided among specific groups of manual laborers, some (i.e., the mechanics) recognized as more skilled and experienced than others (i.e., the materials handlers), and work was carried out with the assistance of tools and machines. The rates at which the machines ran and the type of staple produced by a specific machine regulated the flow of staples from the machine to the work surface, where packers sorted clumps of staples and stuffed them into cartons.

Jerry worked his 32 machines at a pace designed "to keep the machines clear." This meant both picking up the cartons of packed staples that machine operators stacked to the side of the work surface and replenishing dwindling supplies of empty packing cartons for the operators use. The cartons, weighing from 10 to 50 pounds, were placed on the dolly and removed to a work station where they were sorted onto palettes, individually stapled shut, and later taken by fork lift to a central loading area. Jerry made separate runs for each of the operations, which were usually completed within less than the hour's time between breaks. Breaks were scheduled at hourly intervals on the half hour for the six materials handlers on the floor. The expectation was that each man would have completed a set of runs so that each machine for which he was responsible was cleared during the course of a given hour. The agreed-upon procedure was "two runs before the first break (at 4:30 p.m.), two runs before lungh (at 7:00 p.m.), two runs before the second break (9:30 p.m.), and two runs before quitting time (11:30 p.m.)" (9/8/83).

Despite the continually deafening roar of the pounding machines, interaction in the shop was almost constant. Themes of playfulness and cooperation predominated in shop floor interactions among materials handlers, operators, and mechanics, the roving crew of skilled and experienced workers who repaired malfunctioning staple machines, as well as among the crew of materials handlers who frequently orchestrated their work at the end of each run to enable the crew to break at the scheduled intervals. Most of the operators were women, and two or three of them were extremely playful.

The most spirited horseplay developed between Jerry and two operators who worked adjacent sets of machines near the end of one of the aisles. One of the packers, Veronica, was about 25 years old while the other, Eloise was in her fifties. Both were tiny women, standing no taller than 5 feet and weighing no more than 90 pounds. Early in his first run one evening, Jerry's cap was snatched from his head by Veronica who grimaced, sneered, and taunted him while wearing the cap, bill backwards, for the first half of the shift. As Jerry approached Veronica's machine on a subsequent run, he muttered to me, "This is about the worst part of this job, I think." Jerry then warily grabbed his cap off Veronica's head. An excerpt from the field notes described what followed:

> Veronica in turn plucks the cap from his head and pulls it back over her ears, saying, "You better ask for a pretty new cap for Christmas." I ask, "Why don't you get one for him?" Veronica replies, "Oh no—he's getting a lollipop. Right, baby?" Jerry grimaces while Veronica reminds him, "You should remember to respect your elders." (12/16/84)

Veronica's co-worker Eloise would customarily pinch Jerry's nose or ears or spank him, reminding him to be a good boy and threatening to tell his mother. This was no idle threat. Jerry's mother had been employed at Slade for 13 years and occasionally "visited" Jerry during his shift, asking him to babysit for his sister's two children the next morning or requesting some other favor.

Jerry's primary work relationship, however, was with the five other materials handlers. Even in this context, Jerry was plagued by his status as the youngest worker on the plant floor during swing shift. In large part, the ethic of cooperation that developed among the materials crew was forged by the patterned, regular nature of the established work schedule. It was reinforced by the foreman, Tom, who by his own estimation spent 95% of his time on the floor. Tom emphasized both cooperation and a spirit of equalitarianism and interdependence among his work crews. He identified himself closely with his subordinates and saw all of the shift workers as those who "knew the business" as opposed to the plant engineers who, although their status as experts allowed them to maintain that an adjustment to a machine looked good on paper, their ignorance of how things really worked on the floor sometimes lead to disastrous results:

> Once I told one of those guys that this certain part he wanted to try would jam the machine. He wouldn't listen, installed it, and sure enough, it jammed the machine. (12/16/84)

Tom did very little to interfere with the materials handlers and, although he might be "on the floor" most of the time, he actually spent very little time directly supervising Jerry and his co-workers: He insisted that the best policy was to allow young workers a free rein in developing their own strategies for doing the job. Although Jerry soon learned a system for pacing his pickups and deliveries, he continually modified his method for stapling and stacking the filled cartons at the end of his pick up run. At times he completed this operation on his own, but most often he did this task cooperatively with his five co-workers. This cooperative activity was accomplished with very little verbal negotiating and resulted in a mutually desired objective—completing a run before the scheduled break at 9:30 p.m.

Fitting into his job at Slade was made relatively easy for Jerry by several factors. First, he had the personal skills, specifically, a capacity to accomplish physically demanding work with relative ease. As a former baseball player for his high school team, Jerry had the physical power to hoist 50-lb boxes as if they were children's blocks. In addition, he had a particularly charming blend of naiveté and flirtatiousness that enabled him to run the gauntlet of factory-floor interactions with machine operators. Second, Jerry's family connections provided him entry to his job, and his community affiliations allowed him to be easily integrated into the factory culture. Employers at Slade stressed the family feeling of this nonunion factory. Jerry's close ties to kin and near-kin employed at Slade helped to ease him into life at the factory. Finally, the stress on cooperation in a work context that allowed for great flexibility and autonomy in designing and carrying out his tasks contributed to his easy accommodation to the work culture at Slade.

CONCLUSION

Cultural transmission in the work setting is an active, negotiated process that seems to be most smoothly accomplished when the novice is easily assimilated into a work crew whose interactions are governed by a code of cooperation and flexibility in accomplishing the task at hand. In other words, the labor process and the pace of work that governs it substantially shape the new worker's accommodation to the work setting.

Management culture is important in this process, but only because the way that it is characterized by the new worker appears to play an important role in the "success" or "failure" of the new worker in accommodating to the job. At best, managment culture through the role taken by the new worker's supervisors is perceived to be actively supportive. At worst, it may be seen as hostile, inflexible, rejecting, and enigmatic.

Certain organizational settings appear to be less likely to provide benign work climates than others. The findings of the Adolescent Worker Study suggest that these are likely to be banks and other large institutions where routine mental labor is carried out by young, entry-level workers, usually females, in accomplishing such tasks as filing, checking monthly statements, and the like. A high level of mistrust flourishes in these settings. In the cases of both Betty and Miriam, relationships become so badly eroded by mistrust that each quit her job. The regulation and control of work tasks by computerized systems in such settings limit and control worker independence and autonomy rather than explanding the job by increasing task variety and enhancing decision-making opportunities. According to management experts, organizations such as banks and insurance firms are "trying to join the new electronic technologies with the old style of rigidly hierarchical management and tightly circumscribed jobs. As computers are introduced, remaining jobs tend to be redefined to require less training or skill" (*New York Times*, Sept. 30, 1984).

In contrast, the appliance repair shop and the fastener factory, like the die cutting shop in the earlier studies of Roy (1959) and Burawoy (1979), promote the relatively easy integration of most new workers, usually males, into the job. To be sure, Don was *not* successful in his accommodation to the repair shop, in large part because his personal values and background experience undermined relationships with his co-workers and supervisors from the very beginning of his employment. Unlike Pete, the other new worker, and Jerry, the factory employee, he is not buffered by having well-established relatives working in the organization. Although Jerry sustains a fair amount of harassment from female packers on the line, he is able to develop strategies for protecting himself against their assaults. Jerry eventually changed shifts and on "graveyard" shift encountered none of the annoying banter that he had endured working the earlier shift. On the whole, the repair shop and the fastener factory both provide far more autonomy in carrying out job-related tasks. The tasks themselves were manual and less alienated than the mental work done by Miriam and Betty in the bank. Workers in the shop and factory settings were well aware of their locations in the flow of production. In the bank, neither Miriam nor Betty had much control over her job. Each was subjected to the monthly cycle of business and personal account activity. In addition, Betty was burdened by the unpredictable and intrusive nature of the computers that functioned to both regulate and control her work.

In both the shop and factory settings, workers were explicitly told to organize their tasks in a manner harmonious with the individual worker's skills and predilecions. Interaction between workers and supervisors occurred on a daily basis and co-worker interaction was virtually continuous despite the deafening noise from machines in the factory. By contrast, the bank's organizational arrangements created a gap between supervisors and workers, and the jobs themselves were inflexibly dependent upon schedules and designs completely out of the worker's control.

So long as employers in their capacity as supervisors remain aloof from new young workers, and especially when their distance is stretched further by technologically innovative gear, young workers will feel threatened and alienated. Supervisors seem to think that young, part-time workers are highly expendable. Few employers will actually express these sentiments directly. However, policies governing hourly wages, break times, and informal conversation on the job as well as expectations for near-perfect performance seem most heavily calculated to promote the failure of young, female office workers in particular.

REFERENCES

Borman, K.M. & Reisman, J. (1986). *Becoming a worker*. Norwood, NJ: Ablex.

Burawoy, M. (1979). *Manufacturing Consent*. Chicago: University of Chicago Press.

Buros, M.E., Kim, C., Santos, R., & Shapiro, S. (1983). Youth looking for work. In M.E. Buros (Ed.), *Tomorrow's workers*. Lexington, MA: Lexington Books.

Izraeli, D. (1977). "Settling-in": An interactionist perspective on the entry of the new manager. *Pacific Sociological Review*, *20*(1).

Moore, D.T. (1983). *Knowledge at work: An approach to learning by interns.* Columbus OH: National Center for Research in Vocational Education. *New York Times,* Sept. 30, 1984.

Roy, D.F. (1959–60). Banana time: Job satisfaction and information in action. *Human Organization*, *18*, 158–168.

Van Maanen, J. (1976). Breaking in: Socialization to work. In R. Dubin (Ed.), *Handbook of work organization and society.* Chicago: Rand McNally.

Wolcott, H.F. (1982). The anthropology of learning. *Anthropology Education Quarterly*, *13*, 83–108.

13
Authority Relations
in Adolescent Workplace*

JANE REISMAN
Pacific Lutheran University

As youth move out of schools and into workplaces, a major transition occurs for them. No longer students, working youth have jobs to do. More than technical skills are necessary, however, to accomplish their work: Typing speed, welding know-how, and a cheerful telephone voice are not enough. Getting along with supervisors and managers and complying with rules in workplaces are also part of most jobs. Numerous studies have shown that employers are likely to criticize young workers as a group for disregarding the rules at work and for resisting supervision (Borman & Reisman, 1986; Hollenbeck & Smith, 1984; Miguel & Foulk, 1984; Wilms, 1983). Miguel and Foulk's (1984) survey of employers in metropolitan labor markets revealed that noncompliance with workplace rules was likely to result in *immediate dismissal* during early periods of employment. These employers' criticisms suggest a deliberate rejection of the formal authority structure in workplaces. A contrasting viewpoint posits that social relationships and rules in the workplaces are complex (Corwin, 1986; Wellman, 1986). As a result, Corwin (1986) asserts that young workers generally lack an understanding of organizations and labor relations that can be transferred across settings such as schools and various workplaces. Behavior patterns of students in schools do not necessarily transfer into workplaces. In particular, recognizing the sources of authority, knowing how authority is expressed differently by different superordinates, and realizing how rigidly or flexibly rules are implemented constitute an important learning enterprise. In other words, the transition from school to work entails learning how to deal with authority.

Max Weber (1958, 1964) defined authority as "the legitimate right to exercise power." Authority is a pervasive feature in modern social organizations like families, schools, and workplaces. Yet, the ways that managers express their authority in workplaces frequently differ from the ways in which authority is expressed in youths' previous organizational involvements such as schools and families. In

*The research reported in this chapter was supported by a grant from the National Institute of Education, under grant number NIE-G-83-0005, through the National Center for Research in Vocational Education at The Ohio State University. The author wishes to thank Kathryn M. Borman, William Pink, Robert Prus, David Wellman, and Michael Wilson for their comments on earlier versions.

general, managers find their authority vis-à-vis young people to be more tenable than is the case for authority figures in other domains. To wit, it is more difficult for a teacher to expel a student or a parent to disown a child than it is for a manager to fire a young worker. Authority relationships in workplaces are therefore appropriately viewed as a new cognitive terrain for inexperienced young workers.

Researchers have paid considerable attention to authority relationships inside schools. How teachers establish coercive control has been a major focus of these studies (see Spady, 1974, for a review of this literature). Recently, ethnographic accounts of schooling provide analyses of authority *relationships* in schools by considering the extent to which students alter teachers' expressions of their authority. For example, Mary Metz's (1979) research on U.S. junior high schools describes how teachers become preoccupied with maintaining order in schools when students reject the legitimacy of their student roles. Paul Willis (1977) in his study of working-class youth in English secondary schools discusses the role played by an oppositional student culture in undermining teacher authority. Opposition is demonstrated in classroom behavior which is more oriented toward recognition from peers whose values diverge from those held by classroom teachers. Finally, Linda McNeil (1983) reports from her research on U.S. secondary schools that teachers engage in "defensive teaching" to protect themselves from continual violation of their practices and rules.

Similarly, authority in workplaces has been studied by industrial sociologists and psychologists. Sociologists have been mainly interested in the ways that power and resistance are expressed in industrial settings. This inquiry fits into a central concern of the discipline, namely, processes of social control (see Hall, 1983, for an elaboration on this concern in sociological studies). Industrial psychologists are keenly interested in authority relationships between supervisors and employees, most especially as these relationships affect motivation toward work. The ways to improve productivity and employees' attitudes toward work are major concerns. (See Steers and Porter, 1983, for a comprehensive collection of articles in this area.) Both disciplines have focused on the outcomes of social relationships pertaining to authority, that is, the expression of authority or reaction to authority. But little empirical attention has been given to the ways that superordinates and subordinates develop a relationship in the first place. Michael Burawoy (1979) in *Manufacturing Consent* provides an exception to this statement as he describes assimilation into shop floor production practices among workers. David Wellman (1986) in his research on longshoremen also describes the way workers learn to fit into (or fail to fit into) their jobs. Attention to these processes is essential to our understanding of how youth come to terms with authority in work settings.

This chapter examines authority relationships in workplaces involving young workers. Descriptions of authority provided by Max Weber and Georg Simmel direct attention to two guiding questions:

1. How is authority established by supervisors and managers?
2. How is authority acknowledged by workers?

These questions are analyzed using field research on adolescent workers.[1] A sample consisting of 25 youth and a constellation of significant actors including their managers, co-workers, friends, family members, and school personnel were observed at work and interviewed in two Ohio cities between May, 1983, and June, 1984. These youth were between the ages of 18 and 21 at the time of the study and included both males (48%) and females (52%), and both whites (80%) and nonwhites (20%). None of these youth were college students or in the military during the early period of the study, although some pursued these courses after some months had lapsed. A single researcher was present in the workplace on the first day of a new job for these young people and continued observations for an average of two shifts per month thereafter. The researcher's role was strictly that of observer. The researcher maintained a continuous log of the activities, interactions, and dialogues which unfolded during work shifts. Interviews were conducted during breaks and outside working hours. When subjects left jobs, either through termination or resignation, the researchers continued to record the youths' experiences during periods of unemployment and/or subsequent employment.

The work settings in which the youth were employed cut across different employment sectors. These sectors include small retail businesses like bakeries, gas stations, and coin shops; service industries like banks, insurance headquarters, and health spas; and production plants like sheet metal shops and metal parts manufacturers. The jobs in these businesses and industries varied widely and included sales clerks, shop hands, waiters, cooks, exercise trainers, and office workers. These interview and observational data collected in varied work settings offer rich and detailed information about authority relations in adolescent workplaces.

MAX WEBER AND GEORG SIMMEL ON AUTHORITY

Authority contains an implicit power relationship between superordinates and subordinates. The presence and acceptance of authority is a means for maintaining control in social organizations like workplaces, schools, prisons, and the family. Yet, we learn from the work of Max Weber (1958) that authority is a privilege vested in an office, not in a person. Authority is but the probability that a specific command will be obeyed (Weber, 1964). Those who have positions of authority bear both a privilege and a challenge to enact this power.

The privilege of authority among officials in modern complex organizations like schools and workplaces is supported by legal sanctions. Nevertheless, the cooperation of subordinates must still be acquired. How individuals gain cooperation, or inspire obedience, relates to the type of social organization in which the power relationship occurs. Weber's typology of the bases of authority demonstrates this relationship between individual behavior and social structure. The typology iden-

---

[1] Kathryn M. Borman and the author were the principal investigators in this research. The other investigators in this study were Margaretha Vreeburg, Beth Penn, Renee Keels, Scott Huff, and Toni Tamburino.

tifies three different bases of authority: (a) charismatic authority; (b) traditional authority; and (c) rational-legal authority.

Charismatic authority occurs where there is the least amount of formal power and control available to its user. It is frequently characteristic of leaders in social movements. Reverend Jim Jones was a charismatic leader as was the Reverend Martin Luther King, Jr. Charisma motivates and stimulates a desire in the governed to follow orders and heed authority. However, a charismatic leader has no authority when no one is charmed.

Traditional authority is available to rulers when social control powers are at a premium. It is characteristic of leaders in early governance structures where a royal family rules and where stratification is indelibly etched in the social fabric: Peasants are peasants; knights are knights, and kings are kings. Maintenance of traditional authority structures turns on a mutual acceptance of stratification. Thus, traditional authority is not viable when the peasants aspire to be knights and the knights aspire to be kings.

Rational-legal authority is the hallmark of modern Western civilization. It is presumably based on competence—not on brawn or personality. Legal contractual understandings, acceptances, and enforcements of roles, rules, and regulations permit this type of authority to prevail. An underlying assumption of this system is that we operate within a meritocratic system where rewards are achievable and granted based on performance. Rational-legal authority is not operative when the governed do not acknowledge the rules.

These bases of authority provide foundations of authoritative behavioral characteristics in different social structures. While, in theory, this typology identifies three distinct patterns of authority, pure forms of these arrangements are seldom captured in practice. Managers in modern bureaucracies, for instance, may find better results using charismatic leadership than using rational-legal leadership. This typology is meant to be treated as a model, or "ideal-type" scheme.

The variation in authority patterns is further explained in the writings of Georg Simmel (1950). A contemporary of Max Weber, Simmel stresses the interactive quality of authority relationships between superordinates and subordinates. We are reminded that authority occurs through compliance by subordinates. This obedience displaces spontaneity. But importantly, the subordinate actor exercises choice and human agency in relationship to the superordinate actor. In Simmel's (1950) words:

> For instance, what is called "authority" presupposes, in a much higher degree than is usually recognized, a freedom on the part of the person subjected to authority. Even where authority seems to "crush" him, it is based not *only* on coercion or compulsion to yield to it. (p. 183)

The choice of an individual to submit to authority, or substitute obedience for spontaneity, is affected by the balance of power in a particular situation. Like Weber, Simmel relates human interactions to the context in which they occur. Some relationships between superordinates and subordinates occur in contexts which allow one party significantly more freedom of choice than is possible for the other party to enjoy. Such is the case for a king and a peasant. Simmel refers to this type of relationship as "societas leonina," or association with a lion. In these instances, subordinates are treated as mere means to ends, as insignificant beings. Spontaneity among subordinates is severely limited in relationships where advantage is one-sided.

This conception of authority guides the examination of how young people learn to manage authority in workplaces. The context in which authority occurs and the social exchange processes between superordinates and subordinates both become important dimensions.

AUTHORITY RELATIONS IN SCHOOLS

In his review of the literature concerning authority relations in schools Spady (1974) reexamines how authority is established in classrooms. A well-entrenched principle in teacher education emphasizes the importance of establishing respect early in the school year. Teachers are instructed to lay down the law with students at the onset of the school year in order to gain control over class activities. Spady contends that such an approach is based on some weighty but erroneous assumptions. This approach assumes that authority is established once and respected thereafter. Second, this approach suggests that strict assertion of the authority vested in a teacher's office provides a compelling basis for student discipline. Conspicuously absent from this approach is a recognition of the human agency of the students—that students must consent to be taught and be disciplined. This approach does not *recognize the social and interactive nature of relationships.* Several recent ethnographies of schooling redress these problems.

In her field research on authority in schools, Metz (1979) examines the challenge of arranging the authority of day-to-day schooling. She asserts that a major aim of school management is to maintain order. Yet, order is fragile in the classroom and ever more volatile in the corridors. In managing the conflicting goals of maintaining order and pedagogical activities, Metz observes that teachers cannot simply insist that students act orderly in schools. Instead, zones of freedom are established between teachers and students. Teachers and students test each others' wills to reach an equilibrium that allows schooling to proceed. The zones of freedom which allow the equilibrium vary according to the characteristics of the student population. Metz found considerable negotiation of authority in a desegregated school where many youths did not accept the legitimacy of schooling. In this case, spontaneous behavior was more prevalent than obedience, making it difficult for teachers to uphold authority. Many students did not freely consent to the subordinate organizational role of student.

Paul Willis's (1977) examination of working-class boys in British secondary schools also reveals bargaining over roles between teachers and students. Using a class analysis, Willis asserts that many working-class youth project a limited range of opportunities for themselves in the workplace. This negative view of the benefits of schooling promotes disruptive behavior in the classroom. Instead of prizing the virtues of learning, schools are used as forums in which to "have a laff." These "laffs" are often directed toward their obedient, well-socialized peers, the "earholes."

To maintain a semblance of control over these working-class boys, teachers tolerate some resistant behavior. Willis, like Metz, reports that the rejection of the legitimate basis of schooling among some students reduces the probability that the authority vested in classroom teachers will be obeyed. Without the consent of students, authority has to be constructed, bargained, and negotiated—not tacitly accepted as a premise of the teacher and student relationship.

Compulsion Versus Consent

The compulsory circumstances surrounding schooling differentiate it from working. Subordinates in schools (students) are not participants of their own choosing, but subordinates in workplaces (workers) do exercise some choice. Within the constraints of a social and economic context, workers and employers mutually select each other. The relative freedom involved in voluntarily obtaining a job in work settings, in contrast to compulsory attendance in school settings, is important in understanding authority relations in these institutions.

The relative freedom in workplaces provides employers with a firmer basis for expecting deference to their authority than is the case for teachers and school managers (principals). The cost of resistance, or spontaneous behavior, among workers can be termination from employment. Still, employers are faced with the challenge of establishing and implementing their authority to govern in the workplace. This challenge is especially relevant when workers are young and consequently have limited experience in workplaces. To borrow Michael Burawoy's phrase, employers must "manufacture consent" in young workers to their subordinate role of employee.

According to Weber's typology, a rational-legal base of authority is present in contemporary organizations in Western societies. This rational-legal exercise of authority presupposes a shared acceptance of the governing rules by both superordinates and subordinates. Barring this consent to subordination, traditional or charismatic approaches to management may become pragmatic. Indeed, legitimate power (i.e., authority) resides in bosses, but employees have the power to choose obedience or spontaneity from moment to moment at work.

The field study of newly hired adolescent workers provides the opportunity to analyze young people's involvements in authority relations. Numerous situations which address establishing authority and acknowledging authority unfolded during work-site observations and follow-up interviews. It is to these situations that we turn next.

THEMATIC PATTERNS

Since authority is a dominant feature of workplaces, authority relations inevitably developed between all the young workers and their employers. These relations were examined across different work settings in order to identify emergent patterns which characterize authority relations. To identify patterns, specific analytical questions were addressed, including the following: Who represents authority in workplaces? How predictable are managers? How rigidly are rules implemented? How are workplace rules enforced? How much similarity exists among authority figures in workplaces? How do young workers behave toward authority figures? To what extent do young workers comply with rules and procedures in workplaces? How much give-and-take is involved in the ways that young workers and their bosses relate to each other? The questions are based on the theoretical assumptions developed earlier, that authority is grounded in social structure, yet is an interactive social relationship that must be consciously developed among the involved parties.

The search for patterns resulted in the emergence of two pervasive themes which held up across the wide array of cases included in this study. The first theme pertains to the tension between spontaneity and obedience in the development of authority relations. Young workers' entrances to working are accompanied by the containment of spontaneous behavior. To some extent, the playfulness of youth must subside when they cross over the workplace threshold. Whether it is the discipline of long and regular work shifts, a no-nonsense boss, strenuous performance requirements, or physical distancing from age mates in adult-dominated work sites, young people come up against the tension between voluntary and willful "spontaneous" behavior and regulated and externally sanctioned "obedience."

The second emergent theme which characterizes authority relations involving adolescent workers is that authority is not always readily recognized, yet it is inescapable. This theme relates to the ways that bosses utilize different approaches to motivate employees and implement workplace rules, practices, and performance standards. Despite the rational-legal basis of modern organizations, some individuals favor charisma or coercion over reason. This variability may occur for simple reasons like personality differences in individuals or for complex reasons like levels of formalization in organizations. Regardless of the reason, young people learn to adjust to different types of bosses without underestimating the official power residing in these bosses. To a lesser extent, there is also some evidence that bosses adjust their managerial styles in their interaction with their employees.

To encapsulate, two thematic patterns characterize the development of authority relations among young workers:

1. Young workers' entrances to working are accompanied by the containment of spontaneous behavior, and
2. Authority is not always readily recognizable in modern workplaces, yet it is inescapable.

These themes will be explored using case illustrations from the work site observations and interviews. The discussion begins with a detailed case analysis of the early months of employment for a young mail clerk in a financial institution. Over a period of several months which included a succession of bosses, Roy made some deliberate adjustments in his understanding of authority and the way in which he related to superordinates.[2]

Authority Relations in a Mail Room

Roy moved away from his rural home town to a metropolis one year after his high school graduation. Financial difficulties caused him to leave the regional college campus where he was enrolled as a business major and to find employment. Roy first became employed on a temporary basis for a financial institution in a security position. When a permanent, yet still part-time opening became available in the mail room, Roy applied and was hired. It was not until he was selected for the permanent slot that he was formally oriented to the organization.

Roy was introduced to the hierarchical and regulative scheme of the financial institution on the first day of his job in the mail room, September 11, 1983. He spent that morning in a training seminar for all unclassified new hires and spent the afternoon in the mail room. The rules of the workplace were presented in the training session—punctuality, attendance, and a suggestion to leave personal problems at home. The privilege of managers was more subtly expressed in explaining differential salary scales:

> It's not fair to pay the teller as much as we pay the manager . . . no matter how good that person is . . . or loyal. This may sound harsh, but many other companies do this, especially large companies. . . . Managers have college education, some experience, and are responsible for 25 to 40 people.

This initial socialization experience instructed Roy in the rational-legal basis of authority in his employing organization. Such was the message provided by the organization's perpetrator of the authority structure, a training specialist.

Roy's initial experience in the mail room exemplifies a tension in superordinate and subordinate relationships in workplaces which have a rational-legal structure. Whereas management would prefer that their authority is perceived as ubiquitous, employees have greater potential to behave more spontaneously in the absence of direct supervision.

Roy had three bosses: Sal, the day supervisor, Pat, the night supervisor, and Len, the general manager, who is later replaced by Paul. The mail room crew varied from about 3 to 10 throughout multiple shifts. Eight people were present during Roy's first day on the job; the majority were also adolescent workers. Sal, the day supervisor, had not been in at all due to an assignment to jury duty. But the mail room crew appeared to be familiar enough with the task demands to carry on without direct instruction. These tasks consist of sorting mail, processing mail through postage machines, receiving deliveries, and delivering mail inside and outside the building. In contrast to subsequent observations, there was a great deal of standing

---

[2] Pseudonyms are used throughout this work to protect the identities of the research participants.

around, conversing, and bringing in snacks from an outside area.

Roy knew some of the employees, since he had held a temporary position in the security area prior to obtaining the mail room job. Co-workers guided him through the work activities throughout the afternoon, primarily showing him how to process mail through postage machines. When not given a specific job to do, Roy involved himself in conversations or sat on a vinyl-padded couch between the mail boxes and the processing machines. Shortly after 5:00 p.m., he finished his final task for the day and departed.

Following this initial observation, I had a brief discussion with Len, the department manager. Len had walked into the mail room once during the 4-hour observation, exchanged some words with Pat, the night supervisor, and departed. Len introduced himself to me at the conclusion of the work shift to provide some information. He wanted it known that the behavior in the mail room that day was more unruly than usual due to the absence of the day manager. No supervisor was present for the crew of young workers until Pat arrived late in the day. This manager heard reports (from unspecified sources) of excessive amounts of off-task activities. The youth had spent long breaks in the cafeteria and had taken long drives in the mail truck. Concerned that the new hire might get the wrong impression about conduct on the job, this manager planned to address the crew the following day about their behavior. Otherwise, he feared that the new worker might be set up for failure. In his words, "I will be doing some yelling and screaming tomorrow. I don't want Roy to get the wrong impression and maybe lose his job" (9/11/83).

This young man's experience on the first day of the job illustrates how relationships of authority are upheld or disavowed at work. This encounter supports Max Weber's (1958) portrayal of authority as a privilege that is vested in an office not a person.

Conversely, subordinates must acknowledge this power and elect to obey rules, practices, or direct commands. In business and industry, managers occupy the offices which hold authority. Without the presence of a manager in this work setting, the rules and regulations were not carefully observed by the youthful crew. Aware of this breakdown in the social order of the workplace, a higher-level manager planned to intervene in order to assist in the new worker's accommodation to this new job. This departmental manager was concerned that Roy might not otherwise understand the message that he wanted to deploy in the mail room—namely, that authority is ubiquitous and tenacious.

A third instance, a few months into employment, shows how Roy had begun to acknowledge the authority of his superordinates and had initiated some resistance to this control. According to Roy, the day and night supervisors were as different as night and day: the day supervisor, Sal, was "nice," the night supervisor, Pat, was "evil." The day supervisor inspired devotion and hard work among Roy's work group through her charismatic approach to management: "The guys get the work done for her 'cause she's so nice" (10/24/84). In contrast, the night supervisor stirred up wrath and venom among the mail crew members through her coercive managerial approach: "Pat yells at you and treats you like a little kid; people our age don't appreciate that" (11/19/83).

Roy was subject to the authority of both supervisors after he was assigned to the position of mail deliverer. This duty meant that he drove the mail truck on a prescribed route to make deliveries at various bank offices. His work shift spanned the hours between 2:30 p.m. and 6:30 p.m. with this specialized assignment. The shift in supervisors occurred at 5:00 p.m.

Roy's prescribed route was supposed to occur on an hourly cycle. He began his route in the main mail room at 2:30 p.m. and was expected to return there by 3:30 p.m. Following essentially the same route, he was expected to repeat his deliveries three more times in the afternoon. Roy often was able to accomplish his route in less than an hour's time. During the day supervisor's shift, Roy used this extra time by talking with his co-workers who were stationed in the confines of the mail room, while they did their jobs as sorters, processors, and receivers. The night supervisor did not tolerate small talk among the workers. If Roy returned early to the mail room, Pat would immediately assign him a filler job. Roy soon learned not to show up early. Instead, if he returned early, he would sit in his truck outside the door listening to music. He did not voluntarily subject himself to her authority.

Indeed, avoidance was a practical way for this young worker to resist coercive supervision. In this vein, Roy's assignment to the delivery route was opportune. As he saw it, "I don't have to deal with the people in the mail room too much since I have the delivery route job. I'm glad I'm not in there" (11/19/83). The multiple supervisors and prescribed accountability patterns (hourly cycles) surrounding Roy's job made authority more visible and powerful than some mail crew members had imagined. Roy's solution was to work hard for those who were charismatic and to attempt to avoid those who were coercive.

One other boss–employee relationship which took shape during these observations shows a small, but significant degree of flexibility and negotiation. This relationship involved Paul, the succeeding general manager. Roy initially viewed Paul as "mean" when Paul first started working. Pat perpetrated this image of the new manager. Roy reports that Pat had warned the crew to watch out, because Paul was going to be "strict." An encounter between Roy and Paul concerning Roy's truck-driving behavior verified this strict image during Paul's first week as boss.

The Playful Truck Incident. I accompanied Roy as he drove the truck out of the parking lot. Crossing his path was his co-worker, Jerry. Roy played with Jerry by pretending to run him down. This event was witnessed by manager Paul. I recorded this scene:

We leave building C and Jerry is crossing the parking lot. Roy swerves and steps on the gas as if he is trying to hit Jerry. Both guys laugh. [Roy and Jerry talk briefly to each other and then Roy continues on.] Roy is going about 15 mph and doesn't slow down for the speed bump. He passes an older, stocky man. Roy waves and the man waves back with a kind of strange look on his face. [Roy tells me that he is the new manager, Paul.] [3] (12/16/83).

---

[3] Notes enclosed in brackets represent paraphrased accounts from the field notes.

Following this delivery route, Roy returns to the mail room and is immediately summoned by Pat. As recorded in the field notes:

Pat says to Roy, "I've got to talk to you."

Roy says, "OK," and begins to walk down the hall to make his building C deliveries.

Pat says, "Paul saw you playing around with the truck."

Roy looks confused. Pat continues, "On your last run Paul saw you playing around."

Roy, "I waved at him . . ."

Pat, "He also saw you swerve and chase Jerry."

Roy, "Oh, that."

Pat, "Well, Paul wants me to warn you. He said you could be taken off this job, or possibly taken off the entire bank job, if he sees that again."

Roy says, "OK."

Pat turns around and goes back to the mail room. Roy finishes his deliveries looking very sullen.

When he returns (to the mail room), he motions to Jerry who then joins him outside. Roy tells him about the incident. Jerry tells him that he also got into trouble for not signing in and leaving the keys in the bank car (a common practice among the crew). Jerry and Roy discuss how strict Paul is. Roy concludes, "I'm not going to be here long." (12/16/83)

The dialogue between the young co-workers revealed a mutual recognition on the part of these subordinates about the coercive approach to management which Paul was attempting to establish. They clearly felt the implicit threat that they must conform to his rules or else they would be fired. This message was administered by him and also extended by his assistant, Pat, without providing an explanation or a forum for understanding the rules through reason (rational-legal authority). The young workers perceived his style to emphasize management through punishment (traditional authority) as opposed to management through reason (rational legal-authority).

This traditional approach to management was particularly problematic when the young workers did not share an understanding of what acceptable behavior looked like to their new boss. Roy had made no attempt to hide his playful behavior in the truck. While this spontaneity was completely unacceptable to Paul, Roy was not purposefully being disobedient. He simply was naïve about the disciplinary climate, rules, and practices which Paul maintained.

Roy had already adopted an avoidance approach to the coercive managerial style of Pat. Similarly, he planned to remove himself from Paul's span of control, as shown in the conversation between the observer and Roy which occurred on the next delivery commute:

Researcher: What do you think of your new boss?

Roy: I think he is worse than Len (former manager) . . . I mean you can be strict, but that's just too strict. We're not little kids . . . I mean looking at our time sheets . . . we're not going to cheat. . . . I guess that's what he thinks. I mean we come in at 2:40, and we'll sign in at 2:30. I guess that's what he's thinking. I mean now we have to sign when we get there. [They used to sign in and out when they were leaving for the day.] ... He slapped the time sheet down on the desk in front of Jerry and said, "Are you going to sign in?" ... (Roy brings up the subject of keys) I mean they have been doing this for years (leaving the keys in the bank vehicle while making a delivery), and no one has stole no cars—now this guy comes out and he thinks everyone is a thief. . . .

Researcher: So how are you going to deal with this guy?

Roy: Stay away from him. That way he can't do nothing. (12/16/83)

Although the former manager (Len) had tried to convey to the mail room crew that authority was omnipresent, Roy recognized that authority was implemented by individuals. By escaping visual purview of authority figures, he also hoped to escape the ramifications of officialdom.

Over the next few weeks, Roy and his cohort of co-workers tried to distance themselves from the new manager. On December 19, Roy reported that he had heard rumors to the effect that Paul did not think the crew liked him. Roy commented, "This is true and you can put my name on the top of the list."

Adjustments in Authority Relations. Close to one month later, on January 7, Paul called a meeting of the mail room crew. Paul reviewed his rules and rationale about such practices as leaving keys in cars and violating scheduling procedures. He also established formal times for employees breaks. In general, he attempted to explain some of his policies and to show their implications to the staff. Roy responded favorably to this meeting which, for the first time, allowed him to view this manager emphatically. In Roy's terms, the manager became "nice," but in Weber's typology, the manager had become more legalistic and less traditional. The following interview affords these insights:

Researcher: How did he approach the meeting?

Roy: He was really telling us rules.

Researcher: He was telling you rules? Were these some rules that you already knew and some new ones?

Roy: Yeah, he was just telling us to be more careful about driving, because a manager or something once got kidnapped.

Researcher: Do they want the people who are out on the road to use more security?

Roy: Yeah, like if you see somebody and they look suspicious, you know, don't take our stuff out, just call the guard and tell him there's someone out there who looks suspicious.

Researcher: Uh, huh, have you ever had cause for alarm yourself?

Roy: *That's it, because I never really even worried about it* (emphasis added).

For Roy, being permitted to know the reason for the rules and being given an allowance to worry was a turning point in his acceptance and acknowledgment of authority. The mail crew was not simply being scolded about leaving keys in the vans for punishment—there was a legitimate reason given for this rule. When Paul convened the employees to discuss rules and the rationales for them, he brought rationality into his approach to managerial authority. This action made him a more legitimate leader to the mail crew. They now acknowledged his authority.

A degree of negotiation is evident in the construction of this relationship between Paul and Roy. While there was no direct discourse concerning who was boss or how bosses and employees behave, Paul had somehow become alerted to the negative impact he had on the crew through his early dictums. Recall that Roy and the other crew members responded to his coercive rules through withdrawal. Paul's meeting provided a forum to allow reason or rational-legal authority to prevail. Furthermore, this approach effectively inspired Roy and others to consent to meeting this manager's expectations for employees.

In essence, Paul's authority never diminished, he simply altered his management strategy. Roy and the others' attempts to remain out of Paul's way helped them avoid confrontations prior to this adjustment. But their avoidance was only obtained by the young workers curtailing their behavior—through constraining their spontaneity—an outcome which Paul found desirable. Paul's meeting did, however, relieve the tension which had started to build inside the mail room. Without such action, over time, Paul may have been faced with the necessity of firing some of the resisters or having to sustain a conflict-ridden mail room.

The thematic patterns earlier identified are continuously woven throughout this account: the containment of spontaneity and the inescapable character of authority in the workplace. In fact, these central themes are themselves closely related, as is especially evident in the playful truck incident. It was while Roy was engaged in playful behavior in the course of commuting on his mail delivery route that he was observed by his manager and unwittingly risked losing his job. Following the reprimand for this act, Roy grew more cautious about his behavior and defensively avoided in-person contact with his boss.

Accounts involving other young workers further demonstrate the tension between spontaneity, in which people behave as they wish, and obedience, in which people subjugate their will to the rule structure of others. These accounts tend to show that youths lack familiarity with rules and acceptable practices to specific managers.

The Tension Between Spontaneity and Obedience

Like Roy, a young man employed as a clerk in a small coin and stamp store upset his employers early in his employment. In this case, Rod had difficulty in maintaining his scheduled hours for working. As one example, Rod was disappointed when his request was denied to come in late to work following Independence Day. He perceived that this denial would put a damper on his late-night celebrating. In another example, Rod infuriated the assistant manager by showing up when the store opened instead of 15 to 30 minutes in advance. Earlier, the assistant manager had stressed to Rod that it would be a good idea to come in early. It wasn't until the assistant manager told him that he *must* arrive earlier that Rod adjusted his schedule. Three men worked in this store, Justin, the manager, Chuck, the assistant manager, and Rod. Considerable concern was paid to Rod's personal well-being, a concern that often made it difficult to see a prescribed form developing between superordinate and subordinate roles.

In contrast to Roy's experience in the mail room of a large, complex organization, both roles and rules in the small shop seemed arbitrary and flexible. Justin expected Rod to develop a sense of loyalty to him and to take initiative in learning the business, a relationship that was more fitting to a charismatic structure than a rational-legal one. While Rod appreciated that his job compared favorably to those held by friends employed in fast food establishments and other "dead-end" organizations, he was reticent about taking on too much responsibility. Instead, he looked for opportunities to lighten up the job—chatting with customers and friends who visited or staring out the window at the pedestrian and automobile traffic. After several months, Justin despairingly reassessed his approach to training Rod. He mused that he would have to become more directive, because Rod was not showing an eagerness to wait on customers, learn how to stock the store, and acquire other skills on his own. Essentially, Justin wished to move forward with the process of replacing spontaneity with obedience in young Rod.

In contrast to Roy and Rod, other examples show that some youth place constraints on their spontaneity. These youth have taken to heart the warnings of teachers, parents, job developers, and others who suggest that the world of work is a serious business. Expecting that work is part of the adult world which is defined by rules and responsibilities, these young workers impose a strict adherence to tasks and orders on themselves. One young shop hand, Al, exemplified this self-imposed obedience. Observations of Al's 8-hour shift making ducts in a sheet metal shop repeatedly showed that Al worked continuously and silently. Even when co-workers initiated conversations, Al uttered one-word responses and did not interrupt his work tasks. This approach to work stood in stark contrast to his behavior at school. I was surprised to learn that Al's vocational shop teacher had been concerned about Al's tendency to converse with his schoolmates during class lessons and with his lack of enthusiasm toward class projects. For Al, the workplace presented an authority structure that he accepted in a way he never did at school. He began reserving his play behavior for evenings and weekends, which he usually spent either at his girlfriend's house or out drinking with his friends.

A young office worker, Miriam, employed as a clerk in a bank, also figured that workplaces were serious places. Miriam obtained her job with the assistance of a job development program which attempted to indoctrinate its participants with a willingness to work and respect for the rules of work. Miriam felt fortunate to have this job, which she perceived as "clean" compared to the dirty factory work performed by her mother. To demonstrate her commitment to the job, Miriam kept to herself and did little to interact with her co-workers. To her surprise and dismay, her attitude was perceived as negative by her supervisor. She simply did not appear to enjoy her work in the eyes of her employers.

Al and Miriam demonstrated a zealous adherence to the formal authority structure of work by keeping a continual pace and restraining from playful behavior on the job. Ironically, in Miriam's case, this reaction to authority was detrimental. By viewing spontaneity and obedience as mutually exclusive, she cut herself off from co-workers and supervisors who never came to know her as an individual. This is not typical of most young workers who tend to engage in spontaneous behavior more frequently. However, for most young people, it is difficult to determine just how much spontaneity is permissible in their work places.

The Inescapable Character of Authority

In addition to resolving issues related to spontaneity as opposed to task orientation, the inescapable character of authority must eventually be recognized during the course of becoming a worker. Although some bosses adjust their approaches to management when they meet resistance from their staff, as did the mail room general manager, the privilege of authority does not diminish even with these adjustments. Al's co-worker, Charles, was fired, ostensibly for resisting rules such as those governing excessive absences and grooming standards. Charles was surprised, since he did not believe his behavior was insubordinate. Moreover, all of the incidents of firing came as a surprise to the young workers who experienced this managerial prerogative. During the first 6 months of the study, 9 terminations occurred. These dismissals were most frequently cited by their bosses as related to the inability of young people to comply with specific work practices. Those young people affected by these dismissals, in direct contrast to their employers, regarded the authority structures as being excessively rigid. Unfortunately, those people who were dismissed and out of work had not anticipated their imminent dismissals well enough in advance to seek other employment. In two of these cases, subsequent periods of unemployment lasted for over 6 months.

Although several incidents of dismissal occurred among youth, employers generally were reluctant to take this course of action. The dismissal of an employee sets up frustrations for managers and may be viewed by some managers as a sign of their own failure. Brian, for instance, a manager of an administrative unit in a corporate headquarters, expressed these sentiments. He dismissed a young clerical worker for unsatisfactory performance after one year on the job. Rather than seeking help with difficult tasks, this worker allowed the tasks to accumulate on her desk while she attended to work which she could adequately perform. Her manager was dismayed that the young woman was reluctant to obtain help from the manager or her co-workers. He imagined that she feared exposing her ignorance, hoping it would not be noticed. When Brian hired this worker's replacement, Val—one of the young worker's under study—he made unusually vigorous attempts to offer her the assistance she needed and to make himself approachable.

Thomas Lupton (1976) has pointed out that managers confront a dilemma in their attempts to establish authority. In the context of factory production work, Lupton noted that employees arc condemned for their failures to comply with managerial expectations, but that managers feel frustrated in their failure to plan and control employee behavior. As Lupton (1976) surmises, "It might well appear to them (managers) as if they have failed to demonstrate technical competence, and that the legitimacy of their authority is being called into question" (p. 180). Yet, for young entry-level workers, dismissal is more likely to result from a conflict over compliance with authority structures than for other reasons.

Indeed, youth may find themselves particularly restricted by workplace rules and the authority of managers in their entry periods of employment. The propensity of managers to expect deficiencies in work performance and "attitude" among young people often results in a manager keeping a close eye on young workers. In one instance on the floor of a fast-food restaurant, two young waitresses congregated around a newly hired worker who appeared in need of help. The manager, assuming that his employees were simply wasting time, hurried over to break up their conference. The privilege of "strategic leniency," a term used by Alvin Gouldner (1964) to describe a manager's discretionary use of leniency toward workers who have earned trust or recognition, does not apply in the case of young workers. If strategic leniency operated for young workers, being three minutes late would not have counted as a major infraction for Betty. Yet the more senior representative stationed alongside Betty smoked cigarettes continuously throughout her work shift, despite office policy prohibiting smoking! This senior worker had not escaped entirely from the jurisdiction of the workplace rules. She simply had been awarded some leniency in her authority relations.

CONCLUSION AND EDUCATIONAL IMPLICATIONS

The inescapable nature of authority relations in adolescent workplaces demands that young workers develop some recognition of the rhetoric of rules and practices which operate in these settings. Even in those contexts where managers are unable to enforce their workplace standards—as in the case of the unsupervised mail room—managers attempt to construct an image of the ubiquity of supervision. Managers utilize varied approaches to supervision: charisma, coercion, and reason. These variations do not seem related to differences in work settings. The three superordinates in Roy's mail room, for instance, used quite dissimilar strategies in overseeing their workers. The location of this mail room in the complex organization of a financial institution would suggest the logic of a rational-legal approach to authority. Yet, the managers were not predisposed to use this approach, developing coercive and charismatic means just as readily. Unfortunately, the rational-legal approach was uniformly most effective with the young workers, because they had not initially been told the reasons behind the rules which they were expected to respect. In another setting, the coin and stamp store, the manager eventually decided to become more coercive with his young employee, because he was not obtaining the results he wanted through reason or persuasion.

It is also apparent that authority relations are changeable. Young people adjust to rules and practices either through greater compliance or through greater resistance, both of which hamper spontaneity. Managers, too, make adjustments, but with the intention of increasing cooperation among young employees. There was no evidence of negotiation between young workers and managers that resulted in relaxed standards or increased flexibility. The numerous instances of termination which managers attributed to young workers' failure to respect the rules and comply with practices affirm the strength of managerial authority in workplaces.

Simmel's phrase "societas leonina" aptly describes the unbalanced relationship between young workers and their bosses. Structural supports, affording managers far greater power, buttress this imbalance. The labor market opportunity structure for young workers is limited—with most jobs available in the secondary market (e.g., health spas, fast-food restaurants, and so on) and positioned at the entry level. Additionally, unemployment rates for the young are substantially higher than the rates for older age groups, especially among nonwhite youth. If these structural factors are coupled with a negative social-psychological predisposition on the part of employers to expect an inadequate performance from young workers, the plight of young workers is increased. Since managers are especially wary about their young employees, workers have but a narrow margin for resistance or insubordination in workplaces. Given their lack of experience, insubordination is frequently an artifact of their general workplace ignorance.

The enactment and recognition of authority is best understood as a set of voluntary and intentional social actions: Young people must purposefully comply with managerial directions in order for authority structures to be upheld and for business as usual to move forward. In view of the purposeful quality to authority relations, it seems that schools should be able to help prepare young people for the authority relations they will face in workplaces. However, this expectation from schools—that they serve as agents in easing the transition from school to work—has its proponents and its adversaries.

The most vocal group of proponents of the view that schools should take an active role in preparing young people for work is the vocational education community. Since the passage of the Smith-Hughes Act in 1917, the vocational curriculum track has been part of American public education. Originally, vocational education supported programs in the occupational areas of trade and industry, agriculture, and home economics to correspond to the work-force needs of businesses and industries in the early part of the century. Reforms have been concerned with instruction in career awareness and development, job search skills, and most recently, vocational ethics. It is this last area, vocational ethics, that relates to authority relations. Curricular material including both books and computerized modules instructs students in learning normative rules of working and in gaining a respect for superordinates. Students get high grades when they master the "proper" attitudes toward work: reporting for work on time and when scheduled, following directions; sharing problems with supervisors; being careful with a company's property; and telling the truth.

The 1980s has witnessed a proliferation of partnerships between business and education which develop further ways that schools can prepare young people for work. A typical part of these programs is a concern for introducing students "to the performance and attitudinal requirements of the workplace" (Boston Public

Schools, cited in Spring, 1986). Some analysts are concerned about the close relationship between education and business to the extent that students learn the specific interests of business and industry at the expense of a broader understanding of social, political, and economic processes. Joel Spring (1986), for instance, described this dilemma:

> Employers might be happy with the schools determining whether or not a person is a compliant worker, but it does not forbode much good for the quality of our future society if this becomes a major goal of socialization within the public schools. A society of people with proper attitudinal requirements for the workplace might be one that has lost its inventive and dynamic qualities. (p. xxx)

Additionally, the target student group of many of the recent job development partnerships are central city youth who are predominantly from lower-income groups and are nonwhite. A limited educational emphasis with respect to skill learning in these job development programs may result in improved adaptability to workplaces among program participants but may also lead to restricted capabilities of movement beyond entry-level employment.

Schools also have informal ways of conveying authority relations to students. As do all complex organizations, school systems design their own internal opportunity structure and sanctions. This opportunity structure is the curricular tracking system. Critics of curriculum tracking point out that an indirect consequence of this system is the construction of a hidden curriculum, or paracurriculum of schooling. This paracurriculum places greater emphasis on obedience to rules and respect for the authority of office among the nonacademic tracks than is the case in academic, college preparatory classes. Since curricular tracks may correspond closely to the socioeconomic status of students, in effect, obedience may be more emphasized among students from lower economic classes who will be assuming a subordinate role in workplaces at an earlier point in their lives—than their college-bound schoolmates in the upper academic tracks.

Whether one examines the workplace-related formal curriculum or similar informal curricular programs in schools, there are some notable differences in people's experiences associated with socioeconomic variables. Certainly, schools alone cannot be expected to remedy inequality in society, but neither are they expected to perpetuate or intensify inequality. How, then, can schools help students become better equipped in dealing with authority relations in workplaces without simultaneously teaching students to be docile, compliant, and unquestioning?

One constructive suggestion was recently proposed by Ronald Corwin (1986). It is Corwin's thesis that work skill levels in workplaces may have become technically downgraded in some jobs, but that organizational skills have become increasingly difficult to master. By organizational skills, Corwin means such abilities as understanding how organizations work, how authority is implemented, and how and why rules are administered. A sufficient body of generalized knowledge about organizational structures and processes has been developed and can be incorporated into the curriculum of secondary schools. The exposure of students to a body of systematic knowledge about organizations would provide a basis for their better-informed participation in authority relations in workplaces.

The young clerk in the coin and stamp shop commented that high school had been a "game" to him, but that his workplace was "a lot different." Once this new entrant to the labor force becomes more familiar with the actors at work, the rules, both formal and informal, how divisions relate to the organization as a whole, and how decisions are made—he may change his view.

REFERENCES

Borman, K.M., & Reisman, J. (1986). Becoming a worker. In K. Borman & J. Reisman (Eds.), *Becoming a worker*. Norwood, NJ: Ablex.

Burawoy, M. (1979). Manufacturing consent: Changes in the labor process under monopoly capitalism. Chicago: University of Chicago Press.

Corwin, R. (1986). Organizational skills and the "deskilling hypothesis." In K. Borman & J. Reisman (Eds.), *Becoming a worker*. Norwood, NJ: Ablex.

Gouldner, A.W. (1964). *Patterns of industrial bureaucracy*. London: Collier-Macmillan.

Hall, R.H. (1983). Theoretical trends in the sociology of occupations. *The Sociological Quarterly, 24*, 6–23.

Hollenbeck, K. & Smith, B. (1984). Selecting young workers: *The influence of applicants' education and skills on employability assessments by employers*. Columbus, OH: The National Center for Research in Vocational Education, The Ohio State University.

Lupton, T. (1976). Shop floor behavior. In R. Dubin (Ed.), *Handbook of work: Organization and society*. Chicago: Rand McNally.

McNeil, M.H. (1983). Defensive teaching and classroom control. In M.W. Apple & L. Weiss (Eds.), *Ideology and practice in schooling*. Philadelphia, PA: Temple University Press.

Metz, M.H. (1979). *Classrooms and corridors: The crisis of authority in desegregated secondary schools*. Berkeley, CA: University of California Press.

Miguel, R.J., & Foulk, R.C. (1984). *Youth's perceptions of employer standards: Effects of employer outcomes and employer evaluations*. Columbus, OH: The National Center for Research in Vocational Education, The Ohio State University.

Simmel, G. (1950). *The sociology of Georg Simmel*. (K.H. Wolff, Trans.). New York: The Free Press.

Spady, W. (1974). The authority of the school and student unrest: A theoretical explanation. In C.W. Gordon (Ed.), *Uses of sociology of education*. Chicago: The National Society for the Study of Education.

Spring, J. (1986). The government and the schools: The new partnerships. In K. Borman & J. Reisman (Eds.), *Becoming a worker*. Norwood, NJ: Ablex.

Steers, R.M. & Porter, L.W. (1983). *Motivation and work behavior*. New York: McGraw Hill.

Weber, M. (1958). *From Max Weber: Essays in sociology*. (H. Gerth & C.W. Mills, Trans.). New York: Oxford University Press.

Weber, M. (1964). The three types of legitimate rule. (H. Gerth, Trans.). In A. Etzioni (Ed.), *Complex organizations: A sociological reader*. New York: Holt, Rinehart & Winston.

Wellman D. (1986). Learning at work: The etiquette of longshoring. In K.H. Baorman & J. Reisman (Eds.), *Becoming a worker*. Norwood, NJ: Ablex.

Willis, P. (1977). *Learning to labour: How working class kids get working class jobs*. Westmead, England: Saxon House.

Wilms, W.W. (1983). The limited utility of vocational education: California employers' views. *Public Affairs Report*. Berkeley, CA: Institute of Governmental Studies, University of California, *24*, 1–7.

14

Life's Not Working: Cultural Alternatives to Career Alternatives*

HARRY F. WOLCOTT
University of Oregon

Life's productive years and efforts, at least as perceived by North American educators who take responsibility for talking and writing about such things, are properly directed toward two complementary and all-consuming activities, school and work. Since entry into school ordinarily precedes entry into the work force by at least 10 years—and up to twice that long in the professions—school is regarded as both antecedent to and prerequisite for work. This common acceptance of schooling as prerequisite for work (and virtually no question that work is what human life in the contemporary social order is all about) provides a comforting *raison d'être* whenever educators entertain self-doubts about their vital role and contribution to the common good.

My purpose here is to serve reminder that *school and work are not the only options perceived by today's youth.* The seemingly invariable sequence of school then work, reflected in titles such as Eli Ginsberg's (1980) *The School/Work Nexus: Transition of Youth from School to Work,* is not so invariable after all. Preoccupation with issues of employment, vocation, career, and the necessary transition from school place to workplace leads us to perceive everyone as falling into one of two critical categories, the already employed and the to-be-employed. With a few categories for the convenient labeling of exceptions (e.g., the retired, "pre-employeds" still in school, the physically incapacitated) we dismiss from immediate purview those who detract from the implicit message: After school comes work. Even housewives (and, more recently, househusbands) have been redefined to be counted among the economically productive rather than to be viewed as nonworkers.

Through the use of life history data from a 22-year-old male, and from his perspective, I want to illustrate the obvious, but often ignored, fact that school and work are *not* the only alternatives. Stated more strongly, the case study presented

*Collection of the original life history data upon which this account is based was inspired and in part supported pursuant to Contract Number NIE-P-81-0271 of the National Institute of Education. However, the focus of the present article is different and is based largely on events that transpired following submission of the original commissioned paper. A version of that report, to which the present article is sequel, appeared in Wolcott (1983). Numerous readers have offered encouragement or insight on early drafts including C.H. Edson, Sue E. Estroff, Bryce Johnson, William Pink, John Singleton, and George Spindler.

here raises a question of whether, at least for some individuals—including white, middle-class, mainstream American youth—school and work offer realistic alternatives at all.[1] Minority status and inner-city life styles only confound the problems further for other youth for whom schooling opens no doors.

My case study is drawn from a young man whom I refer to here as Brad. I have written elsewhere about Brad in an account contrasting *schooling* and *education* and in which I discuss how, although Brad's schooling had stopped several years earlier, his education had continued apace (Wolcott, 1983). As in that earlier account, this one draws on an extensive dialogue with Brad held over a 2-year period, although comments concerning events subsequent to those conversations are of necessity more speculative.

Brad was not part of a systematic research effort on my behalf to collect life histories in order to examine alternatives to school and work as young people in similar straits perceive them. To the contrary, I cannot imagine that I would have written this account had I not happened to encounter Brad, for my own everyday existence is comprised of that very world of school and world of work of the sort already mentioned. Those two worlds dovetail nicely for me in the career of a professor who is at once an educator and an anthropological observer of educators and the educational process.

Nor do I write about Brad because he is "typical" or "average." It will become apparent to anyone who has read the earlier account, as it has become increasingly apparent to me, that Brad is not typical or average at all. Nevertheless, there are many like him; if he is not typical, neither is he one of a kind (for another firsthand account see, for example, Brown, 1983). I think his story is worth relating, because its implications extend far beyond the case of one seemingly "screwed-up" kid.

I first came to know Brad through what ethnographers doing fieldwork refer to as serendipity. Literally as well as figuratively, I discovered Brad in my own back-

---

[1] I have not sought to document my observation that "school or work" is generally accepted as the normal order of things; volumes and professional lifetimes have been made out of the problems of career education, youth employment and training, and the school's role in preparing young people for "the marketplace." In 1983 the National Commission on Excellence in Education released a widely circulated report, *A Nation at Risk: The Imperative for Educational Reform,* that presents the "school or work" option in classic form: "More and more young people emerge from high school ready neither for college nor for work" (p. 12).

The point of the present article is that college and work may be the most apparent options for young people—and they are certainly perceived so both by educators and by their critics—but they are not the only options. The specific reference to Ginzberg's work is included because I find the phrase "school/work nexus" a convenient way to underscore the pervasiveness of our work-focused view of the world, not to any particular issue I take with Ginzberg. For an illustrative bibliography on the school-work transition and interviews with high school juniors relating their views of its inevitability, see Sherman (1983). For a historical review of the circumstances that so firmly established the relationship between work and schooling in American education, see, e.g., Edson (1982). For contemporary views of that relationship, see, e.g., LeCompte (1978) and Wirth (1983).

yard several weeks after he had managed, unannounced and uninvited, to construct a 10- by 12-foot cabin at a far corner of the 20-acre, densely wooded slope on which my own home stands. At the moment of our first and unexpected meeting, I felt hesitant about allowing him to remain on my land; yet I felt even greater reluctance in insisting that he leave, especially when he affirmed what was already quite obvious: He had no money, no job, and no place to go. Food stamps provided his major source of income, and most of what he needed in order to build and live in his rather hastily constructed sapling cabin he either found or stole. I did not expect or encourage him to stay, but as time went on and he continued to make improvements (a sturdy roof, wooden floor, windows, shelves, plastered walls, a wood stove, kerosene lamps), he gradually became as much a fixture about the place as was his cabin.

Although Brad "wished" for a regular job, he made no effort to find one. At one point, his failure to engage in ritual employment-seeking—during a period of staggering local recession and unemployment—cost him the previously dependable source of welfare dole that he had found in food stamps. I tried to underwrite his modest but recurring need for cash by letting him work for me whenever he needed a few dollars. Several large projects he undertook earned him sums adequate to allow major purchases.

Brad's early life, as revealed first through bits and pieces of conversation and later through formal taped interviews, had many elements familiar in contemporary middle-class American life. After his parents' divorce, Brad's mother moved to southern California, and Brad was shunted back and forth between his parents and their new spouses, a "hassle" in one household usually resulting in his being dispatched to the other. He was no longer welcome (i.e., allowed) in either parent's home; however, in the course of two years he spent at the cabin, both parents did visit his homestead, his mother making a special trip from California to see him for the first time in several years.

Brad was proud of the cabin and of having done virtually everything on his own to get his life together. As his material circumstances improved, however, his social orientation seemed to deteriorate. An impending and once eagerly anticipated 21st birthday that would mark the completion of two full years "on the mountain" found him instead growing despondent and increasingly preoccupied with events and people largely the creation of his imagination. Through a casual acquaintance he found what he described as "the best job I ever had" working as an occasional helper for a gardener-landscaper. Yet after a few weeks he convinced himself that he was no longer wanted on the job, and he stopped reporting for work. Following several days of aimless wandering and musing, he announced abruptly (but after what appeared to have been an agonizing decision), "I'm hitting the road. Something's gotta happen. There's nothing for me here."

Knowing Brad's impulsive nature, and realizing that he had been preoccupied with the decision to leave but probably had given little thought to where he would go or what he would do, I urged him to postpone his departure for a few days while he considered his alternatives. Reluctantly, he agreed.

There were several things I hoped might be accomplished by the delay. First, I wanted Brad to have time to renege, if his thoughts of departing were merely an ill-considered whim. Although he had stated more than once his intent to stay at the cabin "as long as two years," and two full years had come to a close just 10 days earlier, this was the first time he had actually mentioned leaving. (As well, I suddenly realized that, in spite of our sometimes stormy relationship in resolving what he could and could not do as an unofficial tenant, I would greatly miss this unexpected intruder into my life and thought.)

Second, although there was little doubt that someday Brad would leave, I felt grave reservation about seeing him depart just then. His recent behavior had become uncharacteristically frenetic. He had begun "hearing voices" and he complained of psychological stress that he described as "a sledgehammer to the brain." I had asked earlier whether he thought talking to a counselor at a local mental health office would help, and I felt he might be willing to go there now. Acknowledging his own concern, he conceded that he "might try talking to them," although he insisted that it wouldn't really help.

Third, if some new precipitating event had occurred in Brad's wide wanderings or limited social contacts during the previous few days, there had not been time to talk it out. Over the course of two years we had communicated with what seemed a good deal of candor. If something specific was bothering him, I hoped eventually he would be able to talk about it.[2]

Fourth, if Brad was going to leave, here was an opportune time for him to take stock of his options and to review what he hoped to accomplish by the move. I suspected that he would identify fewer options than he really had, and I thought I could help him review his choices. "After all," I argued, "once you get to the freeway, at least you have to decide whether you'll head north or south."

"South," Brad replied, without a pause. Then he added, "Yeah, staying awhile will give me time to get my story, too." If you're going to be hitchhiking, it seems, people want to know why you are traveling. You've got to be ready for them. Deep inside my cutomarily reticent young friend lurked a practiced storyteller.

APPROVED CAREER ALTERNATIVES: SCHOOL OR WORK

The remainder of this account deals with a review of the options that Brad saw as he set out, deliberately and self-consciously, to take the next major step in his life. Some of these options were considered explicitly during the ensuing five days before Brad "hit the road." Other options had been pondered over the course of the preceding months. There was, of course, no systematic review in the sequenced array in which I now discuss the options, but the essential range of alternatives as Brad perceived them are the substance of what follows.

---

[2] To forestall anticipation: if there was a single precipitating event, I never learned what it was. On reflection, I also wonder whether we had the level of candor that I once perceived. Brad did reveal a great deal of himself—but he kept a great deal to himself as well.

As my title suggests, Brad's quest was not undertaken in search of a career. Let me begin by discussing the two alternatives that reflect mainstream society's orderly world but that now seemed of little consequence in Brad's life: school and work.

In brief, school had not "worked" for Brad and work had not "schooled" him—in the sense of teaching him or socializing him. If experiences of both schooling and working were inevitable at some point in his life, neither had given him any sense of satisfaction or accomplishment. They may be society's alternatives, but they had not become his.

Brad's earliest recollection of schooling was of a kindergarten teacher's threat to wash his mouth with soap for using objectionable language. Things seem to have gone downhill from there. Even in his early school years he was frequently excluded from class for disciplinary reasons. While still in the primary grades, he and a pal found themselves in serious trouble after a weekend break-in to their school.

After his parents' divorce, Brad bounced between families and states and was constantly being re-enrolled in different schools. Apparently lacking any other sense of school achievement, and forever feeling "behind the rest of the class," he boasted that in his upper elementary grades he "must have had the world's record for ditching school." That was his only accomplishment and his only recollection of grades 5 and 6.

Brad recalled "a pretty good year" after he enrolled in junior high school and earned marks that assured him he was not stupid. Relatively speaking, that may have been a good year from Brad's point of view, but a school counselor remembered Brad as a somewhat troubled seventh grader who had spent most of his time either in a counselor's office or "seeing the vice principal," the school disciplinarian.

Grades 8 and 9 were spent in southern California. Though little seems to have resulted other than the performance of the ritual itself, school personnel were forever testing him. He was eventually assigned to what he described as "an EH [educationally handicapped] class with the other stonies." He preferred that assignment to otherwise big and boring classes, but psychologically he had already dropped out of school. Even *during* school he regularly left the rest of the class; while they went for physical education, he enjoyed a daily respite in a nearby orange grove:

> I wasn't interested in sports. So I'd go get stoned. I'd take a walk during that class, go kick back in an orange grove, maybe eat an orange, get high, smoke a cigarette, and by the time I'd walk back, it was time for another class. I did it for a long time and never got caught. Anyhow, then I switched schools.

Another family hassle during grade 10 found Brad again "on a bus back to Oregon." He had no intention of re-enrolling in school, but this time his parental hassle resulted in a sentence to reform school. Once more, his "work" was school. Recognizing that his lack of diligence at classroom assignments was prolonging his stay, Brad finally "started to speed up and do the stuff, and then I got out."

At age 20, reflecting over his academic achievement, Brad claimed, "I was doing ninth grade work. I probably did some tenth- and eleventh-grade stuff, but not a lot." In voluntary testing he underwent as part of my collecting his life history, Brad's reading level tested at grade 9. His grade-level achievement at spelling and arithmetic was about 3 years below that. He was remarkable in his phonetic spelling of a language that is not, unfortunately, all that phonetic: *edgucate, beleve, preshious, angsiaty, conchens, phisithion, egsagurate*; yet he was sufficiently intrigued with words he wanted to understand or to spell that he would try patiently to locate them in an old dictionary he procured for the cabin. Hunting for unfamiliar words proved no easy task for a phonetic speller who had to recite the alphabet as his first step.

Brad was proud and confident of his ability to read, and he shrugged off poor performance at other school skills such as multiplication facts "kind of forgotten." When he once expressed interest in looking for a job as a waiter, I asked how he expected to write an order the cook could read. "That's easy," he explained. "I'll just write down what they say, good enough for me. Then I'll go around the corner and copy the words off the menu."

Clearly Brad had gotten something out of 10 sporadic years spent at school, but equally important to him, he had gotten out of school itself. It was barely conceivable to him that he would ever again subject himself to the frustrations of a classroom, to didactic instruction (he hated being told *anything* by *anybody*), or to having to display in public his marginal spelling or computation skills or slow reading speed.

If Brad is a classic case of a school underachiever, a kid whom the schools simply could not reach, he was a learner, nonetheless. As he himself summarized, "I've always liked learning. I just didn't like school." He would pore over instruction manuals, disassemble and reassemble machine parts to see how they worked, devise and refine improvements for the cabin, and, in the evening, select among the more educational and informative programs to view on his battery-operated TV. In his fiercely independent mode, learning, like everything else, had to be something that occurred strictly at his own pace, in his own time, for his own purposes.

Brad's experiences as an employee ran afoul of similar considerations: He could not find work that he could do at his own pace, in his own time, and subject to whether or not he was in the mood to work. He reported having worked briefly at a number of jobs, all of which entailed hard physical labor, required no special skills or previous experience, and offered no future. The pattern at each job seemed to have been the same, whether planting trees, washing dishes, doing yard work, or working for his father in light construction: at the beginning, high hopes, a clean slate, and a fresh burst of energy; at the end, reduced hours and take-home pay, "misunderstandings" about what was to be done or when he was next expected to work, and, usually, a final verbal confrontation in which the job was lost but pride regained. Against a real world of jobs he had done or might possibly get, Brad had a vision of jobs he would like, such as waiter at a fancy restaurant making big tips (although he had never worked as a bus boy) or driver of heavy equipment (although his driver's license had been revoked). "Just any job" would not do. Furthermore, Brad abhorred the fruitless ritual of job hunting. He disliked having to ask for anything and the likelihood of being refused.

If in my own experience I have become less than euphoric about the intrinsic value of work, in conversations with Brad I nonetheless found myself arguing on behalf of very traditional views; e.g., everyone should work, you have no self-respect without work, you should take whatever work you can get. I felt that I was helping Brad "build character" by doggedly insisting that he earn every penny I gave him. He avoided the lesson by working for me only as a last resort.[3] True, the security of being able to earn ready cash did help him. He was well paid; in turn, he worked hard for his money. But I was less altruistic than I thought; there was no future for Brad in working for me, so he worked only for the present. He liked to goad me with his conviction that it was easier to steal what little he needed than to put in the time and effort necessary to earn it. If he had more than a dollar or two in his pocket, he usually chose not to work at all.

On an escalated scale, Brad expressed the same antipathy toward holding a regular full-time job that he felt about working occasionally for me. Before he "took to the woods" he experienced what he described as "having a second-class job so you can live in a second-class apartment and lead a second-class life." Having reduced his cash outlay to under $100 a month, he did not need to put himself in bondage to ensure survival. The possibility of a regular job also posed a threat to his new-found security. Living in a cabin at the edge of town made getting to and from work difficult, requiring either a long walk to public transportation or a bicycle ride of several miles with a strenuous uphill return. His semi-outdoor life style, as well as tramping through the perennial northwest rains and along a network of muddy trails, also created difficulties in keeping himself presentable, should a job demand it. A dependable income meant not only the loss of food stamps, but also dedicated his earnings either to purchase and operate a motorcycle or an automobile or to move back to town and thus back to the second-rate life style again.

I thought I would be able to present Brad with a convincing argument on behalf of work, but I never succeeded. The best argument I could muster had virtually nothing to do with work itself: A job might help him become socially involved and therefore reduce his self-imposed alienation. Yet the thought of working with others, particularly in a job where "everybody sees you," was another of Brad's expressed concerns (as well as a cue that his publicly stated reasons for not working were not necessarily his only reasons).

As a consequence of conversations with Brad, I now pay more attention to menial jobs and to the people performing them. I am far less certain that being a bus boy, clerk, waiter or waitress, maid, usher, counter person at a fast-food chain, or gardener's helper really builds character or warrants a lifetime of occupational commitment. There are a lot of dull jobs, and employment projections are that dull jobs will increase in number in the years ahead. Because many working-class and

---

[3] I am intrigued here with word choices that make me appear as benefactor: I *gave* Brad jobs; I *offered* or *provided* him work; I *let/allowed* him to work for me. From Brad's point of view, my seeming "generosity" went unremarked, particularly because I let him work anytime but steadfastly refused to advance money for work not yet completed.

middle-class youth have the skills, connections, or social savvy to make the leap from early experience at menial jobs to the opportunity of better ones, work "works" for them, but it does not work for everyone. Without skills or connections or savvy, it takes grim determination and great faith to start at the bottom, dutifully to put in one's time day after day, year after year, and to sustain a belief that some-day it will prove worth the effort. Brad had watched his parents engage in that struggle. He was not sure what it got them; he had rejected it as a worthwhile goal for himself. As he said of his father, "He's worked hard all his life, but he doesn't have any fun."

What Brad quite consciously had set out to do in heading for the hills and "hiding out from life" was to learn something about life's minimal essentials, an exploration that led him away from customary and (to him) unattractive alternatives. As he summarized, "I don't have to work my life away just to survive." The material aspects needed for survival, particularly for a stoic 19-year-old, were surprisingly few: food and water, either on a meal-to-meal basis or with ways to get, keep, and pre-pare meals for himself; clothing enough to keep warm, dry, and presentable; satisfactory places for sleeping, for toileting, and for washing himself, his utensils, and his clothes; a sleeping bag or blanket; and—the pervasive problem of accumulating even so modest an inventory as this—places for the safe storage of any possession that he did not wish to carry everywhere with him.[4]

Armed with little more than determination, an old sleeping bag, and a handful of tools and nails, the immediate essentials in Brad's new life style were not hard to discern. The location he selected for his cabin, a site discovered in earlier wander-ings, was fortuitous. Young trees for building a cabin were there for the cutting. Within a radius of two miles were new house constructions, several shopping centers, and hundreds of unlocked cars and well-stocked sheds and garages. Such resources, coupled with years of successfully "being sneaky" and acquiring what he could not or would not purchase, hastened the initial construction and provisioning of an ade-quate shelter. Food stamps underwrote his basic menu.

Primal needs adequately attended to, humans look for ways to make life more satisfying, if infinitely more complex. In that quest they are guided by cultural norms so embracing that they even tell us how to go about being alienated or dif-ferent or socially marginal. For Brad, first-order luxuries such as cigarettes, "pot," being able to listen to rock music on the radio, a camp stove, or a sturdy pair of boots soon became second-order necessities. In turn, new items like the stove en-tailed procuring additional items such as fuel and containers. The young hermit, at first hiding his every movement lest he be discovered, grows proud of his home-stead and wants others to see what he has built. A painfully shy teenager-cum-adult now "showers," shampoos, and carefully combs his hair, dons a clean shirt, and sets aside one pair of shoes exclusively for wearing to town (rather than walking on

---

[4]It is the need to carry some sort of bedroll that makes the self-sufficient wanderer in temperate climates so conspicuous, be it student traveler, mountain backpacker, or transient hobo.

muddy trails) before making even the quickest trip to the store, ever alert to the possibility of a brief exchange with "someone my own age" and the remote possibility of meeting the girl of his dreams.

Socially ill at ease as he was, I think Brad was nonetheless responding to social impulses he could no longer contain when he decided to "hit the road" and give up the security of the cabin. If his departure was not people-centered, he himself probably would subscribe to the idea that the time had come to embark upon a new experience. Brad measured his life in "experiences" the way others mark periods of their lives through promotions or the social events of birth, marriage, and death:

> I've lived in a lot of different places. Like going to California. Living out in the country. Living different places in town. Dealing with people. Living at the reform school. Living in Portland. Living here. I've definitely had more experiences than some of the people I went to school with and I've had my ears opened more than they have. In some things, I'm wiser than other kids my age.

Although Brad needed money while hitchhiking, his quest was neither for work nor riches. Nor was it an ideological search for an alternative life style. Brad held "hippies" in low regard, observing categorically: "They are dirty." In the same breath that he once wondered aloud if he ought to try living in a commune (there are many such groups on the backroads of western Oregon), he dismissed the idea because of the social involvement he anticipated: "They'd never just let you be by yourself." Brad was too antisocial to become part of a socially inspired counterculture movement. Nor was he really at odds with his own middle-class background. He was not making a social statement in his decision to leave. His problem, simply stated, was that neither of the two traditional alternatives—going "back" to school or going "on" to a job—appeared as a realistic possibility to him.

CULTURAL ALTERNATIVES TO CAREER ALTERNATIVES

In what follows I have tried to portray options that Brad saw, in the way he saw them, during the days after his sudden announcement about leaving. The categories themselves are mine. Wherever possible, I have expanded the discussion to include related thoughts Brad had shared during earlier conversations.

Join Up

For Brad, the idea of enlisting was not new but neither was it his own. More than four years earlier, his father had "encouraged" him to join the army, to the point of virtually insisting on it. Brad took and passed the necessary paper tests, including the G.E.D. (General Equivalency Diploma) exam attesting to his acquisition of basic literacy. Overnight in a Portland hotel as a guest of the government prior to undergoing the routines of the regional military processing station, he had second thoughts; in the morning, he was gone. His view since that time was that he would go into the military only if drafted, he would never volunteer.

Now, on impulse, but also older, stronger, and wiser, he was willing to reconsider enlistment, on one condition: They had to take him immediately. Like a flash, he was off to the local recruiting station, only to discover to his surprise that the U.S. Army had a minimum waiting time of 6 months, the Navy even longer. Only the Marines offered the prospect of quick processing. Brad made a formal appointment with a Marine recruiter for the following day, elated by easy questions asked during a screening interview and bolstered by an overheard comment definitely intended for his ears, "That looks like officer material."

Back at the Marine recruiting office next day, the military option suddenly vanished. High school graduates were preferred; tenth grade was the absolute minimum, at least without the delay of undergoing an entire battery of tests. The G.E.D. test was no longer sufficient. At reform school, his last "school of record," Brad had been classified a ninth grader. School had failed him one more time! Eventually, the reasons that had gotten him into reform school would also have been subject to review, but for now, his lack of formal education was enough. Brad was not acceptable.

Stay Put

"If you just had a job now, you'd be all set," Brad's mother told him during her visit 6 months earlier. Even without a job or close friends, however, he did seem to have succeeded in his goal of getting his life together. In a rare display of contentment, he once summarized his circumstances with the observation, "For me, it's great." Later he found a "perfect job" working as a landscape gardener's helper. He voiced little objection to the facts that the job demanded hard work, had more days off than on, was slow to pay, and, as often happens to people who must take such jobs if they want to work at all, part of each hour's earnings were withheld—without receipt—for purported tax purposes. Nevertheless, the job provided the prospect of at least part-time work. Brad also liked the young man he worked for: "I can relate to him," he said in the argot of his generation.

After Brad failed to appear for several days, his new employer made a special trip to the cabin to see what was wrong and to disabuse Brad of his illusion that he was no longer wanted on the job. But it was too late: As he had done before, Brad had decided to run away. For once, he was not in trouble with anyone else; this time the trouble was within. Nonetheless, the dearly gained life style and security of the cabin were not enough to hold him.

Be Crazy

The months immediately prior to his 21st birthday became a time of emotional stress and increasing personal anguish for Brad. His wanderings in town seemed to lack their earlier purposefulness, and his activities at the cabin often appeared aimless and repetitive. On dreary, rainy days he sometimes sat for hours gazing into the flames of his wood stove, interrupting his reveries only to roll a cigarette or joint or to prepare a snack. Not only was it an exceedingly difficult time for him (his food stamps had been summarily cut off, job searches seemed futile, and he was

penniless), but he began to brood over his "hard life" and things that seemed forever beyond his reach: job, car, friends, a girlfriend.

With the approach of spring, the weather gradually improved, and so did Brad's
luck (with the new part-time job), but his outlook did not. Momentary highs (several consecutive days of work; payday and the purchase of a new cook stove; the
birthday itself, which did get celebrated) were eroded by days of brooding. Distant
"voices," usually approving and just within Brad's hearing ("Boy, look at that
guy—how strong he is—I wouldn't want to mess with him") were reported more
often, along with occasional headaches, and finally Brad's acknowledgment of the
incessant "sledgehammer to the brain."

For at least a year I had noticed Brad's tendency to preoccupy himself with
one—and only one—major purpose or thought at a time, seeming virtually to get
"stuck" on any problem until it was resolved. I hoped—but with a rapidly dim-
inishing basis for such hope—that his persisting state of mental turmoil centered
around some new and unresolved question, but I also broached with him the idea
that perhaps we could—and should—find someone in addition to me for him to talk
with, someone who might provide more help than my patient listening seemed now
to accomplish. I doubted that Brad would be receptive to the idea—and he was
not—but I laid part of the problem to my own seeming inability to be of help, and
he did not appear to take offense at my concern for his mental state. On my own,
and anonymously, I contacted a local mental health office to learn what resources
were available either to me or to Brad should we want to use them. Having overcome my reluctance to consider "professional help," I inquired how I could ever
hope to get an even more reluctant youth to talk to a counselor. I received what I
thought was reasonable advice that subsequently proved effective: "You might ask
whether the things bothering him seem to be making him uncomfortable. Maybe
we can get him some help so he won't feel so uncomfortable."

Brad operated at or near a level of constant mental "discomfort" during the days
leading to his decision to leave. He was so distraught on the day he announced the
decision that he agreed at least to a telephone conversation with a counselor, but
his guarded revelations provided little basis for anything more than encouraging him
to come in for a visit. Brad took the unsatisfactory exchange as proof that counselors "don't do anything but talk."

Two days later, following the crushing announcement that his educational
attainment did not satisfy the required minimum for joining the Marines, Brad was
so distraught that he agreed (or at least acquiesced) to my suggestion that now
might be the time to talk to someone at the mental health agency.

Responding to my tone of urgency, a counselor set an appointment for that
afternoon. After a short consultation, Brad was asked to return the following morning to meet with a staff doctor. As we drove away, Brad reviewed the kinds of questions he had been asked. "Dumb questions," he related, like "Do you know what
day of the week it is?" "Today's date?" "What month?" Brad knew it was Wednes-
day and probably was still April; cabin life does not give priority to such information. He said that the two options offered him were to receive outpatient attention

(their preferred alternative) or to commit himself to a mental institution until he could "get things straightened out." He was adamantly opposed to medication and outpatient care, but he seemed intrigued with going to a mental hospital where he would be clean, comfortable, and cared for. "Hmmm," he mused aloud as we drove home, "Crazy Brad." In that moment, a new alternative seemed to be forming in his mind.

In order to ride to town with me to keep his appointment, Brad was at the house bright and early the next morning, but his demeanor was anything but bright. He had not washed his face or combed his hair, and I wondered whether he had slept. He summed up his strategy in one sentence: "I'll tell them whatever I have to tell them to make them think I'm crazy." He appeared convincing enough as Crazy Brad that I wondered whether I would see him again that day. It seemed thinkable he might get them to commit him straightaway.

Returning home that afternoon, I set out immediately on the steep trail to the cabin to see whether Brad was there. He was—along with a new sleeping bag and a new backpack. He had already packed his personal gear. He announced that he might start hitchhiking that very evening. His mood seemed lighthearted, although with the actuality of his departure now virtually assured, his ambivalence was even more apparent.

And what had been the outcome of his visit to the mental health office, I asked? "They wouldn't help me," he announced, and the subject was dropped. But he *had* been offered help; instead, he had experienced a change of heart. He was not ready to be Crazy Brad after all. He had been given the choices outlined the previous day: drugs and therapy as an outpatient or voluntary commitment, if he so chose. He declined both options. As if to punctuate his decision, he had "acquired" the new sleeping bag and backpack along the route of his return to the cabin.

Brad did not deny that he was still experiencing a great deal of mental stress. He assured me he would find a mental health clinic or seek out a halfway house if he needed help.

Suicide

I am reluctant to include suicide among Brad's alternatives, but I am equally reluctant to ignore it. My intuitive sense was that Brad was not a suicide risk. Even if it is at the outermost periphery of alternatives for him, however, it was not entirely unthinkable. For many youth, middle-class whites as well as young people (males especially) in certain ethnic groups, suicide offers a patterned response for coping with the unmanageable; Brad's own pattern was to run rather than to give up.

From my conservative, middle-aged perspective, Brad was an impulsive risk-taker. He liked to impress me with stories of street drugs he had tried and of dangerous (or at least foolish) things he had done, ranging from driving a motorcycle "115 miles an hour" to creeping out with his companions on the runway of a busy southern California airport at night when jets were landing. His high-climbing and high-swinging antics in towering fir trees near the cabin were enough to convince me of his youthful daring, but I came as well to appreciate that he was not as foolhardy as he sometimes appeared.

I never felt that this risk-taking reflected suicidal tendencies. Moreover, at the time of his greatest stress, there was not the slightest hint that "ending it all" was an option he was considering. Nevertheless, he did use the phrase, "I'd kill myself first," to underscore circumstances that to him seemed beyond the pale. And on one occasion, finally talking through a problem that had weighed heavily upon him, he confided, "I even thought of pulling myself up by a rope, and when you came up here looking for me you'd be staring at my feet swinging from a tree."

Welfare

Brad once offered the opinion, "Food stamps are society's way of paying me to drop out." He was first-generation welfare; I doubt that either of his parents had ever sought it; most likely they would meet an emergency in some other way should an occasion arise where welfare was an option. For some people, seeking welfare is virtually unthinkable. Brad held strong feelings against begging—as he said (and did), "I'd steal before I'd ever beg." But welfare was different.

Even at 19, Brad had been down and out often enough that he saw welfare—particularly the receiving of food stamps—as one of his rights, albeit a capriciously or conditionally given one. He also knew he could count on handouts any time in a big city. All he had to do was to locate its missions or meal stations, something he often had done before. In Brad's experience, it was all right to go for a free meal if you needed one, but in general you were better off keeping to yourself. For him, a mission handout was a last resort: Missions were places where too many people congregated, and they were not Brad's kind of people. That type of charity was the emergency solution; government welfare was preferable.

Getting Locked Up

In just three days of pondering, Brad's options seemed at first to increase, only to narrow again to his original idea to "hit the road." Adamant in his feeling that he had to move on (thus excluding consideration of the possibility of remaining at the cabin), his two most attractive long-term alternatives appeared to be the institutional ones that had now been ruled out: military enlistment or mental hospital.

Strikingly different in my perspective, to Brad these two institutions shared common and even appealing properties (regular meals; a warm, dry place to sleep; clothing; opportunity to keep onself and one's clothes washed; things to do and other people to do them with) that compensated in large part for some obvious drawbacks (regimentation, everyone telling you what to do, large groups of people, lack of privacy or autonomy). The military rejected Brad, at least on his "now or never" terms; he, in turn, rejected institutionalization in a mental hospital. One additional institution was also a possibility: jail, leading perhaps even to prison. Brad had no qualms about going to jail; he had been there before and had no fear of it. Even prison was not unthinkable to someone who had already spent the better part of a year in reform school.

I recognize my inclination to focus on differences among institutions; Brad tended to see their similarities. From his perspective, jail had certain attractions over other institutions, provided one's presence was not for anything too serious.

Going to jail offers a chance to clean up, to sleep, and to be fed, and one does not have to stay as long as in the army or a mental hospital. In Brad's view, born of experience: "They have to let you out sometime."

With jail as his most likely risk, the idea of simply "moving on," living by his own resourcefulness and cunning, came around again not only as a good alternative but as the only realistic one for a young man in a hurry to be on his way but with no particular place to go. Easily acquiring a new sleeping bag and backpack for his anticipated travels served to reassure Brad that his skill as a shoplifter—seldom used in the past year—remained intact for the adventure ahead. As always, he would take only what he needed; he emphatically had explained that he was not a "super thief" who made a living by stealing, he was merely resourceful in obtaining necessary items he could not afford. He could get by. The mixed blessing of a few days in jail was the most likely consequence of getting caught at petty theft.

Hustling

As for the long-term future, Brad's strategy was simply to "see what happens and not worry too much about it." On the streets, he would remain alert to whatever possibilities came up. "Dealing" drugs, for example—particularly to younger kids, just as older kids once had sold drugs to him—was a likely possibility.

Brad recognized a new sexuality and physical prowess in himself, only recently having outgrown an adolescent agony over what he had regarded as his youthful puniness (another of his personal reasons for deciding originally to take to the woods and live by himself, a topic broached only after months of discussing less personal issues). He now remarked casually about the possibility of marketing his body. His ideal sex-for-hire scenario was, predictably, to have a "beautiful woman" offer him a ride and immediately take him home with her, where he would enjoy the good life as a handsome young consort.

Brad also acknowledged that at his age and with his physique he would be attractive to males as well, and the idea of easy money and no work had its appeal. Along certain well-known boulevards of the metropolitan areas where Brad was headed, "San Francisco, maybe even as far south as Los Angeles," young males regularly hustle customers under the guise of hustling rides. Brad had caught glimpses of the hustler's role in exposes on television and may have experienced them firsthand on the streets of the larger cities in which he had lived or traveled. The moral issue was not particularly at stake: "I can drop my morals whenever I want." Brad doubted that he would try it—but the issue was largely academic until a real occasion presented itself. One had to be open to any possibility. After all, if he got to Hollywood, he might end up as a rock star *or* a hustler.[5]

---

[5] I have used the term *hustler* here to refer specifically to young males hustling sexual partners. In Bettylou Valentine's (1978) *Hustling and Other Hard Work: Life Styles in the Ghetto*, hustling constituted a major category of activity in what she presented as a threefold solution to the hard work of making a living in the ghetto: jobs, welfare (perceived as the *effort* required to obtain what one could, rather than the dole itself), and hustling.

I am unaware of any systematic anthropological attention to young male hustlers. Such studies would seem rife with possibilities for examining the rapid transmission and acquisition of culture as well as with the balancing of paradoxical norms and self-sustaining belief systems that

Going Home

Brad's world was confined essentially to the West Coast, from Portland to southern California. He told me he might go as far south as Los Angeles, so I asked whether he would return to the community where he had spent several years as a youth and where his mother resided. Currently expressing feelings of deep alienation from both parents, he insisted that he had no intention of going near his mother's home, reminding me that he was neither welcome nor allowed in his stepfather's house. Brad seemed to regard his departure more like *leaving* home than heading there. More than once while growing up he had run away from both his father's and his mother's homes. Once again he was resolving his problems by running away, but this time it was from a literal as well as a figurative home—and life—of his own making.

That Brad felt utterly rootless was evident in a new and poignant concern expressed during the brief interim where he was considering the military: "When everyone else goes home on leave, like at Christmas, I won't have any place to go to." I reminded him that the cabin would still be standing, and that he could return there (or to my home, if in the semi-stoicism of the peacetime military he had grown used to such creature comforts as hot and cold running water).

Underscoring that the cabin did now represent home, Brad sorted through his assortment of tools, parts, and utensils, carrying rubbish to an accessible pick-up point and storing valued items in cartons packed safely in my basement. Moments before his departure he suddenly changed his mind and, in the bizarre fashion that had come to characterize his behavior, he began sorting through his possessions looking for anything that might bring a few dollars at a pawnshop. (I hadn't realized our town had a pawnshop.) Then he was off.

Prior to that final, dramatic, and seemingly defiant act ("These are my things; I can do whatever I want with them"), I thought Brad might return after a few weeks or even a few days. But as of this writing I have not seem him again.[6]

---

assure people that they are not *really* doing what they are in fact doing (see, e.g., Reiss 1961). A journalistic account by Lloyd (1976) provided some perspective into the sociological *role* but not into the fuller human context of its young and transient occupants; see also a perceptive "novel" and subsequent writings by John Rechy (1963) and a study by Weisberg (1985).

Brad was aware that the same youthful attractiveness he might "hustle" casually on the streets would not be a casual commodity were he to find himself in prison. In the fewest possible words, a wise jailbird had conveyed to Brad how quickly the decisions might be made. The scenario, as Brad related it: "Hey, kid, wanna smoke a joint? You'll be *my* 'punk' now." Ironically, the same qualities of self-reliance and independence exhibited by young white males like Brad, so culturally appropriate outside prison walls, are the qualities that make them more susceptible than members of minority groups to victimization once inside them (see, Wooden & Parker, 1982, especially chap. 6, "The Punks in Prison").

[6] In the interim between completion of the manuscript and publication of the book, Brad did return, just as several readers of early drafts predicted. Within hours of his arrival he provided sufficient evidence of "craziness" to be incarcerated. Long beyond the moment for timely help, the state's resources for dealing with him punitively seemed limitless.

I do not yet understand those events or their meaning in terms of Brad's life or my own well enough to relate them; I am not sure I ever will. Bizarre as they are, the ensuing events do not change what I have written. In retrospect, my comments seem almost prophetic. But Brad had been equally prophetic years earlier when he reflected on what had been and what was yet to be: "I always seem to screw things up at the end."

EPILOGUE TO THE STORY

The range of alternatives as Brad saw them serves to make the point of this writing in the way that attention to individual cases makes its impact. Here is a young man for whom neither school nor work held much attraction and who saw and reviewed his options in rather different light from his mainstream middle-class cohorts. Like all human stories, his is, in its specifics, unique, the combination of body chemistry, social experience, local circumstances, and the particular sense he made of the world as he perceived it. But Brad is also part of the story of all humankind as each of us goes about defining and locating himself or herself in a social world. In particular, Brad's story speaks for those of similar age and circumstance who fail to get caught up in the work ethos dominant in our society and who therefore seem oblivious to the forced choice they are given between school and work.

Our attention is more often drawn to highly visible and less transient groups in this "neither school nor work" population such as unwed welfare mothers, the job-seeking unemployed, or identifiable groups like "inner-city black youth." Young people like Brad ordinarily do not show up on official rosters until they are in trouble. But that does not mean they are not there. Like Brad, they may regard themselves as essentially alone, facing a "tough life" (Brad's phrase), largely forgotten or even unwanted, and, as they perceive it, entirely dependent on their own resources to survive in a social system that constantly threatens that very survival. For Brad, the solution offered by those about him—myself included—was apparent and simple: "Why not get a job?"

Brad's story—at least to the 22nd year of his life and to the extent I was able to piece it together—had not taken a course I might have predicted, yet it is intriguing how well it accommodated many of the seemingly disparate strands among his alternatives and underlying motives.

Almost from the moment Brad left, I expected either to see him reappear at the cabin—hale, hearty, and resigned, if not content, with his lot—or to receive a long-distance telephone call from (or about) him, informing me that he was in serious trouble. Instead, more than 2 months after he departed, I received a call from his mother. By a circuitous route that had included "waking up in Phoenix," hustling on the boulevards of West Hollywood, and spending several days in jail in a suburb of Los Angeles on a shoplifting charge, and following a series of increasingly frequent collect calls from localities throughout southern California that gave his mother her first hint of Brad's current mental state, he had finally gone home.

Brad's mother reported that she found a motel room for him, but as she listened to him drift between fact and fancy in relating events, she began to realize that Brad was home to stay. She rented a small place where he could live, and discussed with him the idea of seeking professional help. Shortly after arriving home Brad voluntarily committed himself to the County Mental Institution for 16 days, but a steadfast refusal to join therapy groups or regularly take medicine left everyone, Brad included, feeling that institutionalization was not likely to be any more helpful than it was necessary. In response to a letter sent in care of his mother, Brad telephoned me once from the institution, but the conversation seemed forced and aimless; he concluded it by saying, "Send me money."

Distraught and, I suspect, somewhat guilt ridden, for several weeks Brad's mother cooked and delivered a hot meal to him daily, did his laundry, and resumed the "mothering" that she had given up years earlier. Dissuaded by a mental health worker (as well as Brad's stepfather) who insisted that Brad was not all that helpless, she subsequently reduced her visits to about three a week.

As soon as he was formally diagnosed as a mental health patient—and thus a disabled member *within* society rather than a renegade from it—Brad became eligible not only for welfare benefits but for additional SSI (Supplemental Security Income) payments as well. In his mother's opinion, given Brad's moodiness, constant daydreaming, and short interest span, it seemed unlikely that he would ever be able to hold a job. She resigned herself to the fact that he was "insane" and to the likelihood that she would have to look after him the rest of his life.

Although Brad purportedly started taking an antidepressant prescribed for him and, in his mother's words (and in *her* meaning of the term rather than in Brad's) eventually became "mellow," he continued to refuse counseling or to attend voluntary vocational therapy sessions. She said he occasionally rode his bicycle, mostly sat in his room listening to rock music, and was leading what she described as a "very boring life."

Perhaps it was boring. It appeared so to his mother. It sounded incredibly boring to me when I reflected on the energy and sense of accomplishment once demonstrated by a fiercely independent youth who now waited for the government to send him money and for his mother to bring his supper and wash his clothes. But from Brad's perspective, compared to the lifetime he could envision as a dishwasher, tree planter, or day laborer, life may have been no less boring as he was living it. He would be the first to admit it was easier. Words once spoken at the cabin could be echoed again: "I don't have to work my life away just to survive."

LIFE'S NOT WORKING: SOME FINAL COMMENTS

Although this case is necessarily incomplete, in part because it examines a young life still in the making, and also because I am no longer privy to Brad's thoughts or actions, I feel the data are sufficient to illustrate that for Brad—and for others like him with similar stories to tell—the "school/work nexus" represents neither *realistic* alternatives nor the full *range* of alternatives that they perceive. For many youth, school represents their first task-related failure; the neat and orderly progression from school success to work success is broken at the first step. Brad failed at school (or, stated more accurately, school and Brad repeatedly failed each other) and seemed now to have failed at work. He had taken a roundabout way to locate himself in a world in which he had nonetheless achieved some modicum of security and control.

As noted in my introduction, I did not seek Brad out as part of a systematic effort to investigate cultural alternatives to career alternatives. That opportunity arose in the course of events of Brad's life, the result of an unanticipated (though perhaps impending) crisis that precipitated an explicit review and choice of a course of action. The anthropologist in me is reluctant to dismiss Brad as (a) an isolated case, of (b) an alienated dropout, who (c) began exhibiting psychotic tendencies and therefore could not do what all normal people do, which is (d) hold a job. There are other possible interpretations—cultural ones—that invite us to examine the social circumstances of such a case and to raise other questions and speculations. Let me conclude by suggesting a few of them.

First, it is difficult for those of us reared under a strict ethos of the propriety of work, and who have in turn subscribed to that ethos in the ordering of our own lives, to fathom that *all* individuals capable of doing so would not choose either to work or at least occupy themselves with some moral equivalent of it. We need to recognize our own deep-seated and unexamined assumptions regarding the inviolability of work. The dignity we associate romantically with "work" is not equally apparent in each of the jobs that comprises the work force; young people appear well aware of the distinction (cf. Sherman, 1983, chap. 3). Brad could get jobs, but they do not lead to careers.

My own role as an educator is ipso facto evidence of having bought into the work ethic. The same holds true of any of the formal role-occupiers with whom a young person like Brad comes in contact: welfare worker, psychiatric counselor, personnel manager, police officer, probation officer, employed staff member at an unemployment office. Brad's encounters of record were held entirely among the comfortable and diligent, the standard-bearers of mainstream American society. They surrounded him in every official role to serve simultaneously as his judges, teachers, counselors, and benefactors. They provide living testimony to the fact that the system "works," because it works for them.

But a dominant ethos is not a universal one. Brad stood not so much in opposition to the work ethos as disengaged from it. He did not seek his identity in work any more than he had sought it earlier at school. He had tailored his hopes and ambitions. He had a keen sense of what for him constituted the essentials; obtaining them provided his driving force. His attention was on what he needed, rather than on what he might become. Survival was his challenge and his work, and he worked full time at it. But work for its own sake cast no compelling spell over him; it was no more than a ready trap back into the second-class life he had already tried and rejected.[7]

Second, Brad's case reveals a far stronger institutional "pull" in our society than I had been aware of, a pull toward compliance and dependency. Yet the case also illustrates both how powerful and how few are those institutional alternatives. The three "total institutions" that beckoned—the military, jail, or a mental institution—seemed in his assessment to provide roughly the same amenities in exchange for a

---

[7] Valentine's (1978) black ghetto residents who include *hustling* and *obtaining welfare* as forms of "hard work" appear to have adopted the ideal of the work ethic even though the *jobs*

full-time commitment.[8] Second-order institutional support—welfare, outpatient mental health services, meals at some mission—required less commitment but offered less in return.

I do not regard these institutions as providing alternative ways to order *my* life, and perhaps that is why it astounded me to hear Brad review them in inventorying possible resolutions for what to do with *his* life. It proved even more astounding to recognize how limited his choices were and the social cost of making them; the commitments are not casual. To me, each of his choices represents what I would take to be at best an interruption in life's work; to Brad, they represented genuine alternatives to it.

Although I have sensed growing disenchantment with the dominance of the role that work heretofore has played in our lives, some lessening of the dignity or pride associated with it, more tolerance for people who retire early even if they are *not* technologically displaced or under doctor's orders, I assume that gainful employment will continue to reflect an American core value, one of the realities of contemporary life. But we might attend more closely to the possibility of providing institutional options to help individuals like Brad find their way and to deal more directly with the social fact that we do not need—and cannot accommodate—every able-bodied person in the work force. One would think that we could come up with more creative primary institutional options than jail, mental institutions, or a reluctant stint in the armed forces.

Rather than foster alternatives that build or nurture institutional dependence, however, perhaps we should examine the ways we currently provide secondary institutional support. With Brad's problems conveniently "medicalized," he received two government checks, one (welfare) rewarding his acknowledged dependency, the other (SSI) rewarding his acknowledged incompetence.[9] During his years at the cabin, Brad was able to live on far less, maintaining his independence through the modest subsidy of food stamps that neither encouraged continued dependence

---

actually available to them are "scarce, poorly paid, unreliable, and often degrading" (p. 2). Here, consistent with both Brad's and my middle-class view of things, I have used "work" in the more restricted sense of holding a regular job and have regarded other income-producing activities as alternatives *to* work rather than alternative forms *of* it. It is interesting to realize that a restricted definition of work excludes much ghetto activity, thereby denying external legitimization of ghetto residents as "industrious." Their own interpretation of their activities suggests that because black ghetto residents *do* embrace the work ethic, they include as "hard work" certain activities that outsiders consider the very antithesis of it.

[8] I have portrayed "the military" as Brad perceived it, an alternative to getting a job, a one-time-only choice with no thought of a lifetime career; at best, "time out," at worst, time wasted. Prior to his reconsideration about enlisting, Brad had characterized individuals who join the service as "mostly black and not very smart." When thinking about enlisting, Brad showed little interest in the branch or term of enlistment; his only concern was which one of the armed forces would take him the earliest.

[9] As Estroff noted (1981; chap. 6) the SSI check that rewards incompetence paradoxically weds one to it.

322   WOLCOTT

nor (initially) punished him for it. Concidence or not, it was in the weeks immediately after his food stamps were "cut off" that Brad began to show dramatic signs
of the stress that eventually consumed him. He needed immediate financial help;
instead, he received an appointment for a hearing. With his newfound and medically
validated social status as "mentally disabled," he became eligible for subsidies that
may last for a lifetime, as well as a life, of not working.

Third and last, I want to comment on the totally unexpected alternative that
Brad followed, an alternative that anthropologist Sue Estroff (1981) described as
"making it crazy." I am inclined to think that Brad "chose" to make it crazy.
Viewed not only as a psychological response but also as a social solution that simultaneously resolved several important problems in his life, he could hardly have
chosen better.

I do not mean to imply that Brad was faking a psychosis. He was rapidly losing
touch with reality during his last few weeks at the cabin, and he steadfastly ignored
my suggestions of ways to test whether the things he had begun to hear and to
believe were true. Nevertheless, there are important cultural dimensions in the
resolution of his problems.

Much as I agreed that enlisting in the military offered Brad a possible option, I
breathed a sigh of relief when the Marines turned him down. Given his mental state
and his natural antipathy toward being ordered about, I doubted that he was ready
for the psychological abuse of initiation into the military even though he would
have reveled—and excelled—in its physical rigors.

Similarly, a customary wariness that heretofore had served him well "on the
streets" seemed to have escalated into a dysfunctional paranoia. Whatever actually
occurred during his brief escapade as a street hustler, Brad subsequently confided
to his mother that he was being followed and that the "Hollywood Mafia" was
after him. The streets had become too dangerous. It was time to go home.

Originally, Brad dismissed the idea of going home. As part of his assertion of
independence, he prided himself on not having (and therefore not being dependent
upon) a home or family he could turn to, faltering in his pose of self-reliance only
at the realization that even Marines go home at Christmas. Because he had been
banished from the home of his stepfather as a result of unruly past behavior, all his
mother could have done had he come to visit would have been to "go out for pizza"
and give him money or buy him clothes. She had steadfastly refused his demands for
a car or another motorcycle until he could demonstrate responsibility; turning up
jobless and penniless would hardly have provided a basis for appeal on that decision.

But turning up as a son now deeply disturbed and obviously in need of help provided a point of entrée that made it all right for him to go home, all right for his
mother to assume responsibility for him, all right for him to cast aside all thoughts
of a job, and all right to accept a new status as a helpless dependent, the very antithesis of the qualities on which he had so prided himself the previous two years.
The physiological basis was there; social circumstances called for everyone to play
it to the hilt.

With Brad-the-social-problem now reinterpreted as Brad-the-medical-problem, the state was willing to assume the economic burden and provide professional help that Brad could not find earlier. The only condition attached to his new status was that he continue to be crazy, or, more accurately, to act crazy enough to be convincing. That became his work. It is relatively permanent, relatively secure; it requires only physical presence, not physical effort. One can, more or less, choose one's own hours. The role requires a certain amount of acquiescence but tolerates a great deal of abberation as well; indeed, as Estroff (1981, p. 190) pointed out, it is important not to become *too* compliant or *too* cooperative.

There is some sacrifice of self-esteem, but since one may remain in relative isolation, the loss of self-esteem is probably no greater than one would find in many demeaning jobs. The only thing one must be careful to do is to demonstrate one's continuing inadequacy at some—but not all—social roles, including "work" in particular. As Estroff (1981) noted in what she identified as "Rules for Making It Crazy," it is all right to "try new things, like working, every once in a while," but you must assume you are going to fail, and when you do, you offer it as proof to yourself and to those about you that you are sick and cannot manage (p. 189). Brad had been rehearsing appropriate behaviors for years.

In anthropological fashion, Estroff (1981) explored paradoxes in the lives of American psychiatric clients, focusing particularly on the seductive pull of income maintenance programs that "may perpetuate the crazy life not only by making it attractive as a source of income but also by rewarding the continuation of inadequacy demonstrated by not working" (p. 171). Estroff (1981) concluded with a broad generalization amply demonstrated in Brad's case:

> Being a full-time crazy person is becoming an occupation among a certain population in our midst. If we as a society continue to subsidize this career, I do not think it humane or justifiable to persist in negatively perceiving those who take us up on the offer and become employed in this way. (p. 255- 256)

I realize that, given the slightest hint that an individual has been professionally diagnosed as mentally disturbed, there is the likelihood that the individual is then regarded *only* in those terms. Thus I run the risk that my efforts to present a study illustrating a range of cultural alternatives to career alternatives can be dismissed on the grounds that crazy people do crazy things and the case demonstrates nothing more.

I hope that readers will feel, as I do, that the case does illustrate something more: that school and work are not the only alternatives, that the school/work nexus is not the only nexus, and that the realistic alternatives for eking out a living—that is, for sheer *survival*—as today's youth perceive them, may vary considerably from the ideal world we like to think has been created for them. Schools and social agencies oriented to a world of a-job-for-everyone-and-everyone-in-a-job address only part of the population and part of the problem of the transition that every human must make to adulthood. That is the message, or at least the reminder, of this case.

If the case is diminished because its young protagonist crossed a psychological threshold and lost some touch with reality, there is still something to be learned.

As noted, being a paid and full-time crazy person is becoming an "occupation" for a discernible portion of our population, a social group whose distinguishing economic characteristic is that they are remunerated on the basis of their *incompetence* rather than their competence. Further, no one is crazy all the time. Even during the moments when they do act crazily, the cultural repertoire from which so-called crazy people draw remains essentially the same as it is for those around them. Even inappropriateness must be exercised in culturally appropriate ways. In his paranoia, Brad did not bury his fingernail clippings, cast a magic spell over his cabin and belongings, stick pins in voodoo dolls, or run amok: rather, he hitch-hiked a thousand miles, cast about for several weeks, and then suddenly began making collect telephone calls to his mother from freeway points conveniently accessible from her home, insisting that he was broke, hungry, and lost.

Against such alternatives as being in jail, joining the military (out of desperation rather than preference), or holding a menial job— and taking into account the dependable income he now "earned"—Brad had opted for what seemed at the moment to be society's best offer. I did not envy his solution to the "school or work" dilemma; nor, apparently, did he envy mine.

REFERENCES

Brown, W.K. (1983). *The other side of delinquency*. New Brunswick, NJ: Rutgers University Press.

Edson, C.H. (1982). Schooling for work and working at school. Perspectives on immigrant and working-class education in urban America, 1880–1920. In R.B. Everhart (Ed.), *The public school monopoly*. Cambridge, MA: Ballinger.

Estroff, S.E. (1981). *Making it crazy: An ethnography of psychiatric clients in an American community*. Berkeley, CA: University of California Press.

Ginzberg, E. (1980). *The school/work nexus: Transition of youth from school to work*. Bloomington, IN: Phi Delta Kappa Educational Foundation.

LeCompte, M. (1978). Learning to work: The hidden curriculum of the classroom. *Anthropology and Education Quarterly*, *9*(1), 22–37.

Lloyd, R. (1976). *For money or love*. New York: Vanguard Press.

National Commission on Excellence in Education. (1983). *A nation at risk: The imperative for educational reform*. Washington, DC: U.S. Department of Education.

Rechy, J. (1963). *City of night*. New York: Grove Press.

Reiss, A.J., Jr. (1961). The social integration of queers and peers. *Social Problems*, *9*(2), 102-120.

Sherman, D.F. (1983). *Views of school and work: Interviews with high school juniors*. Unpublished doctoral dissertation, Division of Educational Policy and Management, College of Education, University of Oregon, Eugene.

Valentine, B. (1978). *Hustling and other hard work: Life styles in the ghetto*. New York: Free Press.

Weisburg, D.K. (1985). *Children of the night: A study of adolescent prostitution*. Lexington, MA: Heath.

Wirth, G. (1983). *Productive work—In industry and schools: Becoming persons again*. Washington, DC: University Press of America.

Wolcott, H.F. (1983). Adequate schools and inadequate education: The life history of a sneaky kid. *Anthropology and Education Quarterly*, *14*, 3–32.

Wooden, W.S., & Parker, J. (1982). *Men behind bars: Sexual exploitation in prison*. New York: Plenum Press.

Author Index

Subject Index